Financial Planning and Control

Financial Planning and Control

Second edition

Edited by
M. A. Pocock and A. H. Taylor

Gower

First published 1981 as *Handbook of Financial Planning and Control*

Second edition published 1988 by
Gower Publishing Company Limited,
Gower House,
Croft Road,
Aldershot
Hants GU11 3HR,
England

Gower Publishing Company,
Old Post Road,
Brookfield,
Vermont 05036,
U.S.A.

British Library Cataloguing in Publication Data

Financial planning and control.—2nd ed.
  1. Business firms. Financial management
  I. Pocock, M.A. II. Taylor, A.H. (Anthony
Herbert), III. Handbook of
financial planning and control
  658.1'5

Library of Congress Cataloging in Publication Data

Financial planning and control / edited by M.A. Pocock and
A.H. Taylor. — 2nd ed.
    p. cm.
  Rev. ed. of: Handbook of financial planning and control. c1981.
  Includes index.
  1. Business enterprises—Finance. 2. Corporations—Finance.
I. Pocock, M. A. II. Taylor, Anthony Herbert. III. Handbook of
financial planning and control.
HG4026.5.F575   1988
658.1'5—dc19   88–10888
            CIP

ISBN 0 566 02713 5

Printed and bound in Great Britain by
Anchor Press Ltd, Tiptree, Essex

Contents

Contents

What is a small business? – Management time and information
requirements – The business plan – The budget – Key ratios –
Sensitivity analysis – Profit and output – Capital expenditure

PART III   SPECIAL ASPECTS

An overview of business computer systems – Availability of
systems – The effect of systems on organizations –
Considerations before installation – Future financial
applications

Significant areas of social performance – Reporting progress –
Money values in social accounting reports – Human resource
accounting – A social reporting model

The regulatory framework – The merger investment decision
– Post merger performance – Method of financing – Defences
against merger

An accounting or economic problem? – Distortions in
reporting – Two schools of thought – Accounting for inflation
in the real world

International operations – International financing – Small
companies

Notes on Contributors

Richard Aitken-Davies, BA, FCCA, ATII (*Cash forecasting and controlling the funds*), graduated in 1971 with an honours degree in Business Studies and has since held a series of accounting and managerial positions in industry. He is presently Central Planning Manager in the Operations Division of the Central Electricity Generating Board, where he is responsible for the development and implementation of management information systems and for co-ordinating the operational input to the Board's strategic and business plans. He maintains an interest in business and management education through work for the Council for National Academic Awards and is active in local government.

Bryan Atkin, BSc(Econ.) (*Pricing policy*), has been engaged in industrial market research and business consultancy for more than twenty years. In 1984, he became a founder director of Research Solutions Ltd and currently specializes in research and consultancy for the Information Technology industry. He has extensive experience of the analysis, through research, of the purchasing process and the role of price in decision-taking. He has also devised and implemented specific research procedures for testing price sensitivity and/or acceptability in relation to a wide range of products and services. Bryan Atkin directed the important 'How British Industry Buys, 1974' report sponsored and published by the *Financial Times* and co-authored a study into industrial pricing practices, 'How British Industry Prices', published by IMR Ltd in 1975. In 1978 he spent six months on secondment to the Price Commission.

Professor Harold Bierman, (*Capital budgeting*), is the Nicholas H. Noyes Professor of Business Administration at the Graduate School of Business and Public Administration, Cornell University. A Cornell faculty member since 1956, Professor Bierman formerly taught at Louisiana State University, the University of Michigan, and the University of Chicago. From 1964 to 1979 he helped the University of West Indies to establish a management programme.

His industrial experience includes work with Arthur Young and Company, Shell Oil Company, Ford Motor Company, National Can Corporation, and Boeing. He has been consultant to a wide variety of firms including Owens Corning Fibreglass and AT and T as well as the US government.

His teaching interests are in financial policy, investments and accounting. He is the author or co-author of ten books, including *The Capital Budgeting Decision, Financial Accounting, Managerial Accounting and Financial Policy Decisions*, and 100 journal articles.

Raymond Brockington, BCom, MSc(Econ.), FCA (*Inflation accounting*), is currently lecturer in Finance and Accounting at the University of Bath. He has followed the debate on inflation accounting with great interest. He holds degrees from the Universities of Birmingham and London and is a Fellow of the Institute of Chartered Accountants in England and Wales. He has taught on a wide variety of courses in a number of educational establishments. An important research interest is in accounting education to which he has given practical expression over many years through his work for the Council for National Academic Awards. He believes firmly that problems such as those presented by inflation can only fully be resolved by a profession made receptive to ideas derived from research by an appropriate academic input to education and training.

Richard Brown, BA (*Cost control*), is Finance Manager of a division of Lucas CAV LTD, and has general management responsibility for a number of companies in the UK and overseas. He obtained an honours degree in Business Studies, awarded by the Council for National Academic Awards, at the School of Business, Ealing College of Higher Education.

Peter Chidgey, BSc(Econ.), FCA (*Internal audit and internal control*), is Technical Director at Stoy Hayward where he is responsible for the technical aspects of audit practice in the UK. He is also a member of the international accounting and auditing committee of Howarth and Howarth International, of which Stoy Hayward is a leading member, and which oversees auditing practices throughout the world. Formerly he was a lecturer in auditing and management accounting in the Department of Accounting and Financial Control, University College, Cardiff.

John Chown, (*Tax planning*), Educated at Gordonstoun and Selwyn College, Cambridge (First Class Honours Economics, Adam Smith Prize 1953, Wrenbury Scholarship 1954), John Chown founded J F Chown and Company Ltd in 1962. He is also a director of Fixed Income Research and Management Limited, Reserve Asset Managers Ltd, and of Anthony Wieler and Company Limited. John Chown's special interest is the relationship between international tax, foreign currency fluctuations and international finance.

An active and extensive writer and lecturer on taxation and international finance, he is co-editor of the *Journal of Strategy in International Taxation* and was, for some years, the contributor to the *Financial Times* of a regular column, 'Taxation and the Investor'. His books include *Tax Efficient Forex Management* (Professional Publishing 1986).

A co-founder and Executive Committee member of the Institute for Fiscal Studies, John Chown is actively involved in tax policy issues in the UK, the EEC and elsewhere, and serves on the tax committee of the Institute of Directors and the technical committee of the Association of Corporate Treasurers.

Richard Dobbins, PhD, MSc, FCCA (*Social accounting and mergers*), is Senior Lecturer in Financial Management at the University of Bradford Management Centre. He qualified as a certified accountant in 1968 after several years' experience in professional offices, industry and public service. He studied for his MSc and PhD in Management and Administration, at the University of Bradford, where he was appointed Esmée Fairbairn research assistant in 1972, Lecturer in Finance in 1973 and Senior Lecturer in Financial Management in 1979.

He is an active consultant, editor of *Managerial Finance*, has contributed to several academic journals, and has lectured on management programmes in Europe, the Far East, Africa, Australia and North America. He is the co-author of *The Growth and Impact of*

Institutional Investors, (Institute of Chartered Accountants in England and Wales, 1978), *Portfolio Theory and Investment Management* (Martin Robertson, 1983, Basil Blackwell, 1986), and *Investment Decisions and Financial Strategy* (Philip Allen, 1986).

Trevor Gambling, BCom, PhD, FCA (*Developments in accounting thought and practice*), is an Emeritus Professor of the University of Birmingham, England. He is the author of numerous books and papers on the theory of accounting and has acted as a consultant to major companies and governments. He has held a number of senior visiting appointments, principally in the USA and Australia. A more curious distinction is the reference to his work by Dr Alvin Toffler, in his book *The Third Wave*.

Desmond Goch, FCCA (*Income and expenditure budgets*), is the managing director of Coster Aerosols Ltd and he has previously held financial executive appointments in the aircraft, newspaper and packaging industries. He qualified as a certified accountant in 1955 and in 1988 was President of the Chartered Association of Certified Accountants. He is the author of *Finance and Accounts for Managers* (Kogan Page) and he has contributed many articles to the financial and accountancy press.

Philip Jones, MSc (*Systems and the computer*), worked in the motor industry for ten years before moving into higher education and then on to founding MagnaSys Ltd, a company providing consultancy and business systems. In Ford of Europe Systems Office he was responsible for the design, development and implementation of management information systems in European plants. He qualified for the degree of MSc at the Cranfield Institute of Technology. In education he taught undergraduate and post-graduate students in the uses of computers in business and management studies.

R.Y. Kennedy, CA, FCMA (*Analysing the financial resources of the business*), served in London with Peat, Marwick Mitchell and Co., after qualifying. He has acted as external examiner for the BA in Business Studies and was awarded a silver plaque by the Institute of Cost and Management Accounts for his services to that body. For ten years he was financial director of Winsor and Newton Ltd before being elected chairman and managing director. Subsequently he joined the Reckitt and Colman Group as chairman of their Leisure Division.

John Lloyd, BSc(Econ.) (*Financial control in the public sector*), graduated in Economics at Leeds University in 1965. He went on to do graduate work in the field of public sector economics, whilst on the teaching staff. Subsequent studies included work in the field of public and social administration at Brunel University.

He has worked closely with many major British firms, including Marley Tile and BOC, and taught on a number of business studies degree courses and management programmes. He spent some time lecturing in America, within the Pennsylvanian State College system.

For the past five years he has concentrated upon the economic and financial aspects of health care. This has been given an international perspective through involvement with courses for overseas hospital and health service administrators, both in London, and in West Africa. He has enjoyed practical planning and management attachments at hospital and at Regional Authority level with North West Thames.

He is currently Principal Lecturer in Economics at the Polytechnic of the South Bank, London.

Professor Charles Magee, FCA, BComm. (*Assessment of performance*), was Professor of Accounting and Financial Control at University College, Cardiff from 1970 to 1977, and Dean of the Faculty of Economic and Social Studies from 1973 to 1976. He was responsible for a continuous research project for the Department of Health and Social Security to develop procedures for a system of costing to be introduced into the hospital service in the UK. He is the author of standard textbooks on accounting and of articles on hospital costing and finance.

Michael Mepham, BSc(Econ.), PhD, Dip. OR, FCA, FCMA (*Financial modelling*), is Senior Lecturer in Accounting at Heriot-Watt Unviersity, Edinburgh. After extensive accounting experience in professional offices and industry, Dr Mepham embarked on a career in accounting education. He has taught at Slough College of Higher Education and at the Unversities of Glasgow, Florida and the West Indies. From 1982 to 1986 he was examiner in Management Accounting for one of the major professional bodies and from 1983 to 1986 he was Dean of the Faculty of Economic and Social Studies at Heriot-Watt University. He has written numerous articles in the professional journals and two books: *Accounting Models* (Pitman, 1980) and *Accounting in Eighteenth Century Scotland* (which is to be published by Garland Press in 1988). His current research activity is centred on Accounting Models and Database Accounting.

Elwood Miller, PhD, CPA (*Accounting problems of multinational businesses*), is Professor of the Departments of Accounting and International Business, and former chairman of the Department of Accounting at Saint Louis University, Saint Louis, Missouri USA. He has had extensive experience in international business operations and is the author of a number of publications including: *Accounting Problems of Multinational Enterprise* (Lexington Books, 1979) *Inflation Accounting* (Van Nostrand Reinhold, 1980) and *Responsibility Accounting and Performance Evaluations* (Van Nostrand Reinhold, 1982).

Christine Parkinson, MBA, FCCA, MIMC (*Mergers and acquisitions*), is a qualified accountant and holds an MBA from the University of Bradford. She has spent all her professional life in industry working mainly in the planning and control function. For five years she was a free lance management consultant operating in the UK and overseas. She is currently undertaking doctoral research at Bradford University. Her topic of study is mergers and acquisitions with particular reference to defended or hostile takeover bids.

Alan Pearson, BSc (*Planning and control of research and development*), was in 1979 appointed director of the Management Course at the Manchester Business School, having previously held posts at that School concerned with Econometrics, Operational Research, Decision Analysis and, from 1967, as senior research fellow and director of the R and D Research Unit. Before joining the academic world he held appointments in industry with Pilkington Brothers and Simon Engineering. His career embraces an impressive list of appointments to various boards and committees, largely connected with R and D at home and abroad. His publications include numerous papers and articles as well as joint authorship of *Mathematics for Economists* (David and Charles, 1975) and *Transfer Processes in Technical Change* (Sijthoff and Noordhoff, 1978). He has carried out consultancy and course design assignments with many leading UK companies.

Alan Robson, BSc(Econ.), FCA, FCMA (*Objectives and practice in financial planning and control*), is Professor of Management

Accounting at the Cranfield School of Management, where he is chairman of Continuing Studies. He is also chairman of the Management Information Panel of the Institute of Chartered Accountants in England and Wales and author of a number of publications on management accounting and corporate planning. His early experience was in professional accountancy practice and in industry. Before joining the academic world he was finance officer for the Engineering Division of the UK Atomic Energy Authority at Harwell.

Maurice Sasieni, BSc, MSc, PhD (*Forecasting demand*), holds a first class degree in Mathematics from London University and a PhD in Operations Research from Case Western Reserve University in the USA. For several years he worked in Unilever's Marketing Division and is currently Professor of Marketing at the University of Alberta.

Professor John Rankin Small, BSc(Econ.), FFCA, FCMA, JDip MA (*Financial control in the smaller business*), is Vice Principal and Head of the Department of Accountancy and Finance at Heriot-Watt University; chairman of the Commission for Local Authority Accounts in Scotland; past president and member of the Council of the Chartered Association of Certified Accountants; member of the Chartered Institute of Management Accountants. He has taken an active interest in international accounting organisations and has extensive knowledge of the financial problems of small businesses in both rural and urban areas.

Stephen F. Witt, BA, MSc, MA, PhD, FSS, FTS (*Social accounting*), graduated with a BA(Hons) in Mathematics and Economics from the University of Warwick in 1969. He subsequently obtained the degrees of MSc in Mathematical Statistics from the University of Leeds, MA in Economics from the University of Warwick and PhD from the University of Bradford. In 1969 he was elected a Fellow of the Royal Statistical Society and in 1985 a Fellow of the Tourism Society. He took up his current appointment as Lecturer in Econometrics at the University of Bradford Management Centre in 1974.

Research interests include portfolio management and security analysis, tourism management and business forecasting, and he has numerous publications relating to these areas. These include *Portfolio Theory and Investment Management* (with R Dobbins), Martin Robertson 1983 (reprinted by Basil Blackwell 1986), *Practical Business Forecasting* (with J Saunders and J Sharp, Gower, 1987), and papers which have appeared in various financial and economic journals.

Avison Wormald, BA(Hons), CBIM (*Financial planning in conditions of change* and *Development overseas*), is executive vice-president of Lansberg, Wormald Humble y Asociados CA, Management Consultants, Caracas, Venezuela; Professor of International Trade at the Universidad Metropolitana, Caracas; author of *International Business*, published by Pan Books. He was director and managing director of Fisons Ltd, London from 1950 to 1962; chairman Grace Bros Ltd (W.R. Grace and Co.) and a director of many companies in six countries. He graduated from London University with first-class honours and is a fellow of the British Institute of Management.

Preface

The purpose of this book is to provide a practical exposition of the principles and practices of financial planning and control in modern business. The book is directed not only to financial executives but also to managers in other functions of business, since their decisions inevitably involve financial consequences.

Since the book was first published in 1981 (as *Handbook of Financial Planning and Control*) significant changes have occurred in the environment of business, and hence in the emphasis given to certain aspects of financial management. These changes have been reflected in this edition by rigorous updating and revision, and the inclusion of a number of new chapters. The new material deals with, among other issues, control techniques in the public sector; mathematical modelling; the resurgence in take-overs and mergers; and a critical analysis of traditional accounting concepts.

The theme of the book is that no business can hope to succeed – or, indeed, to survive – without preparing plans and controlling performance in relation to those plans. The plans must be expressed in financial terms because the various business activities are measured in the common language of money. Greater emphasis should be given to strategic planning since much of the investment made by industrial undertakings is for the long term. At the same time a fiercely competitive world imposes a need for flexibility and adaptability both in planning and action. Adjustment to external change often demands rapid and sometimes radical reorganization of the marketing, buying, production, research and administrative functions.

Implicit in the following pages is the need for managers at all levels to participate in the financial planning and control processes. These processes are not, and never have been, the sole prerogative of the accountant; they are the responsibility of the managers acting as a multi-disciplinary team. Business functions are necessarily inter-dependent and must be integrated. The corporate plans and their revisions will reach down to the grass roots of the organization, to the shop floor, section and department so that eventually the various sectional and departmental plans will form an intricate and closely linked framework. Initially the plans will be based on quantitative measures, such as units of output, quantities of material, numbers of sales, etc. In the end they will be expressed in financial terms leading to the corporate profit, capital and cash flow. Thus money becomes the co-ordinating influence.

This book takes a wide view of the scope of the subject and some chapters may seem to be, but are not in fact, ancillary to financial management. The reality is that planning and control embrace all aspects of business, and we have selected those topics which we consider to be of the greatest current importance. Inevitably some matters which others may view as significant have been omitted, but the bibliographies at the end of most chapters should be useful to those who seek further information. The book is arranged in three Parts of which the first deals with Formulating the Plan, the second with Controlling the Performance, and the third with Special Aspects. The chapters tend to overlap to some degree, as do the planning and control functions; but this tendency gives the reader the advantage of contrasting viewpoints and at the same time helps to integrate the discussion.

PART 1 FORMULATING THE PLAN

The corporate objectives

Several writers in this Part refer to the need for defining the corporate objectives as a first step in the forward planning process. Clearly the objectives must be communicated to first line management, if not right down the line, as is the practice in preparing military formations for battle. The corporate objectives will normally be of a long term nature but must provide for the crisis situation or unexpected oppor-tunities.

The achievement of the objectives will require the preparation of divisional and departmental plans, but before these can be drawn up, clear guidance must be given on the resources available for their implementation. This part of the book deals with the review of resources and then goes on to discuss in detail the process of formulating the various departmental plans.

The resources of the business

The resources of the business include physical assets such as land and buildings, plant and equipment; human assets of management and employees; accounting and administrative services; and the overall limiting factor of finance.

The purpose of reviewing resources is so that management can consider the extent to which they are appropriate for the proposed future operations. Undoubtedly additional resources will be required for a plan of development, but in any situation some assets will need replacement and some may have become redundant. The financial controller has the responsibility not only of advising on the extent to which additional funds can be raised within the organization or obtained from external sources but also on the investment of surplus funds.

The departmental plans

The next stage in the planning procedure is for departmental and divisional managers to consider their plans for meeting the corporate objectives. Since these objectives are likely to be long term, the plans for each proposal must extend for a similar period of years, subject to more detailed projections for the short term. Because the departments are interdependent there is a problem of reconciliation. In particular the volume and nature of the forecasted sales have to be reconciled with the potential to produce or procure the products.

An aid to the co-ordination of departmental plans is for the first forecast to be prepared by what may be called the dominant function of the business; that is to say that function which will dictate the scope of planning by other departments. In most cases this will be the sales forecast; but in a situation of under-utilization, the production capacity may be the deciding factor and a special effort must then be directed to finding means of selling that capacity, maybe at marginal profit. In any event various limiting factors will become evident during the planning process and, in addition to potential output or sales, these may include the availability of materials, equipment, space, skilled personnel and support services.

A necessary preliminary to the sales plan is a forecast of demand, the approach to which is examined in Chapter 3. The demand forecast leads to the assessment of potential sales and, after adjustment and reconciliation with production and/or procurement, of the sales achievable. For the purpose of formulating monetary budgets the orders receivable must be priced and converted into required deliveries of the finished products. The critical subject of pricing policy is considered in Chapter 4.

The following chapter takes an overall view of the construction of the array of interlocking departmental budgets which are eventually amalgamated into a Master Budget. Projects of capital expenditure on, for example, plant and equipment, will be necessarily included in the departmental plans, and methods of evaluating those projects by the use of discounted cash flow techniques are analysed and illustrated in Chapter 6. Developments in financial modelling as a means of facilitating the planning processes are explained in Chapter 7.

The ultimate limiting factor is the availability of finance, both working capital and, where necessary, further long term or permanent funds. For the purpose of assessing the funds required it is essential that before the budgeting system is finalized a cash forecast be prepared for the long term as well as the short term. If it is impracticable or inadvisable for the additional funds required to be obtained then appropriate adjustments must be made to the forward plans. The principles and methods involved in the preparation of the cash forecast are explained in Chapter 8.

Part I of the book concludes with an analysis of the repercussions of change, risk and uncertainty on the business plans, and emphasizes the consequent need for the greatest flexibility in the planning and control processes.

PART II

Controlling the performance

Although forward planning is in itself a rewarding exercise for all levels of management it is otherwise ineffective without systems for controlling the performance of the various activities. This aspect of the general subject is given detailed consideration in Part II of the book. However, planning and control are often concurrent operations, so that there is inevitably some overlap with Part I.

In Part II much practical advice is provided by authors of wide experience on such topics as methods of assessing performance, control of costs and of funds, research and development, overseas operations, the small business and the public sector. These chapters once again emphasize that financial control is a matter for all managers acting as a team; whilst the financial executives supply information and interpret the results, remedial action is the responsibility of the operating management.

Control action is initiated by a process of comparison. Basically the results are compared with the budget. But, where the budget becomes out of phase with the reality of the situation, other relationships or 'indicators' are appropriate, as outlined in Chapter 11, Cost Control, and in Chapter 17, Financial Control in the Public Sector. For these purposes it is essential that the accounting service provides relevant up-to-date information which can be understood by the manager for whom it is prepared.

Unfortunately the conventions applied to the preparation of formal accounts are often quite inapplicable for planning and control purposes. For example, as many contributors to this book indicate, marginal costs and the contribution are more positive indicators than apportioned costs and conventional profit. In many cases the most realistic measure of projected or actual performance is cash flow.

Likewise the budget which is fixed and unalterable can inhibit action and obstruct enterprise. Budgetary control needs to be a flexible and continuous process rather than a stop-and-go exercise. Furthermore, any kind of dynamic situation requires regular and frequent appraisals of activities, and to this end the system of internal audit and internal check, described in Chapter 13, can be invaluable.

In addition to the methods of control which, as outlined above, are common to all businesses, special techniques need to be applied in particular situations. Chapter 14 examines the control of research and development expenditure of which the eventual benefits are largely unpredictable. In Development Overseas (Chapter 15) and Accounting Problems of Multinational Business (Chapter 16) the problems discussed include currency risks, relative rates of inflation and taxation, transfer pricing, and the consolidation of results from different countries. The development of control systems in the public sector (Chapter 17) has many implications for private enterprise.

A further area where special conditions apply is in the smaller business (Chapter 18). The importance of the small business unit in the context of this book is not only that it represents an important sector of the economy but also that it may be a branch or subsidiary of a large company, or closely associated with the latter. This chapter suggests that control systems in the small business should have regard to the fact that managers of those concerns are normally in close contact with shop floor operations and that the keynote must be simplicity.

PART III

Special aspects

Part III deals with a selection of special aspects of importance to all managers. Chapter 19 shows how modern improvements in computerized systems can ease the burden and sharpen the impact of both planning and control procedures. The obligations of business to society and to employees are of growing importance and are discussed in Chapter 20. The resurgence in take-over bids and mergers is the subject of the next chapter. In Chapter 22 the unresolved problems of inflation accounting are analysed and it is argued that whilst inflation appears to be under control in the UK and elsewhere its incidence still needs to be reflected in forward planning. Then follows a chapter on tax planning which, because of the complexity of the subject, concentrates on the tax implications of overseas operations and the small business. A thought-provoking final chapter examines the effect of change on the traditional concepts of accounting.

The editors are indebted to the authors, many of whom are of international repute and all of whom are experts in their respective fields. They are a mixture of business executives and academics with close business connections, so that the emphasis throughout is on practical applications. Where appropriate the views expressed are unconventional, sometimes controversial. In these changing times there is a continuing need for managers, as well as accountants, to think afresh about traditional techniques of financial planning and control, and we hope this book will make a useful contribution to that process.

M.A. Pocock
A.H. Taylor

Part 1
FORMULATING THE PLAN

Part 1 Formulating the plan

This part examines the essential stages involved in formulating the forward plans of a business and the expression of those plans in financial terms. The translation of the operating plans into monetary language will exercise a co-ordinating influence, as well as acting as a constraint, and will provide a measure of the extent to which the combined plans of the various functions are likely to achieve the business objectives. Furthermore the statement of the plans in terms of money will form a basis for responsibility accounting, and the establishment of standards and budgets for operating managers.

The Preface has emphasized the prime importance of defining objectives, considering alternative courses of action, and setting up a system of appraising performance. A further essential preliminary to sound planning is the analysis of the financial resources of the business, and this topic is developed by an experienced chief executive and accountant, Robert Kennedy. He also discusses the need to establish an effective organization of the financial function, which must include a system for forecasting and controlling cash flow.

On such firm foundations the formulation of the business plans may be developed, and the first of such exercises is the forecasting of demand, as examined by Dr Sasieni. He points out that the demand forecast will be influenced by demographic and economic factors and eventually converted to an assessment of the attainable market share. The preparation of such a demand forecast will be aided by statistical devices as well as by the application of judgement and experience.

On the basis of the demand forecast the detailed process of preparing budgets of income and expenditure will be inaugurated.

The fourth chapter is thus concerned with the approaches to successful budgeting and here another executive, Desmond Goch, maintains that the budgets must be primarily directed towards the achievement of a satisfactory return on the *current* value of capital employed. Guidelines to budgeting for capital expenditure are given incisive treatment by an acknowledged expert on the subject, Professor Harold Bierman of Cornell University. The crucial problem of pricing policy is discussed by Bryan Atkin, a founder director of Research Solutions Ltd.

1

Objectives and Practice in Financial Planning and Control

A.P. Robson

In this opening chapter the author seeks to clarify the objectives of financial planning and control as a means of assisting managers to choose between alternatives, plan action and check performance. He distinguishes between strategic and tactical decisions, emphasizes the motivating influence of the exercise, and stresses the importance of discounted cash flow and marginal costing. The author gives due attention to human aspects and sees future development resting largely on the growing body of financially numerate managers, growth in communications, development of more relevant management information and advances in computerization. The ideas outlined by Professor Robson are taken up in greater depth, and with appropriate variations, by contributors to subsequent chapters.

The financial planning and control function in an organization has the main objective of assisting the management of that organization. This assistance is directed primarily towards the planning and control activities of managers; but other activities will benefit as well, if the system is well conceived and used: for example, the co-ordinating and motivating aspects of management. A good financial planning and control system is one which is 'in context': what is done is relevant to the purposes of that particular organization and the managers who work for it, whatever those purposes and however they may be measured and appraised. Inevitably, financial planning and control systems in practice fall short of this ideal, either in their design or in the way they are used. This chapter concentrates on those aspects of financial planning and control where improvements in practice might be made.

If a financial planning and control system is to assist managers, it will be useful to clarify, at an early stage, those activities which can receive particular benefit. They are: (a) choosing between alternative courses of action; (b) planning the action which is to be taken during a specified period of time; and (c) checking performance once action has been taken.

ALTERNATIVE CHOICE DECISIONS

Choosing between alternatives is one of those activities which managers carry out several times every day. Every time someone comes into a manager's office and asks, 'what do you think we should do about such-and-such?', the manager must either suggest doing nothing or recommend a course of action. In making his reply he is involved in choosing. But some of the issues he gets involved with are of sufficient importance to warrant some sort of formal financial analysis – and it is with these types of decisions that we are particularly concerned.

Two sets of these types of decisions may be identified. Each set has particular characteristics which give rise to the need for a specific kind of financial analysis.

The first set of decisions may be characterized as strategic. The use of the word 'strategic' indicates that these decisions are of sufficient importance to warrant the attention of relatively senior managers. 'Strategic' also implies that the decisions are likely to affect the organization's survival and well-being in some fundamental way. Therefore, these decisions tend to have long-run effects, lasting over several years. Often they change the capacity of the organization, for example, by expanding or contracting the assets in use. Examples of decisions which have these characteristics are: the acquisition of an additional business; the closure of a factory; the closure of an activity accompanied by a switch to sub-contractors; the launching of a new product; and the re-equipment of a transport fleet.

A second set of decisions which managers are involved with may be thought of as being more tactical. This implies some sort of manoeuvring to achieve an improved result with given resources and a given organization. 'Tactical' also implies the involvement of middle and senior managers, rather than senior and top managers. In many cases it is likely that a tactical manoeuvre will not commit the organization for lengthy periods of time, since the essence of tactics is to be flexible in the face of a changing environment. Perhaps the most frequently found example of a decision in business which has these characteristics is the product-mix decision: a choice between alternatives, in which the managers have to decide which products they prefer to emphasize in their selling and marketing, so as to obtain whatever additional profit is latent in the market conditions which they face. Hotel companies which operate weekend holidays at lower than normal prices are examples of businesses involved in such a decision. They are trying to improve their profitability by filling the spare capacity which exists in the off-season. Their decision as to which hotel to include in the bargain rate scheme, and at what price, is aimed at securing whatever additional profit is available in a limited market. Should the decision appear to be wrong, the consequences are not too dramatic and can be reversed without undue delay and penalty. If the hotel is fully booked and inundated with enquiries, it is a simple enough matter to remove the hotel from the list in the next season's publication. Contrast this with the strategic situation where a company builds a new hotel of the wrong size, or in the wrong location or to the wrong design!

ACTION PLANNING

Planning the action which is to be taken during a specified period of time is the second of the management activities listed earlier as likely to benefit particularly from the financial planning and control function. Planning of this type is much more detailed than the decision making first described. The extent to which the one type of planning is detailed and the other 'broad-brush' may be highlighted by the following simple example: suppose an organization has an accommodation problem and has identified two possible sites for relocation of staff. Evaluating these alternatives is decision making of a relatively broad-brush nature, involving an overall appraisal of such issues as the capital and running costs of the two locations, their convenience from the point of view of access to Head Office, the amenities they provide, the spare capacity which they offer for future growth in staff numbers and so on. Once a particular location has been chosen, it will be necessary to prepare a much more detailed plan involving such issues as: surveyor's reports, legal negotiations, deciding on facilities to be provided, appointment of a project team to supervise contractors, appointment and terms of reference of a project manager. The project manager will, in turn, need a detailed plan covering such issues as the specification to be followed, the sequence of work to be performed, the time to be taken, and the cost to be incurred. She or he will need to plan the information required and the communication system to be set up. Of course, detailed action plans are required in organizations, not only to facilitate the implementation of strategic and tactical decisions, but also to ensure the smooth running of all those operations (probably the majority) which are to be carried on without any changes being introduced.

Preparing such a comprehensive action plan in an organization of any size is obviously a considerable administrative task, involving many managers, and often spread over several months. If the organization is to function effectively (in that it achieves its purposes) and efficiently (in that these purposes are achieved without undue loss of resources) the plan which the managers produce needs to be a co-ordinated one. Fitting the pieces together involves cutting and shaping the component parts, which usually means someone cutting and shaping someone else's plans. The object is that the organization functions as nearly as possible as a harmonious whole, even though the management tasks are in the hands of individual managers who are organizationally subdivided.

Few activities are more liable to arouse heated debates than this, so that action planning is also tied up with motivating. If action planning is well handled, the managers in the organization will acknowledge the interests of the organization as a whole and will be committed to pursuing those interests even if this means some sacrifices on their part.

Another feature of detailed action planning is that it covers a specified period of time, in contrast to the decision making referred to earlier, where the planning period covers the expected life of the decision. Plans which repeatedly cover the same period of time become routine; and routine can become a chore and a nuisance. Unless the planning process is well managed, it can degenerate into a ritual of little effect, or an exercise which people undertake because they have to, rather than because they want to. While it is unusual for people to be indifferent towards the task of choosing between alternatives of a strategic or tactical nature, it is quite possible for these same people to be unenthusiastic about detailed planning. For this latter activity, creativity has to give way to bureaucracy; and initiative and imagination are seen to run into the dull, restrictive world of the administrator! Yet the issues covered by organization-wide action planning are of considerable importance, dealing as they do with the acquisition, storage and consumption of resources in the supplying of sevices or products; the financing implications of this activity; and the cash flow consequences.

PERFORMANCE APPRAISAL

Checking performance is the third important management activity which the financial planning and control function aims to assist in particular. This activity is clearly linked to the preceding ones, in that choosing between alternatives logically precedes action planning, which is logically followed by checking performance, which may, in turn, lead to re-choosing and/or re-planning, and so on. Checking performance implies the existence of a benchmark against which actual results can be compared. This is usually, but by no means exclusively, the current plan of action. Checking also implies high-lighting people's failures as well as their successes: failure to set achievable plans based on accurate forecasts, or failure to act as they should have done. Checking also implies analysis of the causes of such failures and successes, and consideration of the action which will eliminate the failure and reinforce the success. All this relies on information being created which is relevant to the manager, in that it relates to that sphere of responsibility and deals with the key issues in that particular job; and, bearing in mind that there is no automatic control reaction on the part of a manager, the information should also invite a reaction as to what is to be done about the results.

FINANCIAL PLANNING AND CONTROL TOOLS

In attempting to assist managers in these areas, the financial planning and control function has developed an impressive kit of tools. To use these tools effectively, both the manager and the management accountant need certain knowledge, skills and attitudes, which will enable them to recognize the potential and the limitations of the tools; and also to avoid misusing them.

Two tools are of particular relevance to the manager who faces the strategic and tactical issues outlined earlier: discounted cash flow and marginal costing. Both are examples of applied logic in which the financial consequences of alternative courses of action are highlighted without reference to a number of the conventions of more traditional accounting.

DISCOUNTED CASH FLOW

Discounted cash flow, as the name implies, focuses on the cash consequences of radical change. These consequences are grouped under four main headings: more cash flowing out, less cash flowing in, less cash flowing out and more cash flowing in, all as a result of the change being contemplated. Cash is the focus because the change is being assessed, as far as is practicable, over the life of the venture. By focusing on the life of the venture and not on the individual accounting periods within that life, discounted cash flow greatly simplifies the collection of relevant information.

The contrast between the cash flow accounting which is needed for such an evaluation and the accrual accounting which is relevant to interim appraisal was perhaps more familiar to businessmen of a bygone age than to some businessmen today! For example, a group of merchants living in Venice who decided to trade in the Far East, could start their evaluation with the pile of gold which they possessed, and which they used to buy a ship and something to sell. They then would set sail; reach the Far East; sell what they had brought; buy something else; set sail for home; reach Venice; sell what they brought back; and sell the ship, ending up (they hoped) with a larger pile of gold than they started with. Profit equalled the difference between the pile of gold at the end of the voyage and the pile of gold at the start. There was no need for accountants (other than tax advisers); and above all, there was no need for accrual accounting. But if someone asked, in the middle of the Indian Ocean on the return trip, 'how much profit have we made so far?', then the whole complicated apparatus of accrual accounting would be needed, involving the preparation of a profit and loss account and a balance sheet, which could in turn involve problems of valuing the stock, matching expenses in revenues, depreciating the boat, etcetera.

It is possible that in the modern world this distinction between cash accounting and accrual accounting has become blurred. People are in danger of confusing decision-making appraisals with accounting for decisions. The danger points are the inclusion of 'sunk costs' and 'ongoing items' in decision-making appraisals. Vital though 'sunk costs' and ongoing items may be for other forms of accounting, financial numbers which are unaffected by a particular decision obviously should not enter into the economic evaluation of that particular decision – if I am stuck with something whichever way I turn, it does not help me decide which way to turn. An important consequence of this is that no matter how much money I have already spent on an asset in an organization (a 'sunk' cost) and no matter how recently I spent the money, this asset's book value has no relevance to the economic evaluation of its disposal, looked at as an individual project in an ongoing organization. Not all users (and, alas, not all producers) of financial information are convinced of the truth of these statements. In effect, some people appear to prefer to keep an asset simply because they have spent money on it, not because it is more economic to do so! If this is the case, they are confusing decision making with review of decisions, and this is more likely to happen when review leads to regret, i.e. when mistakes have been made in the past, and losses on disposal are coming home to roost.

MARGINAL COSTING

Marginal costing in practice has always been fraught with difficulties. The commonest are probably the difficulty of determining the fixed or variable costs associated with a particular decision; an unwillingness to abandon one of the longest-serving members of the management accountant's list of ideas – the allocated and apportioned fixed overhead – and a failure to readjust to new percentage margins when setting selling prices. These are points which have been difficulties facing management accountants for many years. For example, some managers will equate fixed cost with committed cost, so that a fixed cost becomes 'one that cannot be altered at the discretion of management', as opposed to 'one that is not directly affected by a change in the level of activity being contemplated'. Similarly, some managers will confuse correlation with cause and effect, when considering variable costs. For them, advertising and order-getting costs generally are variables in that they usually move in relation to sales – more advertising usually means more sales. On the contrary, of course, advertising is a fixed cost in the terms of the definition given above, leaving the word 'variable' to be reserved for those costs which are 'caused by volume changes', such as the postage cost in a mail-order business.

The allocated and apportioned fixed overhead is a concept of value in a number of settings, for example, as a component in making a pricing decision, and as part of a calculation designed to assess the economic viability of a venture. But, as a component in a marginal cost calculation, an allocated and apportioned fixed overhead, such as rent, has little, if any, place. Perhaps the reluctance which some managers feel about leaving out fixed overhead is born of the feeling that there is such a thing as *the* cost of something, so that a cost figure produced for one purpose is automatically seen as being useful for another. But, of course, a cost figure which is a valuable tool in one setting need not be a valuable tool in another – in the same way that, say, a hammer is a very useful tool for putting in nails but not much use for putting in screws! Perhaps management accountants should always ask their managers a question before supplying a cost figure: 'what are you going to do with it?'

Readjusting to new margins when the base number is on a marginal cost basis is, of course, another old problem. And yet, the finer points of accountancy can tend to get overlooked in practice, particularly when price competition is keen, so that contribution costing can be introduced, even though contribution pricing may be inappropriate, in that it yields too low a return on investment, or in terms of locking up spare capacity at low margins and perhaps preventing the organization from accepting more profitable orders in the future.

ADMINISTRATION AND MOTIVATION

It has already been seen that two important problems associated with action planning are administrative and motivational problems; and since budgeting and action planning go hand in hand, the former is as much subject to those problems as the latter. For example, preparing a set of budgets which includes figures relating to labour costs, purchases, stocks, material usage, overhead support in the factory, overhead support in administration, marketing, personnel, research and development and distribution – with all the detailed sub-schedules itemizing the nature of these overheads, such as salaries, stationery, travel, etc., together with budgets for equipment, vehicles, debtors, creditors, cash flow, and fund-raising – all takes a great deal of organizing, and often a great deal of time. Add to this the fact that most budgets go through an evaluation phase, whereby first drafts are criticized and amended, resubmitted and perhaps further amended before final approval, and the administrative task becomes even more evident. Most accountants are adept at this: arranging for the preparation and processing of paperwork is a task for which they are trained and for which they usually have the right temperament. But herein lies a degree of danger: that the preparation and evaluation of budgets will be seen to be primarily exercises in processing paperwork as far as the accountant is concerned. Even if the task is seen to include assisting in the development of alternatives so that budgets which are both achievable and desirable emerge, a main feature of the process will have been underplayed. This is, of course, the motivational aspect. Budgeting is part of the process of getting ready for action and as such should be considered as being clearly associated with leadership. What matters is not simply what figures are put together and whether all likely alternatives have been assessed, but also how the people involved feel about the outcome.

As already noted, co-ordination invariably means some sort of compromise whereby original proposals are modified in the light of other people's requirements, or in the light of externally imposed constraints. So, for example, the advertising manager may have to sacrifice some of his draft budget to the research manager, simply because top management feel that they cannot afford to spend all that was asked on developing business for the future, either because of cash constraints or because of likely reaction of the shareholders to the lower profit margins and lower return on capital which such expenditures will invariably bring, at first. But the alteration of one proposed budget and not another, or the alteration of a budget to accord with the interests of the organization as a whole, is something which needs to be handled very carefully. Otherwise a nonsense will be encouraged: the insertion of 'fat' into the figures at first draft stage, in anticipation of subsequent cuts, so that these cuts can be tolerated in the event. A system which then reinforces this, allowing people a budget in line with their previous year's actual (plus an appropriate allowance for staff and other changes such as inflation), is positively encouraging waste, as the 'fatted' budgets are spent so as to ensure a sufficiently large budget-base for next time. Techniques such as using a zero-base for budgeting are obviously useful in this connection, but they only provide a palliative to a problem which centres on the motivational aspects of financial planning and control.

INFORMATION FOR CONTROL

Checking performance and the use of variance analysis is likewise an activity involving both accounting technique and psychology: accounting technique to distinguish such results as labour efficiency, rate and mix variances, materials usage, mix, yield and price variances, overhead expenditure and under/over recovery variances, etc.; and psychology to be able to use these results productively when they highlight, for the employee and the boss, what has gone wrong (as well as what has gone right).

In considering information which is being produced as a basis for control, it is essential to question if the information currently being produced is the most effective for this purpose. Control information needs to concentrate on key result areas. In so far as results in those areas can be measured, the numbers used need not always be financial; but if good results are being achieved on these numbers, then the organization is a long way along the road to creating good financial results. For example, in the monitoring of the performance of branch managers in a commercial bank (where most of the local costs are commitments and many are determined by people other than the local branch manager), indices such as the value of month-end and monthly average credit balances, the monthly average value of approved loans, the number of new instalment loans granted, and the number of new accounts opened (excluding transfers from one branch to another) was felt by one bank to be more relevant for control purposes than preparing branch profit and loss accounts. Producing useful information for control purposes implies that the management accountant needs to adopt an imaginative approach which goes behind the balance sheet and profit and loss account to factors which determine financial results.

'Information for control must always be tailored to suit the circumstances' is something with which most accountants agree, but not all practise. Deciding just what is a relevant information package for a particular manager in a particular job is not an easy task. This is a subject with which the academic accountant should be concerned as well, since there is an inadequate basis of ideas and information for the practitioner to draw on. Each location will have its own particular elements which need to be categorized and taken into account. For example, the different functional managers have different problems to cope with, ranging from the relative uncertainty and discretionary nature of the world of research and development, to the relative certainty and degree of commitment which forms much of the world of administration. Choosing a package of control information also involves choosing the criteria by which managers are to be judged by their superiors in the management hierarchy. These criteria must not only relate to the things that matter locally, but they must also encourage action (or inaction) in the interests of the organization as a whole. Much has been written on this subject, of achieving what is often called 'goal congruence', especially in the context of divisionalized businesses, where the division heads have a great deal of autonomy and are treated as profit or investment centres. And the special case of the division head invariably raises the issue of transfer pricing. This, too, is an area which can repay attention in practice. In any event, the management accountant may well find that he or she is thrust into a discussion on what constitutes an appropriate transfer price for a particular set of circumstances, since the subject can arouse a great deal of emotion among the managers involved, and the management accountant can be found acting as arbitrator between embattled transferor and transferee divisions.

Transfer pricing problems can also arise in practice in the area of decision making, where the system used to measure performance can give rise to unwise decisions, especially of the kind which involves weighing up whether or not to trade within the organization. For example, transfer prices will be a major element influencing the decision whether or not to buy from inside the organization. The possibility of using a transfer price which encourages the wrong decision is obvious: for example, a decision to buy from outside, because it is 'cheaper' on a full cost basis, when what in fact ensues is a double cost – the additional cost incurred by buying outside *and* the ongoing cost of maintaining the (partly used) facility inside.

FUTURE DEVELOPMENT

As all subjects are evolving in the field of management, it will be useful to consider some of the factors which are making for change in the area of financial planning and control.

One such element is a growing body of financially numerate managers, who are aware of the techniques in outline, know the jargon and are anxious to make proper use of their knowledge in their decision making, planning and control. Potential exists for a more fruitful relationship between managers and accountants, provided the latter are willing to respond and do not see the financially numerate managers as some sort of threat. Even greater potential would exist if management accountants were to make special arrangements for on-the-job training of these managers who are working in the other functional areas. An ideal would be for the managers who have attended a basic course in management accounting techniques also to attend an in-company course on the way these techniques are applied in the specifics of their own department, including the organization and procedures that are adopted and the priorities which currently exist.

This is one aspect of employee communications as they affect the management accountant. Employee communications, generally, is a theme which is likely to increase in importance in the future. Already, companies have adopted varying forms of employee reports, and it is likely that developments will continue in this direction, so that there will be an increasing requirement placed upon the management accountant to make clear to the layman what financial figures mean. It is unlikely that the general mass of employees in an organization will have received the same financial training as their managers; most will have received none. So this development in communication may pose a particular challenge for some management accountants whose orientation hitherto has been towards the preparation of figures, as opposed to their presentation and interpretation.

But even in the preparation of figures there are challenges to the management accountant, which are already with us and are likely to intensify. These stem from the growing influence of computers, not so much to perform complex calculations as to explore the consequences of alternatives. An obvious computer application of this type is when alternative assumptions are being made concerning a major project, and the computer is used to calculate the effect of variations in the financial outcome of the project. For example, the effect and likelihood of a delay in the start-up of the project, or the effect and likelihood of more or less buoyant sales can be rapidly seen by those involved in the project appraisal. This 'sensitivity testing' and 'risk analysis' is, of course, fairly common among larger organizations. With the advent of cheap computers, the practice of this type of calculation is likely to spread.

Similar approaches using computers may also be applied to the evaluation of budgets, other than project budgets. In the working capital area, for example, the effects of alternative stock, debtor and creditor policies and different cost and selling prices, either separately or in combination, can be quickly seen via the computer. Such calculations are not merely a speeding up, so that what took a week to do on a batch basis, now takes only a matter of minutes via a terminal or a table-top machine: the new dimension which has been added is the repeated interaction of calculation and judgement. As managers mull over the issues in the process of reaching a decision, they can explore alternatives, quickly see their likely effect if adopted, perhaps be surprised at the outcome and consequently shift the emphasis. There is potential here for considerably improved understanding of the economics of situations, leading to improved predictive ability and more soundly based decisions. Added to the administrative and motivational problems of budgeting already referred to, the management accountant will have to understand how to enable interaction between people and computers so that the judgement of the smoke-filled boardroom and the rapid calculation of the computer reinforce each other.

2

Analysing the Financial Resources of the Business

R.Y. Kennedy

An important preliminary to the establishment of an effective system of planning and control is to define and analyse the resources available for implementing whatever plan may be adopted. The author of this chapter discusses the subject from the essentially practical viewpoint of his long experience in industry both as chief financial officer and as managing director. He distinguishes between material and intangible resources and emphasizes the need for careful analysis of the availability of finance as it affects long-term cash flow. The importance of cash flow, which has already been given prominence in the introductory chapter, will be referred to on many occasions later in this book.

Mr Kennedy highlights another resource of great importance to financial planning, that of the organization of the financial department in a business and its division into various co-ordinated activities. He discusses the effect on planning of degrees of delegated authority and the special importance of dispersed operating units. An analysis of the significance of the smaller business unit is examined in depth by another contributor.

A business in a free society exists to perform a service for the community in which it operates (including the gaining of foreign currency from exports) and in so doing to allow people working in it to earn a living. An employee cannot be forced to perform a specific task if he or she does not wish to. Nor can a customer be forced to buy if the goods are not attractive. The environment is always changing and what may have been a successful market for many years may disappear quite suddenly. Businesses do not exist in a vacuum – they must interact successfully with their environment. Some develop products which become household words for generations; others become famous for a time and then disappear; others again remain relatively unknown to the public but provide a service for many years.

It is the task of a company's financial organization to ensure the availability of financial resources and to produce the financial information which will enable the business to succeed. Unless the revenue generated by a business exceeds its expenditure through time, the community will not allow it to continue indefinitely. Regardless of whether the business is operating within a free or a mixed economy, the community will either tire of filling its begging bowl and allow it to disappear or a new management will be appointed to reorganize it in such a manner that it will become profitable.

The environment tends to be hostile and the continued success of a business is always in jeopardy from one source or another. This gives rise to the element of excitement experienced by those engaged in the business. The information flowing from a company's financial organization will not eliminate risk but it should provide data adequate to indicate trends on which action may be taken in time to avoid future dangers. The tasks of the financial organization include ensuring the availability and control of finance; the evaluation of future plans in money terms; monitoring progress for the use of those responsible for controlling and co-ordinating the activities of the various parts of the business and the preparation of the annual balance sheet and profit and loss account for the information of the providers of finance and interested members of the public.

BUSINESS OBJECTIVES

Any group of active people tends to fragment unless strong control is exercised from the centre. A business will, however, lose much of the enthusiasm of its executives if too many decisions are taken at the centre. Yet without general directives each executive will tend to develop each section according to a personal interpretation of the future of the business, possibly in a manner different from that desired by senior management. This problem will be minimized by the preparation and adoption of parameters for the business in the form of business objectives.

Though many difficulties will arise in drawing up the statement of business objectives, it is more important to have some statement, however inadequate, than none at all. The statement should err on the side of brevity. Experience alone will identify where improvements may be made but a lengthy document will tend to be ignored. At regular intervals all statements should be reviewed and amended to take account of changes in the environment and the development of the business. However, too frequent reviews may merely irritate and confuse members of the organization, and it is therefore preferable that the statement should be limited to the permanent and more important aspects of the business.

FINANCIAL POLICY

The financial organization should analyse its role within the framework of the business objectives and should secure the approval of senior management. Such an analysis will be the basis of a statement of financial policy without which it would be impossible to make a meaningful assessment of the state of the resources of the business. The reports and recommendations emanating from the financial organization will affect the activities of almost every executive and their justification must be related to agreed objectives, so that, though critical, they do not disturb good relations in the team.

The financial policy statement would cover such subjects as:

1   the owning and leasing of fixed assets;
2   borrowing;
3   the desired level of profit in relation to sales volume and capital employed;
4   the proportions in which profit should ideally be allocated to development, the suppliers of capital and the employees and, if applicable:
5   rules regarding inter-company pricing;
6   the conversion rates of foreign currencies.

THE STATE OF MATERIAL RESOURCES

In a small business, management is so intimately involved that members are subconsciously aware of the state of the material resources. This familiarity is impossible in larger businesses and, to remedy the deficiency, the financial organization, with the assistance of experts in particular areas, should provide a statement of the material resources at regular and frequent intervals. Material resources give rise to upkeep costs and incur money costs as they represent finance tied up in the business. The advantages to be gained by a close control of the size of the investment in material resources may be illustrated in the following simplified example. If the general interest rate on borrowed money is 12 per cent p.a. and the business turns over its investment in material resources twice a year, then 6 per cent has to be added to the cost of the products to pay for the capital employed. This falls to 3 per cent if the investment is turned over four times a year.

The statement should give an assessment of the resources both quantitatively and qualitatively and should indicate the use made of the resources by the business as a whole. Where applicable, reference should be made to risk elements, measuring the risk in bands. When dealing with resources located overseas notes should be made of significant legislative and foreign exchange trends. A report should accompany the statement commenting on the assessment and making recommendations with a view to improving the effectiveness of the material resources investment.

The following notes on classes of material resources indicate aspects which should be considered in making the assessment.

Land

Businesses engaged in such activities as building, mining, agriculture etc., depend on their tenure of suitable undeveloped land. Other businesses will benefit from their location near supplies of raw materials, availability of skilled labour and ready access to markets etc., in varying degrees according to circumstances. In such cases undeveloped land in close proximity to the established site is a hedge against the disruption and costs of moving to accommodate future expansion. Only a fixed fund of land overall is available, although its supply may be to some extent variable for particular uses, and competition for it will always be severe. The continued holding of suitable land is of great importance to a business. Reserves of undeveloped land to provide for expansion are always desirable and a necessity in the building and extractive industries.

Buildings

Modern industrial buildings remain valuable assets for many years provided they are regularly maintained. The relative advantage of purchasing, leasing or renting is a policy matter but amenable to financial evaluation. Where the industrial process requires a specialized building, the risk element in providing the resource is considerable because the opportunities of realizing the initial cost in the event of a subsequent sale are minimal, and it may be wise to treat the building as part of the plant.

Plant and machinery

This group of resources is highly specialized and the operations executives should be invited to take a leading part in the assessment. Up-to-date plant registers, planned maintenance, and planned plant replacement will form the basic control. The actual time spent on installation should be controlled against the original estimates.

Stocks

Stocks of goods will be found in all parts of the organization. Each executive will aim never to go short through lack of the materials necessary for carrying out tasks and the total value of stocks held is usually a substantial proportion of the total investment in material resources. The ratio of stock held to usage is one of the best indicators for use in controls. Stocks no longer of value to the business are written off and should be disposed of to release space. Because stocks on consignment are held outside the business they call for special care.

Trade debtors

Customers can be trained to pay promptly by the use of strict credit control. This enforces good accounting on them and the less efficient outlets are weeded out. Granting cash discounts is relatively expensive and would only be worthwhile if used as a marketing incentive, e.g. in lieu of additional trade discount. The twin controls of ageing individual debts, and the overall ratio of debtors to sales by markets are usually adequate if allied to a special check on the history of new customers. The assessment should include a review of the number and purpose of the issue of credit notes to ensure the adequacy of the system for billing customers.

Trade investments

Circumstances may arise when it is advisable to invest in the businesses of suppliers and customers to secure preferential treatment, or as a preliminary to acquisition. Such investments tend to become permanent and the assessment of their value to the business should be rigorous to ascertain whether the original reasons for investing remain valid.

Liquid resources

These are subject to a slightly different approach. They fall into three categories:

Small funds held by various individuals to meet out-of-pocket expenditure. They are controlled by imprest. The assessment should include reviews of the amounts and of the necessity for holding any funds at all. In total, they can add up to a large sum and in practice they become fixed.

Bank balances held for the payment of purchases and expenses and the receipt of payments by customers. The timing of receipts and payments can vary widely during the year and as a result the total finance tied up may be considerable, particularly in a group. Appreciable savings can be effected by developing a central banking system in which all the group receipts and payments are balanced each day and surpluses invested on an 'overnight' basis. Movements of foreign currency can be handled in a similar manner, but this operation should be carried out by experts if losses are to be avoided.

Reserve funds. However excellent the planning system, the outcome of a year's operation does not equate with the planned profit and cash flow. The unexpected always intervenes. Some years everything goes well and in others a run of bad luck is experienced and the liquid resources have to bear the strain. Recourse is made to temporary borrowing and if this occurs in a period of recession, which is likely, interest rates will be high and their cost will increase the trading profit shortfall. The resources of the business should include funds to meet such contingencies. In good years the excess cash flow is invested outside the business to 'earn its keep' and to provide a resource to finance the years of cash shortages. The assessment should evaluate the size and effectiveness of the use of these funds.

INTANGIBLE RESOURCES

Intangible resources emerge as a result of effort expended and are of permanent use to a business. In economic terms they have a value. However, the accounting convention treats such resources as of nil value on several practical grounds, e.g.:

1 Intangible resources have an exchange value only on a change in ownership, an event which is incompatible with the continuing business basis on which the annual accounts are drawn up.
2 The economic value of intangible resources tends to rise and fall in step with trading profits. Consequently changes in a value for such resources merely emphasize the up and downs in trading profits.
3 There are no objective bases against which these resources can be measured; their valuation in money terms would be highly subjective and introduce undesirable obscurities.

Nonetheless, accountants have traditionally given values to the intangible resources listed below based on past expenses and/or profits modified by estimates of future profits.

Assessments of the state of intangible resources can be of assistance to management by determining the trend of their effectiveness through time.

Research and development

There is no difficulty in recognizing a successful completed project. But it is difficult in advance to assess whether or not the resources required for a new project will be wasted. It is hardly a matter to be left to the judgement of the Head of Finance, whose research and development colleagues are usually too involved to be able to take objective views. Once a project is running, a monitoring procedure should be instituted to assess the resources likely to be required, evaluating them in money terms, setting successive 'go'/'no go' decision points, and comparing actual expenditure with the forecast.

The assessment should investigate each completed project to obtain an indication of reasons for its success or failure. The data will assist in deciding the areas to be exploited and the methods to be followed in the future.

Patents

One of the more difficult business decisions is to decide whether to make public the details of new products and obtain the right to attack plagiarists, or to allow competitors to deduce the new technology and copy it without fear of reprisals. Much will depend on an assessment of competitors' activities and strengths, and on the customs of the industry. Possibilities may exist for using patents aggressively to enter protected markets by offering licences for local manufacture and/or marketing in return for royalties. They can yield sizeable contributions toward the costs of research and development for a negligible outlay. The wider distribution should enhance an international reputation and reduce the opportunities available to competitors.

Trade marks

Marketing policy may call for the registration of trade marks to deny their use to a competitor who might hope to persuade the public to buy a product carrying a near imitation. Registration fees are not high but the process of defending a trade mark in the courts can be costly. As the renewal periods of registration are infrequent and not uniform in all countries there is a tendency for the files to be neglected. The assessment of the value of trade marks will rely heavily on the strength of marketing opinion.

Reputation (traditionally termed 'goodwill')

Profitable selling is much easier if the business has developed a good reputation for fair prices, reliable deliveries, consistent quality of product and generous settlement of grievances. A good reputation is not earned quickly but it can be lost overnight by changes which do not find acceptance with customers, e.g. new products which do not fulfil expectations, better or more acceptable products introduced by a competitor, etc. An outstanding reputation may inhibit change and innovation from fear of adverse market reaction.

Personal relations

A framework of good personal relations in a business will be provided by the introduction of adequate techniques to ensure good pay and conditions at each level, the welfare of employees, fair retirement benefits, comprehensive induction and training techniques, and sensible regulations for the settlement of disputes. However, it should be recognized that while employees are quick to detect in their superiors bluff, sloth, unfairness, meanness etc., they appreciate firm control, fair judgement, acknowledgement of extra effort and an intelligent interest in their affairs. A business is a closely integrated social group of human beings and attention to these factors is essential for the effective functioning of the techniques.

Access to reliable sources of supply

Businesses depend on the effectiveness of their suppliers. Many large and successful businesses have spent much time, energy and money in assisting their suppliers to improve their manufacturing methods and techniques, recouping themselves by paying less for purchases and reducing stock levels as a result of more reliable delivery forecasts. They regard their suppliers of essential materials as an extension of their own business and have been known to assist in the provision of manufacturing facilities close to their own operations. This option is frequently preferable to incurring the capital cost and risks of entering new fields of activity in which expert knowledge is lacking. It is impracticable to adopt these procedures with all suppliers but purchasing departments can do much for the business by building up goodwill with suppliers' representatives. Good access to reliable suppliers of goods and services is a valuable business resource which is often overlooked.

THE AVAILABILITY OF FINANCE

Finance has been called the life-blood of a business. Without an adequate supply of finance all the activities of a business are restrained and progress is impaired. It is not sufficient for a business immediately to have an adequate fund of finance; sources of further finance must be available to meet future commitments and survive inevitable setbacks. Lack of finance is a major cause of business failure.

A successful business will have less difficulty in obtaining additional finance when credit is freely available. But, like commodities its supply and price may fluctuate. Its supply is particularly subject to changes in government policy. If proper steps are taken in the better times, finance will be more readily available for survival in the lean times. Consequently a business should keep its suppliers of finance informed of its financial progress, how it is dealing with problems arising from the state of the economy and what modifications it is making in its future intentions.

Study of long-term cash flows

The experience of the rapid change in outlook which followed the investment boom of the early 1970s and the subsequent sharp rise in oil prices are a reminder to business people that they operate in an uncertain environment. Reserves of minerals, fossil fuels, and so on are dwindling. Developments in computer technology threaten to alter radically our way of life. On the other hand, mankind has consistently demonstrated an ability to adapt successfully to changing environments. Against this background a basic study has to be made of the probable levels of cash flow through the foreseeable future, for without such a study rational estimates of the timing and quantity of future requirements are impossible.

The length of the 'foreseeable future' is determined by the nature of the products being considered and the stability of the market. Ten years might be reasonable for an established general-purpose machine manufacturer, but three years could be too long for articles made for a newly developed fashion market. It is a subjective management estimate of the time which it will take to complete a current long-term programme.

Borrowing finance

Although small businesses, particularly those starting up and proposing rapid expansion, often complain of difficulties in attracting the finance they require, surveys indicate that the amount of available finance is more than adequate. Applicants for finance tend to assume that the more optimistic they are, the more successful they will be; whereas the suppliers (the party to be convinced) look for realistic assessments of demand trends, costs and profitability, basing their assessments on their experience of similar businesses. Borrowers should always frame their applications for finance in a manner which will win the goodwill of the lender, without underestimating the difficulties of developing a successful business.

In a period of rapid inflation, the borrowing of finance for medium terms at fixed interest rates is often attractive compared with the issue of ordinary share capital. The cost of the dividends on the latter increases with the rising profits of the business, whereas the amount of interest paid on loans remains constant in money terms and becomes a lower and lower percentage of trading profit in a period of inflation. On the other hand if the rate of inflation drops, the borrower may find that relatively high interest charges are being paid out of declining profits.

Policies should be established for long- and/or short-term borrowing based on the study of cash flow and after review of the sources of finance.

Long-term finance

Stock exchanges at home and overseas are the main sources of long-term finance for the larger businesses. Strict rules about conduct and disclosure of information have to be accepted by the borrower, but stock exchanges do give access to a continuing and broadly based financial source.

The form of long-term finance for an established business will be determined by a variety of factors including the existing capital structure, the stock market preference at the time of the issue reflecting an assessment of future currency inflation, the trend of interest rates, the incidence of taxation and the current degree of optimism. Rights issues are popular when the market is buoyant.

Medium- and short-term finance

There are many sources including joint stock banks, merchant banks, finance houses, financial institutions, pension funds etc. Sources tend to specialize in particular outlets and businesses have the opportunity of choosing the source likely to be most satisfactory to them. There are advantages in cultivating more than one source of finance. The chosen sources should enjoy a substantial reputation, have some knowledge of the field in which the business operates, and be of a size relevant to the size of the borrowing business. A check should be made to ensure that the lender has access to reliable sources of new funds.

Lenders will expect to receive guarantees of good faith such as (a) preferential rights over some fixed assets, (b) guarantees of performance executed by a third party, (c) a share of the profits of the business by the issue of preference or ordinary shares or a mixture of such options.

Other sources of finance

As an alternative to seeking additional funds, approaches can be made to any of a wide range of bodies prepared to share in the cost of specific material resources, such as:

Central and local government and other agencies whose function is to make available grants and subsidies or give preferential treatment at specified locations. Assistance is widely advertised and available to help achieve socially desirable objectives, e.g. reduction of unemployment where it is high, aid to an important sector of industry experiencing a cyclical slump, care of the disabled and elderly, housing to encourage people to move from overcrowded areas etc. The terms and conditions alter, often at short notice, as a result of changes in government policy. However, nothing is given free – the business will be required to forgo some of its freedom of choice. The only reason for offering special treatment is to tempt business to accept a course of action which it might not have followed otherwise. In many instances, a slight adjustment to planned decisions will enable a business to make successful deals in partnership with these agencies.

Leasing. A wide range of plant, machinery and equipment can be obtained by means of a leasing contract with one of the many finance companies specializing in this type of transaction. Contract details vary but the leasing company generally pays the supplier for the equipment on delivery and charges a fixed sum for an agreed term of years. The company offering the leasing contract compares the total cost of payments over the period of the lease with the estimated cost of other methods of financing the purchase. Savings may arise from the incidence of tax and interest rate charges. Benefits in the form of favourable repurchase terms and specialist advice on maintenance etc. are frequently offered. The implications of the contract terms should be carefully weighed as future changes in tax regulations, interest rates etc. may impose unfortunate liabilities on the party accepting the lease. The lease will run for several years and the outcome may well be different from that envisaged at the outset.

Commodity 'futures'. Commodity prices are subject to frequent and wide fluctuations owing to changes in supply and demand. As a result the profits of companies which consume a large quantity of a particular commodity, it might be wheat, copper, lead, will be seriously affected by changes in the buying price of their principal raw material. There are specialized markets dealing in the more important commodities on an international basis. Dealers in these markets, using their expert knowledge and experience, offer quantities of the commodity for delivery at a future date at a fixed price known as the 'futures' price. Companies using the commodity have the option of minimizing the effects of commodity price fluctuations and variable storage costs either by a substantial investment in high stocks or by placing forward orders through the commodity 'futures' market. The latter course saves storage and interest charges but the prices include the dealer's profit.

Factoring trade debtors. Companies offering this service purchase for cash about 80 per cent of the value of trade debtors at a discount and/or fee. They collect the money from customers when due, and remit the balance of 20 per cent to the business. Factoring can often be an advantage to a business but many managements who have organized an efficient control of credit are averse to losing personal contact with customers.

Borrowing for export

Bills of exchange are short-term instruments of credit and are inadequate for financing long-term, large-scale capital projects. The speeding up of international communications has lessened their use but the bill discount market is still very active and operates on narrow margins. Bills of exchange arising from a trade in which short terms of credit are granted can be discounted at very fine rates. They form a useful, continuing and flexible source of semi-permanent finance.

Export credit guarantee department. This government department was formed originally to provide a type of mutual insurance against the possibility of an overseas customer defaulting. Loans against export sales at advantageous interest rates are now available to those who use the department's services.

Joint stock banks, merchant banks and others have government support for the provision of special financial facilities to assist British exporters to compete in overseas trade. Consequently, they are able in suitable cases to provide finance to cover export trade at preferential interest rates and guaranteed terms.

Internal generation of funds

In a discussion of the availability of finance, perhaps the most important rule is to reduce the need for it. The internal generation of a surplus cash flow is the cheapest source of finance. The level of investment in material resources should be strictly controlled. As much credit should be obtained from suppliers as is consistent with their own liquidity and the standard of service they are prepared to offer.

ORGANIZING THE FINANCIAL CONTROL

Businesses grow from a more or less well defined idea in someone's mind but finance must be available before the idea can become a reality. Financial backing is required to acquire those things necessary to give a physical structure to the business – the building, the equipment, the stocks of material and the people who will run the business. As the company develops, the original idea, if viable, will take on a unique form; control of the various activities becomes more defined and information about the efficiency of the organization becomes increasingly essential. Experience has shown that the best general basis for the measurement of efficiency is in money terms and is achieved through an adequate system of financial control.

The development of the financial organization

In the early development of the business financial control will be rudimentary and little more than that required by every household in the conduct of its affairs. As the business grows in size it becomes a more complex entity, and a more structured form of financial control is needed to handle the increasing flow of information required in managing the business. Although the financial control becomes more important its role will always be to assist the business in achieving its objectives. In due course, the financial organization will itself have to expand and the work pattern of the sections be reviewed in the light of developments and improved work techniques.

The staff should be asked for their ideas and several alternative solutions may be put forward. Some will involve substantial changes. The founders of the business probably held definite views of organization and their influence may permeate the fabric of the company long after they have retired. The results of radical changes are often disappointing, partly because of a failure to appreciate the psychological and practical value of retaining continuity. Frequently the best solution involves only the essential changes. There are always difficulties which inhibit the will to institute changes and usually the best time to make alterations in settled routines is 'now'.

Annual accounts

The developed financial organization will provide the annual and interim reports which have to be made to shareholders and the wider public. In addition to the financial figures and supporting notes, the reports will include a varied selection of information regarding the company's corporate activities, such as internal reorganization; provisions for health and safety at work; staff consultation; the policies being followed toward Third World countries; charitable, educational and sporting contributions made to the community at large.

Internal reporting

In practice, however, the larger and more important work effort is directed toward the marshalling and recording of the flows of data and their presentation to management in a manner suitable for the control, administration and development of the business. The process can be immensely facilitated by the use of computers. The computer configurations produce output designed to supply the various sections of the financial organization with the information required in the desired format, e.g. operators' wages, staff salaries, payment for supplies, customers' invoices and statements etc. Collated reports are issued for the use of line managers covering such aspects of the business as the levels of income and expenditure actually achieved compared to budget, measures of output and efficiency and so on. The economic service at headquarters will receive copies of the current results for incorporation in comparative studies of the progress of the business in relation to competitors' activities and general trade experience.

Costing. When profitability is measured only in terms of the units of the business, some products will tend to be overpriced and some underpriced in relation to a fair assessment of the proportion of expenditure attributable to them. A knowledge of the margin between the cost of a product and its selling price is an essential element of financial control. The amount of cost attributable to a product depends on such things as utilization of the productive capacity of the factory, the prices at which the buying department obtains the raw materials, the efficiency of the work force and the qualities required of the finished product. The net price at which the product is offered for sale depends on a variety of considerations including the quantity to be purchased, costs incurred in effecting the sale and competitive prices. In quoting prices the marketing department relies to an important extent on the adequacy of the information provided by the costing department. A number of costing techniques have been developed to assist the preparation of product costs, e.g. marginal, standard, replacement and batch costing. The chosen technique should be the one most applicable to the needs of the business. Product costing involves a considerable amount of repetitive and detailed calculation which can be performed by a computer utilizing data held in the memory store for other purposes. It may be preferable to limit the computer operation to routine calculations and print-out, leaving to skilled accountants the interpretation of the output.

Cash control. The financial organization can make a direct contribution to the profitability of the business by its handling of liquid resources. The units holding cash and bank balances should send by teleprinter to central control their opening balances, receipts and payments for the day and their estimates for the succeeding five days. Transactions involving foreign currency are reported separately. The information is collated at headquarters where the groups' liquid resources are treated as one fund. Staff are in a position to maximize very short-term investment, hold back payments to even out cash flow and organize the timing of foreign exchange transactions.

Specialist activities. A number of specialist activities are often treated as part of the financial organization, e.g. registrar's duties relating to share transfers and dividend payments, taxation, insurance, pensions and patents, although in some companies these tasks are carried out by the legal department or by outside specialists.

Computers and centralized organization

The increased standard of living in the industrialized countries led businesses to expand rapidly to satisfy the growing demand from consumers and to look for greater efficiency through economies of scale. To benefit from the advantages of large-scale operations, they tended to centralize their activities in a small number of large locations. These large units required increasingly complex organizations which became unwieldy unless serviced by efficient financial departments. The volume of data became more and more difficult to handle by manual systems. In the early 1950s digital computers became available and commercial models were introduced into financial organizations. It was soon realized that these machines could speed up the collection and processing of data across the functional boundaries of the business and improve the effectiveness of centralized control.

However, largely as a result of the growth of centralization in large businesses, shop-floor operators, first-line supervisors, office managers and their staffs began to feel so remote from those responsible for decision making that they saw themselves as mere cyphers in a vast impersonal organization. In consequence efficiency and morale declined. 'Wild-cat' strikes were more frequent per employee in large organizations than in the small- and medium-sized businesses. Top management often felt out of touch with what the ordinary people in the business were thinking and doing. The development of greater consultation at all levels should ease the sociological problems, but consultation may, by its very nature, nullify a main advantage of centralization, namely the ability of top management to put decisions into effect quickly and decisively.

Although a large computer system is a necessity in the financial organization of a centralized business operating internationally, the system carries within itself factors which tend to inhibit its full potential. Systems planning is complex and calls for a rare degree of understanding of the interlocking nature of the various activities in the business. At no time are the systems in a settled state, for the business itself is continually changing in various small ways and the available computer hardware is constantly being improved.

Principles of the delegation of authority

The problems arising from a centralization of activities as enumerated above indicate that a departure from full centralization would improve industrial efficiency. This would involve a greater degree of delegation of authority for the taking of decisions than is practised in a centralized organization.

As an administrative convenience the many activities within the financial organization are accomplished through an adequate delegation of authority over the various specialist sections of the organization. A manager is responsible to a superior for the proper carrying out of duties, and in turn delegates to subordinates. The responsibilities inherent in the job and those activities in which he or she is an acknowledged expert will not be delegated. A clearly defined range of activities should be agreed with an assistant and the authority to take the related decisions transferred.

The supervisor will find it relatively easy to arrange for immediate subordinates to follow directions but in situations where responsibility is held for several command levels, particularly at separate locations, it is more difficult to ensure that given methods are adopted in first-line operations. Visits should be made to the various offices at regular intervals to talk to the staff at this level and observe weaknesses. Subsequently a discussion with the immediately responsible subordinate should have the object of encouraging an improvement in working conditions in the office concerned.

The structure of the business described in the objectives of the business will determine the degree of delegation practised in the financial organization. Preferences range from a predominately centralized system of control to a decentralized system but whatever the degree of centralization, the foregoing principles of delegation will apply.

Dangers inherent in an organized financial control

Two aspects of organized financial control may, if overlooked, involve the business in serious difficulties.

A well ordered and adequate financial organization contains information on most of the vital aspects of a business: the state of its assets and liabilities; profitable and unprofitable activities; the propress being made toward the planned future of the business etc. When well organized, financial control can be the most far-reaching and effective management tool at the disposal of the chief executive. But it is a tool to be used with restraint and discretion lest it become the dominant function of the organization, producing endless information with too little regard for the objectives of the business.

It is not yet fully appreciated to what extent the future will be affected by (a) the growing realization of the limits of oil and other resources and (b) the developments in the use of micro-transistors in control mechanisms. Both will lead to basic changes in management practice. Financial organizations will be called upon to evaluate in money terms the effects of fundamental changes. They must be adequately staffed with assistants well qualified to assess ways of meeting the new challenges and able to present their findings to each management level in a clear unbiased manner.

Financial control of dispersed operating units

The terms branches, subsidiaries, divisions, and groups are used to describe the departments of a business which operate at a distance from the centre. Joint ventures with other companies may be designated subsidiaries with minority shareholders, associated companies, consortia etc. according to the form of the relationship. Their operations may be carried out at home or overseas and will embrace a wide range of activities. A complete review of financial controls covering the range of dispersed operating units is beyond the scope of this chapter which has concentrated on a brief statement of a general approach to the problems involved in their control.

Complex structures are to be avoided as they give rise to differences in the interpretation of laws and regulations unconnected with the task of achieving business objectives. Subsidiaries are an example. They are legal entities structured according to statutes which define, among other things, the duties and responsibilities of the directors regarding separate financial accounts whereas a divisional structure enables managers to limit their attention to the general financial requirements of the total group. Matters are further complicated in situations where there are minority shareholders whose interests have to be safeguarded.

The basic, albeit oversimplified, objective of the financial control of dispersed operating units is to enable management to deduce an answer to the question: 'Is the trend of returns satisfactory?'

To provide the information on which such an assessment can be based the financial organization will be required to assist in establishing the tasks in terms of the local currency for the dispersed units to achieve in the immediate and more distant future. An accounting system will be developed to report, as a minimum, the values of monthly sales and profits compared with the forecasted tasks. The ratios of sales to profit, stocks and trade debtors wil be calculated and compared with the ratios reported in previous periods and those used in the forecasts. A balance sheet of assets and liabilities with, in the case of jointly owned units, a local audit certificate would also be required.

Accounting conventions should be agreed. Although they will generally conform to accepted accounting principles it is important that they are agreeable to local practices and the needs of the business. This is particularly relevant in overseas units where national laws govern the methods of conducting business and preparing profit statements – some international companies which have raised capital overseas publish separate financial accounts for some of the countries in which they operate. The agreed conventions would cover such subjects as the bases on which profit is computed (depreciation; valuation of stocks; quantifying future liabilities; intangible and reserve assets; etc.) and the rules for inter-company pricing which would provide incentives to the manufacturing units and take account of the fiscal regulations of both the exporting and importing countries.

The financial organization at headquarters would be responsible for converting the reports from the dispersed units stated in local currencies into consolidated statements by adjusting for changes in rates of exchange and inflation.

The method of financing the dispersed units, sharing profits and making distributions, should be described in the agreement which establishes the unit. Local residents can assist in ensuring that alternative courses of achieving local objectives are not overlooked and there may be advantages in involving local residents in the financial management of larger units even where such a course is not obligatory.

3

Forecasting Demand

M.W. Sasieni

It is inconceivable that any business, or new venture in a long-standing business, could be successfully established without some forecast of the demand for the products or services which it is intended to supply, even if such forecast is purely intuitive. In more sophisticated situations, particularly where large-scale operations and heavy investments are involved, the forecast of demand on which the business plans are to be based will represent the result of a rigorous and scientific assessment of the future market. Such assessment will itself be founded upon a study of the economic and demographic factors which have affected and will continue to affect the demand.

Depending on the scope of the operations envisaged – or maybe the ambitions of the entrepreneurs involved – the forecast of demand will normally be followed by an estimate of the market share which the business aims to obtain. The extent to which that market share can be exploited and expanded will depend upon the several constraints on the organization imposed by such factors as production capacity and the availability and cost of essential resources such as manpower, equipment and materials. One over-ridding constraint will be the finance which can be made available. For the latter reason alone, the long chain of exercises leading from the forecast of demand to the eventual sales budget, although falling naturally within the ambit of the marketing function, must also be regarded as a vital element in financial planning, and justifies discussion in a work on that subject. Of equal importance, the subsequent financial control procedures should be directly related to the business plan which, it has been argued above, will logically be based initially on the forecast of demand.

In this chapter the author points out that for substantial businesses methods of forecasting have become somewhat specialized and, for that reason alone, require at least the general understanding of all members of the management team. The author refers, interalia, to demographic factors, the level of economic activity, input/output analysis and demand/price elasticity. The discussion covers both consumer products and industrial products and particular attention is given to forecasting demand for new products. The technique of concept testing is examined and so are consumer trials and the application of various statistical devices. As a practising consultant Dr Sasieni acknowledges that judgement and experience may be vital factors in the accuracy of the forecasting exercise.

All planning is a matter of assessing the task to be accomplished, deciding what resources this will require and making sure that the resources become available as and when they are needed. Financial planning is, of course, primarily concerned with a single resource – money – but it should be stressed that money alone will frequently fail to ensure that resources appear and tasks are accomplished on schedule. We only have to consider problems arising from crop failures to wartime shortages, from labour unrest to lack of technological and managerial skills, to see that while money is important it is by no means the only factor entering into planning and control. There are large organizations (including some state-controlled enterprises) that regularly and consistently fail to spend their capital budgets. The reasons are often complex, but they seldom include shortage of liquid assets.

Russell Ackoff (1965) has defined planning as 'anticipatory decision making' so that, by its very nature, planning is concerned with the future. It is therefore necessary that the planner has some understanding of the techniques available for forecasting, particularly for forecasting demand. Every business, whether privately or state-owned, and many government and local government departments are in existence to supply goods or services. To plan their future they need to understand how much of their goods or services will be required by customers. Of course the demand is partially within their control. We could say that the purpose of the large marketing departments, which exist in many organizations, is to ensure that demand reaches levels which the organizations considers acceptable.

Demand forecasting ranges over a continuum. At one end we have commodities at a worldwide level. Over the next few years what will the world's requirements be for wheat? for edible oils? for mineral oils? for coal, steel, etc? At the other end we may be selling chocolate candy bars under a particular brand name and we wish to know how many we will sell next year. In principle any technique can be used across the range, but in practice methods of forecasting have become specialized and some of these will be considered here.

Averaging

It is well-known that the average of several measurements is likely to be more accurate then a single measurement. Thus, if we wish to know the percentage of alcohol in a blood sample and a single analysis has an error of ± 1 per cent, the average of four independent analyses can be expected to be within ± ½ per cent. Notice that the analyses should be *independent* and that quadrupling the effort (four analyses) only reduces the error by half. In recent years these concepts have been applied to forecasting. Estimates of future demand are made by several methods and the results are averaged to give a 'best estimate'.

Forecasts do not quite fit the structure of repeated laboratory measurements. If two managers have different models, both cannot be right at the same time. For example, to estimate demand for bricks next year, one manager may plot a simple graph of annual production (which need not be the same as demand – what about stock level changes?) and extrapolate to next year with a free hand sketch. Another may first estimate the likely levels of new housing and other constructions, and estimate the quantity of bricks needed. To this must be added the likely requirements of such industries as mining, quarrying, and steel making, all of which use bricks. When there is a clear reason to prefer one model over another, there may be little logic to using their average, but where there is no a priori reason to accept one model (or the views of one expert) averaging several estimates has been found to yield good results.

The estimates should be made by different people, so that some semblance of independence is preserved. However, even individuals who do not work together may share a common bias. Field sales staff are notoriously optimistic and averaging the estimates of sales representatives with those of area and regional sales managers may merely compound the error of any one of them.

Scott Armstrong (1984) in a brief but very readable note surveying forecasting methods wrote:

For the practitioner the implications are clear: relatively simple extrapolation methods . . . are adequate . . . use more than one method. My suggestion is to spread the budget over three or four inexpensive and easily understood methods, then calculate an average forecast.[1]

It is to some of these simple approaches that we now turn.

COMMODITIES AND INDUSTRIAL TOTALS

Even a small manufacturer is likely to find that the demand for one firm's products varies directly with the total demand for products of a similar nature. On top of the variation associated with the commodity or industry there will also be changes brought about by the marketing activities of the manufacturer. These will be considered later, but first some of the factors which enter into predicting the demand for commodities will be reviewed. It should be realized that their relative importance depends on the timescale involved. Thus population growth may be of little consequence in next year's demand for, say, motor vehicles. It may be the single crucial factor in assessing demand for wheat or rice five to ten years from now. Changing demographics (by which is meant all aspects of population, including birth rate, age distribution, family size, level of education, geographic distribution etc.) are always candidates for consideration in forecasting demand over any horizon beyond the next year or two.

The second major factor is the general level of economic activity. This concept need not be defined here with any degree of precision. Suffice it to say that demand for most goods and services is likely to increase in periods of economic boom. There are exceptions; demand for cheaper substitutes is likely to be stimulated when times are hard. Such businesses are called counter-cyclical and may be much prized by companies with 'normal' products who wish to preserve a more uniform level of activity despite the ups and downs of the business cycle. The machine tool business is notorious for the way in which

---

[1] In a subsequent conversation, Scott Armstrong has suggested that instead of using an arithmetic mean, the median of several estimates would be better. The median is a value such that half the estimates are above it and half below. When we only have three or four estimates, calculation of the median is only possible by making some assumption about the distribution of estimates from which the actual estimates constitute a small sample.

peaks and troughs exceed those of other industries. One firm discovered that during depression the government had a tendency to stimulate the economy with road building programmes. By producing a range of medium-weight earth-moving equipment some of the worst fluctuations could be ironed out.

The use of economic activity to forecast, other than in general fashion, is a highly skilled matter, and a discussion is beyond the scope of this chapter. However two techniques are worth mentioning. In principle a lead-indicator can be used. If some activity is found which moves ahead of the one it is desired to forecast, observation of the indicator can be used to predict. Thus changes in today's wholesale price index are likely to be reflected in retail prices three to six months hence. Current prices of raw materials will appear in wholesale prices later and so on. Unfortunately such indicators are not always easy to find and the relationship between them and the forecast variable may be weak. However they can be useful when our planning horizon is the next few months. Beyond this the only indicator may be population. After all, the adult population a few years hence already exists (partly as children) and a knowledge of death rates will enable a fairly good prediction of future age distribution, subject only to emigration and immigration.

A method which has received much attention over recent years is called 'input–output analysis'. Consider a particular industry, say steel, and ask what input from other industries is required to produce a ton of steel. Among other items there will be iron ore, coal and lime. There will also be less obvious requirements. Thus bricks and cement, motor vehicles, electric energy, even perhaps time on a computer will be needed. A table can then be drawn up, showing for each major sector of the economy the number of units of input required from others to produce a unit of output.

It can then be seen how changes in the output of any one industry affect all the others. Thus one ton of steel will require say one ton of coal. This in turn will require steel, bricks, cement, vehicles etc. Models of economic systems used to be built with perhaps twenty or so 'industries'. Nowadays, the availability of large computers has permitted models with hundreds of industries. The current limitations are probably the availability of data for deriving the input–output matrix, rather than computing resources.

One of the appealing features of this approach is its ability to model technological change. The data matrix represents current technology. Thus if steel is made in electric arc furnaces, the direct input of coal will be reduced and the input of electricity will rise. The coefficients can be changed to reflect beliefs about changing technology and thus forecast the impact of these changes on various industries.

It would not be appropriate to conclude this section without a reference to prices. In classical economics the major factor which influences demand at the commodity level is price. In practice there are many other factors, but price remains important. Unfortunately it is no easier to forecast price than demand, but sometimes both can be successfully predicted simultaneously.

Suppose that from past observations (world) production of a commodity against its price can be plotted, and in addition a relationship between demand and price can be developed. On the assumption that supply and demand balance in the long run the level of price and quantity at which equilibrium will occur can be determined. The effects of other factors can be allowed for, by envisioning them to cause a shift in either the demand or supply curve. Thus increasing popularity of coffee would cause the demand for tea at any given price to be reduced. The graph of demand versus price will be shifted downwards and to the left. Similarly a new production process may shift the supply curve so that the quantity produced at any specified price will change. Thus forecasting quantities and prices is

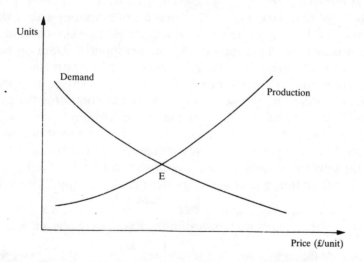

Fig. 3.1 Supply and demand curves for a commodity
Note: At the point E the quantity demanded just matches the production and there is equilibrium.

reduced to understanding how these curves react to changes (see Fig. 3.1).

ESTABLISHED CONSUMER BRANDS

The volume for brands within established product fields is usually estimated in two stages. First a forecast is made for the product field and then brand share within the total can be estimated. The simplest approach to forecasting is to say that the future will be similar to the past and the latest available share figure is a good guide to next year. If it is wished to predict for next year it would be as well to use share over a twelve-month period, because the latest monthly figure may reflect all sorts of temporary or seasonal fluctuation. The estimate is then adjusted in the light of any other relevant information. For example it might be known that a competitor was about to open a new plant which would give increased capacity at a lower cost. Alternatively, it might be known that distribution had finally been achieved through a retail chain which hitherto had not stocked that particular brand.

If a price change which could affect the volume is considered, more sophisticated analysis can help. To start, a graph of market share against relative price[1] (i.e. price compared with competing brands) would be plotted (see Fig. 3.2). Then a price–volume curve which appears best to reflect their relationship would be sketched in. All this can now be done automatically on a computer. Data on actual volumes for the main brands and others together with revenues or prices are input. The machine not only computes shares and prices, but in addition plots the necessary graphs and computes the price–volume curve. It will also assess the statistical significance[2] of the curve, and the price *elasticity*. The latter is a convenient and widely used method of expressing the way volume varies with price. Elasticity is the percentage gain (fall) in volume for a 1 per cent fall (rise) in price. It has an immediate and important profit interpretation. If the

---

[1] The use of relative prices and volumes usually eliminates problems of seasonality and inflation.

[2] It is possible that even if price and volume were unrelated, sheer chance would produce a plot in which a limited number of points lie on a line. It is usually desirable to know the probability that this has occurred. If it is low it reinforces the belief that price and volume are related.

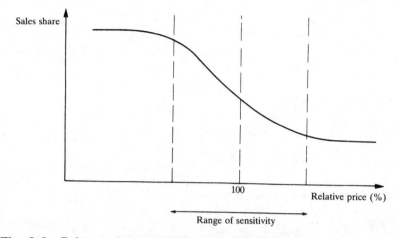

Fig. 3.2 Price–volume relationship for a brand
Note: Typically share is not price-sensitive at very high or very low prices.
Share may change markedly at prices near the market average (100 per
cent). Most brands usually operate within a fairly narrow price range and
within this range the curve can be treated as a straight line – plot the graph
and use a rule.

variable margin per cent is divided into 100 and the result exceeds the
elasticity it will pay to decrease the price[1], thus increasing both gross
profit and volume. On the other hand if the result is less than the
elasticity gross profit can be increased by increasing the price.[1] There
will be a decrease in volume and this is a side effect that the profit gain
may not be large enough to justify.

In some markets the only variable which has a measurable effect in
the short- and medium-term is price, but often several others should
be considered. Among potential candidates are:

1   advertising levels
2   distribution
3   product quality (including packaging).

In practice, distribution and particularly quality may not have varied
in the past enough for their effects to be measurable (if there have
been no changes, it cannot be said what the effects of changes would

---

[1] Recall that calculations were made in terms of relative price so that to achieve the
volume changes discussed a relative price change is needed. Competitors may not
permit this as they can easily change prices to match.

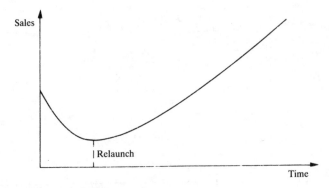

Fig. 3.3   The hockey stick forecast

be). Of course the graphical plot will hardly serve if there are additional variables, but they present no special computational problems.

Product quality only enters the forecast if it is expected to change, either because of a change in brand, or to a change in a competing brand. When either is expected some allowance must be made. Often a change in brand is part of a relaunch by which it is hoped to give the brand a fresh impetus. Volume changes are often forecast by the well-known 'hockey stick' approach. This derives its name from its graph which resembles a hockey stock (see Fig. 3.3). Such a graph may be wildly optimistic and examination of relaunches of other brands may yield a more realistic estimate of the likely gains.

Advertising differs in one important way from price. Experience shows that, much of the time, the effects of a price change on volume are over within the month in which it occurs. This is in marked contrast to advertising effects which may persist for several months or even longer. In analysing how advertising affects volume these carry-over effects must be considered. Furthermore, while a straight line may be an acceptable representation of the way volume (share) responds to (relative) price, it may be expected that the effects of each successive pound spent on advertising will diminish.[1] This means that advertising response cannot be represented with a single

---

[1] People will already have heard the message. Since the number of good (TV) spots is limited, ever increasing funds will force buying of poorer spots.

There may be an opposite effect at very low budgets. Many writers claim that there is a threshold below which advertising has little or no effect. The evidence for this is not strong.

straight line and more complicated curves are required. All these problems can be surmounted by a competent statistician, provided sufficient data exist. A complete understanding may require more than 60 observations. At one a month this means five years' data. Even if this much were available, market and economic conditions are likely to have changed so much as to make the early observations irrelevant. In these circumstances it is often best to settle for a simple model, which captures those aspects of the market which experience shows are important.

In many businesses established products account for the bulk of the turnover and profits. Any forecast of company performance will require their accurate assessment.

Although sophisticated analytical methods are available for forecasting, the results must always be 'hand polished' for those non-quantitative aspects which modify past history. The economic climate, competitive and retail trade activity, technological and political change are all likely to influence volumes, but often experienced judgement is the only way to incorporate them into forecasts.

NEW CONSUMER PRODUCTS

Most businesses find that the demand for long-established products tends to diminish over time. This view has been enshrined in the so-called 'product life cycle theory' in which three stages in the life of a product (or brand) are envisaged. First there is a growth period in which more and more people learn to use it. This is followed by a mature stage in which sales are steady; finally the item goes into decline and ultimately disappears altogether. The pattern fits many brands, but the reader can probably think of some notorious exceptions. Some brands, by constant modifications and improvement have been household names for forty years and more. Be that as it may, there is no doubt that a firm that wishes to stay in business is likely to find it necessary to launch a stream of new and/or improved products. In planning it is clearly necessary to forecast demand for any proposed product.

At this point it is as well to distinguish three types of forecast which are frequently confused. Ideally the three should be estimated independently, and preferably by different people. Very often a single figure is used for all of them without any clear view as to which was the one actually estimated. The first forecast is the estimate of what the demand will prove to be. This will reflect the sum total of relevant experience and will take into account, as explicitly as possible, all the 'hard' evidence available. Such a forecast has nothing to do with how profitable the product will be, or whether the launch is desirable. It merely reflects the best thoughts about future demand.

This must be distinguished from an action standard. Very often there are a number of stages between the initial concept and final market success. At each of them a go/no go decision is necessary and frequently action standards are set as an aid to the decision process. Thus considerations of profitability might dictate that if the product fails to get 10 per cent in a test market it will not be launched nationally (or not in the test market form). Such a standard might be quite different from the estimate of what the actual share will be.

Finally there is the target figure. So much of the eventual outcome depends on the incentives, motivation and confidence of the staff involved that it is necessary to give them something to strive for, usually referred to as a sales target. It must be realistic, in the sense that while not so low as to be easily reached, it is not so high as to be considered impossible by those whose task it is to meet it.

In forecasting demand for a new product the purpose of the forecast needs to be understood, otherwise totally unsuitable numbers may be produced. For planning purposes the best estimate of actual sales will often be required, but sometimes action standards together with the chances of meeting them will be more appropriate.

This section concludes with brief notes on some of the techniques which provide relevant data for new product forecasting. Unfortunately none of them separately or in combination is infallible; there are many new products which fail and prudent financial planning will consider this possibility even if the sales manager's address to the sales convention does not!

PRODUCT FORECASTING TECHNIQUES

Concept testing

Once a product concept is considered a possible new entry by management, the next stage may be a group discussion. A small sample drawn from the demographic groups considered to be potential customers is invited to a meeting and a trained leader focuses the discussion on the product area. For example the groups might be asked to consider the problems of dirty dishes. From such a meeting the consumers' views as to the strengths and weaknesses of existing products will emerge for comparison with the new entrant. Quantitative estimates of sales volumes are not the normal outcome, but some feel for the potential can be obtained.

Consumer trials

Once the product is available, even in very limited quantities, potential purchasers may be invited to try it and to comment. A group discussion could be used, but often a simulated purchasing situation will be more revealing. Respondents may be told they have so much money to spend (say enough for two packs of any brand in the product area) and they are asked to choose between the new brand and other existing brands. Usually any money remaining will be theirs to keep and they may keep all the money if they wish. Such a test involves pricing the new entrant, which is highly important to its ultimate success. The actual choice may be made from a catalogue list or from a mock-up of a real store.

Such a test is aimed at measuring repeat purchasing. The eventual sales depend on two factors: (a) what proportion of the population will try, i.e. buy, at least once; and (b) what fraction of their subsequent purchases will consist of the new brand. The first factor is called penetration and the second, repeat rate. The eventual share is the product of the two.

There are many ways of stimulating trial, including heavy advertising, free samples, special price offers and so on. However the repeat rate depends largely on the product itself, so that it can be estimated from test data of the sort described above. An attempt would be made to estimate penetration from previous experience of the proposed levels of advertising, promotion and sales effort. An important intermediate variable to be considered is the level of distribution (i.e. proportion of shops handling) which will be obtained.

If somewhat larger amounts of product are available, and if there are samples of the pack, a form of test, much closer to the real marketplace, is the mini-van. This is a van which calls on a selected panel at regular intervals and offers a fairly complete range of groceries at competitive prices. By accepting orders only on the special form provided a complete record of purchases is obtained. It is easy enough to insert new items into the range for test purposes. As far as the customer is concerned, the van is merely a door-to-door selling operation, but it has been found to provide good estimates of repeat buying rates. It is less effective at estimating penetration, as it is difficult to simulate normal advertising activity, particularly television. Also missing are the effects associated with distribution levels. In some countries special mini-stores are used rather than vans.

The closest that can be come to the full national market is an area test market. Here the intention is to reproduce every aspect in a small area where the costs and risks are less than in a national launch. It is usually necessary to commission special market research in the test area to provide the required information. This is because routine sources seldom cover small areas in sufficient detail.

How well do test markets predict national sales? Apart from sampling errors associated with their size, there are some other problems. By their nature, small test areas may receive an undue level of sales-force attention. This should not happen but it does, because all concerned are aware of head-office interest. Competitive reaction is sometimes on a scale which could not be maintained on a national level. Finally the effects of regional differences must be considered. Different products do sell differently across the country and this too must be considered in grossing up to national sales.

Before leaving test marketing it should be noted that it cannot be kept secret (unlike a mini-van). Often competitors can learn just as much from a test market. If the product can easily be copied it may be preferable to avoid a test market altogether.

INDUSTRIAL GOODS

Forecasting the demand for industrial goods differs in many ways from that of consumer products. The difference lies in the nature of the buyers, and often in the frequency of purchase. Typically the buyers are relatively few in number and technically competent to evaluate the objective properties of their purchases. This means that it is often possible to place prototypes with potential customers for evaluation.

Before this stage is reached it is usual to analyze the industrial uses of the product and to form estimates of the future development of the users. Thus the market for a new roof tile must depend on future housing starts, together with the rate at which existing roofs will require replacement. Once these estimates are available, they can be used together with the customer trials to estimate the volume we are likely to obtain.

It is likely that in estimating consumer sales potential, the bulk of the effort will go into field work to obtain data. In industrial markets a much higher proportion will be desk work in which data already published will be studied for the light they throw on the product.

ANALYTICAL METHODS OF SHORT-TERM FORECASTS

In all practical forecasting problems, the relevant information consists of a series of, say, monthly observations. These might be sales or production data. At any point of time the past history of the series is available and it is wished to predict the next few numbers. If the data are plotted on graph paper two things will be noticed. There is a broad pattern which relates the data to the passage of time – a pencilled-in freehand curve reflects this relationship. In addition there is a random pattern of deviations from this curve. To forecast, the freehand curve needs to be extended in advance of firm information. To see how accurate the forecast is likely to be, the pattern of the deviations must be understood (see Fig. 3.4).

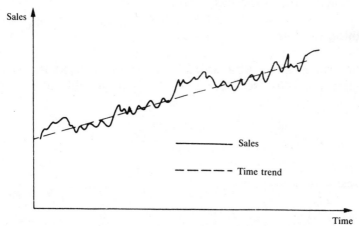

Fig. 3.4   Actual sales and underlying pattern

Moving averages

Intuition suggests that random fluctuations 'ought to average out' and this leads to the simplest possible method of computing the underlying time pattern. An appropriate number of observations is averaged. Quarters might be taken, which means adding the first three observations and dividing by three. Then observations 2, 3, and

4 and so on are taken. The result is a quarterly moving average. This could be computed just as well by multiplying each observation by one-third and adding the results in sets of three. The quantities 'one-third' are called weights.

Moving averages not only iron out random fluctuations; they also iron out seasonal patterns, provided the length of the cycle is the same as the number of observations being averaged. For this reason they usually exhibit a much simpler pattern than the original data and it is easier to guess the next few moving averages for prediction purposes.

There is no reason why the weights used should all be equal and for many purposes it is better to use unequal weights. Thus 60 per cent of last month's sales might be taken, plus 30 per cent of the month before and 10 per cent of the month before that. Such a weighting system reflects the belief that recent events are more relevant to the future than the remote past. Most of the currently available forecasting formulas are equivalent to some form of weighted moving average, but frequently this is not readily apparent as it is convenient to compute with other formulas.

Smoothing models

As time passes more observations are obtained and the size of forecasting errors is ascertained. It seems reasonable to take past

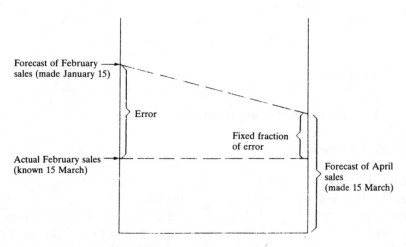

Fig. 3.5 How smoothed forecasts are made

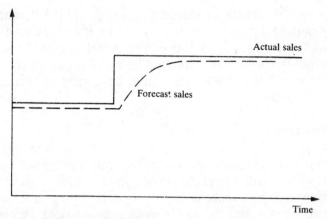

Fig. 3.6 Tracking a step rise

errors into account in making further forecasts. One way to do this is to add a fixed percentage of last month's error to last month's actual sales and use the result as a forecast for next month. This is equivalent to using a weighted average of actual and forecast sales.

If there is a time trend the same can be done for the trend measure, which is defined as the difference between this month's and last month's actual sales.

Figures 3.5, 3.6 and 3.7 illustrate some possibilities with simple smoothing methods. Such methods seem to give quite good short-term forecasts, but perhaps too short-term for financial planning.

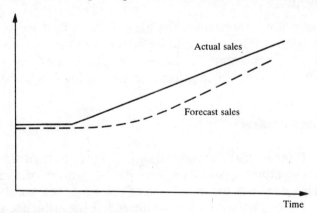

Fig. 3.7 Tracking a trend

Note: Unless the trend is also smoothed, the forecast will lag behind the actual sales.

They are very useful for production planning and stock control. As with any 'automatic' methods results can be improved by the judicious use of extraneous information. For example, it might be known that this month's sales were affected by a strike or by raw material problems; abnormally high sales might be anticipated next month because of a price offer.

Large time series

The smoothing method just described can start with very few observations and will often settle down quite quickly to yield reasonable forecasts. When there are several years' listing more sophisticated methods can be used to determine appropriate weights. The best known of these is named 'Box–Jenkins' after its originators. It uses a weighted average of sales over several months, together with a weighted average of past errors. The system starts by using the data to determine how many months of each to take and then computes the weights. The basic criterion used is to make the (average) forecast error as small as possible, but Box and Jenkins recognized another principle which is helpful.

> As long as successive errors are not independent of each other, a knowledge of past errors could be used to predict future errors and hence to improve forecasts. Thus if calculation shows that errors are related to each other the forecast formula can be improved.

This approach not only permits the past history of a time series to forecast its future, but it can also be adapted to take into account other relevant information. For example in predicting sales it might be much better to use data on prices and advertising levels instead of sales alone.

Causality and control

In order to forecast sales a lead indicator might be discovered and Box–Jenkins methods used to ascertain the nature of the relationship. This does not mean a cause of sales has necessarily been found or that altering the indicator would control or influence sales in any way. There may merely be a pair of variables which move together under the influence of a third, possibly unknown factor. Thus there is a major difference between forecast and control. The latter will require a much deeper understanding of the underlying mechanisms than the former. It is probable that control will require designed experiments to ascertain the nature of these mechanisms. A discussion of these points is beyond the scope of this chapter.

REFERENCES AND FURTHER READING

Ackoff, R.L. and Sasieni, M.W., *Fundamentals of Operations Research*, Wiley, 1965.

Armstrong, J. Scott, *Long Range Forecasting: From Crystal Ball to Computer*, Wiley N.Y., 1978.

Armstrong, J. Scott, 'Forecasting by Extrapolation: Conclusions from 25 years of Research', *Interfaces*, **14**, No. 6, November/December, 1984.

Bunn, Derek, W., 'The Synthesis of Predictive Models in Marketing Research', *Journal of Marketing Research* **16**, No. 2 (May), 1979.

Gabor, A., *Pricing*, 2nd edition, Gower, 1988.

Kotler, P., *Marketing Management: Analysis, Planning and Control*, Prentice-Hall, 1976.

Lewis, C.D., *Industrial Forecasting Techniques*, Machinery Publishing, 1970.

Makridakis, S. and Winkler, R.L., 'Averages of Forecasts: Some Empirical Results' *Management Science*, **29**, No. 9 (September), 1983.

Wilson, A., *The Assessment of Industrial Markets*, Cassell/ABP, 1973.

Worcester, R.M. and Downham, J. (eds), *Consumer Market Research Handbook*, Van Nostrand Reinhold, 1972.

4

Pricing Policy

Bryan Atkin

Financial executives will surely agree with the author of this chapter when he says that the pricing decision represents perhaps 'the most delicate and important of the problems facing a company'. Those who are responsible for financial planning and control will also be acutely aware that 'relatively small differences in price can have a dramatic effect on the profitability of a product or service'. For the latter reason alone an error in establishing the price can nullify at one stroke the reality of the forward plans and the most efficient control of the subsequent performance.

Pricing policy is therefore an essential element in the financial planning of a company's affairs. The many and diverse implications of establishing that policy are proper subjects for study by financial executives for it may well be incumbent on them to give advice, from their particular viewpoint, of the financial effects of that policy or, indeed, to assist in the framing of the policy.

Nevertheless, the determination of price is generally the direct responsibility of the marketing, commercial or contracts department, if only because that exercise involves so many interacting and complex aspects of marketing policy. Thus it was appropriate that this chapter should be written by one who essentially takes the marketing viewpoint although throughout he acknowledges the critical influence of financial considerations.

The chapter discusses economic theory related to price, especially the concepts of elasticity and break-even levels. The author accepts the importance of economic theory in analysing the general way in which markets behave, but finds it of little help in the practical business of determining a price.

The chapter is concerned with pricing strategy as a long-term aspect of the subject, and with pricing tactics as representing shorter-term manoeuvres. Whereas in principle the strategy should exercise a broad influence on the tactics, there are circumstances in which the constraints and the opportunities arising from the tactical situation demand a review of the long-term strategy.

Although the writer is largely concerned with marketing tactics and strategy, he takes the attitude that those aspects of the general subject must be applied to achieving corporate objectives and long-term profitability. He carefully examines the role of costs but implicitly recognizes the old adage that 'cost is a convention and price a policy'. He pays due attention to the alternative policies of 'skimming' and 'penetration' pricing in relation to new products, and analyses both the benefits and the short-comings of market research. His discussion of the possibilities inherent in mathematical models and computer simulation of pricing mechanisms will be of particular relevance to those interested in the potentialities of those approaches.

It is a reflection of the paradoxes inherent in the realities of business life that there is probably no area of business activity in which practice differs so widely from theory as the area of pricing. The simple – and well attested – truth is that in a great many firms, large, as well as small, prices are set in a way which is disorganized, inconsistent and often just illogical. The reasons for this are not hard to find. Pricing decisions, even under the best of conditions are difficult to make and frequently have to be taken against what can often seem overwhelming odds – inadequate information; time pressures; corporate demands; changing and sometimes unpredictable competitive situations; higher than budgeted R and D and other overhead costs; inflationary pressures on labour, material and other production costs. Added to this, those responsible for pricing in the firm are often managing directors, sales or marketing managers or financial managers who face a great many other demands on their time.

The purpose of this chapter is not to describe at length theories of pricing, which are well covered in other texts, but to provide a framework within which the reader can evaluate the opportunities for greater profitability available to his or her own firm through the development of a more rational pricing policy and implement the practical procedures leading to the shaping, introduction and control of this policy.

ECONOMIC THEORY AND PRACTICALITY

There is a substantial body of economic theory dealing with price and pricing. The practical business person can, however, expect little direct help from the academic in applying economic theory to the solution of everyday pricing problems. Certainly, theories of price are effective in describing *in general* the way markets behave: demand and to some extent supply volumes do respond to price approximately as predicted by theory and markets do vary in the degree of responsiveness to price changes (as provided for by the concept of price elasticity[1]). The problem is that the theory breaks down when applied in particular cases largely because the assumptions on which theoretical calculations are based turn out to be inappropriate in real life. For one thing firms rarely possess, or are able to generate, the empirical data required to construct actual demand or revenue curves for their products and are often unable to distinguish costs sufficiently clearly to construct cost curves. Second, the goals which business people set themselves and the constraints which surround their achievement are usually far different – and less rational – than the idealized principles and responses of the theoretical firm. Third, markets do not in practice display the assumed characteristics of perfect competition and rational purchasing behaviour on which theory is based.

Nevertheless, since it has long enjoyed a certain popularity, an adaptation of economic theory worth mentioning at this point is the concept of 'breakeven'. The concept, in its simplest form, purports to show the minimum quantity of its product(s) a firm has to sell simply to cover its costs. Figure 4.1 shows the classic breakeven chart in its most widely reproduced form.

The attractiveness of the 'breakeven' idea – which in principle can be applied both to individual products and to the firm as a whole – is obvious in the context of a chart on the managing director's wall dramatizing what the firm has to do to stay in business *once selling*

---

[1] Technically, price elasticity is measured by dividing the percentage change in the volume of demand (or sales) brought about by a change in price by the percentage change in price. 'Elastic' markets are ones where demand increases (or decreases) by more than a proportionate price change and 'inelastic' markets where a change in price is greater, proportionately, than the effective increase (or decrease) in demand.

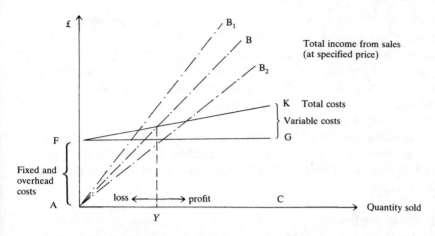

Fig. 4.1   Simple 'breakeven' chart

price has been determined, by indicating the volume of sales which have to be achieved to reach breakeven. However, the concept is of little help to the pricing executive in actually setting prices because of the crude and unrealistic assumptions which the basic theory assumes about the level of, and relationship between, price, demand and costs. In particular, the breakeven quantity (Y) is still a 'formula' calculation, not a forecast of actual sales which would still need to be made to determine the profits likely to be generated at a particular price.

At best the 'breakeven' concept – which is closely associated with cost-based pricing formulae described later – is mostly of value as a simple 'rule of thumb' method for evaluating pricing options in the context of other market-oriented information on (potential) demand and competition.

PRICING POLICY, STRATEGY AND TACTICS

Before looking in more detail at pricing decisions and the way they are arrived at, it is useful to draw a distinction between three terms often used rather interchangeably by business people. These terms are *pricing policy*, *pricing strategy* and *pricing tactics*.

Pricing policy refers to the framework of rules and constraints within which, and perhaps by which, pricing decisions are taken. The nature and scope of this framework and the degree of formalization or precision can vary widely from one firm to another, on no better basis than management preference or style, even within the same industry or between firms with apparently similar pricing problems. At one extreme pricing policy can be little more than a rationalization of rule of thumb judgements or historical practice. At the other end of the scale can be policies devised and spelled out in considerable detail. An example is the policy operated by the Metal Box Company (1978) described by the Price Commission as comprising the following elements:

1 an immediate objective of raising return on capital to 17 per cent;
2 through the discount structure to pass on to large customers the cost savings commensurate with the scale, continuity and stability of their demand;
3 for non-standard containers to price these at a level related to the operating costs of the lines while producing these containers;
4 to ensure that customers share with the company the benefits arising from productivity improvements and reductions in specification;
5 in the case of new business, selling prices are to be set on the basis of (achieving) 70 per cent capacity usage of (production) equipment (If demand fails to reach target volume, a decision has to be taken whether to increase selling price or to eliminate the product.);
6 to obtain high export prices wherever possible but retain flexibility to use marginal cost techniques for opportunistic business;
7 regular review of standard margins to ensure equity across the range.

Simply having a pricing policy, however formal, does not imply that it is either logical or sensible in the broader arena of the market place. Nor does the existence of a policy guarantee that it will be observed in practice – policies are often more honoured in the breach than the observance. Indeed it is entirely feasible for a firm to trade without a pricing policy at all or for decisions to be justified by reference to a policy which is to all intents and purposes a *post hoc* rationalization. This is often the case with small companies where pricing, like many other decisions, is in the hands of one forceful personality – a situation in which whim, intuition and ignorance can easily play a powerful role.

Whereas *pricing policy* is the outcome of largely internalized objectives of a financial or other corporate nature, or of statements of pricing principles, *pricing strategy* reflects the (longer-term) market-orientated (or externalized) objectives of the firm. In effect, *pricing strategy* involves the systematic manipulation or planning of pricing decisions and policies over a period of time in the context of achieving the broader objectives contained in corporate and marketing plans. It implies recognition of the role of price as an active, and important, component of the overall marketing mix rather than a largely intractable obstacle which marketing has to overcome in order to compete successfully. In so far as pricing policies and strategies are the expression of needs and objectives over different time periods and on different planes it is not unusual for firms to have a pricing policy but no pricing *strategy*.

While pricing strategy is 'the art of projecting and directing the larger pricing issues within a marketing campaign in the longer term (i.e. ignoring short-term fluctuations in market or trading conditions)' (Wilson, 1972, p. 132), pricing tactics are concerned with the manipulation of prices themselves and the way they are presented in order to achieve the optimum response in a competitive situation from a targeted customer group. Pricing tactics therefore take as much from an interpretation of the psychology of the buyer as from more rational 'economic' judgements. Tactics are, by their nature, often short-term and may be changed several times during the life of the strategy of which they form a part – the practical means of responding on a more day-to-day basis to changing conditions in the market place. In practice pricing tactics, of which there are a great many variations (some are desribed later in the chapter) are often mistakenly elevated to the level of pricing strategy.

Oxenfeldt (1960) sees the pricing process as one involving a series of sequential decisions which can be taken over a period of time rather than a single all-embracing solution. The six steps he proposes are:

1 indentification of target markets,
2 choosing an appropriate image,
3 constructing the marketing mix,
4 selecting a pricing policy,
5 determining price strategy (and tactics),
6 definition of a specific price.

This multi-stage approach has a particular relevance to new

product development but can be recycled wholly or in part as a means of reappraising existing products. The approach is particularly interesting in the emphasis it gives to broader issues of market segmentation and planning the marketing mix as the essential framework for pricing decisions.

PRICING POLICIES AND TECHNIQUES

Wilson (1972) has observed that pricing 'is an exercise which must be undertaken on two dimensions. First it is necessary to think in terms of establishing the right price and second of using the correct methodology for arriving at it.' In a way, this observation neatly encapsulates the practical dilemma facing most firms with respect to pricing.

At one level the pricing process take place within a framework which is the product of a variety of factors and influences, both internal to and external to the firm itself. These factors, which provide the basis for defining pricing policy, strategy and tactics, include:

Internal	*External*
Corporate objectives and business goals – both generalized and specific	The nature, strength and pricing behaviour of competition (direct and indirect; existing and potential)
Cost structures – direct and indirect	The role and importance of distributors and their attitudes and needs relating to price (including need to create/maintain acceptable margins)
Existing prices (e.g. of other products in the same or other product lines)	(Pressure from) suppliers of raw materials, components etc. used in the product
Historical practice and precedent in price setting within the firm	The size, structure and perceived price sensitivity of demand
Degree of market knowledge (or ignorance) of key executives	The purchasing procedures and motivations of (potential) customers

Internal	*External*
Pressures from feedback of other individuals within the firm, e.g. salespeople	Existing and anticipated government policies
Levels of R and D and pace of new product development.	General conditions prevailing in different markets (especially where export markets are concerned).

At the second level the pricing process involves (or more correctly, perhaps, should involve) the application of a sensible and coherent procedure for actually determining the final price at which the product will sell. This procedure or methodology needs to be conceived and operated within a broader framework of attitudes and subjective judgements which may not always be logical and may even be in conflict.

However, pricing policies and strategies do not necessarily define, or even imply, a particular methodology or technique for arriving at the selling price itself. In many cases this is set as much by guesswork, trial and error, historical analogy and simple entrepreneurial judgement as it is by some more formal procedure or formula.

There is not single correct methodology or golden rule for arriving at the right price. For example, the pricing decision process and the degree of flexibility available to the pricing executive in setting prices are heavily conditioned by whether prices are *declared* or *negotiated* (the pricing system). At one extreme the executive responsible for setting catalogue or list prices is in theory creating a structure of 'ruling' prices which will remain in force for all or a substantial proportion of sales until a change is notified; at the other extreme the executive involved in contract or tender pricing is faced with a new pricing decision with each new order or customer.

The right price is not necessarily what theorists would call the 'best-selling price' in the sense that it maximizes profits for a given product considered by itself. In any meaningful sense what is right can only be assessed in the context of what the firm identifies as its general strategic or operational goals. Because these differ according to the size, product range, historical development, future ambitions, geographical trading pattern, financial resources and management philosophy of individuals so the concept of the 'right' price will also vary.

The precise combination and weighting of factors determining pricing policy and price setting will depend on the product, the market and other circumstances. The following paragraphs look in more detail at five categories of factor which both shape pricing policy and contribute to a greater or lesser extent to the process of actual price setting. To the extent that one of these categories may carry the greatest weight in the pricing process it is possible to talk about pricing which is profit, cost, competition, demand (or customer) or distribution system orientated.

Profit targets and other corporate objectives

Perhaps the most widely quoted of all business aphorisms is that it is the objective of every firm to maximize its profits. The most cursory examination of this proposition in the light of actual business practice, however, shows it to be one which should not be taken too literally. Firms rarely set out even with the *theoretical* objective of maximizing profits (or return on capital employed) and often introduce criteria into pricing strategies and policies the deliberate effect of which is to contain profits at a level which is below that which otherwise might be achievable.

Few would deny that, in a free market economy, a firm exists to make a profit and, indeed, needs to make a profit to exist. More fundamentally, perhaps, the profits generated by the firm have to be sufficient to satisfy the providers of the capital – shareholders, bankers, etc. – on whom the firm's existence and future ultimately depend. Simply making a profit does not itself guarantee the continued flow of funds required to renew current plant and invest in facilities for producing new products. Equally, given the scarcity and cost of capital, it is nonsense to suggest that a firm would be able, even if it wished, to continue to pour capital into the production of a product until the last drop of profit has been extracted from the market.

Profit (which can be defined as total gross sales returns or revenue minus the total of fixed and variable costs, before tax) is therefore a less meaningful criterion for judging business performance in the longer term than return on capital employed or 'return on investment' (which is usually taken as the relationship between a firm's profit before tax and the whole of its assets). Thus the Price Commission commented with respect to UG Glass Containers Ltd that, 'for (the company's) profit to be adequate it must be sufficient after paying for the cost of capital to fund all expenditure on fixed and working capital necessary to maintain the fabric of the business and to make a contribution towards capital required for expansion' and went on to state that the company's corporate strategy provided specific targets relating to pre-tax profit and return on capital employed to be 'achieved and maintained' (UG Glass Containers Ltd, 1978).

The question of time dimension also needs to be considered. A quick glance at the city pages of any national newspaper shows that profits achieved by even the largest firms fluctuate from year to year for reasons, often connected with the general economic environment and trading conditions, over which the firm has no control. Financial objectives can therefore be expressed both as long-term and immediate.

Longer-term financial objectives tend to be set in the context of achieving a targeted average level of return on investment or profit for the whole of the company which is considered by the firm to be 'reasonable' taken over a period of years (and across all products). This is usually expressed as a percentage but could also be a money sum. Judgement of what is reasonable is in this context largely a pragmatic affair, owing more to general perceptions within society of what might be considered as 'fair trading profit' or to historical experience or analogy, than to the projection of a mechanistic formula. In the short term, different targets may be set either for return on capital for profit or for margins or contributions (difference between selling price and *direct* costs usually expressed as a percentage) which reflect prevailing economic and market conditions in individual years or even short planning periods.

As we have indicated earlier, however, financial objectives are not the only determinants of corporate policy and are therefore by no means the only factor underlying a pricing decision. Other considerations affecting either individual price decisions or the internal climate within which decisions are made include:

● (Market) growth objectives and quantitative targets
● Market share targets or aspirations to 'market leadership'
● Development of products and businesses to meet more broadly conceived goals concerning the longer-term stability and growth of the firm as a whole
● Pursuit or rejection of a course of action in the light of judgments about the way the company wishes to be seen in the market place, including both the protecting of existing image and the development of a targeted new image

- The level of costs incurred in Research & Development which will need to be recouped
- Cost reduction and efficiency objectives contained in corporate plans
- Implementation of strategies for pre-empting, containing or meeting competition
- Achievement of an acceptable level of use of production capacity.

An example of the way various strands of corporate policy link together to affect prices can be found at BOC Ltd.

> The company's central thinking is based on the need to manage a portfolio of businesses. Essentially, this is to invest for market growth and to increase market share on the assumption that scale benefits on costs will be obtained. This gives the investor market dominance based on competitively low cost which in turn provides the power further to secure market position by keen pricing. When the growth slackens off the rate of investment can be reduced to yield a positive cash flow which may be reinvested in another growth market . . . (BOC Ltd, 1979).

The role of costs in pricing

It has often been claimed that the pricing of industrial products is derived from or based on costs and very little else – a process which Wilson has derided as, 'faith, hope and fifty per cent'. The argument runs that the cost accountant and the engineer have dominated the pricing process and that neat formulae based on cost are most easily comprehended by these types of executive whose knowledge of, and exposure to, the market place itself is limited. Research into pricing behaviour has tended to support this view of the pricing process: when asked directly about the pricing of their products firms will indeed claim that they arrive at their prices largely by the application of some formula related to costs.

How rigidly companies stand by such formulae or, indeed, whether they actually have a formula at all, is very much open to doubt. Gabor claims that, 'pricing is not in fact carried out by the alleged mechanistic application of cost-based formulae' and goes on to quote Edwards: 'the manufacturer has a "hunch" as to the price at which his article can be sold and makes use of "costing" or "estimating" to justify that price'. In other words a price 'derived from cost' can often be in effect the reverse procedure with margins and contributions justified *post hoc* by reference to costs when in fact they are sub-sumed from price. Nevertheless if prices are rarely based exclusively on cost, it is equally rare for costs not in some way to form the starting point or platform either for calculating prices or for evaluating the profit consequences of various prices indicated or set by reference to other factors.

In order to use costs at all in the pricing process it is obviously necessary for the firm to have a clear idea of what its costs are and how these should be allocated to individual products. This is all very well for the firm producing only one product since all costs are, by definition, attributable to that product. Where more than one pro-duct is concerned, as it is for most firms, the issues of cost allocation can be exceedingly complex and the solutions at best arbitrary. The costs of producing and selling a range of products can be classified broadly into three main components:

1 *Variable (including direct) costs* – costs which vary in relation to output, e.g. materials and components, labour, advertising.
2 *Fixed costs* – costs which do not vary in relation to output except in the longer term, e.g. buildings, machines, vehicles.
3 *Overhead costs* – costs attributable to management.

The problem of allocating management overheads will be obvious but what of variable and fixed costs? *Shared costs* are a common feature with respect, say, to vehicles and buildings but can also occur with respect to materials and labour. Consider, for example, the furniture factory which uses the same labour force, the same machin-ery and to some extent the same materials to make beds, wardrobes and dining room tables. Add to this a constantly changing balance of production volume between these different product lines – and within each product line between different model ranges – and the problems of allocation assume daunting proportions. The cost accountant might be able to devise an acceptable formula for allocation if each product was always produced in the same proportions but the formu-la becomes increasingly unworkable and arbitrary where these are constantly changing. Basing a formula on historical experience is equally undesirable as it makes pricing for the future dependent on past and possibly greatly outdated sales levels. The scale of difficulty increases still further where several products are produced by the same process (as in oil refining or dairy processes) and therefore incur, not so much shared costs as *joint costs*, or where a marketable product is a by-product of the production process for another good.

The problems outlined above become highly relevant when costs are used as a means of calculating price. There are two main concepts or procedures for cost-based pricing – *absorption or full cost pricing* and *variable cost or incremental cost pricing*.

Absorption cost pricing, to put it simply, involves the principle of adding a predetermined mark-up to total unit costs derived from the formula

$$\frac{\text{total of fixed and variable costs attributable to the product}}{\text{total units producted}}$$

By this procedure, sometimes known as 'cost-plus', each product produced by the firm is made, in theory, to cover all of its costs and make a known profit on each unit of sale or order.

Variable cost pricing is based on the principle of relating prices not to total costs but to variable costs only with the mark-up on costs (or the price less variable costs if the price is set by a procedure independent of costs) making a *contribution* to fixed costs and to profit, the scale of which depends on sales objectives being achieved. Gabor (1988) distinguishes two variants of variable cost pricing: one is based on average variable costs (for a predicted level of output) and the other, which he calls incremental cost pricing, is based on the incremental or additional cost of producing a particular batch of the product which may be different from the variable costs of total production when considered in unit terms. Incremental cost pricing is a concept particularly appropriate to pricing individual orders, in cases where demand is made up of discrete orders or batches, or in evaluating the relative contribution of alternative possible orders where the price available is fixed by some other means perhaps beyond the firm's direct control.

Absorption cost pricing is a method which has had particular appeal to the firm with a substantial proportion of its total costs in the form of fixed costs and overheads, since it places all products, in theory, on a sound profit footing and eliminates cross-subsidization and below-cost trading. It is particularly useful in tender or contract pricing as a reference basis for pricing where there are no other useful indicators and in setting some practical limits to prices of new products with no relevant competitors. However, absorption costing has a number of major drawbacks as the basis for pricing. The arguments can be summarized as follows:

1   It is, as has already been shown, not always easy to isolate the total costs attributable to a particular product where there are several, possibly disparate, product lines and ranges. Depending on the conventions and assumptions used to apportion costs, the outcome of the application of absorption cost pricing techniques could be substantially varying price levels for individual products.

2   There is, anyway, no compelling reason why any particular segment of the business, individual product, or specific order *should* be made to bear its proportionate or 'fair' share of overheads even where these can be calculated. Looked at in an overall corporate sense, the ability to offer a full product range, stability of production, attraction or retention of a major customer, response to change in the competitive environment and many other factors may in individual cases and pricing decisions be considered to carry greater weight.

3   Absorption costing takes no account of demand. The fact that a price can be computed by this method does not guarantee that consumers will buy the item at that price or at the predicted volumes. Nor are firms willing in reality to implement one of the apparent implications of the method which is *to raise* prices when demand falls short of expectations or declines from a previous level (since total costs will be spread over a smaller volume of output). The inclination of most firms in this situation would be to *reduce* prices.

4   Absorption costing takes no account of competition. No firm can guarantee that its competitors will play by the same rules either by adopting the same method of costing or by allocating its overhead and fixed costs to particular products on the same basis. The firm rigidly applying absorption cost pricing would find its products highly vulnerable to a competitor using direct or incremental cost methods or simply pricing irrationally.

The proponents of incremental cost pricing tend to use arguments which are the obverse of their criticisms of absorption cost pricing emphasizing the flexibility of the method as a means of responding to (changing) demand and competitive conditions. Thus it is pointed out, for example, that since market conditions vary between different industry segments of a given national market and even more, perhaps, between different national markets it is logical to seek (or accept) prices which reflect those conditions. Using a direct or an incremental cost approach enables the firm to operate at different prices in different markets while maintaining overall control over the aggregated contribution derived from sales to these various markets and to assign supply priorities between them in the event of demand outstripping capacity. Similarly the method enables the firm to consider and respond to individual orders in a way appropriate to specific circumstances. Thus, for example, at times of high demand a means is provided of selecting orders or pieces of business which yield the greatest contribution and at times of low demand of indicating how far the firm might reduce its prices before an order ceases to make any contribution at all.

Despite its apparent pragmatism, variable or incremental costing is not without its attendant dangers. In the first place, it has been said with some truth that all costs become variable if the firm is to survive – that is, in the end, the firm depends on making sufficient revenue from its sales to cover all costs incurred whether variable, fixed or overhead. Incremental cost pricing cannot therefore be pursued unchecked. As we have seen earlier it must be conducted within some framework or yardstick of required contribution based on profit targets or targets for return on capital invested.

Second, firms using incremental cost pricing to justify accepting an order at reduced contribution may find they have made a rod for their own backs in subsequent dealings with the same customer. However logical the concept of variable pricing might be to the seller, the buyer is given a weapon which will be all too easy to use in subsequent negotiations when general demand conditions have improved and the firm has been able to command higher prices. If the seller gets to the point of refusing an order offered at too low a price there is a danger that the buyer may simply eliminate that supplier from future consideration or allow a competitor to gain entry.

Third, there is always a risk of provoking price retaliation from competitors resulting in reduced margins all round and a steep hill to climb back to acceptable profitability in a market environment which can become accustomed with remarkable rapidity to low prices.

Finally, it must be appreciated that it is not always easy to determine clearly either the variable costs attributable to a particular product or the incremental costs associated with a particular batch or order. Some so-called variable costs are not, in fact, more than marginally variable, at least in the shorter term. Few firms are able or willing, for example, to manipulate the size of their labour forces constantly to reflect changes in the level of orders. Unionization and a natural desire on the part of firms to keep a trained and effective work force together play an important role here. It is easy for firms to delude themselves therefore as to what the incremental or marginal unit cost of a product actually is. Similarly, taking on an additional order in certain circumstances may have its own hidden incremental costs in the form of overtime working, loss of efficiency in output in machines pushed closer to maximum capacity, extra blocks of production space requiring heating, lighting and maintenance and many other items.

Pricing is not only difficult in practice to base entirely on costs but even should it be feasible it renders the firm vulnerable in other respects. In a strictly competitive sense it hardly matters a jot how reasonable a profit mark-up or contribution target a firm sets in relation to its own costs if these costs are higher than those of competitors. Indeed it has been observed that the costs which ultimately matter are those of the lowest-cost producer. Of course, most markets support producers who vary in efficiency, but the greater the disparity in efficiency, the greater is the pressure exerted on the least efficient producers.

More broadly, cost-based pricing formulae often provide little encouragement to company management to consider the prospect for improving margins by reducing costs as distinct from raising prices. The degree to which costs are in themselves controllable will depend on individual production circumstances and quality of management. Firms rarely explore as rigorously as they might the various ways in which costs might be cut, from better materials purchasing to tighter control of office costs. This is not, however, the only way costs can be cut and here we return again to the need to be alive to *market* needs and conditions. Research has consistently shown over the years that products and services can quite simply be 'over-engineered' – that is contain features to which the user attaches little economic significance in the purchase decision or which are designed to a quality standard which exceeds customer needs. By eliminating these features from the product or changing the product specification the firm may well be able to make considerable savings in costs without comparable reductions in price.

Competition and pricing

There are few products or services indeed for which there is no effective competition. Even when a firm has no direct competitors – as in the case of an innovative product – it usually has to take into account products capable of acting as alternatives or substitutes in some way, or the prospect of competition developing.

Long-term monopolies are therefore rare outside the realms of state enterprises but it is possible for short-term monopolies to develop on the basis of new products, particularly where high technology is involved. Firms may be able to protect themselves for a time from direct competition by the taking out of patents – as Xerox Corporation did with plain paper copiers and Polaroid Corporation with instant photography – but in the end competition will come either through expiry of patents or through a competitor finding a means of entry which does not infringe the patents. The short-term monopolist needs to consider pricing in the context of the breathing space available to establish the product in the market place before competition develops, rather than in terms of the apparent freedom of action of the true monopolist.

At the most fundamental level, the product competes on the basis of its usefulness or value to the buyer compared with the many other items on which income or resources can be expended.

Price acts as an element in competition therefore at up to three levels: it can help determine whether or not a product is bought at all (or whether the decision to purchase is taken now or at a later date); it can help determine in which of a number of alternative ways a particular need is satisfied; and it can help determine which supplier's product is selected.

It is not surprising then that in most cases prices are set and maintained with some reference to the general level and range of competitive prices. In a more specific sense, however, pricing against competition can become in itself a technique of pricing. This can work in one of two main ways:

1   By establishing the prices being charged by all (or a selected cross-section) of the competitive suppliers active in the market and positioning one's own price to occupy a certain position in the range. This may reflect either 'safety' pricing (pricing in the middle of the range) or 'aggressive' pricing (pricing at either extreme).

2 By gearing prices to those charged by a specific competitor on the basis of achieving parity with them or of achieving a designated discount or premium. This approach is often used where one company has achieved a position of such pre-eminence in the market place that both sellers and customers accept its prices as a reference level.

In so far as competitors' prices are declared or easily established, competition–orientated pricing is relatively straightforward and has the advantage of placing prices within the known parameters of the market place. The price structure of markets is not, however, always easy to establish. Published price lists often give a highly misleading guide to actual price levels which may be arrived at largely by discounting or special negotiation. Further, buyers are frequently reluctant to indicate even to independent researchers, let alone company salesmen, the terms of a bargain struck with a competitor. There is always a danger therefore that prices may be set on the basis of a competitive price structure which is different in reality from that assumed.

The extent to which firms are willing and able to take a competitively independent line in setting and maintaining prices is partly a reflection of factors such as market share, established reputation, financial strength, distinctiveness of product and relative costs of production, and partly a reflection of competitive psychology. Many writers on pricing have drawn attention to the fact that price competition often tends to be of a muted and controlled nature in which a few (perhaps only one or two) dominant suppliers (price leaders) both set the price levels and pricing systems around which competition is fought, and determine the timing and scale of price changes. Other firms (price followers) are essentially content to respond – raising and lowering prices in line with the price leaders. Markets operating on this basis can become highly conservative and regulated structures in which price competition is to all intents and purposes eliminated. As Japanese companies have demonstrated repeatedly in European markets, complacent and conservative competitive environments – which in turn lead to reduced interest in increasing efficiency and cost savings – are highly vulnerable to a bold and determined aggressor.

The attitudes and motivations of the buyer

Price is rarely, if ever, the only factor entering into the purchasing decision and is sometimes only secondary. The success of pricing decisions is therefore highly dependent on the ability of the firm to comprehend and respond to the purchasing environment into which its products are sold. Many ineffective, even disastrous, pricing policies can be traced back to misconceptions about the attitude of buyers to price and the role of price in the purchase decision. These misconceptions are often rooted in a popular industry folklore the credibility of which has been reinforced by constant repetition to a point at which the desire or willingness of firms to go against this conventional wisdom has been almost totally sapped. The philosophy of price cutting as the only effective means of competition which pervades some industries is often due more to uncritical acceptance of this folklore than to a sober analysis of marketing options.

Distinguishing fact from fiction in the market place is therefore the first task of the would-be rational pricing executive. A key concept in this contest is that of 'product differentiation'. This relates to the differences in functions, performance, design and other product-related or physical attributes which a manufacturer can introduce to distinguish the firm's products from those of the competition. The greater the differentiation, it is argued, the more invidious direct price comparisions by the buyer become, thus giving the firm greater flexibility in turn to gear its prices to the value it believes, or can persuade buyers to believe, attaches to the features or benefits it is offering.

The principle of segmentation – designing and pricing products to cater to a particular target group of customers within the market as a whole – derives from the concept of differentiation.

Economists usually assume, in theorizing on purchasing behaviour, that the buyer, being rational and efficient, will tend to purchase at the lowest price prevailing in the market place, for the product which best fits her or his needs and requirements. Where there is little or no product differentiation, such as in the case of electrical cable or industrial fasteners, the customer might be expected to look for the lowest price *per se*; where there is substantial differentiation such as in an industrial engine or a conveying system, then the buyer will weigh up all the economic aspects of the alternatives to arrive at the product which offers the highest cost-benefit. As consumer goods companies and advertising agencies have long appreciated, the domestic consumer is neither rational nor efficient but there is a widely held belief that the industrial buyer, being a 'professional', cannot be deceived as easily and will go unerringly to the 'bottom line'. Research into the buying decision has consistently shown this simply not to be true when considered in any detail.

In the first place, economic factors are not the only criteria employed in the purchase decision. Even in the case of non-differentiated products, many other factors can intrude to justify purchases at other than the lowest price which may be available. These include:

1 delivery (firms are often prepared to pay more for fast delivery or guaranteed delivery or for a delivery particularly convenient to the purchaser);
2 after-sales service/availability of spare parts;
3 previous good experience of the product or other things produced by the same manufacturer;
4 proximity of supplier to the purchaser;
5 security of supply/risk spreading (e.g. by dividing requirements between two or more suppliers);
6 general reputation of supplier/advice and recommendation of own staff and other firms in buyer's industry;
7 the volume of other goods purchased from the same supplier;
8 good personal relationship with salesman, technical staff and other aspects of the supplier's organization.

Second, economic considerations can go far beyond the 'price' of the product. In the case of a capital product such as a commercial vehicle, a forklift truck or a machine tool, the purchase price of the product is only one of several cost-related considerations such as running costs and method of financing.

Third, industrial buyers are perfectly capable of being irrationally influenced by factors such as a persuasive salesman; clever advertising; cosmetic product features such as a design; fashion trends within the industry and simple prejudice. A manufacturer of circular knitting machines for whom the author once carried out a research project found it hard to accept that many customers rejected his technically well-engineered but old-fashioned looking product in favour of a streamlined, push-button import with, by objective standards, an inferior price/performance relationship.

Finally, buyers rarely have perfect knowledge of the markets for all the products they have to buy. Thus the buyer for a fabrications firm may have an extensive and systematically compiled knowledge of the suppliers and prices for the steel products which make up a substantial proportion of the firm's costs but has neither time nor the inclination to develop the same knowledge for less significant items such as paper clips and toilet rolls.

It has rightly been said that the price the final buyer is prepared to pay for a product is, in the end, the best guide to optimum pricing. Because it is the best guide, however, it is inevitably the most difficult concept to employ as a practical technique in pricing. The attraction of cost-based pricing formulae and using competitors' prices as a yardstick for price setting can be attributed at least in part to the fact that they are simple to understand and employ information which, in theory at least, is readily to hand or easily generated. By contrast it is often exceedingly difficult to establish in a direct way how much customers for a product are prepared to pay for it. Nevertheless it is within the capacity and resources of most firms to develop sufficient information from their own knowledge and experience of trading in particular market places or by talking to some potential customers, or by some experimentation or by extrapolating the results of market research surveys. Then they can make broad assumptions about the size and structure of demand for a product and responsiveness to price in a competitive context which can be used to narrow the limits within which price should be set and define the strategy and tactics which best fit market conditions.

Distribution structure

Where a product is sold direct from manufacturer to end user, as many industrial products are, the pricing executive has only to consider pricing at a single level. The situation becomes more complex when distributive intermediaries – agents, wholesalers and retailers – are involved, as the consideration is then not just the price at which the product is sold to the immediate customer, say a wholesaler, but also the price at which it ultimately sells to the final consumer after it has passed through one, two or even three sets of hands each of which have added their own mark-up. Wholesalers and retailers tend to price by adding a designated percentage mark-up to the price they buy-in the product in order to cover overhead and sales costs and yield a profit. It is, however, relatively unusual for a single fixed percentage to be applied to all products. Rather the percentage mark-up is manipulated between products according to circumstances or design around some overall average (which may itself reflect long-standing practice or folklore in a particular industry rather than any independent judgement on the part of the distributor).

Since the ending of resale price maintenance the manufacturer is unable to dictate the ultimate selling price of products (and therefore in effect distributors' margins). Distributors may therefore manipulate margins in a way which favours or disfavours the products of the individual manufacturer and therefore impacts on ultimate sales. Pricing to the *distributor* but with an eye to reselling prices is therefore a special component of the art of pricing.

It should also be recognized that the effect of passing on, say, a reduction (or an increase) in the cost of materials or components is heavily affected by the length of the distribution chain. Not only might the change be much smaller proportionately in respect of the final selling price than it is to the ex-factory price but distributors can choose to pass on the change across a spectrum of options ranging from no price adjustment at all to one in excess of that made by the manufacturer.

AIDS TO PRICING

Models and computer simulations

Various attempts have been made to construct 'models' of a more formal nature designed to help the firm fix the optimum price of its products under actual competitive conditions. These models differ widely in their nature, purpose and origin, but most frequently relate to the pricing of goods for retail sale (particularly fast-moving goods such as baked beans and washing powder) and pricing in a competitive bid or tender situation.

Basically, all models work by simulating, in terms of mathematical relationships, the interaction of the variables – company-, competition- and demand-related – which govern the pricing decision. They share therefore inevitable problems in defining and assigning a value to each variable. Their success depends on the quality of research or of the market knowledge or insight the firm is able to feed into the model, and on the manipulation of the variables which normally requires access to a computer.

Market research

Whether or not a pricing model is being developed, firms still require information to help them to reach sensible pricing decisions. This information is rarely readily available 'off the shelf' and some level of active information gathering is therefore required. The most widely employed source of intelligence is the sales staff. In practice, however, sales people are a highly unreliable source of pricing intelligence and tactical judgement (Atkin and Skinner, 1975). Where key pricing decisions are concerned, therefore, it is probably prudent to think in terms of conducting more systematic market research.

The market research industry can contribute to the pricing decision in three ways:

● by providing effective and up-to-date intelligence on the prices being charged by competitors (by reference to actual prices paid or discounts received by customers) and on the impact of specific pricing tactics employed by competitors for short-term advantage;
● by testing the sensitivity of different target customer groups to various possible price levels for a product, or by seeking to define acceptable/tolerable price levels, through carefully controlled sequences of questions (a number of 'models' have been developed by research companies for this purpose);
● by placing price and price-related issues in the broader context of the purchase decision process.

DEVISING PRICING STRATEGY AND TACTICS

Entry strategies

The concept of pricing strategy as a means of using price as an element in the achievement of specific marketing goals was mentioned earlier. This involves the co-ordination of pricing decisions in the context of their longer-term impact and implications rather than their short-term or tactical benefits and requires the firm to take an extended view of such factors as probable product life; volume and price sensitivity of potential demand; opportunities for segmentation of demand by price and the optimum phasing of segmentation; pace of likely consumer acceptance taking into account competitive, alternative and substitute products; build-up of production capacity and the opportunity for scale economies in unit costs; timescale for recovery of R and D costs.

The most sensitive, and probably the most important time for strategy formulation is before the launch of new product – whether or not the product concerned is an innovative or unique one with no direct competitors or is a new brand entrant to an established market place. It is frequently stated that at the stage of market entry the firm has a choice between two basic strategy options known as *skimming* and *penetration*.

Skimming strategies involve the deliberate setting of an initial price which is high in relation to anticipated long-term price levels towards which the price will be progressively lowered as competition and demand conditions change. The benefits of this strategy derive from the high gross margins achieved at the outset against which R and D and other 'sunk' costs and often heavy initial promotional costs can be set and from the flexibility afforded for using subsequent price changes as a means of controlling market expansion (since, setting aside inflation, the direction of price changes will be downward) and meeting emerging competition by aggressive pricing.

Skimming enables the firm to cream off that component of demand prepared to buy the product at its highest price before attacking the broader potential market which may exist for the product at a lower price. In so far as the progressive effective price reductions can be implemented on a 'step-wise' basis, the market may be, in effect, creamed off at different (and progressively larger) levels. This strategy has, for example, been expertly exploited by IBM in the personal computer market.

The firm employing a skimming entry strategy also gives itself the option of approaching the anticipated longer-term downward adjustment in price by introducing variations of its original product or even a different brand rather than by simple price reduction, thus enabling it to maintain a premium price on its original product. This strategy might be termed progressive segmentation.

An advantage of skimming which should not be overlooked is that it conforms to the well attested dictum that it is easier to correct a pricing mistake in a downward direction than in an upward one.

Penetration strategies are intended to generate the highest possible volume of sales from the outset by keen (low margin) pricing. In practice they can be divided into two categories – demand-orientated and competition-orientated strategies (see Table 4.1). Demand-orientated penetration strategies are based in the main on a combination of an expected high level of price sensitivity among potential buyers and a need for a high volume of demand to justify plant

Table 4.1
Evaluation of entry price strategy

Skimming	Penetration – demand-orientated	Penetration – competition orientated
Anticipated short product life (technological changes, fashion)	Anticipated long product life	Anticipated need to tempt users to try new product rather than continue with existing functional alternatives (gain foothold especially where differentiation not immediately clear to, or valued by, consumers)
Slow initial consumer acceptance (new applications, new technology	Belief in rapid consumer acceptance/high price elasticity	
Uncertainty over ultimate scale and elasticity of demand	Economies of scale in output – threshold sales level before economies can be achieved	Pre-emption of competition – exclude prospective competitors by raising entry costs/establishing entrenched position
Market segmentation – 'cream' those prepared to pay high price before moving to mass market (perhaps with lower priced variants)	Expectation of rapid competitive response – establish sound market postion/market leadership before competition can develop	
Inelastic production costs/capacity constraints	Exploitation of established reputation/sales, marketing distribution strengths	Displacement of entrenched competition by aggressive pricing in directly competitive market (market launch of similar or identical product)
Recovery of high R and D costs		
Generation of funds for mass marketing	Create platform for continued sale of related products e.g. labelling machines and labels	
Competition slow to develop due to patent protection, research lead time, high production entry costs		
Exploitation of established reputation/ differentiation aspects of product		

investment or achieve projected economies of scale in production
(i.e. some products have to be produced in volume or not at all).
Competitively they have the advantage of potentially creating a

strong market position or an image as market leaders before competition emerges (although this will depend on the speed and strength of the competitive response).

One specific variant of demand-orientated penetration strategies is worth mentioning – this might be called the 'razor and razor blades' strategy. Basically it involves pricing a unit of hardware (e.g. razor, labelling gun, copier, computer printer) at a level which achieves the maximum market penetration or placement so that profits can be achieved on repeated sales of related consumables (or 'add on' enhancements to the original hardware). If the consumable can be made unique in some way to the hardware, at least initially, a curious combination strategy of penetration for the hardware and what amounts to skimming on the consumable presents itself.

Competition-orientated penetration strategies tend to fall themselves into two main types – we can call them 're-active' and 'pro-active'. Re-active strategies reflect a situation in which a new market entrant is responding to an existing competitive environment. In this situation, the new entrant may determine to take market share by 'undercutting' the prices of the market leader(s), either with an alternative, simplified product (which, nevertheless, still meets the needs of users) or by 'copying' the market leader's product as closely as legally possible. The personal computer market dramatically demonstrates the impact of such strategies, with the development of low priced 'clones' of both the top selling computer (the IBM PC) and of best selling software packages, which appear to offer comparable functionality and performance for a much lower price than the copied original. Pro-active strategies involve the use of price as a means of deterring potential competitors by pressuring the margins which can be achieved to offset the costs of entry implicit in product development, investment in production facilities and marketing/promotion efforts. However, the history of recent high technology market places suggests that it is unlikely to deter competitors for very long.

Two situations exist, however, where the strategy may be one of low entry price and an underlying plan for either a sharp or gradual increase in price. First, where a new product is being launched in a market where the competition comprises substitute or alternative products, price has been used as a means of persuading potential users to try the product (about which they may have, for example, technical doubts) on the assumption that when it has proved itself they would be prepared to pay a price equal to, or higher than, the existing alternatives. The second example concerns the use of a low entry price as a means of displacing or forcing out entrenched competition from an established market place or of gaining a substantial market share on the basis of which prices can subsequently be increased to a more profitable level. This highly aggressive strategy is one which has been successfully employed by Japanese companies in European markets for a wide variety of products. An example is marine engines. 'The prime target for the Japanese . . . was the European market and the view in the trade was that their strategy would follow the familiar pattern of gaining a large initial market share at cut prices, forcing the opposition out and then raising prices' (*Marketing*, 1979, Oct., p. 32).

The temptation to use price as an entry wedge becomes increasingly great the more difficult it is for the firm entering a well established existing market to differentiate its product sufficiently clearly from those already available. It can be a high-risk strategy if competitors have the resources to fight a rear-guard battle or even to step up the price war or if customers do not respond to the entry price as expected.

However, it can also be spectacularly successful as the Amstrad company has proved, first with HiFi and video products and now with personal computers. Amstrad has employed a deliberate penetration strategy, based on highly aggressive pricing, which, in the personal computer market at least, has had the effect both of expanding the. overall size of the market by attracting customers unwilling to pay the prices of more expensive competitors (demand-orientated strategy) but also of taking market share from these competitors (competition-orientated strategy). Even so, it is interesting to note that other suppliers are beginning to respond even to this extreme example of an attempt to command the market by price.

In general terms the more innovative the product the more the firm is likely to incline towards a skimming rather than a penetration strategy, particularly if R and D costs have been high and production capacity is limited, at least in the short term. However, there are no 'hard and fast' rules – the right strategy will depend on the firm, the product and the market.

Reviewing strategy after entry

Although pricing strategies are conceived as operating over a period of time, ignoring short-term fluctuations or pressures which may demand a tactical response, this does not mean that the strategy does not need to be kept under regular review. Nor that it is not necessary for strategies to be changed if conditions in the market place become sufficiently different from those that prompted the original plan.

The firm which has adopted a skimming strategy is faced with the need to decide when to implement the price cuts envisaged by the strategy and how large these should be on each occasion. There can be no hard and fast rules to guide these decisions. Depending on the pace at which competition develops – and this may be slowed down by patent protection, high entry costs and other factors – a high initial price might be retained for some considerable time before it needs to be reduced. On the other hand it can be advantageous to make the first cut well ahead of competition as a pre-emptive measure. Equally the timing and size of the cut may be best related to taking advantage of the demand interest opened up by initial entry to boost sales by a substantial cut in price justified by reference to cost savings from increased scale of production and greater efficiency. Similar considerations apply to subsequent cuts.

The firm which has implemented a penetration strategy has less room to manoeuvre in terms of price adjustments in the face of developing competition. The major problem facing pricing executives is maintaining a long-term view of price developments when competitive pressures appear to be forcing the firm into a growing number of reactive or short-term tactical decisions most probably associated with price cuts. In order to maintain its strategic grip the firm must be able to retain a broader view of the development of demand, its sensitivity to price changes and its susceptibility to non-price differentials.

It is probable that for many products, pricing decisions shade from the strategic to the tactical in the longer term whichever entry strategy is adopted as competition develops, as product differentiation becomes increasingly difficult to sustain and as sales approach saturation. Even so it would pay the firm to be alive to the opportunities which exist for using a deliberate change in strategy to revitalize its position in the market place or improve profits. The variations of strategy option are legion but include:

1 Switching from a skimming strategy to a penetration strategy to exploit mass market potential of a product initially pioneered at a high price – perhaps by introducing a simplified and cheaper version rather than by cutting the price of the original product.

2 Introduction of replacement or second generation products which can be differentiated sufficiently to command a premium price (return to skimming strategy).
3 'Re-packaging' of products in a way which takes them out of the competitive arena. A good example is the development of 'electronic office' concepts linking more conventional pieces of equipment in a unique total way (return to skimming strategy).
4 Concentration of attention on more profitable market segments even at the cost of volume – diversion of released production resources into other products.
5 Improve margins by concentration on cost savings through more efficient production rather than by increasing prices (although the ability of the firm to use this strategy is limited by the long-term tendency of all production methods to ape the most efficient).

Tactical considerations

In theory, strategy precedes tactics in the pricing process, the latter providing the short-term dimension to the implementation of strategy which governs the actual prices charged and the way these are expressed to the customer. In practice it is not always easy to separate the two. Tactics can be considered at two levels. First there are tactical decisions which relate to gearing actual price levels, and the form they take, to what might be termed the 'psychology' of the customer and the nature of the purchasing process. Such tactical considerations, in so far as they hold true over a period of time, in effect form part of strategy.

The semantics of such pricing tactics tend to be those of the consumer market and retail pricing. However, many have a more universal relevance whatever the product or service being sold. Probably the most widespread tactical device is discounting and this is considered in more detail below. However, mention might also be made of such tactics[1] as:

1 *Offset* – low basic price, 'lost' margin recouped on extras, replacement parts or consumables.
2 *Diversionary* – low basic price on some products (in range or line) developing overall image of low cost.
3 *Discrete* – tailoring of price to bring product within the purchasing

---

[1] Based on Wilson, 1972.

competence of a given seniority of buyer (relevant where the
location of purchase decision is determined by corporate price
ceilings).

4 *Price lining* – price kept constant but quality of product or extent
of service adjusted to reflect changes in costs.

5 *Financing* – alternative options to purchase such as leasing and
rental (can be used as a specific means of extracting greater profit
by changing the bases on which 'price' is assessed by the customer); might be coupled with special credit terms, trade-in allowances and special offers.

The information technology market place, in particular, reflects the
development of three further categories of tactic:

6 *Bundling* – offer of a package consisting of one or more items,
usually sold separately, at a special price which is less than the sum
of the individual components; a widely used example is the
inclusion of one or more software packages (or a printer, or extra
memory/storage, etc) with the basic computer in order to appear
to be offering more value than a competitor. The promotion of
these 'bundled' offers uses the retail prices of the extra items to
demonstrate how much 'discount' is being offered to the customer; however, in practical terms, the package may be designed to
prevent discounting of the basic computer.

7 *Upgrade* – offer of upgrades to an originally purchased product
(especially software but also, in some instances, hardware) at a
very much reduced price aimed at extracting additional revenue
from a customer who might otherwise have chosen to stay with the
original product. In this objective, 'upgrade' pricing is a true
reflection of the principle of marginal pricing and is quite different
from the practice of offering 'trade-in' incentives as a form of
discount to stimulate new sales in a saturated market place.

8 *Multi-user licensing* – in the computer software industry, how to
price copies of software to a customer wanting several (or many)
copies is a particularly sensitive issue – especially as customers
have proved hostile to copy protection practices aimed at confin-
ing the use of a copy of purchased software to a single machine or
user. Software suppliers are devising licensing systems whereby
customers pay a special price to secure multiple copies of the
software for use on a network, site or company-wide basis. Pricing
of these licences has called for particularly fine judgement of the
balance between unit price and volume.

The above tactics are basically concerned with price. However, these need to be considered alongside what might be termed non-price differentials – ways of competing which command customer loyalty outside the framework of direct price competition, such as delivery services, after-sales support, technical back-up and advice and advertising and promotion effort.

In addition to these 'tactics of strategy' there are tactical questions of a more practical day-to-day level: what is the best way to pass on a price increase forced by rises in costs? Should ways be sought of keeping prices stable by modifying the product? Is it better to make price changes at regular and infrequent intervals (as until recently was mainly the case) or often in line with cost changes (as inflation is increasingly forcing on firms)? Should prices be changed to take into account positions of short-term strengths or weaknesses in the market place? How should the firm react to changes in competitors' pricing – is it necessary to react at all? By how much?

The combination and application of tactics requires, if they are to have the desired effect, a detailed knowledge of the customer groups to which they are applied and the way these take purchasing decisions as well as a good appreciation of the likely response from competitors and the tactics which they are using themselves.

DISCOUNTS AND DISCOUNTING

The principle of discounting, whether formal or discretionary, is entrenched in most sectors of manufacturing industry where list prices of some kind or other are employed. The variations in discounting practice in everyday use are numerous. Four main types of discount: quantity discounts, trade discounts, cash discounts and seasonal/load shedding discounts are summarized in Table 4.2. Other types of discount include those based on geographical factors (e.g. zonal pricing based on delivery distance); delivery method (e.g. discounts for customer collection); trade-in allowances on old equipment; 'free' supply of related consumables (e.g. labels used in price marking equipment).

There are various ways also in which discounts are actually effected: they can be based on physical volume or money sales; be a percentage discount or a cash difference from a 'list' price; be shown as a flat sum rebate or a net price; be made 'on-invoice' or 'off invoice'. Discount structures can be formal (with details published

Table 4.2
Types of discount

	Method of operation	Reasons for use
Quantity or discount/ rebates	1 Single order – discount based on physical volume purchased at one particular time	1 Respond to individual purchasing power of customer in a competitive environment
	2 Cumulative – discount based on physical volume purchased over a fixed period of time (usually one year)	2 Pass on cost savings involved in servicing larger orders
	3 Guaranteed offtake – version of cumulative discount involving commitment by the buyer to take up either a fixed minimum quantity over the period as a whole or in specified amounts at fixed intervals (e.g. monthly) or both. Sometimes penalties in the form of surcharges are made for exceeding a contract offtake as well as for falling short. In other cases bonuses can be paid for exceeding contract minimum	3 Encourage customers to purchase in larger quantities than they might otherwise do 4 Discourage small orders which are expensive to process or unprofitable 5 Promote repeat purchasing 6 Create stability in demand and foster greater regularity and consistency in supply
Trade discounts	Usually percentage discount from a specified 'list' price, designed to represent the distributors' operating expenses and profit. Alternatively may be represented as net trade prices available only to recognised 'trade' customers Trade discounts may be characterised as a flat rate trade concession (e.g. 25 per cent to trade, list to other buyers) or combined with a quantity discount	1 Aid in controlling or guiding final selling price (subject to legislation) 2 Means of discriminating between different types of distributor 3 Simplicity – easily understood by distributors 4 Economy – reduce need to keep changing catalogues (since discounts, not 'list' prices can be manipulated) 5 Protection of distributor against direct buyers

contd.

	Method of operation	Reasons for use
Cash discounts	Deductions offered by the seller if payment of an invoice is made within a specified time period	Encourage immediate or early payment thus saving costs involved in the extension of credit and management of overdue accounts
Seasonal discounts/ load shedding	Differential prices according to season, day of week or time of day, where demand has a cyclical pattern and supply is fixed or intractable – most appropriate in consumer markets	Encourage spreading of demand, diversion of peak loading, boosting of demand at low periods Examples – electricity, coal, hotels, cross channel ferries, public transport, cinemas

for customer use) or discretionary (in the form of guidelines within which sales managers can negotiate) or a combination of the two. Special contract or 'net price' arrangements with key customers are, in effect, an extension of the discretionary discounting principle but with the essential difference that the terms of the sales agreement are usually the result of direct negotiation between buyer and seller rather than a development of the existing discount formula.

Of course in theory and in practice there are excellent reasons for operating a discount policy, some of which are indicated in Table 4.2. Carefully operated and controlled, discounting provides firms with a flexible facility for fine-tuning response to (changing) demand and competitive conditions while retaining the overall integrity of catalogue and list price structures. The danger of discounting as general practice is that it can lead to inconsistency and lack of control.

Discounts and special details in effect represent the reality of pricing while formal price lists and formulas represent the theory. Thus, for example, 'special terms' (discounted and negotiated prices) covered approximately 80 per cent of the sales of the Metal Box Company (open top group) in 1977. The greater the flexibility or informality of the discounting procedure, and the more discretion which is granted to individual sales executives in negotiating actual prices, then the more the difficulty the company faces in maintaining a firm grip over the effects of its pricing activities. Anticipating revenues and profit is a basic component of financial budgeting and contol. However, the ability to make realistic forecasts and impose meaningful controls is directly related to an appreciation of the way prices are actually arrived at, the extent and 'mix' of sales at discounted prices and the relationship these prices have with formal price structures.

PRICING AND NEW PRODUCT PLANNING

It can be said that the only time a firm genuinely has complete discretion in pricing is before it has committed itself to developing and marketing a new product at all! Once resources start to be committed to R and D, and even more once production facilities have been invested in, the pricing options available to the firm become progressively narrowed by practical considerations: the costs 'sunk' in bringing the product to market; the fixed costs represented by the scale of plant laid down to produce it; the direct costs of production consequent on choice of production process and scale of production; the constraints imposed by demand and competitive conditions and by the pricing of existing product lines with which the new product might be expected to interact.

New product development has always been a high-risk activity – various studies in the USA have shown failure rates among those actually launched running as high as 60 per cent. Many others are abandoned before they reach the production stage after large sums have been spent on R and D. The risks are moreover tending to become greater on average as the pace of technological change and competitive pressures force up development costs.

The process of new product appraisal is one which involves a large number of corporate and marketing considerations. However, anticipation of the price ranges at which the product is likely to sell and market conditions or assumptions underlying those ranges is something which should normally take place at the earliest stages of product planning and be held under review throughout the development process. In effect it is argued that firms should think far more concretely about gearing new product development to a broad target selling price derived in turn from a realistic evaluation of potential demand and the nature of competition than they do at present. This would have several major benefits:

1 It would contain the tendency in R and D to 'over-engineer' products (since the price target will also imply production cost targets which would have to be met if satisfactory profits are to be made).

2 It would prevent the development of products based on unrealistic assumptions about likely sales volumes (which often result from the use of cost-plus formulas to project price, at the planning stage).
3 It would provide a framework for 'fine-tuning' the product during the later stages of development to maximize competitive success within the selected price range.

Admittedly this approach is not easy to apply to the product which is itself a dramatic technological breakthrough or creative innovation for which existing price indications in the market place are inadequate and hypothetical testing of consumer responses at best unreliable. However, the great majority of new products do not fall into this category but relate in some reasonably direct way to established applications and existing products against which price targets can reasonably be set.

PRICING AND PRODUCT LINES

The existence of product lines raises particularly complex issues of pricing because of the way demand of each individual product interacts. Product lines as a whole may be mutually supportive but individual products within the line can easily be competitive with each other, particularly if encouraged by lack of care in pricing. Simply applying a common mark-up to each individual product is clearly unsatisfactory since it is probable that each product will vary in its production and marketing cost profile and in the opportunities and constraints implied by demand and the competitor environment it is selling into. This argues for a pricing policy which provides for each product in a line to be individually priced according to costs and market conditions subject to certain broad principles of consistency.

SUMMARY

This chapter has sought to demonstrate why pricing is perhaps the most complex and demanding – and least clearly understood – of all tasks facing company management. What conclusions can be drawn which might help the financial executive, in particular, contribute more effectively to pricing policy formulation and price setting?

1 *Pricing is much more of an art than a science.* There is no universal formula or golden rule for arriving at the right price. Those responsible for price setting have to balance and allow for a variety of factors and influences both internal to and external to the firm itself which, far from the ordered and rational world of the theoretical economist, may not always be logical and may even be in conflict. Nevertheless, profitability can significantly be enhanced by injecting greater coherence into the rules and principles, whatever these may be, which govern the way prices are fixed and maintained. The financial executive has an important part to play in the preparation and implementation of pricing policy.

2 *Successful pricing decisions cannot be based on costs alone.* Prices are far less often arrived at by the mechanistic application of cost-based formulae than is widely believed. Even so, costs and cost-related profit targets remain a major obsession of many firms in pricing, particularly in the case of industrial products. Financial executives have tended on the whole to encourage and reinforce this essentially inward-looking approach. The success of pricing decisions is, however, highly dependent on the ability of the firm to comprehend and respond to *market* needs and conditions. The contribution of the financial executive to pricing decisions would be substantially enhanced by greater recognition of the role of such factors as competition, buyer attitudes and motivations and the impact of distributive systems in optimum pricing.

3 *Price is a much neglected and potentially powerful element in the marketing mix.* Price is widely treated more as a handicap which has to be borne rather than as a positive tool for achieving designated marketing goals. This chapter has looked at the ways pricing can contribute to overall marketing plans both in the longer term (pricing strategy) and in the short term (pricing tactics). The financial executive should be prepared to be 'sufficiently flexible in his own advice and policies not to inhibit sales and marketing personnel from manipulation of price as a marketing weapon'.

4 *Pricing considerations are a key element in product planning.* Anticipation of price ranges and market conditions are an essential precondition to effective investment and product planning. The financial executive should seek to ensure that pricing factors are introduced at the beginning and not at the end of the planning cycle for new products.

REFERENCES AND FURTHER READING

1 Atkin, B, and Skinner, R., *How British Industry Prices*, IMR, 1975.
2 Gabor, A., *Pricing*, 2nd edition, Gower, 1988.
3 *Marketing*, p. 32, Oct. 1979.
4 Price Commission, *Open Top Food and Beverage Cans and Aerosol Cans* (Metal Box Ltd), HC 135, 1978.
5 Price Commission, *Prices of Glass Containers* (UG Glass Containers Ltd) HC 170, 1978.
6 Price Commission, *Compressed Permanent Gases and Dissolved Acetylene Sold in Cylinders, Cylinder Rentals and Fixed Charges* (BOC Ltd), HC 223, 1979.
7 Price Commission, *Report for the period 1st February to 30th April 1980.*
8 Oxenfeldt, A.R., 'Multi-Stage Approach to Pricing', *Harvard Business Review,* July/August 1960.
9 Wilson, A., *The Marketing of Professional Services*, McGraw-Hill, 1972.

5

Income and Expenditure Budgets

Desmond Goch

We now assume that the business has defined its objectives, considered its resources, and assessed the demand for the goods and services which it was set up to supply. The next major stage in the planning process is to formulate the budgets of income and expenditure, for both revenue and capital items. The author of this chapter deals with income and expenditure on revenue account and the succeeding chapter will examine capital budgeting. He divides the process of revenue budgeting into (a) long-term strategic planning, incorporating the forecast demand changes referred to in Chapter 3, and (b) short-term, tactical planning. The author refers to the budgeting process as representing 'a distillation of experience and judgement. . . of the management team', thus echoing a similar thought expressed by Dr Sasieni when examining the forecasting of demand. Another significant comment by the present author on the budgetary system is that it should combine 'an element of motivation with a dash of scepticism'.

Emphasis is given to the importance of the objective of a profit target based on the current value of capital employed (for further discussion of the assessment of current values the reader is referred to the chapter on inflation accounting); and of reconciling the sales and production viewpoints. One of the key planning considerations in preparing the sales budget is to give priority to those product ranges from which the greatest contribution will be derived. The importance of sound pricing policy and the need for control of research and development are referred to by Mr Goch and taken up in greater depth in other chapters.

STRATEGIC AND TACTICAL PLANNING

Business planning can be divided into two broad categories. The first is strategic planning which is primarily concerned with forecasting and shaping the way the business is to be developed in the longer-term so as to take advantage of perceived changes in the market for its existing products or services and to be ready to exploit new commercial opportunities and technological developments whenever they arise. This kind of planning has a time-horizon that may extend forward for a decade or more, particularly where the industry concerned is one that requires a lengthy gestation period for its major capital expenditure schemes before they start to make a contribution to profits. For example, an oil refinery or a complex chemical plant is bound to be subjected to lengthy environmental planning permission procedures and even then the ensuing design and construction phases may be spread over several years. In these circumstances forward planning entails looking a long way ahead in commercial terms.

The second kind of business planning – with which we are concerned in this chapter – is the shorter-term tactical planning that reflects the current trading environment and makes its impact through the annual trading budget. With its much shorter time-horizon, usually no more than a year or so ahead at a time, it aims to assess the current business outlook and to plan accordingly so as to make the most economical and profitable use of resources in exploiting potential market opportunities. This budgeting exercise imposes a discipline on management by requiring a regular appraisal of the way in which the long-term planning objectives are being met and determining the standards by which subsequent performance will be measured. It has to be emphasized at the outset that the preparation of a trading budget of this nature is an exercise that should, where possible, involve all those senior line managers who will subsequently share the responsibility for seeing that it is being implemented. Although the budget is ultimately expressed in financial terms, it is essentially concerned with planning the effective and profitable use of the human, physical and financial resources of the business during the trading period under review. It should accordingly represent a distillation of the expertise and judgement of the full range of opinions represented on the management team and in this way it is more likely to be accepted as being an achievable target.

In the sense that the targets set by the budget should be ones that demand a concentrated effort to achieve, the planning process should aim to combine an element of motivation with a dash of scepticism – the latter being necessary as a counterweight to the over-optimism that sometimes pervades the discussion when sales and production targets and potential sales opportunities are being considered. Such optimism should not, of course, be discouraged too hastily but there is obviously the need to make an entirely objective assessment of the underlying planning assumptions if the trading budget that eventually emerges is to provide a sound base for the consequential decisions that may need to be made with regard to possible provision for extra production facilities and working capital requirements.

KEY PLANNING CONSIDERATIONS

The starting point for the planning exercise should be an appraisal of the proposed business strategy in the context of the current economic and trading environment and of the marketing conditions that might be foreseen as prevailing during the trading period covered by the budget plan. In making this appraisal the strategy will need to be conditioned by the business climate and related factors such as the degree of competition to be expected and the likely strength of consumer demand. The nature of the industry will, of course, be a material factor in determining the precise approach. Different considerations will apply when forecasting the potential demand for a fast-selling consumer product compared with, say, the prospective order book for specialized machinery being sold in overseas markets against worldwide competition.

Most forms of business activity are affected to some extent by the external trading environment and the level of economic activity in the territories where business is being contemplated. A key factor in assessing market possibilities and shaping the trading budget will therefore be the accuracy of the assessment of the probable course of the national economy during the budget period under review. Whether the business be one of organizing and selling foreign holiday package tours or of involvement in selling high-technology electronic equipment to overseas customers around the world, the prospect of finding sufficient customers to take up the potential output or production capacity that is available will be influenced to some degree by the state of the internal economies of the countries in which these activities are being planned to take place. In some instances, of course, the underlying political stability of national governments will be a material consideration when deciding where to concentrate marketing effort. There may also be a need to take account of difficulties likely to be encountered in remitting back to the parent business the proceeds of sales made in countries that impose stringent exchange control restrictions on currency transfers. Where the nature of the business is such that there is a markedly seasonal pattern to sales, the success of the trading forecast on which the budget is to be based may be conditioned by the potential buoyancy of trade in the immediate months ahead. An example of this kind of business is the toy manufacturing industry which has a large part of its annual sales turnover concentrated into the immediate pre-Christmas shopping period. The level of demand in the shops at that time is bound to be influenced by the amount of disposable income in the hands of parents and other relatives when the Christmas-present buying season is at its peak. If at that time the national economy is running at a high level of consumer demand and there are no adverse factors such as transport strikes to mar the spending spree, then there is every likelihood of a good selling season for the toy industry.

However, the decisions about which toys to stock, and at what level of output, have to be made many months beforehand, and at the time when production programmes and sales campaigns are being planned the economic outlook may appear to be very much less favourable. In such circumstances the budget planners might well wish to consider the views of the more reputable and influential economic forecasting institutions and to study available surveys of business opinion such as those conducted by the Confederation of British Industry. Equally important, of course, will be such feedback as can be obtained from customers when they are being visited by sales representatives as this will give an indication of opinion in the market places in which the business operates. A further view on the prevailing industrial climate can usually be given by the senior marketing executives, and their contribution to the budget planning sessions is very often the most sensitive and closely informed guide to likely trends of trade.

It is against the backdrop of external economic factors and intelligence gathered about the known intentions of competitors, actual or potential, that the budget planners will have to make their assessment of the prospective order book and the market opportunities that are likely to be presented. If the company is a divisionalized or multi-product business, then this task ought to be delegated as much as possible to those managers who are responsible for the marketing operations on a day-to-day basis and their individual assessments can then be presented for analysis and discussion by the central planning group. Such a procedure is more likely to encourage the formulation of a broadly based consensus of views on the probable trend of trade.

MARKETING POLICY AND THE BUDGET

It is the essence of business activity that firms exist to meet the demands of the market-place and ultimately the customer rules. The preparation of the sales budget therefore offers an ideal opportunity to make a detailed appraisal of marketing policy with the intention of re-defining objectives and considering new opportunities in terms of products and territories.

If, for example, one such objective is to increase market share – and what business does not have that aim? – then its achievement will almost certainly have implications for pricing policy. It is therefore important that the senior sales executives should in the first instance spend some time examining and agreeing on their broad policy objectives so as to establish the parameters to the detailed budgeting exercise.

The problems of forecasting demand and of pricing policy are analysed elsewhere in this book but for our immediate purpose an appropriate quantitative starting point for preparation of the sales budget might be the current forward order book. Lead times for production and delivery will vary greatly from firm to firm, according to the nature of the business, and in some instances forward orders may customarily extend only a few weeks ahead. In other kinds of business the production capacity may be fully committed for many months in advance. However, the current trend of order-placing can be expected to give an indication of the way in which demand may be expected to develop over the coming months.

From this base of the forward order book, projections can be made for each major product range or group and at this stage the opportunity should be taken to involve sales personnel who have direct customer contact. The sales representative who is making daily calls on customers is likely to have a closer feel for the immediate state of the market and be better placed to discern any early indications of changing trends than the senior executive in head office who may have fewer opportunities to meet customers face-to-face.

In the course of preparing sales estimates it is important to make appropriate allowances for intended product changes and the introduction of new product lines. The potential effect of proposed price changes must also be considered, although final decisions in this respect may need to be deferred until a later stage of the budgeting exercise. If the sales projections include a contribution expected to accrue from the introduction of new products or services, then consideration should be given to any launch promotion costs or other special promotion campaigns which may have to be run to achieve sales targets.

It cannot be emphasized too strongly that it is extremely important to produce a sales forecast as close to achievable reality as prediction will permit. Even a quite modest under- or over-estimate of projected revenue can have quite dramatic consequences for the bottom line of the trading forecast and could lead to decisions being made in relation to provision of production and financial resources which might have a significant knock-on effect.

THE SALES/PRODUCTION EQUATION

When sales budgets are under discussion it is often the case that attention is focused on maximizing sales turnover and insufficient consideration is given to the contribution it can be expected to make to profit. Sales turnover is vital in the context of gaining or maintaining market share and this is often regarded as an all-important yardstick for judging success. However, unless it is accompanied by adequate gross profit yields it will do little towards enhancing the net profit figure on the bottom line of the trading account.

Where the assessment of potential demand and market opportunities indicates that there is an element of choice in deciding which sectors and product ranges should be given priority, then this requires close consultation with the production management executives (or the executives responsible for procurement and supply where the organization is one engaged in an activity such as retailing and does not itself manufacture) and also with the financial members of the planning group.

In such circumstances the selling effort will probably need to be concentrated on those product ranges that yield the highest profit contribution and a close analysis should be made of the kind of sales that will be most likely to achieve this objective. The profit contribution per unit of output represents the difference between the revenue yield and the directly related incremental costs arising from production activity and it is commonly referred to as the 'contribution margin'. By way of example, if the unit of sales is a canned food product, the incremental costs would comprise the cost of the bought-out can and the ingredients that go to make up the contents. When assessing the relative profitability of this product compared with an alternative, it is essential to know their respective contribution margins after taking into consideration the hourly production rates assuming that they are both suitable for being produced on the same preparation and canning lines.

The following example based on this imaginary food product illustrates this important concept of the contribution margin as a factor when making a sales/production decision in such circumstances. It is assumed that the management of the food factory is faced with the situation that it has only a limited capacity on its can-filling lines and has to choose between three alternative products when it is planning the production programme. The three food products are sold to wholesalers and large retailers and the respective contribution margins have been calculated as in Table 5.1, thus:

TABLE 5.1
CONTRIBUTION MARGINS

	Product A	Product B	Product C
Net sales revenue (p)	22	24	28
Incremental costs (p):			
Can	4	4	4
Ingredients	6	8	10
Other direct costs	2	2	2
	12	14	16
Contribution margin (p)	10	10	12
Hourly production rate	3600	3400	2800
Contribution per hour (£)	360	340	336

It will be noted from this example that although Product C has the highest unit selling price and the highest unit contribution margin, it is Product A with the lowest unit selling price which yields the highest contribution per hour of production and it is therefore the higher hourly production rate which is the deciding factor. The contribution margin represents the gross profit from which the production over-heads, selling, distribution and administration expenses and the net profit margin have to be met and consequently it is important that it should be maximized by choosing the mix of product that is most likely to achieve this objective.

Although this particular example has been based on a manufactured product, the contribution margin principle applies equally to businesses engaged in distribution and service industry activities. A retailer will obviously need to look closely at the gross profit margin (a synonym for the contribution margin in this context) when deciding which ranges of goods should be given prime selling space when planning counter and window displays.

MATCHING DEMAND TO RESOURCES

When planning the sales budgets for individual products an essential aspect of the exercise is to ensure that the forecasted off-take can be matched by the production capacity of the manufacturing and supply side of the organization. It may be that when the sales department's forecast of its requirements is related to the capacity that will be available, it will be found that the sales targets cannot be achieved without bringing into use additional resources. In this event it will probably be necessary for the budget planners to examine the implications as it might be necessary to seek authorization for capital expenditure on plant and to incur additional operating costs.

If, on the other hand, it is considered that there is a possibility that the existing production facilities will not be fully utilized, then it may be necessary to plan for the introduction of new product lines or services so as to achieve a satisfactory level of activity. An example of this approach to the exploitation of under-employed capacity is to be found in the magazine and periodical publishing industry where new titles are launched, or existing ones are relaunched, so as to use printing capacity that would otherwise be standing idle. A takeover of titles from another publisher might even be contemplated by an aggressive management seeking long-term solutions.

A comparable situation in a service industry might be the package holiday travel business where when popular resorts have reached their capacity in terms of available hotel accommodation, marketing effort is turned to promoting the virtues of newer resorts and centres which have not hitherto attracted a large tourist following. By setting out to create a demand for these newer holiday centres the travel companies and air charter firms hope to maintain full utilization of aircraft and other facilities that have been committed on time charters, and continue to spread their administration overheads over a wide range of turnover.

When the broad outline of the sales/production plan has been agreed, it will be necessary for the production members of the budget planning team to break it down into manageable sectors so that the manpower and materials requirements can be allocated to departments concerned and costed out in financial terms. This part of the exercise is probably the most complex and tedious aspect as it involves translating physical measurements into manning and machine-loading programmes and thence into monetary cost terms. In addition, an appraisal must be made of requirements for ancillary facilities such as maintenance services and toolroom back-up. Most of the problems in this area are likely to arise when an extension of existing production capacity is being planned or a major product change is put in hand.

It is possible, of course, that where the pattern of sales has seasonal or other cyclical characteristics, then the production programme may have to be planned on the basis that goods are to be made for stock when sales are at a cyclically low ebb. On the other hand, where levels of production are based on forecast demand from retailers, rather than being matched against specific orders, provision may need to be made in the labour budget for possible overtime working at peak periods when the demand on production is at an exceptionally high level. Peaks and troughs in demand can make for production planning difficulties and the ideal solution, albeit often unattainable, is to develop new products or sales outlets that will fit into the slacker periods in the current programme. This, in turn, needs to be remitted back to the sales department for further consideration.

Having translated the production requirements into physical and manpower resource terms, it is necessary to determine appropriate control factors for monitoring subsequent performance against the budget. If standard costing systems are already in use they will provide the basic data for building up a system of flexible budgeting. Such a system is valuable where budgeting assumptions have to be made within a range of possible output levels as some items of expenditure will fluctuate proportionately to volume while others will vary hardly at all. Indeed, it is often the case that in the short-term very few overhead expenses will vary in relation to output levels – with the possible exception of some items such as consumable materials and the variable element of charges for gas or electricity.

With longer-term variations in the level of activity there will, of course, be pressures to reduce items of overhead expenditure that are left untouched in the short-term. It may therefore be advisable to classify the various elements of overhead expenditure as either 'fixed' or 'variable' so that the budgeted expenditure limits can be flexed according to the level of activity.

It is essential to the preparation of a soundly-based trading budget to appreciate the significance of fixed costs and variable costs within the overall cost structure of the business, particularly in terms of the effect on gross margins. The variable costs are those which fluctuate in proportion to the level of output: as do the cost of the can and the ingredients in the example of the canned food product given earlier.

In the short-term most of the other operating costs of the typical business can normally be categorized as fixed costs. These short-term fixed costs would include such items as workforce and management payrolls, fuel and power, insurances, maintenance expenses and the many other items of a like character which are incurred in the course of the day-to-day running of the business. Longer-term fixed costs would include rent, rates, capital expenditure amortization, etc.

All these fixed costs, whether categorized as short-term or long-term costs, have to be met from the gross margin surplus accruing from sales turnover and it is vital to the financial viability of the business that the projected gross contribution is sufficient to cover all the fixed costs and also yield an adequate surplus by way of net profit.

The relationship between fixed costs, variable costs, sales revenue and the profitability break-even point can probably be best understood by being illustrated in diagrammatic form (Fig. 5.1).

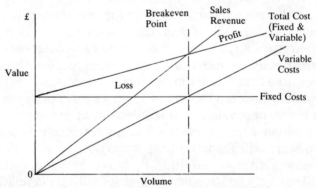

Figure 5.1　Costs – revenue relationships, showing break-even point

Note: This chart is also discussed in Chapter 4, page 59.

At the point where total costs (i.e. variable costs plus fixed costs) are exactly equal to total revenue, the break-even position will have been reached and any further sales turnover will take the business into profit.

The lesson to be drawn from this somewhat over-simplified example is that the greater the contribution margin earned on sales turnover, the sooner will the break-even point be reached and the larger the eventual net trading profit that will be earned.

BUDGETING FOR OVERHEADS

Concurrently with the planning of the sales and production programmes, an analysis should be made of the expenses that go to make up the remainder of the operating expenditure that comes under the general classification of factory overheads. In the case of a manufacturing organization these expenses will embrace a multitude of items ranging from period costs such as capital expenditure amortization charges to the day-to-day spending on maintenance spares, small tools, consumable materials, etc.

The periodic budgeting exercise provides an opportunity for a detailed scrutiny of the many items of expense that tend to be concealed in the nooks and crannies of overhead expenditure and accordingly a careful appraisal should be made of the justification for continuing to incur commitments simply on the basis that they already exist. For example, careful study of the telephone account sometimes discloses charges for rent of equipment or services which are no longer actively used and this may equally be the case with regard to equipment-leasing agreements.

For many businesses the payroll comprises by far the largest single category of expenditure and in addition to the direct wage and salary costs there are the related costs such as national insurance contributions, superannuation scheme contributions, sickness benefit and medical insurance schemes, employer's liability insurance and similar payroll-related commitments. It therefore follows that with labour costs becoming such a large element of total costs for many businesses, particular attention needs to be given to the properly planned use of labour resources and to any aspect of the budget that might entail recruiting additional employees. Indeed, there is much to commend the practice of many organizations of drawing up a total manpower budget which, when it has been approved, represents the upper limit of the payroll commitment and which cannot be exceeded without specific authorization by a senior management executive.

Planning the labour element of the budget is one of the most crucial phases of the whole exercise as there is a natural human tendency on the part of many departmental managers to aim to achieve as large a manpower establishment for budgetary purposes as can be negotiated. Underspending being so much easier to justify than overspending, and with the possibility of absenteeism and sickness in mind, they will sometimes seek to hedge their bets when asked to spell out their manning requirements for inclusion in the budget. When evaluating manpower requirements for production-line work it may not be too difficult to assess the strength of the case that is being made for additional people, but when it comes to extra indirect employees the budget planners may have to exercise a degree of scepticism. Jobs such as storekeeping, quality control, packing, labouring, cleaning, etc., have a tendency to multiply and swallow up the profit margins unless they are closely controlled. A similar approach needs to be adopted when considering budgets for administrative personnel. The budget exercise provides an opportunity often denied at other times to impose proper management control over payroll costs, but leaving individual department managers to decide their own priorities within the framework of financial resources represented by their budgeted allocation for labour costs.

ACTIVITY BUDGETING

For some types of business the planned level of business activity may need to be capable of significant variation as the year progresses if new opportunities arise. For example, a multiple retailing organization operating a chain of shops in major towns and cities will often find that the opportunity may arise at short notice to acquire new premises or to take over existing premises as additional outlets and this may represent an expansion of trading turnover and profit expectation beyond that envisaged in the original budget.

For this kind of business the approach to budgeting would probably need to be based on the assumption of a target rate of turnover and gross profit contribution from each retail outlet calculated according to floor area in terms of selling price, and any new acquisitions during the year would be added to the main budget on such a basis. Similarly, of course, any shops which are closed down during the year would result in a corresponding downward adjustment to the budget from the time when they ceased to trade.

The sales staff payroll budget and the shop-related overheads budgets could be built up in the same way, according to the number of shop units, and the emphasis of the budget plan would thus be directed at the operating level of the retail shop outlets rather than at the consolidated results of the group as a whole. Indeed, with this kind of multiple retailing organization the essence of sound budgeting and control would be the formulation of appropriate budget standards based on experience gained in operating the more efficient outlets.

The principle of applying predetermined budget standards has, of course, got other applications and has the virtue of combining the forecasting of operating costs with the setting of standards which can be applied as a yardstick for measuring subsequent performance. It may be possible to devise similar control factors to those used in many manufacturing businesses and thus relate target cost levels to the degree of activity. Companies employing a force of outside sales representatives might well adopt a similar approach when forecasting and controlling selling costs in terms of salaries and expenses and the same technique can also be applied to operating costs for a vehicle fleet measured on a volume/mileage basis.

RESEARCH AND DEVELOPMENT BUDGETING

For many companies – and typically those in the aerospace and pharmaceuticals industries – long-term survival depends on the ability to maintain a technical or scientific edge over competitors and this entails supporting a continuous programme of research and development. The nature and extent of this commitment will vary considerably according to the type of business, but in many instances it will entail financing the cost of a permanent research establishment with the attendant running costs that have to be incurred to maintain such a project. A detailed analysis of the commitment of resources to research and development appears in a later chapter but the following paragraphs are relevant to our consideration of expenditure budgeting.

At the end of the day, of course, the expectation is that such an investment will fully justify its existence when the pay-off comes in the form of new products and improvements to existing ones. During their commercial lifetime they will thus contribute to earnings on a scale that will recoup the expenditure incurred in running the research facility and make a proper contribution to trading profit, while at the same time helping to enhance the company's reputation as an innovator and leader in its industry. Setting up such a facility often represents an act of faith in the future as there can never be absolute certainty that the investment will pay off in clearly identifiable financial terms. It is almost inevitable that some research projects will prove abortive and perhaps only a small proportion of them will offer the possibility of commercial exploitation on a profitable basis.

However, having made the decision to set up such a facility it can be assumed that the parent organization has accepted a commitment to finance a research programme and the question that now has to be asked is how much is it prepared to underwrite on an annual budget for the project. It is perhaps understandable that the staff who are employed on this kind of work might feel that it can be best carried on in premises that are separated from the day-to-day activities of the production units, but it has to be understood that isolation from the normal commercial pressures may make it more difficult for them to accept the financial disciplines and constraints that are normally imposed elsewhere in the organization. It will therefore make for a better relationship between the senior management of the company and the senior research staff if there is a clear appreciation on both sides of the broad objectives of the research and development programme and of the financial limitations within which it has to be conducted.

To achieve this end it is essential that the research establishment should be fully integrated into the annual budgeting exercise. To the extent that the main research establishment budget will comprise premises and payroll costs, these elements of the total allocation can be readily evaluated in financial terms. In addition, it is probable that there will be some non-recurring expenditure to be incurred in acquiring or using specialized test equipment and possibly on projects placed with outside research organizations and institutions. In quantifying the projected expenditure in these sectors it is desirable that the head of the research department should be asked to outline the year's programme so that priorities can be defined and a global total be determined for inclusion in the overall budget. Once such a programme has been accepted by the budget planning group, then it must be regarded as an upper limit of expenditure which must not be exceeded without specific Board approval.

Although this budgetary discipline will almost certainly seem to be excessively bureaucratic and irksome to the staff members of the research department – as, indeed, it will be to staff elsewhere in the organization – it nevertheless provides them in the long run with a greater measure of personal security and helps them to recognize priorities that are consistent with the commercial objectives of the business as an overall entity. In many industries a sound research and devleopment programme is essential to long-term survival but it has to be contained at a level that can be comfortably sustained within the financial structure of the parent organization. Hence there is a need for soundly-based budgeting and adequate monitoring and control.

THE OVERALL BUDGET REVIEW

When all the individual departmental forecasts and projections have been completed they will have to be assembled and correlated by the budget planning team in a format that matches with the presentation adopted for the organization's internal management accounting and reporting system so that the overall result can be studied and evaluated according to the broad strategy and the financial and commercial criteria which were determined at the outset of the budgeting exercise.

In this context it will be helpful, if not essential, that the trading figures are presented in a format that clearly identifies the significant elements of costs and revenues under their principal product or activity classifications.

For example, projected sales revenue should be analysed under each main product sector or other appropriate classification. Against each category of revenue there should then be deducted the directly attributable costs such as materials and components and those labour and overhead costs which can be positively identified as relating wholly to those activities, see Table 5.2.

The objective in presenting the budget summary in this format is to identify the profit contribution that can be foreseen as accruing from each main trading activity and so enable managerial judgements and decisions to be based on meaningful data. In budgeting responsibility terms it is preferable that this divisionalized or departmental form of presentation should be matched to coincide with the management lines of responsibility so that the senior managers concerned are able to participate in and appreciate the trading implications of their forecasting and budgeting decisions.

It would be surprising, indeed, if the first draft of the master budget were to be found to show an acceptable forecast of trading profit and

Table 5.2
Trading Budget

	Product A £	Product B £	Product C £	Total £
Budgeted sales revenue	9700	15 000	7300	32 000
Material and components	2000	4400	2600	9000
Direct labour and related overheads	4500	6200	2800	13 500
	6500	10 600	5400	22 500
Gross contribution	3200	4400	1900	9500
Gross contribution ratio	33.0%	29.3%	26.0%	29.7%
Other directly attributable costs:				
Distribution	500	1000	500	2000
Promotion	100	300	100	500
	600	1300	600	2500
Net contribution	2600	3100	1300	7000
Net contribution ratio	26.8%	20.7%	17.8%	21.9%
Non-attributable overhead costs				4000
Budgeted net profit				3000

the budget planning team will have to make an assessment of the acceptability of the projected performance of each department or divisionalized activity. It is not practicable in a study of budgeting procedures of this nature to attempt to define the kind of yardstick that might be applied for this purpose, but obviously the assessment would have to evaluate key factors such as the forecasted trading profit expressed as a percentage of sales turnover and, where appropriate, the resulting rate of return on capital employed. Most important, however, will be the plausibility of the underlying assumptions as to the level of forecasted sales turnover and allowances for cost inflation, both of which are fundamental to the validity of the whole exercise. Comparison would need to be made with earlier years on a physical volume basis, so far as this is practicable, and any asssumptions as to increases in such volume, both absolute and relative to market share, tested for the soundness of such expectations. If there is an assumption of an increase in market share, then the budget planners would need to be sure that proper account has been taken of the possible reactions of competitors in the face of potential loss of some of their own market share. If the forecasts are based on an assumption of an overall increase in the market, then they would need to consider whether this presumed growth is consistent with national economic trends and other market indicators. These are the kinds of question the members of the budget planning team could be expected to ask when testing the validity of the projections on which the sales forecasts have been based.

So much for the demand side of the equation; but what about the supply side? Here again there is a need for rigorous scrutiny of the assumptions about the level of output that will be needed to service the projected order book. Any significant increase in the sales volume requirement must be looked at in the context of the existing plant capacity. If the demand on resources is likely to be such that additional capacity will have to be installed, then this will have to be made available in time to produce the extra volume required. Failing that, does the budget make a realistic provision for any extra overtime working or additional shifts that might be needed to meet the demand placed on the existing plant capacity? Do the production plans provide for an adequate supply of bought-out components and materials?

Depending on how satisfied the budget planners are with the replies given by departmental and divisional managers to these questions, it might be necessary to ask for re-working of some sectors of the budget so as to get the balance right. In the final analysis, of course, the overall budget must plan for a level of profit that is acceptable in relation to the financial and other resources employed in the business. It may be that after a full appraisal has been made of the trading possibilities, consideration might have to be given to the case for withdrawing from activities that show little prospect of earning an adequate return within the foreseeable future when measured in this way.

As already mentioned, the budget plan will need to make adequate provision for cost increases which can be foreseen as likely to materialize during the period under review. Where the business is one that operates in an industry in which wage rates are influenced by the outcome of national negotiations, then it will be necessary to formulate a view on the likely outcome of any settlement that will have an impact on wage rates payable during the budget period. On the basis of this view, an appropriate allowance will have to be included in the cost projections.

In the case of a manufacturing business, the likely trend of prices of major raw materials can be difficult to forecast with any certainty, particularly if they are traded commodities such as metals or certain agricultural products. The problem is compounded, of course, where such materials are imported and buying prices are therefore subject to fluctuations in foreign currency exchange rates. The company must weigh carefully whether the premium for buying forward is worth incurring to discount this risk. This latter problem of exchange rates will also arise in the case of service industries where facilities or services have to be paid for in foreign currencies. Holiday tour operators have to pay many of the suppliers of the services and facilities they offer in foreign currencies and airlines pay their fuel bills at prices which are calculated by reference to the US dollar. However, despite these complications, best guesses have to be made so as to give an indication of the likely outcome of trading.

When these various cost inflation contingency factors have been incorporated into the budget forecasts a view can then be taken on the probable effect on profit margins and thus on prospective pricing strategies. Trading budgets which are subject to these kinds of variable can be criticized as being little more than an informed guess at future prospects, and managers who have been involved in business planning at this level will acknowledge that there is an element of truth in this assertion.

However, despite these reservations the fact remains that a soundly constructed budget plan that has been based on reasonable assumptions as to the surrounding economic and business environment will provide an invaluable management tool for monitoring trading performance. As the business moves forward into the trading period covered by the budget, and the actual out-turn can be compared with the forecast, it acts as an early warning system in the event of a deterioration of trading performance and will indicate those areas where action may have to be taken to deal with adverse trends.

Finally, the planning exercise helps to impose a mental discipline on individual managers in that it requires them to make a rigorous appraisal of their department's performance and its prospective contribution to profitability. By becoming involved in the planning processes across the wider spectrum they can be encouraged to take a broader view of their responsibilities and so help to develop their full potential within a controlled and monitored environment.

APPENDIX – RETURN ON CAPITAL EMPLOYED

Return on capital employed is universally accepted as a yardstick for measuring profitability where the undertaking is one that requires a significant investment of capital in the form of land, buildings, plant, machinery and working capital to finance trading stock, materials, work in progress and customer credit in order to carry on the business. Since the capital funds which have to be provided (normally by shareholders and long-term lenders) to finance this investment need to be remunerated in the form of dividends, loan interest and, perhaps, bank interest, then the test of commercial viability and managerial efficiency is the ability to earn enough profit to meet these commitments after tax has been paid and to provide sufficient surplus thereafter to meet the additional capital requirements for progressive expansion in the future.

In setting this financial objective a decision must be made as to the appropriate rate of return to be expected from the employment of capital funds in this way. One approach is to express the target rate in relation to rates being achieved by comparable businesses in the same or in similar industries and this is the one that is most likely to be accepted as a fair yardstick. However, where the business is one that does not require the use of substantial capital investment such as an advertising agency or an architectural consultancy then the ROC measurement will not be appropriate and the profit target might be better determined as (say) a percentage rate of return on gross income (i.e. fees or commissions earned).

In determining this capital employed base it is reasonable to make an adjustment to the historic book cost figures at which the fixed assets are normally shown in the balance sheet so as to reflect current cost values. The following specimen balance sheet of an imaginary company is used to illustrate the calculation of a capital employed base figure for this purpose. It is assumed that the relative price index for 'Land and buildings' stood at 115 at the date of purchase and at 140 at the date of the balance sheet, thus showing an increase of 22

XYZ Ltd – Balance sheet at 31 December 19XX

	£		£
Capital and reserves		Fixed assets	
Share capital	800 000	Land and buildings	750 000
Reserves	400 000	Plant and machinery	280 000
	1 200 000		1 030 000
Deferred taxation	200 000	Investments	100 000
Current liabilities		Current assets	
Creditors	150 000	Trading stock	200 000
Taxation	70 000	Debtors	400 000
Bank overdraft	120 000 340 000	Cash	10 000 610 000
	£1 740 000		£1 740 000

per cent in round figures. The 'Plant and machinery' index stood at 125 at the date of purchase and at 169 at the date of the balance sheet: an increase of 35 per cent.

The adjustments made to the balance sheet figures to bring them to current cost values for the purpose of determining the capital employed base figure are as follows:

	Balance sheet £	Excluded assets £	Indexing factor	Adjusted values £
Land and buildings	750 000	100 000	1.22	793 000
Plant and machinery	280 000	–	1.35	378 000
Investments	100 000	100 000	–	–
Trading stock	200 000	–	–	200 000
Debtors	400 000	–	–	400 000
Creditors	(150 000)	–	–	(150 000)
		Adjusted capital employed		£1 621 000

For the purpose of this example it has been assumed that not all the land and buildings represented by the book value in the balance sheet are employed in the activity for which a profit target is being determined and hence an adjustment has been made to exclude the appropriate figures. The current cost indexation factor has been applied to the adjusted book value. Similarly, the investments have been excluded as they, too, are not part of the capital employed base for this purpose.

It will be noted that the bank overdraft has been omitted from capital employed as being a source of long-term funding rather than as a current liability.

The appropriate target rate of return required by the trading budget would be expressed as a percentage on the capital employed base figure of £1 621 000. Thus, if the budget planners are seeking a target rate of 20 per cent, then this will represent a monetary profit target of £324 000.

REFERENCES AND FURTHER READING

Batty, J., *Management Accountancy*, Macdonald and Evans, 1982.
Cowe, R, (ed), *Handbook of Management Accounting*, Gower, 2nd edition 1987.

Dobbins, R., and Witt, S.F., *Practical Financial Management*, Blackwell, 1988.

Saunders, J.A., Sharp, J.A., and Witt, S.G., *Practical Business Forecasting*, Gower, 1987.

Scapens, R.W., *Advanced Management Accounting*, Macmillan, 1985.

Tucker, S., *Profit Planning Decisions with the Break-even System*, Gower, 1981.

6

Capital Budgeting

Harold Bierman, Jr

This is a subject for which there is already a voluminous literature, by no means all of which reflects recent developments. In this chapter Professor Bierman reviews the progress of thought on the subject.

The author sees the capital budget as the specific plan of action which allocates resources for the long-range plan. The objective of the process is firmly stated to be to maximize the net present value of the stockholders' position. The errors which result from using for capital appraisal purposes the accounting concept of profit are clearly exposed, and accrual accounting is compared with the simpler idea of cash flow. Capital projects are considered under the two essential headings of independent investment alternatives and mutually exclusive investments and we are informed – perhaps to our surprise – that 'there is no reliable objective way to rank independent investments'.

The author explains the defects of using return on investment and payback techniques of assessing capital projects, and compares the net present value method with the internal rate of return. A particularly interesting section is the discussion of risk; 'there is no reason for assuming that risk is compounded through time' and the author maintains that it is incorrect to take risk into account via the discounting technique, but indicates how a risk premium may be quantified and refers to the capital pricing model of William Sharpe.

In a later chapter on the assessment of performance, Professor Magee takes up a development of capital budgeting by emphasizing that a post audit of each project is an important function of financial control.

After the top management of a firm has completed its planning exercises, the resulting long-range strategy has to be translated into a specific plan of action which actually allocates resources. This specific plan may be called the capital budget and the process of arriving at the plan may be called capital budgeting.

It is convenient to divide investments into two general classifiations. The first category is all investment opportunities that are economically independent of each other. Thus a firm might consider replacing its automobile production line with a more labour-efficient set of machines, or it might consider entering the airline industry. These are two independent investment alternatives.

Once the independent investments have been determined, the second type of classification must be considered, that is to gather information on all investments which perform the same economic function. These are 'mutually exclusive' investments.

Once it is decided that the airline industry should be investigated as a possible investment all the different investment possibilities in aeroplanes that are mutually exclusive have to be considered. That is, there can only be one type of aeroplane fleet. The fleet might actually consist of a mixture of types of plane, but there can only be one type of mixture at a given time.

The objective of the capital budgeting process is to make accept-or-reject decisions involving independent investments (they can all be undertaken if they are desirable) and 'best of the set' decisions involving mutually exclusive investments (only one of these investments can be undertaken). In making these decisions there is implied some known and agreed objective for the firm.

As a first step it should be clearly indicated what objectives are not affecting the capital budgeting process. The aim is not to maximize total sales or percentage share of market. Growth is not the goal (though it might occur if the correct decisions are made) nor are earnings per share and total earnings being maximized. It will be seen that the goal is to maximize the net present value of the stockholders' position and it is assumed that in doing so wellbeing of the stockholders is being maximized. The decisions are being made from the point of view of the stockholders and it is assumed that their interests are best served by a procedure that systematically assigns a cost to the capital that is utilized in the production process.

The capital budgeting process that is recommended must take into consideration a cost on the capital that is being utilized or equivalently the process must take into consideration the time value of money.

As a second step, after enough sophistication to include complexities is gained, it can be recognized that the process must also take into account the existence of uncertainty and adjust for the risk of the project being considered.

Capital budgeting decisions generally involve immediate (or nearly immediate) outlays and benefits that stretch out through time. In some cases the benefits may be deferred for many years. The primary problem facing management responsible for making capital budgeting decisions is to incorporate time value and risk considerations in such a manner that the wellbeing of the stockholders is maximized.

This chapter will first review briefly the development of capital budgeting decision making over the past thirty-five years and then describe the present state of theory and practice. Most importantly, the basic principles of capital budgeting about which theoreticians are in general agreement will be described.

THE PAST BRIEFLY REVIEWED

In 1951, two important books were published, one written by Joel Dean and one by Friedrich and Vera Lutz. These books immediately started people thinking about investment decisions and first a trickle and then a flood of papers and articles was written. At the time of publication of the two books the largest number of business firms were using a mixture of payback, a naïve return on investment (average income divided by average investment) and in the machine tool industry some variation of the MAPI[1] formula was just being introduced. An article in the *Harvard Business Review* by Dean (1954) was particularly important in bringing capital budgeting to the notice of business managers. In this paper Dean recommended the use of the rate of return method. This method consisted in finding a percentage (rate of discount) that caused the sum of the present values of the cash flows to be equal to zero and was a particularly important measure since it described the profitability of an investment in terms that were analogous to the yield of a bond or other monetary investment. This was intuitively appealing to practical business managers. The internal rate of return technique rapidly became accepted by a wide range of industrial firms (the chemical and oil firms led the way), but there was some confusion about the

---

[1] Machinery Allied Products Institute

relative merits of the internal rate of return (a percentage) method and the net present value (a dollar amount) method. A famous issue of the University of Chicago *Journal of Business* described the confusion that existed: the classic paper by Lorie and Savage (1955) summarized difficulties associated with the internal rate of return method in evaluating mutually exclusive investments, and in other situations where investments had to be compared.

The confusion between net present value and internal rate of return persisted in theoretical literature until Jack Hirshliefer published a paper in the *Journal of Political Economy* (1958) which drew heavily on the classic book by Irving Fisher (1930), *The Theory of Interest*. In this paper Hirshliefer laid the foundation for understanding the similarities and differences between the net present value and internal rate of return methods of making capital budgeting decisions. Later Bierman and Smidt (1960) published *The Capital Budgeting Decision*.

William Sharpe (1964) published a classic paper that introduced the capital asset pricing model. Since that time scholars have attempted to link that model to the capital budgeting decision problem. Particularly important links have been forged by Hamada (1969), Fama (1968), Linter (1965), Mossin (1966), and Stapleton (1971). Future progress will build on these foundations.

In 1973 Fischer Black and Myron Scholes published their important paper that defined the valuation of options. Efforts have been made to apply the option pricing theories to capital budgeting. The most successful authors have been M.J. Brennan and E.S. Schwartz in their 1985 *Journal of Business* paper, where they apply the technique to valuation of natural resources. To date application possibilities are very limited.

The remainder of this chapter will describe the basic elements of capital budgeting and in the process will indicate how the conflict between net present value and internal rate of return may be easily resolved.

RANKING OF INVESTMENTS

Some managers think it useful to classify investment decisions as being of three types:

1   Making accept-or-reject decisions involving investments whose

cash flows are independent of each other.

2   Choosing the best of a set of mutually exclusive investments; that is because of their characteristics only one of the investments can be undertaken (for example, you only place one roof on a factory).

3   Ranking of independent investments in order of their desirability.

This third classification requires explanation. While investments can be ranked subjectively in the same manner that one can rank the ten best movies of the year, there is no reliable objective way to rank independent investments. This disclosure is generally disappointing to managers who like to rank investments in order of relative desirability and then cut off when all investable funds are committed. In fact, some 'solutions' have been offered which claim to accomplish such rankings. Unfortunately, no simple exact solution exists.

However, all is not lost. Most importantly the investments can be separated into two classifications, acceptable and not acceptable. If a manager then wants to rank the acceptable investments using subjective or quasi-quantitative techniques, given the degree of uncertainty that exists in the world, this practice is relatively harmless. Second, the need for a ranking can be avoided by a 'programming' technique that chooses the best set of investments, given the resource limitations and a well-defined objective (such as maximization of present value).

In some very well-defined situations investments can be ranked, but these cases are not likely to be the normal situation in the real world.

USE OF CASH FLOWS

The investment analysis should be performed using the after-tax cash flows of each period as the inputs into the calculations. The results are consistent with the use of a theoretically correct income measure and easier to compute since they do not require a measure of depreciation expense and other accounting accruals and assumptions.

The debt flows are generally excluded from the measure of cash flows. Thus profitability measures are obtained that are independent of the method of financing. For some purposes the decision maker may want to include all debt flows (not just interest) to obtain stockholder equity profitability measures. These measures must be used with care since they are not comparable to measures that exclude the debt flows. A major error is to include some of the effects of debt, but not all.

The accountant measures yearly earnings based on complex 'accrual' concepts. The cash flow calculations of capital budgeting decisions are much simpler. The net amount of cash receipts and expenditures for each time period need to be found (an implicit cash outlay will be included, as when an office space is used rather than rented out). Conventionally the cash flows are those of the investment excluding the financing cash flows.

Why can cash flows be used for the capital budgeting decision? The objective is to evaluate the investment over its entire life and there is no need to determine the year-by-year profitability (as with accounting) in order to decide whether or not the investment is acceptable.

Discounted cash flow

The discounted cash flow (DCF) methods of evaluating the investments have now gained acceptability and are used by almost all the largest industrial firms and their use is spreading among the smaller firms. Twenty years ago less than 10 per cent of the Fortune 500 firms used these procedures (the estimate is from the Stanford Research Institute study published in January 1966). Today it is difficult to find a Fortune 500 firm that does not use one or more of the discounted cash flow procedures.

All firms face capital budgeting decisions where the timing of the cash flows and the uncertainty of the cash flows of an investment are relevant factors. For many years managers did not know how to take time-value into consideration in a theoretically correct manner. Now two basic methods are widely used and they are both DCF methods. One method is to find the average return on investment earned through the life, where the average is of a very special type. The second method is to apply a rate of discount (interest rate) to future cash flows to bring them back to the present (finding present value equivalents). The first calculation described will be called the 'internal rate of return' method and the second calculation 'net present value'. A wide range of different titles is used and there are also different variations of calculations, but these two methods are the most common and the most useful.

THE TIME–VALUE FACTOR AND INVESTMENT EVALUATION

All investments have three basic elements that an investor is likely to take into account in some fashion:

1 the time-value of money; funds at different times have different values;
2 the outcomes are uncertain; attitudes towards risk are relevant;
3 the value of the information; the uncertain flows are spread out through time and at present there is no information as to the outcome.

It is not surprising that there are markets that enable different individuals to attain their own preferences relative to the three elements listed. There may be some people whose near-term plans are completely independent of the actual outcomes of an investment, so they would pay nothing for information relative to the outcomes of an investment. Others (say someone planning the education of children) may be very concerned with the fact that they will not know the outcome of their investment for a number of years. The same types of differences among the individuals with respect to time-value of money and risk lead to a conclusion that exchanges will take place if there is a market for such exchanges.

The conventional net present value method of making capital budgeting decisions takes the time-value of money into account using the firm's cost of capital as the discount rate. The essence of this approach is that the average cost of a particular source of capital is defined as the discount rate that makes the present value of the expected proceeds that will be received by the capital supplier equal to the market value of the securities representing that capital. With a business corporation, proceeds expected to be received by the capital supplier have some degree of uncertainty. This is clear in the case of equity capital; and so long as there is a probability of default, it is also true of debt. The excess of the cost of corporate capital sources over the discount rate that applies to default-free cash flows presumably reflects an adjustment for risk. Raising the discount rate to compute present values may not be an effective or useful way of allowing for risk of an investment in a real asset.

It will be assumed that it is wished to take the time-value of money into consideration and that initially the uncertainty question does not exist.

Pitfalls of bypassing time-value

Consider the following two investments:

	Cash Flows ($) at time:		
	0	1	2
Investment A	− 10 000	1000	11 000
Investment B	− 10 000	11 000	1000

A casual inspection reveals that the second investment is to be preferred to the first (the total amount received is the same for both investments, but the second investment receives some cash earlier than the first). Several methods of evaluating investments will fail to reveal the superiority of B to A. For example, the total income over the life of either investment is $2000 and the average income is $1000 for an average investment of $5000. This is a 20 per cent return on investment (ROI) and both investments have this return. The ROI measure cannot detect the superiority of B. Either of the DCF methods will reveal that B is better than A.

Time-value calculations

It is well-known that money has value and that a dollar in hand today is worth more than a dollar to be received one year from today. For example if money can be borrowed and lent at 0.10 per year then $100 held today and invested to earn 0.10 will be worth $110 one year from today. In like manner $100 to be received one year from today has a present value now of $90.91 ($90.91 invested to earn 0.10 will earn $9.09 interest and will be worth $100 after one year).

Assuming that we can lend and borrow at an interest rate of r, the following formula enables us to move cash flows back and forth through time:

$$A = (1 + r)^{-n}S$$

where r is the interest rate

n is the number of time periods

S is the future sum to be received in the nth period from now

A is the present value or present equivalent of S.

If r, n and S are properly specified then one is indifferent between S dollars at time n and A dollars now.

For example assume a firm is to receive $1 000 000 two years from now and r is 0.10. Then

$$A = (1.10)^{-2}1\ 000\ 000 = \$826\ 446$$

The firm is indifferent between a security offering $826 446 now or a security offering $1 000 000 in two years. The following calculations show the indifference:

Initial sum	$826 446
Year 1 interest earned	+ 82 645
	909 091
Year 2 interest earned	+ 90 909
	$1 000 000

If $r = 0.10$, the present value of $1 000 000 due in two years is $826 446. Tables give the present value factors for different values of r and n. To find the present equivalent of a future S, multiply the appropriate present value factor by S. Values of $(1 + r)^{-n}$ are contained in tables or alternatively most hand calculators can be readily used to determine the values as can personal computers.

METHODS OF CAPITAL BUDGETING

There are many methods of capital budgeting used by business firms, but just about all of them are based on one of four methods to be described here.

Care is needed with the terminology in this area. The same words are used differently by different people (including authors). In this chapter terms will be used consistently but this does not mean that the next time the terms are encountered they will be used in the same manner.

The most widely used method of making investment decisions is the 'payback' method. The length of time required to recover the initial investment is computed and this measure is compared to the maximum payback period. For example, an investment costing $1 000 000 and recovering $250 000 per year would have a payback period of four years. Well-informed managers will state that they understand the limitations of payback (not considering the time-value of money and the life of the investment after the payback period) but they use the payback measure as an indication of the amount of the investment's risk (a payback of one year would not indicate less risk than a payback of four years). Unfortunately, payback is not a reliable risk measure. For example, gambling at Las Vegas has a shorter payback period than the purchase of a US savings bond but it has much more risk.

The second most popular method of measuring profitability of an investment (though it is rapidly losing ground to better measures) is return on investment (ROI). The ROI of an investment is the average income divided by average investment. Since the income and investment measures used are conventional accounting measures, the ROI measure fails to take effectively into consideration the time value of money. The conventional ROI measure is a very unreliable way of evaluating investments; however, there is an even worse way of applying the technique. A common practice in industry is to compute the ROI of the first complete year of use. Since this ROI, as conventionally computed, will tend to understate the actual return on investment, this creates a bias against accepting investments that should be accepted.

The other methods that require explanation are the several discounted cash flow measures. These measures are more reliable measures of value than the payback and ROI measures described above. The discussion in this chapter will be limited to the internal rate of return and the net present-value methods. These two measures are chosen since they are widely used and also because they will do everything that alternative methods will do and in some cases will avoid errors introduced by these other measures.

The net present-value method

The net present-value method of evaluating investments has been increasing in use for the past 30 years. It is now difficult to find a large industrial firm that does not employ the net present-value method (it is generally used in conjunction with other measures), somewhere in its organization.

The first step in the computation of the net present value of an investment is to choose a rate of discount (this may be a required return or 'hurdle rate'). The second step is to compute the present-value equivalents of all cash flows associated with the investment (on an after-tax basis) and sum these present-value equivalents to obtain the net present value of the investment.

The net present value of an investment is the amount the firm could afford to pay in excess of the cost of the investment and still break even on the investment. It is also the present value of all future profits, where the profits are calculated after the capital costs of the investment.

Example

Consider the investment costing $902 740, that promises cash flows of $1 000 000 one period from now and $100 000 two periods from now. Using the present-value factors for $r = 0.10$ we have:

Time period	Cash flows ($)	Present-value factors (0.10)	Present-value equivalents
0	−902 740	1.0000	−902 740
1	1 000 000	0.9091	909 100
2	100 000	0.8264	82 640
		Net present value	$89 000

The firm could pay $89 000 more than the $902 740 cost and break even (that is, would just earn the 0.10 capital cost). Thus the $89 000 is in a sense the 'excess' incentive to invest and is a measure of the safety margin that exists.

Assume the following arbitrary depreciation schedule (any other schedule would give the same present value of income):

Year	Depreciation ($)
1	842 740
2	60 000

Year	Revenues ($)	Depreciation ($)	Income before interest ($)	Interest on book value ($)	Income ($)	Present-value factors	Present value ($)
1	1 000 000	842 740	157 260	90 274	66 986	0.9091	60 900
2	100 000	60 000	40 000	6 000	34 000	0.8264	28 100
					Present value of incomes		$89 000

The present value of the after-interest income is $89 000 which is the amount of net present value of cash flows obtained above. This value is independent of the method of depreciation.

The argument is sometimes offered that the net present-value method is difficult to understand. Actually it is the simplest of the procedures to use. If the net present value is positive the investment is acceptable. Also, the interpretation of the measure is easy and useful. The net present value is the amount the firm could pay in excess of the cost and still break even, and it is the present value of the income after capital costs.

The internal rate of return method

The net present-value method gives a dollar measure. Some managers prefer a percentage measure that is most frequently called an investment's internal rate of return. Other terms applied to the same measure are yield, DCF or discounted cash flow, return on investment, time adjusted rate of return, profitability index, and to complete the circle, present value.

The internal rate of return can be defined as the rate of discount that causes the sum of the present value of the cash flows to be equal to zero. This definition can then be used to compute an investment's internal rate of return. The internal rate of return is found by a trial and error procedure (when the net present value is equal to zero, the rate of discount being used is the rate of return).

Continuing the above example, the net present value is found equal to zero using a 0.20 rate of discount. For discount rates larger than 0.20 the net present value would be negative (see Table 6.1).

Table 6.1
Present values with different discount rates

Time	Present value: 0.00		Present value: 0.10		Present value: 0.20
0	−902 740	1.0000	−902 740	1.0000	−902 740
1	1 000 000	0.9091	909 100	0.8333	833 300
2	100 000	0.8264	82 640	0.6944	69 440
Net present value	+197 260		+89 000		0

The internal rate of return of an investment has several interesting and relevant economic interpretations. For example, it is the highest rate that the firm can borrow, use the funds generated by the investment and repay the loan. Assume funds are borrowed at a cost of 0.20. The following repayment schedule would then apply:

İnitial amount owed	$902 800
Year 1 interest (0.20)	+180 500
	1 083 300
Repayment using cash flows	−1 000 000
	83 300
Year 2 interest (0.20)	+16 700
	$100 000
Repayment using cash flows	−100 000
Amount owed	0 000

The cash flows generated by the investment are just sufficient to pay the loan costing 0.20.

If incomes and investments are properly measured taking time-value into consideration then the ROI (that is, income divided by investment) of each year will be equal to the internal rate of return of the investment. This will not occur using conventional accounting.

The decision rule to be used with the internal rate of return method is that all investments with an internal rate of return greater than the required return be accepted (this assumes the cash flows are those of a normal investment, that is, one or more periods of cash outlays followed by cash inflows).

THE NET PRESENT-VALUE PROFILE

For any investment we can compute its net present-value profile. Figure 6.1 shows the net present-value profile for the example of this chapter. On the x-axis are measured the different rates of discount and on the y-axis the net present value that results from the use of the different rates of discount. The intersection of the net present-value profile and the x-axis defines the internal rate of return of the investment (the net present value is equal to zero).

Inspection of Fig. 6.1 shows that for a normal investment (negative cash flows followed by positive) the present-value profile slopes downward to the right. Thus for an investment with an internal rate of return greater than the required return the net present value will also be positive. Thus with normal independent investments the present-value method (a dollar measure) and the internal rate of return method (a percentage) will give identical accept and reject decisions.

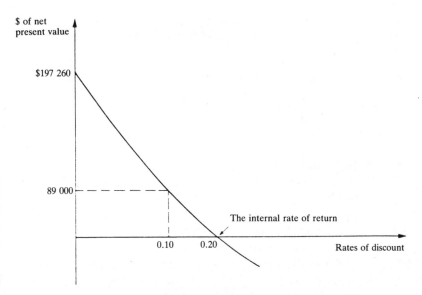

Fig. 6.1   Profile of net present value for an investment

COMPARING NET PRESENT VALUE AND INTERNAL RATE OF RETURN

Figure 6.2 shows why internal rate of return and net present value may seem to recommend different alternatives.

The curve AA represents the net present-value profile of investment A with a rate of return of r_a. The intersection of the curve with the x-axis is defined to be the internal rate of return. Investment B has an internal rate of return of r_b. The present value of the investments is measured on the Y-axis for a given rate of discount. It can be seen that B has a larger internal rate of return than A. However, for all rates of discount less than i, investment A has a higher net present value than investment B. Thus, if A and B are two mutually exclusive investments (only one can be undertaken), the internal rate of return criterion incorrectly indicates B is to be preferred. The present-value method indicates that A is preferred if the appropriate rate of discount is less than i.

If the investments are independent and if the required return is less than r_a then both investments are acceptable. With independent investments the internal rate of return and the net present value procedures both give consistent results. If the internal rate of return is

Table 6.2
Two mutually exclusive investments

Investment	Cash flows 0	1	Internal rate of return	Net present value (0.10)
A	−80 000	100 000	0.25	$10 910
B	−20 000	26 000	0.30	$ 2 364

larger than the required return, then the net present value will also be positive. If the required return is greater than the internal rate of return the investment is not acceptable and the net present value is negative.

Table 6.2 is a concrete example of the type of situation shown in Figure 6.2. Assume A and B are mutually exclusive.

Investment B has a larger internal rate of return than A but if the appropriate rate of discount is 0.10 investment A has a higher net present value. At a 0.233 rate of interest the investor would be indifferent.

RISK AND INVESTMENT

It is not correct to assume that it is appropriate to take the risk of an investment into acount via the discounting (and compounding) procedurc. There is no reason for assuming that risk is always compounded through time, and that $(1 + r)^{-n}$ can be used to take risk and time value factors into consideration in one computation.

Assume an investment is available that costs $100 000 000 and promises to return either $200 100 000 or $0, the events both having 0.5 probability. The pay-off occurs in a time period shortly after the outlay. The expected rate of return is thus very large. While this investment is 'obviously' acceptable using the criterion 'accept when the expected rate of return is greater than 0.10', it is not all clear that investors who are currently expecting a return of 0.10 for a moderately risky firm would want this investment accepted because of the 0.5 probability of losing $100 000 000.

William Sharpe published a paper (1964) that introduced the capital asset pricing model (CAPM). The CAPM is relevant to capital budgeting since if investors are well diversified, certain types of risk are less important than other types. With perfectly diversified in-

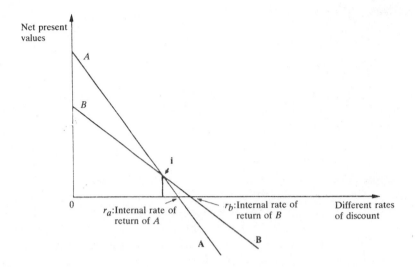

Fig. 6.2 Two mutually exclusive investments

vestors, risks that are specific to the firm can be diversified away by
the investor and thus are not relevant to the decision maker. The risk
that is relevant to the investor is how the investment's profitability is
correlated with the return of the other investments available to the
investor.

This can be translated mathematically into an expression that
allows us to quantify risk premiums. The inputs into the calculation
are the measures of the market return risk trade-off (analogous to the
use of the market interest rates to measure the time-value factor), and
a measure of the degree to which the profitability of the investment is
correlated with the market return. Other problems arise in application because many investors are not perfectly diversified, and more
will have to be learnt about the importance of this consideration and
how to handle it. Another complication is that there are other parties
(such as managers) who have interest in the firm's continuity of
existence, and care must be taken to consider their welfare as well as
the welfare of the common stockholders. Finally, the specific mathematical models only apply to certain limited probability distributions
or utility functions. Thus it does not appear that the CAPM will
supply easy exact solutions to the problem of making capital budgeting decisions under uncertain conditions.

CONCLUSIONS

In the career span of one manager a move has been made from the use of measures (payback and return on investment) that failed to consider effectively time-value to an acceptance of a discounted cash flow measure, internal rate of return. This measure was then found to give faulty directions, in situations involving mutually exclusive investments and the net present-value procedure was found somewhat easier to apply and gave results that were somewhat more reliable indicators of value.

While the cost of capital has been recommended as the discount rate or the hurdle rate to be used by firms, and was used by a large number of firms, the measure implicitly incorporated both time-value and risk considerations, and the compound interest calculation using the weighted average cost of capital did not result in a reliable value measure for all investments.

A default-free time-value factor followed logically from the conclusion that risk did not necessarily compound through time. However, this left risk considerations out of the analysis. Sensitivity analysis and simulation, while giving useful insights, did not lead to explicit accept or reject recommendations. Finally the capital asset pricing model was offered as a possible solution to the problem of how to include time-value and risk. Unfortunately, the calculations require unrealistic assumptions and the model is not apt to apply to the specific investment of the firm being analysed.

Despite the limitations of the capital asset pricing model, business managers should be aware of its existence, because they will be hearing more and more about this theoretical construct for the remainders of their careers. It offers a way of quantifying and incorporating risk considerations if the facts of the situation fit. Investments rejected under conventional analysis using the cost of capital would become acceptable, and investments previously considered to be acceptable would be rejected because of their 'systematic' risk, that is, the risk that they will go down in value if the general market conditions deteriorate.

Capital budgeting is too big a subject to be covered in one chapter. The objective of this chapter has been to make clear the nature and uses of the basic discounted cash flow methods. Some complexities in their use have been omitted as have descriptions of alternative, but inferior, calculations. Too frequently managers have been unnecessarily confused about the basic nature of the net present-value and the internal rate of return methods, and are thus reluctant to use them. The net present-value profit graph makes clear the relationship of net present value to internal rate of return and why they may lead to different recommendations in cases involving mutually exclusive investments.

The DCF calculations are powerful tools for evaluating investments. This chapter has not attempted to deal with all the complexities of using these tools, nor has it fully explained their wide range of uses. It is hoped that the reader will want to become more familiar with these tools. They are extremely useful. While the uncertainty questions occupy the largest part of the academic literature, the operating business person should realize that the basic DCF calculations are still the most reliable way of evaluating investments, and are an important tool in deciding whether or not an investment is acceptable.

REFERENCES AND FURTHER READING

Bierman, H. and Smidt, S., *The Capital Budgeting Decision,* 6th edition, Macmillan, New York, 1984.

Black, F. and Scholes, M., 'The Pricing of Options and Corporate Liabilities.' *Journal of Political Economy*, pp. 637–659, 1973.

Brennan, M.J. and Schwartz, E.S., Evaluating Natural Resource Investments, *Journal of Business*, pp. 137–157, 1985.

Brigham, E.F. and Johnson, R.E., *Issues in Managerial Finance*, 2nd ed. Hinsdale, Ill.: The Dryden Press, Division of CBS College Publishing, 1980.

Crum, R.L. and Derkinderen, F.G.J., *Capital Budgeting Under Conditions of Uncertainty.* Boston: Martinus Nijhoff, 1981.

Dean, Joel, *Capital Budgeting*, Columbia University Press, New York 1951; 'Measuring the Productivity of Capital', *Harvard Business Review*, pp. 120–130, 1954.

Fama, Eugene F., 'Risk, Return and Equilibrium: Some Clarifying Comments', *Journal of Finance*, 23, pp. 29–40, 1968.

Gitman, Lawrence J. and Forrester, John R. Jr., 'Forecasting and Evaluation Practices and Performance: A Survey of Capital Budgeting.' *Financial Management*, 66–71, 1977.

Fisher, Irving, *The Theory of Interest*, Macmillan, New York, 1930.

Hamada, R.S., 'Portfolio Analysis, Market Equilibrium, and Corporation Finance', *Journal of Finance*, 24, pp. 13–31, 1969.

Hirshleifer, Jack, 'On the Theory of Optimal Investment Decision', *Journal of Political Economy*, pp. 329–352, 1958.

Levy, H. and Sarnat, M., *Capital Investment and Financial Decisions*, 2nd ed. Englewood Cliffs, N.J.: Prentice-Hall, 1983.

Lind, R.C. *Discounting for Time and Risk in Energy Policy*, Baltimore, Md.: The Johns Hopkins University Press, 1982.

Lintner, J., 'The Valuation of Risk Assets and the Selection of Risky Investments in Stock Portfolios and Capital Budgets', *Review of Economics and Statistics*, **47**, 1965.

Lorie, J.H. and Savage, L.J., 'Three Problems in Capital Rationing', *Journal of Business*, pp. 229–239, 1955.

Lutz, Friedrich and Vera, *The Theory of Investment of the Firm*, Princeton University Press, 1951.

Mossin, J., 'Equilibrium in a Capital Asset Market', *Econometrics*, pp. 768–775, 1966.

Sharpe, W.F., 'Capital Asset Prices: A Theory of Market Equilibrium Under Conditions of Risk'. *Journal of Finance*, pp. 425–442, 1964.

Stapleton, Richard C., 'Portfolio Analysis, Stock Valuation and Capital Budgeting Rules for Risky Projects', *Journal of Finance*, **26**, pp. 95–118, 1971.

Weingartner, H. Martin, 'Capital Budgeting of Interrelated Projects: Survey and Synthesis.' *Management Science*, pp. 485–516, 1966; 'Some New Views on the Payback Period and Capital Budgeting Decisions.' *Management Science*, pp. 594–607, 1969.

7

Financial Models

M.J. Mepham

Dr Mepham emphasizes that the developing art of financial modelling is intended to capture the essential features of a complex business situation and to eliminate irrelevant detail. The use of financial models is thus an aid to simplification in business planning, especially in representing alternative situations. The author classifies the main types of models and explains the terminology of the subject. He provides a number of practical examples, ranging from the simple application to the somewhat more sophisticated, involving the use of computers and spread sheets. Dr Mepham concludes with a forecast of rapid developments in a subject with which all executives need to be familiar.

This chapter is an introduction to modelling, in particular, the use of financial models to help solve business problems. A model is a representation of some part of 'reality' but in the context of financial modelling the word 'reality' is interpreted very widely. Business problems are frequently concerned with the future and the 'reality' that we seek to model is often an hypothetical state of affairs. In the same way as a set of financial plans elaborated in a budget can be considered as accounting for the future, an identification and representation of the possible effects of future strategies may be regarded as modelling the future.

There are two main reasons why organizations find it useful to build financial models. Firstly, business and financial problems are frequently complex and there is a need to focus attention on essential features and to separate these from confusing detail. An intelligently constructed model can assist here because its structure is intended to capture the essential features of an object system whilst being less complex by omitting irrelevant noise.

In addition to the simplification available through modelling, there is often the hope that experimentation with the model will assist in locating a solution to the real problem. This is the second reason for the use of financial modelling. In many branches of science repeated experiments can be carried out to test alternative theories or in search of the solution to a problem. It is not possible to do this in many business problems but experimentation can be carried out on a model. This facility linked with the power of the modern computer has led to a dramatic growth in the use of financial modelling by managers, financial analysts and accountants. Often such models are important features of sophisticated computerized decision support systems. Many of the developments in financial modelling derive from Operational Research (Operations Research in the USA). Operational Research emphasizes the scientific approach to problem solving and the scientific approach relies extensively on model building.

MATHEMATICAL MODELS

Models can be of various types. An *Iconic Model* is a physical representation of the real system although often it is on a different scale. For example, a model of a space rocket may be much smaller than the rocket itself, whereas a model of DNA molecules will be much larger than the real thing. In contrast, *Analogue Models* may not look at all like the original but they have the feature that an attribute of the real system is represented by a more convenient medium in the model. A model of the economy which represented the flow of goods and services among sectors by the flow of water in a series of interconnected pipes, would be an analogue model.

Financial models are not iconic or analogue; they are invariably *Symbolic Models*. Symbolic Models represent features of reality by symbols which can be manipulated more readily than reality. Usually mathematical symbolism is adopted and the models are mathematical models. Commonly the models are computerized.

Mathematical models describe the object system by means of mathematical expressions, such expressions are then manipulated in an attempt to gain insight into the real problem. To describe the system mathematically some features of the real system are represented by variables in the model: for example the total cost of a proposed development could be represented by TC and the level of activity could be represented by AL. Other features of the real system are represented by linking the model's variables appropriately so that if total cost is considered as being affected by the level of activity at which the new development is operating then it might be appropriate to assume that:

$$TC = FC + VC*AL$$

In this simple linear cost model FC is the fixed period cost, VC is the variable cost per unit of activity and * is used as the multiplication sign.

TERMINOLOGY

The simple cost model, $TC = FC + VC*AL$, is an example of a mathematical function where a function is a rule which will yield a value for a dependent variable (in this case TC) when a value is specified for one or more independent variables (in this case FC, VC and AL). When the model is to be used to estimate the total cost which will arise for various levels of activity it will be necessary to specify values for FC and VC. If values of £1000 and £5 are specified for FC and VC, then the model would be:

$$TC = 1000 + 5AL$$

In this case there is only one independent variable (AL). FC and VC (or more properly the values currently attributed to them) would now be described as parameters where parameters are variables whose values are established before the model can be used. This operational form of the model provides the estimated total cost for any level of activity.

In modelling it is useful to distinguish exogenous variables from endogenous variables. The distinction is that the values for exogenous variables must be supplied from outside the model whereas the values for endogenous variables are supplied by the model. In the case of the cost model, $TC = 1000 + 5AL$, AL is an exogenous variable whereas TC is an endogenous variable. In computer models, exogenous variables are often called input variables and endogenous variables are output variables.

DESCRIPTIVE MODELS AND PRESCRIPTIVE MODELS

The simple cost model outlined in the last paragraph is an example of a Descriptive Model. Such models describe the system in a manner which is helpful for a particular problem or task in hand. For example it is usual to create a data model when designing a database management information system. This model will be constructed with the anticipated informational needs of the users in mind.

Examples of descriptive models abound in business and many business 'systems' can be regarded as being based on underlying descriptive models, although this fact is often unrecognized. The database management information system itself can be regarded as a descriptive model of a slice of reality and an accounting system can similarly be described. Remembering the comments on the wide meaning given to 'reality' in financial modelling, it is appropriate to emphasize that descriptive models will often provide 'descriptions' of the future. Sometimes such models are called Simulation Models as they simulate the effect of alternative decisions or alternative assumptions as to future conditions.

Prescriptive Models go further than providing a description, they prescribe a course of action. Operational research models are frequently of this type. When installing a stock control system, for example, it may be considered useful to provide more than a system based on a descriptive model (i.e. a system which only describes the stock levels on hand). There might be a wish to extend the model so that it can indicate the best time to reorder stock and the best amount to order at any one time. Such inventory models are called Economic Order Quantity (EOQ) models where the EOQ is the optimum size of order to place. The simplest form of EOQ model for a single type of merchandise starts with the cost function:

$$TC = D*PP + D*OC/Q + Q*HC/2$$

where TC is the total cost for a period, PP is the purchase price of one unit of the commodity, Q is the order size adopted, OC is the cost of placing an order, HC is the cost of holding one unit of the commodity for one year and D is the annual demand.

Repeated experimentation with a simulation model would enable the optimum order size to be identified but by using the calculus a general solution can be obtained which is applicable to all problems that have this form of cost function. Using this approach it can be shown that the best order size is where:

$$Q = \sqrt{(2D*OC/HC)}$$

The advice given by any prescriptive model must be viewed critically until it has been tested. The standard EOQ model is certainly not appropriate for many inventory systems and it should not be adopted until its advice has been validated by thorough testing on historical data.

The EOQ model is a prescriptive optimizing model but such models are not appropriate or possible for all situations. Certain conditions must apply if an optimizing model is to be adopted:

1   There must be a solution method for the problem – in the EOQ model the differential calculus provides such a method. Examples of other optimizing techniques which may be useful are linear programming and dynamic programming.
2   There must be some clear cut criterion for ranking alternative courses of action. In the case of the EOQ model the objective is to minimize the period's ordering/storage cost but in reality many business problems are likely to be characterized by multiple goals with some of these goals conflicting and the lack of any agreement as to how they should be ranked.

The use of a given mathematical technique to determine the optimum answer to a problem entails casting the problem in a mould which is suitable for that technique. This usually means doing some violence to the facts and often quite 'heroic' assumptions have to be made to allow a particular solution method to be adopted. Such assumptions can only be justified if the resulting model is found to give useful advice. In some cases the model is so complex that there is no convenient optimizing algorithm. In such circumstances extended experimentation with a simulation model might enable a satisfactory strategy to be located but this may be very time consuming. An alternative approach may sometimes be available in the form of a heuristic method. Heuristic methods are methods which lack scientific justification for their adoption and yet seem to give acceptable answers in practice. For example in some combination problems (e.g. vehicle scheduling problems) the number of possible combinations (vehicle delivery routes) is so large that resort to rule of thumb (heuristic) methods which seem to give good results, without guaranteeing optimality, is justified.

It may not always be possible to use an optimizing model but it may still be possible to give advice to the decision maker by developing a satisficing (prescriptive) model. Satisficing models are less ambitious than optimizing models in that they aim to give good advice or satisfactory advice rather than optimal advice. In many important problem areas it is not possible to specify problems clearly enough to have a clear cut objective function. In developing the budget for an organization the maximization of shareholders' wealth may be one goal but there may be other corporate goals that relate to the organization's workforce (minimizing the number of redundancies) and to the local community (stemming from a 'good neighbour' policy) and to the customers (e.g. a moral commitment to maintain a service function for old equipment). Although some would claim that the maximization of shareholders' wealth should be the unambiguous overriding objective for organizations in the private sector, many organizations would not wish to adopt such an approach. A satisficing model which attempted to achieve a satisfactory budget would commonly be used for the budgeting exercise. One type of satisficing model is the Goal Programming Model which enables the users to specify multiple goals and even allows for conflicting goals. The solution procedure will then identify solutions which achieve these goals as far as possible.

Some models are general purpose whilst others are special purpose. Accounting models and database management information system models are frequently general purpose in that they are designed for multiple end-users with a wide range of problems. The EOQ model on the other hand is special purpose. It is constructed explicitly to answer the question, 'How many items of this stock item should be ordered at one time?' It is much easier for special purpose models to be optimizing as it is more likely that there is an unambiguous objective. Although there are advantages in using special purpose prescriptive models, it is often true that the more fundamental problems faced by management are not capable of being described in this way. Descriptive general purpose models can be used in a wider range of situations.

DETERMINISTIC AND PROBABILISTIC MODELS

Models can be either deterministic or probabilistic. Deterministic models are models which are constructed as if the parameter values are known with absolute certainty. Even when it is known that there is inherent uncertainty in the environment, it may still be useful to adopt a deterministic approach. The best estimates of the parameter values can be used and then the sensitivity of the solution to errors in these values can be tested. Sensitivity Analysis is a useful tool and should always be used for important decisions when there is doubt as to the correct values to use in a model. In some cases it will be discovered that quite large variations in the values attributed to certain problematic variables have little effect on the outcome. In such cases the model is referred to as robust. In other cases the reverse happens and minor changes in one or more variables can result in major changes in the model's output. In the latter case it may be appropriate to spend more time in deciding the values to attribute to these sensitive variables.

Although the 'What if . . .?' (sensitivity analysis) approach is an attractive method which can be used for quite complicated situations, it has its limitations. It cannot deal adequately with situations where there are many probabilistic variables and it gives no indication of how likely (or unlikely) the various outcomes are. Probabilistic (or stochastic) models incorporate uncertainty into the model itself by incorporating probability distributions for the probabilistic variables. For example, in building a stock control model it might be appropriate to recognize that the monthly demand (D) is best described as a normal variate with mean value of 10 000 and a standard deviation of 2500. The normal distribution tables indicate that this means that, although the expected level of demand is 10 000, there is a 0.16 probability that demand will be below 7500 and a similar probability that it will be above 12 500. If it is considered that this is the case then it may be important to incorporate the information into the model.

Sometimes the specification of the required probability distributions can be obtained from records of similar variables in the past but often the distributions will be subjective estimates obtained by quizzing a manager or group of managers. When subjective probabilities are being used it is usually easier to obtain these in the form of discrete probability distributions. Frequently it is appropriate to use three point estimates (pessimistic, most likely and optimistic) with their associated (subjective) probabilities: if the introduction of a new product is under consideration and the accountant is attempting to estimate its unit (variable) cost, he might be able to say that this is £5 with a probability of 0.6; £4.50 with a probability of 0.1 and £6.25 with a probability of 0.3. Similar probability distributions for the monthly demand for various selling prices could perhaps be obtained by questioning the sales staff and the following table might be prepared:

Sales price	Monthly demand	Probability
£6.75	9000	0.3
	9500	0.4
	10 500	0.3
£7.00	8000	0.3
	8500	0.5
	9500	0.2
£7.25	7000	0.3
	8000	0.6
	9000	0.1

When discrete probability distributions are being used there is a finite number of possible outcomes and the outcome of each of these, and its associated probability, can be calculated. For the £7.00 selling price the calculations would be:

Selling price	Monthly revenue		Monthly variable cost		Monthly contribution	
	Pr.	£	Pr.	£	Pr.	£
		56 000	0.3	50 000	0.09	6000
	0.3	56 000	0.6	40 000	0.18	16 000
		56 000	0.1	36 000	0.03	20 000
		59 500	0.3	53 125	0.15	6375
7.00	0.5	59 500	0.6	42 500	0.30	17 000
		59 500	0.1	38 250	0.05	21 250
		66 500	0.3	59 375	0.06	7125
	0.2	66 500	0.6	47 500	0.12	19 000
		66 500	0.1	42 750	0.02	23 750

The foregoing is a numeric approach to solving probabilistic models. In many cases this can be considered as an extension to sensitivity analysis. A second type of probabilistic model uses an analytical approach. The properties of many standard probability distributions have been investigated thoroughly by statisticians and it is possible to formulate optimizing models which can be solved analytically. The third type of probabilistic model is used when the problem is too

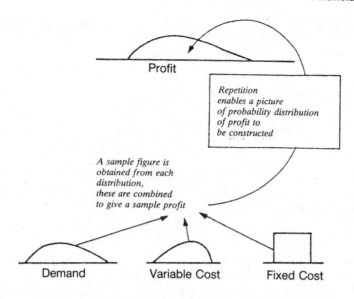

Fig. 7.1 The probabilistic simulation approach

complex to approach in this manner. This approach is a probabilistic simulation approach which is sometimes called the Monte Carlo method.

The Monte Carlo Simulation method requires that continuous probability distributions be established for all the stochastic variables. It is likely that the analyst will have to construct these distributions from information elicited from the specialist staff. If, for a given variable, only upper and lower bounds can be obtained then a rectangular distribution may be assumed. If estimates of the most likely, pessimistic and optimistic values and their associated probabilities are provided then the analyst could attempt to fit an appropriate curve, such distributions can take into account all the available information on the spread of values, skewness etc. The details of the distributions are fed into a computerized simulation model and then the computer, via a random number generator, takes a sample from each distribution and combines these to give an outcome and the associated probability. Figure 7.1 illustrates the process diagramatically.

The sampling procedure is continued for a sufficiently large number of iterations for a frequency distribution of the outcome to be constructed. Liao (1975) describes the procedure and a method of fitting a smooth curve to the resulting outcome frequency distribution.

COMPUTER MODELS – SPREAD SHEETS

The implementation of a mathematical model on a computer requires that the model must be written in a language which can be understood by the computer. From the financial modelling viewpoint two types of 'high level' language can be distinguished. First there is the general purpose language (such as FORTRAN, COBOL, BASIC); secondly there are specialized languages (such as FCS–EPS, PlusPlan). The specialized languages are very useful because, although computer models are built for specific purposes for specific organizations, there are many features which are common for many types of model. This factor has enabled the development of computer packages which can be utilized for many modelling situations. The most useful of these specialized tools is the electronic spreadsheet, a package which facilitates mass production calculations on tables of data. Spreadsheets have proved to be so useful that a class of model, the spreadsheet model, can be identified.

Spreadsheets were first developed for microcomputers and were designed to enable them to deal with multi-column, multi-period financial statements. The first spreadsheet package was VisiCalc which was introduced in 1979. This rapidly began to displace the accountant's laboriously hand written work sheets and it is claimed that the facilities of this package alone persuaded many accountants to purchase a micro. Since 1979 the range of suppliers has expanded and the capabilities of the package have developed to cover, inter alia, graphing capabilities, word processing and database facilities. Here we will describe some of the more common spreadsheet facilities in a typical micro computer spread sheet package.

A spreadsheet package provides a tabular framework into the cells of which can be entered values, letters or formulae. This table or matrix or grid can be viewed on the VDU and the values, letters and formulae are typically entered from the computer (or terminal) key board. Each cell in the spreadsheet has an address made up of its column number (or letter) and its row number, thus C4 refers to the entry in cell which is at the intersection of column C and row 4. The contents of any cell can be linked to the contents of any other cell, or cells, in a straightfoward manner by the use of formulae. Thus if C4 contains the physical stock holding of a particular commodity (say 120 units) and D4 contains its unit cost (say £5), then the total cost of the stock held can be displayed in E4 by inserting the formula C4 multiplied by D4 (i.e. +C4*D4). This will not be shown on the screen as:

	A	B	C	D	E	F
1						
2						
3						
4			120	5	+C4*D4	

Instead the calculation will be performed and the VDU will show:

	A	B	C	D	E	F
1						
2						
3						
4			120	5	600	

Cell E4 shows the result of the calculation not the formula. This means that if the stock holding is reduced to 100 and this change is recorded in C4, the entry will immediately alter to show 500. The fourth row will then appear as:

4			100	5	500	

New stock level – input via keyboard (under C column); New stock value – calculated from formula (under E column)

This feature has clear application in sensitivity analysis as the values of certain key variables can be adjusted and the effect of such adjustments on profit or cost (or any other important dependent variable) will be immediately displayed.

If a spreadsheet model is being constructed it is often useful to include some text e.g. to describe the contents of particular cells or rows and columns of cells. For the example being considered this might be done by keying in the labels 'stock level', 'unit cost' and 'total cost' in cells C1, C2, D1, D2, E1 and E2.

If the table is intended to be a warehouse stock model it will probably be necessary to cover many different types of commodity and this will require another column label in cells A1, B1 and A2 and a row label for each type of commodity. The spread sheet model might now be:

	A	B	C	D	E
1	Commodity	Code	Stock	Unit	Total
2	Number		Level	Cost	Cost
3					
4	XN1209		100	5	500
5	AB5601		406	3	1218
6	NN4403		10	900	9000
84	AQ9988		672	31	20832
85	Grand Total				1875435

The figures in column E are calculated by using the following formulae:

+C4*D4

+C5*D5

+C6*D6

+C84*D84

@SUM(E4..E84)

Usually, as with the above example, the spreadsheet is too big to be seen in its entirety on the VDU screen. The maximum size of a Lotus 123 spreadsheet is 256 columns and 8,192 rows but only 8 columns and 20 rows can be viewed, at any one time, on a typical VDU screen. The user can travel around the larger spreadsheet and can print out the full spreadsheet as desired. The spreadsheet contents can also be saved on disk for future use and further processing.

The major spreadsheet packages make available a number of standard financial formulae (such as compound interest formulae) and statistical formulae for data analysis. There is also usually a random number generator which enables Monte Carlo simulation models to be built.

For complex models, templates can be constructed. These templates contain the basic fomulae for a particular type of business problem. They may be written in-house but for many problem areas templates can be purchased.

CONCLUSION AND FUTURE DEVELOPMENTS

Although it is true that models are built to simplify reality, the use of financial modelling is developing fast and the developments whilst they are geared to the creation of more useful and hence more realistic models, inevitably lead to more complex models. The use of computers and computer spreadsheets provides the tools for the construction of more comprehensive and more detailed models. This move is also a by-product of the integration of accounting and budgeting systems within comprehensive database Management Information Systems. Such developments will require a comprehensive model of the organization. In large organizations, computer models which encompass the whole organization will be very complex and specialist staff are required to operate them.

At present much of the complexity of financial models is one of detail and the volume of data covered since such models are usually descriptive and deterministic simulation models rather than being prescriptive and probabilistic. This, however, is not due to a limitation of the technology but to a user preference for such models. Managers frequently have a sceptical attitude towards the more complex optimizing and probabilistic models but it is to be anticipated that there will be changes as users become more confident with sophisticated models.

One development which can be expected to encourage the use of more sophisticated models is Expert Systems. Expert systems are based on models which attempt to capture a human expert's expertise. An important feature of such models is that they should be able to deal with queries and to provide an explanation for the advice that they give in a similar way to the questioning that a human expert might expect. This should help to give the user confidence in the model.

FURTHER READING

Bhaskar, K., *Building Financial Models: A Simulation Approach*, Associated Business Programmes, London, 1978.

Bhaskar, K., Williams, B., Pope, P. and Morris, R., *Financial Modelling with a Microcomputer: Software Choice and Hardware Selection*, Economist Intelligence Unit, London, 1984.

Carter, L.R. and Huzan, E., *A Practical Approach to Computer Simulation in Business*, Allen and Unwin, London, 1973.

Liao, M., Model sampling: a stochastic cost–volume–profit analysis, *The Accounting Review*, pp. 780–790, Oct. 1975.

Mepham, M.J., *Accounting Models*, Pitman, London, 1980.

Sherwood, D., Financial Modelling: A Practical Guide, Gee, London, 1983.

8

The Cash Forecast

R. Aitken-Davies

The system of budgets as outlined in the previous chapters cannot be finalized until management is assured that the funds necessary for their implementation will be forthcoming. The cash inflows and outflows which will arise from the budgets need therefore to be assessed and set out in a cash forecast. In this chapter R. Aitken-Davies explains the techniques involved in preparing this essential statement. As he points out, the importance of preparing a careful forecast of the cash position is that the ultimate consequences of a cash shortage are the collapse and dissolution of the business. He gives examples of the ways by which a temporary shortage of working capital may be overcome, but indicates that the forecast may show that additional long term capital will be required. This chapter is associated with Chapter 12 on Controlling the Funds.

Introduction

This chapter examines the principles and practices of cash forecasting and the steps which a business needs to take to ensure short term liquidity. The subject increases in importance as business, and the society in which it operates, becomes more complex, especially with the development of plastic money and cashless transfers of funds. Mr. Micawber's famous dictum is as true for a corporate body as it is for an individual. The result of expenditure in excess of income is misery but, of course, where there is reasonable confidence that things will get better soon temporary borrowing can meet the shortage. Nevertheless, the ultimate consequences of a cash deficiency are the collapse and dissolution of the organization.

Cash control is therefore one of the primary concerns of management in any commercial organization. It is customary to delegate to the financial controller the responsibility for ensuring that the forward plans will be adequately funded, and this gives his role a sense of relevance, reality and urgency, not associated to the same degree with the more mundane aspects of financial recording and statutory accounting.

Whilst in the long term an organization cannot survive with a deficit of receipts over payments, it is also generally inadvisable for large cash holdings to remain idle. Such surpluses should be placed in long or short term investments, pending their use by the business, or distribution to the shareholders as dividends, assuming adequate profits are available.

CASH BUDGETING

Cash budgeting can be viewed as an element in the construction of the working capital budget which is dealt with in detail in Chapter 12. As with so many other aspects of the financial controller's work, this is an exercise which lends itself to the use of computerized financial models (see Chapter 7) by which means there can be several iterations of the initial view, reflecting changed assumptions in each and every aspect of the budget.

However, it is still necessary to understand the basis upon which the cash budget is constructed.

A format for the presentation of a cash budget is shown in Table 8.1. Receipts will be represented chiefly by the discharge of indebtedness by the company's customers and/or by cash sales; and payments by the settlement of creditors' invoices. In addition, there will be substantial cash transactions which fall into neither of these categories, such as remuneration, capital items and dividends. The headings in Table 8.1 show some typical areas in which cash movements are likely to occur and the following paragraphs describe the nature of these in more detail.

Sales of assets

From time to time the company will sell assets such as obsolete and

Table 8.1
Format for cash budget

SOURCE/APPLICATION	Review period	CASH BUDGET 19—										(−) = Deficit (£000's)	
		1	2	3	4	5	6	7	8	9	10	11	12
OPENING BALANCE[1]													
RECEIPTS													
Debtors and cash sales													
Sales of assets													
Government grants													
Miscellaneous income													
Other													
SUB-TOTAL													
PAYMENTS													
Creditors and cash purchases													
Wages and salaries													
Capital investment													
Appropriations													
Other													
CLOSING BALANCE[2]													

[1] Closing balance in previous review period.
[2] Estimated cash balance/amount overdrawn at end of review period.

redundant equipment, vehicles, and scrap, and may also from time to time divest itself of investments made outside the normal course of trade (e.g. stock market investments).

Government grants

Whilst the scale of grants coming within this category has diminished markedly in recent years, there are still circumstances in which these may occur, such as where employment subsidies and innovation grants are payable. Consideration should also be given to the availability of grants from the EEC and other quasi-governmental sources.

Miscellaneous income

Most companies have income not immediately associated with their normal course of trade and this will include income from investments (e.g. dividends received) and rental income from property.

Debtors and cash sales

Whilst cash sale projections are fairly straightforward, it should be borne in mind in deriving the debtors cash flows that there will be delay between the projected sale and the receipt of cash. The financial controller must consider the historic levels of credit taken together with any proposed changes in policy anticipated during the budget year and make an allowance for bad debts in arriving at his receipt profile in the cash budget.

Creditors and cash purchases

As for debtors, allowance must be made in the cash flow forecast for the normal credit allowed by the Company's main suppliers.

Wages and salaries

These payments may be obtained from the appropriate budgets, but they should be calculated to include projected salary increases, overtime and bonus arrangements.

Capital investment

Payments should be provided in the appropriate periods according to contracts placed, or in the case of projects which have not begun, in accordance with the assumptions made in appraising the investment. It would also be sensible to include here any payments for leasing transactions.

Appropriations

Important items in the cash forecast are payments anticipated for taxes, financing costs and dividends.

Extraordinary and exceptional items

Finally, the forecast must include the estimated cost of abnormal items, such as impending litigation and the receipt or payment of compensation.

At this stage an initial forecast can be prepared and the purpose of this preliminary statement is to foresee any substantial surpluses or deficits of cash which are likely to arise from the existing operational budgets. A temporary deficit may be met by short-term borrowing or other financial arrangements. A serious long-term deficit will involve the provision of further long-term capital or a complete revision of the organization's forward plans. Such revision might mean, for instance, rigorous trimming of costs, a reduction in the investment in working capital, and a modification of the capital investment programme.

Having resolved longer term requirements, the stage will be reached when funding policies are broadly settled and the financial controller can assume full responsibility for management of short term liquidity fluctuations. He or she will then wish to review the range of short-term financing sources available and/or to establish, in principle, where short-term surpluses can be deposited to the greatest advantage.

SENSITIVITIES

In all budgeting activity nowadays, there is an increasing tendency to test the strength of the central assumptions against a range of sensitivities, a task greatly facilitated by microprocessors and software packages. These are of particular value in the production of a cash budget against which the financial controller wishes to test the effects of variations in the key parameters. To those not willing to embrace the tools of modern technology or who wish to find a short cut to sensitivity tests on their cash budget, the best and worst scenario approach may commend itself. This means calculating or assessing the most pessimistic and most optimistic outcomes for each of the base assumptions upon which the organization's master budget is constructed. A budget is then constructed of what would happen if the pessimistic view were realized in each case and a similar view on the basis of the optimistic view. It is important in undertaking such studies that the series of best and worst assumptions are intrinsically compatible. An example would be that a pessimistic view of sales should be reflected in the level of debtors anticipated (although the debtors figure may well also be amended for adverse drift in the credit periods taken and/or in the level of bad and doubtful debts). Conversely, on an optimistic view it would be appropriate to match an increase in the projected sales by a proportionate increase in debtors (although, here again, the optimistic assumption might envisage a reduction of credit periods and/or in the level of bad and doubtful debts).

The advantage of the best and worst approach is that it should give a feel for the extremes of what the company might conceivably expect during the budget period in question and can at least initiate thinking ahead of events on how the organization should respond.

Sensitivities can be more sophisticated by interpolating a range of scenarios within the extremes established on the best and worst cases around the central assumptions made for the purposes of the adopted budget. Figure 8.1 gives diagrammatic representation of this approach.

One of the great advantages of sensitivity analysis is that during the implementation of the budget, a quick assessment can be made as to which of the series of assumptions the company's performance is most closely correlated and budgets can be flexed and steps taken to accommodate the new circumstances in good time before disaster strikes.

A sensitivity analysis could be presented in many other ways, for example, by reference to net working capital requirements, sales, net profit, debtor/sales ratio.

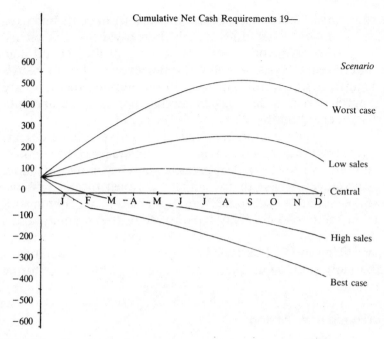

Cumulative Net Cash Requirements 19—

Fig. 8.1 Scenario Budgeting (A presentational example)

We now describe some of the principal methods of securing short-term finance.

Bank accommodation

The most obvious means of avoiding temporary financial embarrassment are overdraft or loan arrangements with the company's bankers. Plainly, an approach to the local manager to discuss an anticipated short-term deficit a year or so in advance is going to be a good deal more impressive than a desperate telephone call a year later from a company on the verge of insolvency. Even if the deficit actually occurs sooner or later than the budget had indicated, the fact that the company is attempting to plan for its cash requirements must encourage its bankers to have confidence in it.

Factoring

An increasingly popular source of short-term finance is the factoring of the company's debts. Such deals can vary from pure financing measures in which the factoring organization advances cash against the security of sums invoiced for a fixed rate of interest, through several intermediate variations to a full takeover of the company's invoicing and credit control function. By this method the debts are actually purchased at a discount by the factors, invoiced and subsequently collected by them.

The advantages of a comprehensive factoring agreement are clear: immediate funds are released and relief is obtained from the administrative burden and frustration of invoicing and accounts collection. The disadvantages are, perhaps, equally obvious: the factors' discount will presumably exceed the sum of the bad debts, administration and financing costs normally experienced by the company, and a crucial link with customers will be relinquished with the attendant risk of sacrificing goodwill as a result of the more stringent methods of securing timely settlement likely to be employed by the factoring organization.

Hire purchase and leasing

For a more fundamental solution, the company could look to converting all or part of its capital investment programme from direct purchase to hire purchase or leasing arrangement. Leases can be of the operational or finance varieties.

Finance leasing as a method of funding capital equipment exploded in popularity after it was introduced in the UK in the 1960s, riding on the back of the substantial tax advantages conferred upon lessors with high profits and low equipment requirements, such as the commercial and merchant banks. In essence a bank, usually operating through a leasing subsidiary, provides funds to a lessee company to purchase its specific equipment requirements but the bank reserves title to the assets so that capital allowances are available for set-off against its other taxable banking profits. Meanwhile the lessees can set the lease rental payments against their profits subject to Corporation Tax as a proper revenue expense, provided those rents are commercial and reasonable in the relevant market circumstances. However, the major economic benefits conferred by these arrangements were substantially removed with the phased abolition of 100 per cent first year allowances as a result of the 1984 Finance Act.

Finance leasing is now principally an alternative method of funding capital requirements on the part of the lessee company. The lessors will almost certainly have no expert knowledge of the equipment subject to lease and although they will retain title to the goods, the period of the lease agreement usually extends over the useful life of the asset and puts the onus for operation and maintenance entirely on the lessees.

On the other hand, an operational lease generally involves hiring plant and machinery from an acknowledged expert in the relevant field in much the same way as one would hire a car. In these cases, the period of the lease may be substantially less than the useful life of the asset and maintenance of the asset normally remains the responsibility of the lessor. The lessee loses the security of tenure and operational control associated with a finance-type lease but gains the advantages of a lower financial commitment to the asset concerned and the removal of the burden of responsibility for maintenance.

Acceptance credits

The acceptance credit is a method of raising funds in the short term, usually for three months. The procedure is that the company draws a Bill of Exchange (i.e. a promise to pay a sum of money at a fixed date in the future) which is then 'accepted' for payment by an 'acceptance house' (i.e. a Merchant Bank) at the expense of an 'acceptance commission' usually of 1–2 per cent. The Bill is then sold for cash by the acceptance house to a 'discount house' (commonly a member of the London Money Market) for a discount charge related to the date the Bill is to be honoured and the prevailing market conditions. Thus the company receives immediate cash from the acceptance house (value of the Bill less acceptance commission and discount charge) and is not required to repay the acceptance house until it has honoured the Bill at maturity in favour of the discount house. The overall cost of this method of finance usually equates to the cost of the more straightforward forms of bank accommodation.

Creditors control

A commonly used means of financing a short term cash deficit is that of delaying payment to creditors either in agreement with those creditors or by default, depending on the nature and desperation of the shortfall problem. In this context, it is most helpful to have creditors pre-classified in priority order starting with those debts which absolutely must be settled by the due dates, then those key creditors whose supplies are essential, down to the creditors of which the loss of supplies and goodwill would be least damaging to the company.

It may also be possible to negotiate with contractors a revised pattern of stage payments for work undertaken, although there will certainly be a penalty in the final cost, and the approach may be regarded as a sign of financial weakness which may be exploited. Another area in which the financial controller may be able to extract some flexibility to help him over short term financing problems is in the payment of declared dividends. Again, this is something which is likely to give definite signals to the shareholders and to the stock market (where applicable) and the relative advantages and disadvantages of this must be weighed up very carefully before going down such a route.

Having dealt with the short term cash management problems highlighted by an initial attempt to construct the cash budget, the financial controller should be in a position to compile the final version incorporating any changes necessitated by proposed funding or investment of cash surpluses. Deficits met by bank overdrafts and surpluses retained as cash deposits at the bank should be left as negative and positive balances respectively, whereas deficits met by loans and acceptances and surpluses invested are in-flows and out-flows of cash and should be reflected as such in the cash budget. Conversely, repayment of loans and realization of investments should be shown as cash paid and received as appropriate in the final cash budget.

CASH MONITORING AND FORECASTING

The need for regular forecasts and formal monitoring will depend on the organization's financial circumstances both in terms of the complexity of the operation and what may be described as the 'liquidity sensitivity'. Where cash is tight, a weekly or even a daily report may be desirable. Also, in those companies where large positive cash balances occur (e.g. retailing), it will be necessary to have frequent monitoring data so that surpluses are quantified quickly and made to work on short-term money markets.

Under normal conditions (those in which the organization is neither on the threshold of classic liquidity crises nor enjoying regular cash surpluses, and where there are no severe variations from the

Table 8.2
Cash monitoring and forecasting report

Figures £000's
(–) Cash Outflow/deficit

Review period ended

	This review period		Year to date		Variations from budget		Forecasts	
	Budget	Actual	Budget	Actual	Period	Year to date	Next period	Year
OPENING BALANCE								
RECEIPTS								
Sales								
Asset Realisations								
Government Grants								
Miscellaneous Income								
Other								
PAYMENTS								
Trade Creditors								
Cash Purchases								
Wages and Salaries								
Capital Investment								
Statutory Creditors								
Capital Costs								
Dividends								
Other								
CLOSING BALANCE								

Commentary

assumptions in the cash budget) a monthly cash monitoring report should be adequate.

Table 8.2 shows a suggested format for the cash monitoring report which incorporates provision for the cash forecast both for the next review period in the budget year and for the year as a whole. Each cash forecast is, in effect, a short-term budget which updates and supplements and eventually replaces the original cash budget. By reflecting changed circumstances since the compilation of the cash budget, the forecast is in the nature of a rolling budget which the financial controller can use as a basis for re-negotiating any financing arrangements which may have been made at the time of the original budget compilation.

CONCLUSION

Cash control is fundamental to the management and success of any business venture. With proper planning and realistic sensitivity analysis of an organization's operations within normal budgetary control conventions, the financial controller can predict and therefore anticipate the effects on the company's liquidity of a whole range of business conditions. Subsequently, by close monitoring of the cash position and continuous updating of cash forecasts, the financial controller can make a significant contribution to the well being of her or his organization.

FURTHER READING

Accounting Standards Committee, Statements of Source and Application of Funds (SSAP 10.) Joint Accountancy Bodies.

Bank of England, *Money for Business*, Bank of England and City Communications Centre, 1987.

Edwards, H., *Credit Management Handbook*, Gower, 2nd edition 1985.

Garbutt, D., *How to Budget and Control Cash*, Gower, 1985.

Lee, T., *Cash Flow Accounting*, Van Nostrand, 1984.

Rutterford, Carter and Smith. *Handbook of U.K. Corporate Finance*, Butterworth, 1987.

Salinger, F.R., *Factoring and the Lending Banker*, Tolley, 1986.

Smith, J.E., *Cash Flow Management*, Woodhead-Falkner, 1984.

Taylor, T.W., *The Financing of Industry and Commerce*, Heinemann, 1985.

9

Financial Planning in Conditions of Change

Avison Wormald

For most businesses of significance change is now the norm rather than the exception, and it follows that one of the most important responsibilities of management is to cope successfully with the various changes, predictable and unpredictable, which affect the fortunes of the business. The author of this chapter classifies the changes which are most likely to affect business as: political change; change in money values; economic change and technological change.

Economic change embraces factors such as economic groupings, EEC for instance, trends in the domestic economy, changes in the distribution of wealth, and in raw material prices and supplies. All these factors have direct repercussions on financial planning and may effect fundamental, but sometimes unnoticed, changes in the nature of a business. For a management team which is prepared to cope with risk and uncertainty, change can lend a stimulus and an excitement to the function of management.

Avison Wormald has seen the pace of change rapidly accelerate and, for the purpose of controlling the situation, he echoes what R.J. Brown maintains in a later chapter – that conventional budgeting and planning techniques are often inadequate and that flexible budgets or alternative 'scenarios' may be most appropriate. He emphasizes the need for an efficient information service to management, presumably computerized, and this would need an audit every two years.

The author illustrates his analysis by a series of short, but pointed case histories which show that growth in business, as well as decline, will demand the highest qualities from the financial controller.

In recent years, the pace of change has been rapidly accelerating. Equally important, the changes seem more violent and more unexpected. The term the 'age of discontinuity' (Drucker, 1969) has been used, which carries these connotations.

In no field have these factors been more evident than in finance, where inflation, monetary instability and enormous changes in the geographic distribution of the world's wealth have shaken the western world, and to some extent, the eastern, to a degree which can only be compared to the impact of world wars.

These changes imply risk and uncertainty, particularly for the financial manager. Risk, by definition, can be estimated and planned for; uncertainty, by definition, cannot, except in so far as general measures can be taken to strengthen the business.

The financial manager's criteria for planning are not uniform; they are to some extent subjective and they are influenced by a particular environment. It has been suggested, as a result of a survey, that three widely applied criteria are:

1 Impact on long-term consolidated earnings per share.
2 Impact on cash flow.
3 Impact on the firm's market value.

These criteria will be used implicitly at least in the subsequent discussion, since they subsume a number of others which might be suggested; e.g. the impact on long-term consolidated earnings per share obviously subsumes a number of criteria about earning power in relation to capital, while the impact on the firm's market value obviously concerns its earning power and asset value. Whether the company is private or public is not really important.

MAJOR POLITICAL CHANGE

In more and more places there is a pervasive feeling that no country, even apparently the most secure, is immune from major political change. If the domestic country goes through a phase of political uncertainty the market value of most companies will suffer as will their share prices. The reply to this threat, especially in 'unstable' countries such as Italy, is to invest abroad, or at least to place substantial liquid funds and even ownership in countries such as Switzerland. Many companies now feel it wise to spread their interests widely.

INFLATION

Inflation is a subject in itself, in its proximate or further consequences perhaps the most important with which the financial manager has to deal.

Since recorded times inflation has been present in virtually all market economies, sometimes at quite low and tolerable levels of 2 or 3 per cent, sometimes rising to 25 per cent. Inflation and deflation are recurring phenomena, and may well be subject to long-term cycles of about 50 years, as suggested by Kondratteff. If the financial manager is obliged to borrow for any but the shortest periods at penal rates of around 20 per cent, clearly this indicates serious trouble. The raising of capital, either loan or equity, must therefore be planned for periods when interest rates are tolerable. We say 'tolerable' because at least it leaves some margin between a 'normal' or 'basic' rate of return of 15 per cent and the cost of servicing capital. Obviously the timing of capital raising is now even more important.

MAJOR ECONOMIC CHANGE

The major economic changes which may affect the financial manager are: changes in economic grouping; major trends in GNP in the domestic economy; changes in the distribution of wealth; and prices of raw materials.

Economic groupings

This is one of the major structural forces in the world today. Entry into the EEC has had profound effects on the UK economy creating greater competition in some areas, larger markets and different currency alignments. One of the directions in which this concerns the financial manager is the trend towards larger operating units. For a company to survive it has to have a strong financial position and good profitability, otherwise the probability is that it will be absorbed by a stronger company.

Major trends in GNP

The relative position of countries in the GNP table is changing, the UK showing a constant trend towards a lower position, and France and Germany in the highest position. Such movements affect the desirability of different countries for investment, a poor market having obviously fewer attractions than a rich one. The trend of these changes may change, as has been the case with Spain and Italy to some extent, so that a long view has to be taken of say 10 years at least.

An offsetting factor may be lower costs of labour which if not accompanied by an equally low labour productivity may make the country desirable as an export base; this would be the case for example for some industries with Eire.

The USA has for some time shown low growth rates and declining labour productivity so that its attractiveness for investment may rest more on the size of the market and its political orientation than on its profitability.

Changes in the distribution of wealth

Various factors have brought this about, especially the transferability of industrial skills and the ability to plan on a large scale. This, native qualities and the existence of reserves of labour in agriculture, has led to the phenomenal growth of the Japanese and Korean economies, and to a lesser extent that of Brazil. The traditionally wealthy countries such as the USA have been affected by the urbanization of the population and the declining raw material base. These changes as already mentioned greatly affect their desirability as sites for investment.

Rising energy prices have had a marked impact on growth trends in many countries especially the USA, Brazil and Japan, and this effect is likely to last 10–20 years unless there is a depression deep enough to restore competition amongst oil exporters.

Raw material prices

Very high growth rates in industry and the entry of many new countries to the list has resulted in great pressure on many raw material supplies, of which oil is only one example. The consequences of this for the financial manager are several. In the first place new investment has to be scrutinized more closely to see if it will be affected by higher material prices; second, working capital may form a higher proportion of total investment in existing or new business areas.

In the short term, for many commodities there are of course the Futures markets, where cover can be obtained at a known price for at least six months ahead. Where there is a long lead time between manufacture and sales, and firm prices have to be fixed a long way ahead, the use of these markets, where they exist, is almost inevitable. The dangers are not few, however, and there have been many cases where prudent coverage of raw material requirements has led to wild gambling either to retrieve losses or to make adventitious profits. Any company which makes use of the futures markets should establish an extremely tight system of authority to purchase or make contracts, where not less than three senior people are involved.

For many raw materials forecasts are available from research organizations. They are obviously not entirely reliable, but repay study since in this way a knowledge of the factors affecting the market is obtained. One of the most important of these is the cost structure of the industry concerned, which frequently is the main factor governing prices and the creation of new capacity.

MAJOR TECHNOLOGICAL CHANGE

Another group of factors is those concerned with technology. In many industries rates of obsolescence for processes and products have become very high, with a consequential need to take a conservative view of the profits over the longer term and to provide for fast write-offs of equipment. Nearly all advanced technology is an increasing risk with patent protection frequently inadequate, high launching costs, possible customer claims and short product lives. Growth industries have their drawbacks as well as advantages, since they tend to attract competition, and may require a 'critical mass' which is very large, as for example in main-frame computers. The financial manager has to consider whether the base is large enough to achieve this minimum economic scale. If not, and if a good estimate has not been made several years before, much money and effort will be wasted.

The opposite case is almost as frequent, that is where an important product is marketed and a large organization created which cannot be sustained once the product has passed its peak. The answer in some of these cases would have been to have licensed the product even though it might have meant less profit.

There is an increasing number of cases which epitomize these problems; large investment in R and D leading to a technical breakthrough, the development cost of which however is many times the cost of the original discovery or invention. This has to be financed through perhaps years of disappointment and difficulties until sales can be made. In this kind of industry the financial manager has to develop a deep understanding of the underlying technical situation, and a healthy scepticism about the timescales of engineers and scientists. In many cases the financial function did not have the status in the organization which was necessary in order to plan adequately; where a ten-year plan is necessary, a system based on annual budgets will lead to disaster. The most successful companies are those where the chief executive has a lifetime knowledge of the business and an acute financial sense. The problems then are more frequently a surplus of cash than a deficit.

CAPITAL MARKETS

The financial manager has to juggle several variables in relation to the raising of capital:

1 The form of capital: basically equity or loan, with a large number of intervening variables.
2 Timing: the needs of the company; the state of the capital markets.
3 Location: in which financial centre, the number of which has constantly increased.
4 Denomination: in what currency.
5 Terms: rate of interest; if loan, repayment, etc.

The changing international economic structure briefly referred to above has had far-reaching effects on capital markets. New York disappeared for a long time, sterling ceased to be used as an international currency, Hong Kong and Tokyo became international financial centres, virtually new currencies, the Eurodollar, the Ecu and the SDR appeared all in the space of 20 years.

The result of these changes has been near disaster for some companies which for example borrowed in German marks for repayment in the same currency; as nearly all currencies declined in relation to the mark there was for most borrowers a substantial capital loss when it came to repayment. Not all the changes were foreseeable by even the most acute observers, and certainly beyond five years requires some superhuman ability.

This type of problem can be solved using a linear program model. A variety of variables can be introduced to test the effect of the more probable occurrences, such as exchange and interest rate changes.

If there is one guiding principle for the financial manager in this highly dynamic situation it is to anticipate the requirement for fresh capital well ahead of time to avoid going to the market at an unfavourable point in one of the recurrent cycles. An immediate penalty has to be paid in that cash balances appear unnecessarily large, and even perhaps tempting to some cash stripping 'raider', but with a generally high level of interest rates in the short term earnings from interest may approximate to earnings from the normal activity of the business.

STRUCTURAL ECONOMIC CHANGES

The return on all types of investment is not of course constant. The financial manager of institutional funds has to recognize this and remain alert to the trends. In the UK for a number of years the return on industrial investment has been declining, while banking and property have shown a more favourable trend. The service economy on the whole is growing faster than the industrial sector, and its rate of return in many cases is higher.

Relative movements such as these may be the result of government policy, particularly in regard to interest rates on mortgages and bank deposits; they may be due to fears regarding inflation or to declines in, for example, the international competitiveness of certain industries. That the overall trend is frequently not easy to discern from close up is shown by the extent to which well-established banks and institutions were over-invested in property in the brief English boom of 1973.

Of all the indicators the most important is that of interest rates; booms of this kind follow low interest rates, but where there is a likelihood of inflation, with consequential negative balance of payments, it is inevitable that interest rates should increase, and share and other prices fall.

GENERAL PLANNING TECHNIQUE

The list of factors making for change is sufficiently long and varied for it to be clear that there can be no one method or technique for dealing with them. Every business has to analyse its economy to see what elements are most important and then study those deeply so that a background of knowledge and a feel for the situation are created. The financial manager should therefore examine:

1 Factors affecting working capital: raw material prices; wages and salaries; selling prices; credit conditions; volume.
2 Factors affecting profitability: the foregoing and taxation; foreign exchange; competition.
3 Factors affecting availability of capital, equity, or loan: inflation and government policy; interest rates; balance of payments; general demand for capital; institutional policies (e.g. property versus equity).

Conventional budgeting and planning techniques have not proved useful in all cases in such unstable conditions. They necessarily tend to give insufficient weight to external conditions. Increasingly 'scenarios' based on a number of different assumptions about the environment are being used as a flexible framework for planning. Planning however can never provide complete safety, the cost of which, if it is possible, is inevitably prohibitive. The story of the New York store group basing all its planning on the assumption of a post-war slump illustrates the point.

THE INDIVIDUAL BUSINESS

Most businesses in their life cycles have periods of rapid change, frequently because of changes in their environment, at other times because of changes in management. All tend to throw a heavy burden of responsibility on the chief financial officer. These changes will be considered under the following headings: changes in the nature of the business; problems of growth; and problems of contraction.

Changes in the nature of the business

Experience shows that this is commoner than generally realized. Some examples within the experience of the writer have been:

1 a commodity trading business became a consumer goods producer;
2 a low-technology business became involved in high technology;
3 a capital-intensive business became involved in a business requiring high working capital;
4 a business trading principally in the domestic market became heavily involved in foreign operations;
5 a financial investment business became involved in manufacturing operations;
6 a large basically unprofitable business acquired a small very profitable activity.

Any reader of *Management Today* (in the UK) or *Fortune* (in the USA) will have seen examples, with their stories of success or failure, of these and similar situations. A rapid analysis will cover most changes of this kind that the financial manager has to contend with.

A commodity trading business

In this case the business concerned was a world-famous cocoa and chocolate company whose primary business had been for many years trading in raw materials, i.e. cocoa powder and cocoa butter. In order to provide more stability (and for historical reasons) the business had been steadily increasing its operations in manufacturing proprietary chocolate goods.

The management of the business, including the financial management, was however heavily oriented to speculative transactions in the Futures markets, which they understood very well. The result was that cost information regarding the more recent manufacturing activities was entirely inadequate, as was budgeting and detailed financial control generally. The change in the nature of the operations and the management and financial control requirements were not realized until the company was acquired by an American industrial group.

A low-technology business

The essential characteristics from a financial standpoint of the low-technology business (fertilizers) were:

1 low rate of change;
2 requirements for very large seasonal finance to carry stocks and finance customer credit;
3 'lumpy' nature of capital investment with large producing units;
4 high cash generation due to capital-intensive nature of the activities.

The financial management had great difficulty in adapting its methods and standpoint to fast-moving, high-risk advanced-technology business, and was consequently very critical of a policy of employing highly paid executives, spending on speculative research and building plants for products for which no demand yet existed. The result was that a new department dealing with forecasting and financial appraisal had to be created parallel to the finance department to provide for the requirements of the high-technology business acquired and created.

A capital-intensive business

The basic business was a well-known fishing organization which was characterized by large fixed investment in ships (largely financed by government however), low working capital and high cash flow. When the business became involved in service businesses, particularly popular restaurants, it was not appreciated that much higher rates of return were required because of higher risk and low depreciation (with a consequential low cash flow). Without high rates of profit it was impossible to justify investment on a DCF basis.

A business oriented to the domestic market

The business concerned, one of the best-known in the UK, embarked on an ambitious programme of overseas expansion, largely through acquisition. Its basic business was relatively slow-moving and the company had ample cash requirements for its normal business. The new overseas business was largely financed by loans, some of which were in foreign currencies. The acquisition programme did not produce sufficient profits, some loans had to be repaid in depreciated sterling, with heavy capital loss, and the group found itself in a major financial crisis. The financial management had little experience of conditions overseas, of making acquisitions or of the foreign loan market. Its financial control in its domestic business was excellent, but the skills required for the new policy were of a different kind, and the deficiencies could not be made good until too late.

A financial investment company

In this case, a large international group, the primary business was the acquisition of companies, the application of rigorous financial controls, and investment or divestment according to the subsequent results. There was little skill in industrial management and virtually no ability to turn unsatisfactory situations around. In this case, however, the higher management of the business had an excellent understanding of its own strengths and weaknesses, and sought in every case to underpin the situation by requiring a strong asset base. If the business was subsequently found to be less profitable than had been hoped, the policy was to sell the assets or the business as a going concern to someone better qualified to manage it.

A basically unprofitable business

Here the basic business was in a traditional conservative low-profit area, with a tendency for profits to decline over the longer term. The business, however, acquired more or less fortuitously a small subsidiary which was highly profitable and whose profits regularly 'topped' up the profits of the main business. The financial management was quite happy with this situation since the company regularly paid a satisfactory dividend. The financial control of the basic business was not sufficiently sophisticated to show that the rate of return, when corrected for inflation, was steadily declining, and that the correct policy was to withdraw progressively from the main business and concentrate on the profitable one. The day of reckoning came when the situation came to the notice of a well-known take-over group, who made a successful bid for the company, sold the assets of the main business, and rapidly expanded the business of the successful small subsidiary.

The basic lesson of these brief real-life cases is 'know your business'.

The only real success story among these is that of the financial investment company whose management had an exceptionally clear understanding of what their expertise was. Since their ability to change businesses radically was very limited, other than in the area of financial control, they took exceptional care with the appraisal of the business to be acquired, and laid down extremely explicit conditions which the business had to satisfy, one of which was, as stated, a strong asset base. This policy was very coherent, its only weakness being that since its outlook was essentially financial, the industrial and commercial make-up of the group was very heterogeneous, with the result that the stock market, and particularly financial analysts, had difficulty in classifying it. This tended towards a rather low share price.

Strengths and weaknesses

In order that a business should avoid the kind of difficulties exemplified by the cases mentioned, what should it do? There is no short answer to this question as to how a business should come to know itself. At present the most powerful tool, in skilful hands, is strengths and weaknesses analysis, proposed by the Stanford Research Institute a good many years ago. However, this does not specify what key questions to ask in the financial area, or indeed in any other. First the basics of the problem have to be understood.[1] What kinds of business are there – what is the taxonomia of the genus? There are obviously fast-moving and slow-moving, market-oriented and production-oriented, high- and low-technology, capital-intensive and the reverse, and many other categories. For the financial manager a possible general form of profile would be as in Table 9.1 adding any special categories necessary in the case of his particular business.

Then a five or ten-year history, preferably in graph form, of the key ratios of the business: liquidity, 'quick' assets, stock-turn, sales/ assets, return on investment, shareholders' funds/total capital employed etc.

But in fact most businesses are multi-faceted so that they have to be analysed as matrices (see Table 9.2).

---

[1] For this there is no better authority than the late Joel Dean whose *Managerial Economics* and other works are full of valuable insights.

Table 9.1
Knowing your business – a profile

	Fixed capital	Working capital	Profit-ability Earnings ——— Investment	Risk	Leverage (gearing)	Cash flow
High						
Low						

The particular characteristics, as regards financial requirements and control, have to be studied for each product group or each 'business' – in effect here, a precision manufacturing and industrial 'business', a mass production industrial 'business' and so on. It is not enough to analyse the overall business from one standpoint.

In the absence of an explicit statement of strategy, obsolete patterns of corporate behaviour are extraordinarily difficult to modify. Where there is no clear concept of what current strategy is, the determination of what might be changed and why, must rest on either subjective or intuitive assessment. This becomes increasingly unreliable as the pace of change accelerates (Tilles, 1979).

(Part of the 'statement of strategy' is obviously the analysis of what the business is now.)

Table 9.2
Analysis of business as a matrix

		Production techniques		
		Precision manufacture	Mass production	Labour-intensive
	Durable consumer		X	
Markets	Non-durable consumer			X
	Industrial	X	X	

In recent years much precise information about the 'laws of the market' has become available from the PIMS project (Profit Impact of Marketing Strategy).

The importance of trends

For many financial managers there is a radical and difficult change in outlook which has to be made, namely to pay more attention to the trends over the significant period than to short-term results – the current quarter or year. In this way structural changes can be recognized and if necessary changed; changes for example in fixed or working capital intensity, return on assets (real, not inflationary), periodicity of earnings, and many other. The head of the successful business referred to above (who is himself a brilliant financial man) spent hours a day pouring over just such statistics from the many businesses controlled. One of the most valuable tools we have is the 'changes in financial position' statement, which is still insufficiently used.

Information requirements

Another lesson of these mini-cases is that different businesses require different types of financial control; some require rapid information, not necessarily extremely accurate, some, broad operating ratios, some, detailed product information. The financial manager, who is frequently the DP manager as well, has a great responsibility to keep the information available relevant to the particular business situation of the company.

In any substantial business there should be an audit not less frequently than every two years (small businesses have quicker reactions) of the whole computerized information system. The IBM information format can be used and a semi-permanent working party should be required to produce a detailed report on necessary changes. If the financial manager can give them detailed directions about any possible structural changes which may be needed, so much the better. Information which is not based on the real nature of the business can actually mask changes which are occurring, as for example changes in product mix, profitability etc.; information that is not regularly reviewed will be too detailed in some aspects, insufficiently detailed in others.

The importance of information in rapidly changing conditions cannot be over-emphasized. In a business of any size, without accurate, well-structured information relating to current and future conditions, there will be a failure to take concerted action, since different parts of the business will be using different information, mostly relating to what are now irrelevant conditions.

The rapidity of change has brought so-called long-range planning into some disrepute because it gives more attention to internal factors, which are more controllable, than to the rapidly changing environment, which is more difficult to forecast. What is more appropriate to changing conditions is to analyse the key features of the business and to consider how each one may be affected by possible changes beyond the control of the business itself. It is not necessary that an elaborate econometric model of the business should be constructed. Since this is a highly sophisticated task where experts have to be used, it may actually interfere with the more important aspect, which is for everyone in the business to reach a consensus about what the business is and what strategy it should pursue.

The most important probable changes are used as the basis for several scenarios, each of which gives a picture of what may be the situation in several years' time. It cannot take account of all the possible variables, nor all possible combinations of them but, for example, a series of three or four financial scenarios developed from the opinions of a cross-section of management will give a better 'feel' of what might happen than a static five-year forecast. This method is increasingly used by companies which feel the impact of major environmental changes. Shell is one company that uses the approach.

Problems of growth

The problems of growth, as far as they affect the financial manager, are generally more apparent than those just considered. They are not necessarily easier to deal with. In the first section of this chapter we have referred to the problems of high-technology business.

In this kind of situation, the financial manager will frequently be fighting a trend of over-optimism on the one hand and a reluctance to provide specific estimates on the other. Dr Eberhard Rees of NASA has this to say: 'It is a strange fact that so few otherwise gifted managers don't see the significance and great importance of proper planning', (Rees, 1976).

In the pharmaceutical, computing or space business, to take a few examples, one product breakthrough can bring an enormous increase in the rate of growth of the business, and much less exciting businesses can have their periods of rapid growth, which we might define as more than 15 per cent per annum. The problem will be financing initially working capital and then probably fixed investment. There will be a variety of different cases.

1   Large increases in sales but low profitability due to write-offs or development costs. In this case the need for working capital will further depress profits, so that the prospect of raising permanent capital will be endangered.
2   Increases in sales and profitability but with a high rate of working capital to sales so that after tax cash flow is insufficient to finance working capital. If the business is in the service area the asset base will probably be small, and the conditions as regards bank loans will probably be stringent.
3   'Lumpy' capital investment, i.e. due to technical factors increments of productive capacity will be very large. The construction and commissioning period will probably be rather long (in the UK 3–5 years) and output low in the first few years of production. In this case the difficulties may be very serious and only capable of solution by treating the venture as virtually a new one to be financed as such; by placing the plant in a highly subsidised development area, or by securing favourable credit terms from the suppliers of the plant and equipment.
4   In high-technology businesses, it is often not realized that the cost of inventing a new product is frequently only a fraction of the cost of developing it to a marketable stage and then subsequently marketing it. In the case of a new drug or pesticide, the cost of actually getting the product accepted by the FDA can easily be $5 million, before any of the product is sold.
5   The pursuit of volume irrespective of profit margins is also a frequent cause of trouble in conditions of rapid growth. If 'direct' costing is used there will be a tendency to think in terms of 'contribution' rather than actual profit, forgetting that if products give an inadequate 'contribution' to overhead and profit, the result must inevitably be an overall loss.

In virtually all cases of rapid growth, finance is a major problem requiring a mixture of sources:

1   Supplier credits – capital or raw material supplies.

2   Customer credits or advances (virtually bringing in the customer as a partner).
3   Government support, direct or indirect.
4   Medium-term bank credit, perhaps in the form of syndicated loans if the amount is large.

Control in rapid growth

It is extremely difficult to maintain tight financial control in times of rapid growth. Even seasoned executives may take the view that growth tomorrow will take care of all the problems of today.

Where capital construction is involved, if the production or engineering department does not maintain a PERT chart, then the financial manager will have to do so. This will show not only the progress of the venture towards revenue earning but also the incidence of payments to suppliers. It is quite common to have revenue earning delayed because construction is out of phase, but payments to suppliers and contractors actually ahead of schedule.

On the revenue side, rapid growth also tends to weaken cost discipline; more overtime is worked than budgeted, raw materials are bought at higher prices and control of accounts receivable is relaxed; the result may be, and frequently is, an impairment of profit margins.

In these conditions, where optimism is too prevalent, flexible budgeting is extremely useful in showing the effects of failure to reach forecast sales, costs or margins. It is also very important to budget for the whole of the development phase, so that the development and marketing people have to make a definite commitment as to when the situation will show a profit – two or three years or whatever – and then how much.

Problems of contraction

A business may find itself on a declining sales or profit trend for a variety of reasons – financial, technological, commercial or managerial. Financial management is not generally in a position to make major policy changes, although it should propose them if they are required. The major problem areas for financial management are:

1   The provision of information which highlights the areas where action is needed: sales, profit margins, costs, etc. Detailed analysis by products and departments will generally be necessary. Ratio analysis will always be useful.

2 The improvement of profits by: (a) cost and expense control; (b) The reduction of capital employed – this is frequently the more neglected term of the ratio profit/capital employed. Redundant assets may be sold, working capital squeezed; (c) Reduction in financial charges (a) and (b) will reduce the amount needed; there remains the possibility of reducing the servicing cost by loans instead of overdraft, etc.

3 Increasing liquidity: reduced investment and release of both fixed and working capital may lead to a highly liquid position in spite of low real profits. Such a position invites bids from cash stripping companies.

4 The undervaluation of the balance sheet, which may include valuable properties and tax losses (credits); management will frequently be reluctant to revalue assets because it will make a low profit position appear even worse.

5 Possible repayment of capital to shareholders: normally there is a prima-facie case for returning capital to investors when it cannot be profitably used for the purpose for which the company was constituted.

THE FINANCIAL MANAGER'S ROLE

The financial manager has a dual role:

1 as the manager of a service department which, like the personnel department, covers the whole business;
2 as the manager responsible for a vital technical function, on which everyone will have views but where she or he has the final responsibility, subject to the Board.

The case studies show failures in both roles, not necessarily exclusively or principally the fault of the financial manager, who may have informed management of the needs of the business. In some cases there was the failure to generate vital information, on costs for example, in others to appreciate the implications of changes in the type of business, in different types of business economy. In financial terms there is a very great difference between a high-technology and a low-technology business, and the principles that apply to one will bring disaster in the other.

It is likely that top management will tend to view the business in terms of marketing or production, relying on the finance manager to interpret the policy in terms of accounting requirements, financial reporting to management and, frequently, capital requirements. He will arrange for the financial implications of policies to be brought out in the annual budget, supplemented perhaps by a three- or five-year financial plan, with a forecast of cash requirements and a budget of capital expenditure.

These estimates and forecasts will all be produced on a basis of sales, production and other departmental estimates, and so will tend to be static. As has been emphasized, and also to place one year's figures in a larger framework of three to five years so that the general trend of the business can be appreciated, the financial manager will need to bring some flexibility into the picture by showing what the implications of higher or lower figures may mean – a 5 per cent increase in sales, ten days increase in accounts receivable etc.

CONCLUSION

Change of whatever kind – in the environment of the business, in the nature of its operations, of growth or decline – are all challenges for the financial manager. Financial managers are increasingly required to be competent economists and acute business people as well as highly qualified accountants.

REFERENCES AND FURTHER READING

Albert-Kenneth, J., *The Strategic Management Handbook*, McGraw Hill, 1983.

Butters, J. Keith, *et al.*, *Problems in Finance*, Irwin, 8th edition, 1981.

Dean, J., *Managerial Economics*, Prentice-Hall, 1951.

Drucker, P., *The Age of Discontinuity*, Heinemann and Pan, 1969.

Rees, E., paper on the 'Apollo Program' submitted to the 1976 CIOS Congress, Munich, Germany.

Tilles, S., 'Making Strategy Explicit', quoted in Ansoff, Igor (ed.), Business Strategy, Penguin Modern Management Readings, 1979.

Part II
CONTROLLING THE PERFORMANCE

Part II Controlling the Performance

Part II assumes that the business plans have been formulated. The efforts of the management team must now be applied to measuring the performance in relation to the plans and taking whatever action is necessary to correct deviations from them. In this stage of the exercise, as many writers point out, it will also be incumbent on the management to consider whether the plans, rather than the operations, need redirection, because of unforeseen contingencies or errors in the original forecasts.

In the construction of a work of this nature it is convenient and orderly to set out the several phases of the exercise of planning and control as being each self-contained, one following the other in apparently neat chronological progression. In fact, as practising managers are well aware, there is inevitably a great deal of overlap between the functions of planning, measuring the results and controlling the operations; and to some extent this overlap is bound to be reflected in writings on the subject which profess to have an applied rather than a purely theoretical emphasis. Thus Part I contains reflections on measurement and control whilst Part II will from time to time refer back to the principles and assumptions on which the forward plans were based.

10

Assessment of Performance

C.C. Magee

Professor Magee begins the discussion on the assessment of perform-
ance by pointing out that, in spite of popular impatience with past
events the post facto *assessment of the financial results constitutes a*
salutary exercise for the managers who were involved in the formula-
tion of the original plans. Thus, in comparing forecasted and actual
results 'there should be no automatic congratulations for managers
who exceed their target'. Nevertheless in making such comparisons it is
important to separate controllable from uncontrollable factors. The
assessment of performance must also embrace investment projects and
should relate to the basis on which they were originally approved. It
will be recalled that the principles and techniques for appraising
projects of a capital nature were examined by Professor Bierman in an
earlier chapter.

The chapter then pursues questions arising from the use of the return
on capital as a standard and a measure of achievement; the rate of
return to be used for such purposes to accord with the social responsibi-
lities of the business. Likewise the capital base, preferably represented
by total assets, needs precise interpretation. The author discusses the
apparently conflicting roles of profit and cash flow in the process of
measuring results and concludes that the two concepts must be re-
garded as 'complementary and not substitutional'. Profits are essential
for the purpose of financing future activities. The chapter lays stress on
the need for sound accounting principles to be applied, particularly in
respect of the valuation of assets, if the dependability of comparisons
over time is to be assured.

An important area of management control is the *post facto* assessment of the financial results of the organization as a whole, that is the examination in retrospect of the financial effects of earlier decisions to invest. Management must regularly commit resources for both long-term and short-term purposes and, because this commitment will always involve risk, a careful assessment of the anticipated results of any project on the financial position should be made before a decision is taken, and before resources are irrevocably committed.

A periodic evaluation is needed, after resources have been invested, to report what has been achieved, to examine the amount of the profit, or the extent of the loss, and to consider the effect of implementing the plan on the financial state of the business, in particular to note whether financial stability has been maintained or alternatively the extent to which it has been impaired. Information on all these aspects of the finances of the business is needed to permit management to assess the quality of earlier plans, the quality of past decisions at strategic level and the effectiveness with which they have been implemented. Finally it is important that an informed base of financial knowledge should be developed from which future activities can be planned.

Production managers in turn require detailed financial information at tactical level about the activities for which they are responsible. General management must be informed about the financial results of all these different areas of activity, with just enough detail to permit it to make a fair assessment of the financial contribution made by each to the overall health of the business. Perhaps emphasis should be placed on the need for information about the extent to which conflicting departmental interests have been responsible for reducing the total profit, and possibly for introducing some element of financial instability.

Profit is an important test of success, but the test can only be satisfactorily applied if profit is one element in a comparison. Profit must be considered for example in relation to a forecast, to the amount of capital resources used to produce it, or to the profit record of a preceding year. Additional comparison may be made in a larger business between the results of different divisions in a particular year, and changes in these relationships over time may be very significant for the long-term health of an undertaking. Profit should be earned at a level that is regarded as adequate in relation to the relevant elements in a comparison, for example to capital employed, and this expected rate of profit is a factor to be taken into account at the forecast stage.

While profit is a good indication of success or failure, however, the accounts that report it give little information about the factors that contributed to its results. An analysis of expenditure will show what items have varied in relation to a forecast or in relation to a previous year, but it provides little evidence of the reason for the change that has taken place.

Explanations of poor results, of reasons for what has happened, must be made available, and the information can then be used to support and interpret what the figures show. This evaluation of the financial results may then be used as a basis for a decision which attempts to bring about an improvement in an unsatisfactory situation during a subsequent period, for example an increase in the profit to produce the expected return on capital. Explanations are just as important if the results are good, perhaps showing an improvement on expectations, and a guide to indicate the steps that should be taken to keep production and profit at this satisfactory level.

An explanatory report on results that differ from expectations is also needed as a point from which to test the forecasting ability of the various groups who contributed to the build-up of the estimates. Results which are better than expected must be subject to the same level of scrutiny as those which fall below the forecast, and this inspection is particularly important when managers who are responsible for operations themselves prepared the data on which the estimates are based. It is not unknown for forecasts to be set deliberately at a low level in order to make achievement easy, and by this means to allow a comfortable margin for the production of an apparently satisfactory result. There should be no automatic congratulations for managers who exceed their target. A failure to forecast a high level of activity may well have made it difficult to produce the goods to meet demand; it may have caused unnecessary expense such as high-cost overtime working, or buying out components. The effect of a higher rate of expenditure, caused by the need to meet this unexpectedly high level of demand, because it is reflected in increased costs, must be to bring the profit down to a level below the potential of the business.

Managers who fail to reach their target must expect to be called on for an explanation. The real responsibility for failure may not be theirs; higher costs may be caused by factors which affect the rate of expenditure but which they are unable to control, and an analysis of data with the object of separating controllable and uncontrollable changes in cost, in order to pin responsibility or to exonerate, is an important exercise in financial control. Systems of standard cost and of budgetary control have been developed as accounting tools which will help to provide information about revenue and about costs on a responsibility basis, and it should be possible, if these procedures are installed and effectively operated, to establish as the result of further equiry what has gone wrong and, if the fault lies within the organization, who is responsible for what has happened. The variances that emerge will normally be investigated if the amount is material, as a part of the ongoing process of detailed assessment, but their effect is likely to become clearer when the comprehensive accounts of the business, showing the reported profit and the general financial position, are under review.

The operation of appraising the results of past investment decisions is important where large sums of money are committed over long periods of time, and discounting is widely used today as a method of selecting the most attractive of a number of different investment possibilities. The mathematical techniques employed can only be put to work on the basis of the data prepared by the accountant or by the budget department and while the mathematical calculations may be perfectly correct, the use of wrong estimates as the basis for these calculations will result in the production of forecasts that can never be correct. The discounting procedures to some extent help to minimize the effect of wrong estimates, especially when they are made in respect of periods that lie well in the future, but they cannot eliminate the impact of such errors completely. Large sums of money are often at stake when long-range business plans are put into effect, and the continued financial health of the business may well depend on the accuracy of the calculations on which decisions to invest are based. Error of a significant amount, especially in connection with receipts and payments which fall in the early part of the period covered, may spell disaster.

There is no way of completely eliminating error from forecasts, but past experience should be used in the attempt to build up the necessary expertise within a particular business. The quality of the forecasts can only be tested satisfactorily if past results are closely scrutinized and compared with the original estimates to discover what discrepancies exist, what has gone wrong and where. This exercise is a first step that must be taken to establish the cause or causes, to suggest remedies for the future, and to provide an assessment of the expertise within the field of forecasting that is available to an organization. The difference between forecast and achievement is not necessarily the result of an operating failure; it may be produced just as easily by a forecasting error, and one that could have been avoided had greater accuracy been achieved when the estimates were prepared in the first place. It should be possible to reduce the risk that a forecasting error will recur and although the exercise will not recover what has been lost, it should at least help to provide more reliable estimates for future planning.

Aids to investment decisions, mathematical or otherwise, are important tools of management, but they do not provide a complete answer because they must depend on forecasts of the future rate of cash receipts and cash payments. Estimates may be wrong *ab initio* or the expectations on which the forecasts were based may change as the result of events that could not have been predicted when the forecasts were prepared and the foundations on which the exercise is built may be completely destroyed. A comprehensive evaluation of the financial results of decisions after the event is needed not only as a check on the accuracy of the calculations on which action was based, but also on the reasons and the responsibilities for an error. Financial reports on the results of individual investment decisions should be produced, in so far as it is possible to identify and analyse the data, but the problem of joint costs often makes it difficult to ensure that adequate allowance has been made for all expenditure relevant to a particular area of activity. There is a very poor case for attempting to analyse joint costs on some arbitrary basis, but there is a very great danger of swinging too far in the opposite direction, and allowing so much attention to be focused on the amount of the contribution provided to meet joint costs that their full impact on profit may be neglected.

There is a wide range of general overhead and administrative expenditure, which may or may not be charged against the operating revenue produced when individual investment decisions are implemented, but which must be covered by the surplus earned from all productive activities. The results of all the investment decisions taken by the management of a particular business must be considered in the light of the profit derived from all operations after all costs have been charged against all revenue. Profit is normally calculated on a period basis and revenue must be charged with all expenditure which has been incurred and which is able to make no future contribution to profit. A decision to carry forward to a future accounting period any part of expenditure which has already been incurred may only be based upon a reasonable expectation that it will provide some future benefit or advantage. Subjective judgement is necessarily involved in any calculation of the amount to be carried forward, that is in quantifying it, but there must exist some objectively established expectation of benefit to justify any carry-forward.

The benefits received from a particular investment plan will not normally be limited to one accounting period, and any analysis of profit on the basis of origin should cover a period of years if it is to permit a full assessment of the results. The analysis must include sufficient detail to identify the revenue derived from each different project together with the expenditure to be matched or charged against it. An important point that must be emphasized is that comparisons of the financial results of individual investment decisions over time must be comprehensive, and they can only be satisfactory if the individual financial results are regarded as an integral part of those produced by the operations of the whole enterprise. Any fragmentation of figures, taking individual items of revenue and of expenditure out of the general context of total income and total expenditure and appraising them as if they represented the results of independent entities, must produce the risk that some items of expenditure will be overlooked and as a result the profit reported from the individual projects overstated. The danger of overlooking revenue is usually much smaller.

The contribution of a particular investment decision to profit is the total benefit it provides during the effectiveness of the expenditure incurred. An evaluation of the results will only be complete however if recognition is given to the total costs, including those which have not been allocated directly to any individual project; these costs must be met before profit emerges, and some undefined part of such expenditure is a legitimate charge against revenue. It may be impossible to charge out some items of costs, but their impact must be recognized.

An important purpose of the appraisal of results is to confirm whether or not the project has produced the expected cash flow. The main function of the financial accounts of a business however is to measure the results in terms of profitability and it is on the basis of success or failure measured in these terms that management will be judged. The resources committed must produce a return calculated on an annual basis at least as good as that which would have been produced by an alternative investment, and this return is measured by reference to actual income available within each year to pay whatever dividend is appropriate and to provide a surplus for reinvestment which it is hoped will in turn be profitably committed.

The evaluation of the results of long-term investment decisions, and in particular the importance of establishing whether or not they have provided an adequate contribution to fixed costs and to joint costs, in short, whether they have been profitable, must be clearly distinguished from the approach to a short-term decision on whether to accept an order which will only provide a small contribution. Long-term expenditure is relevant to an evaluation, anticipatory or *post facto*, of the long-term decision; sunk costs are of no consequence to a short-term decision, and if the business will be worse off by refusing to accept a contract which will do little more than cover marginal costs, the contract should be accepted. The evaluation of long-term expenditure on a long-term basis calls for different considerations and for a different approach.

PROFIT AND FINANCIAL STABILITY

The primary function of business management is to employ the resources committed to it in a profitable manner. The immediate objective is a profit sufficient to cover a dividend on the invested capital, together with a surplus which will be at least sufficient to ensure continued financial stability. A normal expectation today is that the surplus will also be enough to support expansion and development. The longer-term objective is to keep the business alive for the foreseeable future and the profit target must be set with this aim in view.

The level of profit sought must be reasonable in relation to a number of significant factors, financial, material and human, and the target must be one that in practice is possible to achieve. The aim must be clearly defined at the outset; it may be modified or changed subsequently in the light of experience or altered circumstances, but at all times the target must be kept in sight. It must be attainable, and its existence must be known, understood and accepted by all the senior members of the managerial team.

Some concession is made to social policy when the aim of continuity is accepted; the availability of jobs for people is an issue here and continuity of business activity provides them. It may therefore be argued that a moderate level of profit should be the aim of management, because such a level is consistent with continuity, and it follows that a moderate level of dividend and for profit retention is implicit in such a choice. The pursuit of maximum short-term profit, and of efficiency in its extreme form may be socially objectionable, but it is important to note in addition that financial stability may be an early victim of an aggressive profit policy.

The important virtue of retained profit to the business is that it provides an addition to the resources, and therefore to the assets, under the control of management. These additional assets may and should be used for expansion; they should themselves generate additional profit, and although there may be setbacks its average level over a period of years should steadily increase. Management which is able to provide resources for expansion out of profit must also demonstrate an ability to employ them fruitfully and the proof of this ability will be a steady rise in profit commensurate with the additional assets employed.

A profit which falls a little short of this desirable level suggests a lower degree of success, and any shortfall must result in a decline in profit retention if the dividend is maintained, or in dividend paid if an attempt is made to stick to preconceived views of profit retention. A more significant fall, which cuts the dividend and eliminates retention, or vice versa, poses more serious problems. Failure to remunerate capital will make a new issue of shares more difficult; failure to retain profit will make a new issue more necessary.

An important financial fact is that the increase in net assets that results from profit will first of all appear in liquid form; retained profit, subject to any investment decision taken by management, will produce a steady increase in the balance at the bank. The new liquid resources provided by profitable activity come under direct managerial control; they are available for, and normally they will be used for further development and, unless they are to remain idle, a series of investment decisions must be taken with this object in view. It is possible, however, for a successful company to anticipate the availability of new resources produced by profit, to borrow on short-term to finance intended development, and to repay as profit emerges. It is normally regarded as unsound financial policy to provide for long-term investment on the basis of short-term finance and, because the profit from the new venture is unlikely to be enough by itself to repay such a loan within the two or three years' credit period, an advance of this type is quite certainly an undesirable method of financing developments in the case of a new business. The profit that can be expected from the general activity of a well-established and successful business, however, introduces an advantage and provides a series of expectations very different from those existing in a new business. The expected results over the next few years can be calculated by projecting the activity of the recent past into the future. The result of this projection and the anticipated profit from the new investment may together provide a very satisfactory expected source of repayment for a short-term loan.

How much can be borrowed if repayment out of profit is to be completed over two or three years, on the assumption that profit from current activities will continue to accrue at its past rate and that there will be a little extra from the new project, is simple to calculate. The retained profit for one year, that is profit after tax and dividend, is the basis of the calculation; three times this amount can be repaid in three years or in a shorter period if additional profit can be expected from the new venture, provided no new investment is made. It may be preferable to omit any profit from the new venture in the loan repayment calculation until the venture has proved itself.

In practice the amount available for repayment each year is increased by the annual depreciation charge, part of the positive cash flow, and the effect is to permit the repayment of more than three times the profit in three years on the assumption that no resources are needed during the period for replacing plant that wears out and no new investment decisions are taken. The extent to which such assumptions are valid in a mature and widely based business must be closely considered and all these factors would need to be very carefully assessed before a decision to borrow is taken.

A very different situation will exist in the case of a business that has suffered a loss, even a short-term one; it is significant of rather more than the fact that there is nothing available for dividend, since it results in an actual decline in the resources under managerial control. If the previous level of resources was satisfactory, their total after a loss will not be adequate to allow the enterprise to carry on without some restrictions on its rate of activity. An attempt to evade the logic of the situation will produce a decline in liquidity, and this is likely to be at the expense of external creditors, unless and until the loss is made good by profit in a later period. A short-term loss means only a temporary set-back, but unless the amount is small and the trend of results is quickly reversed, its implications are clear and must be recognized.

If losses persist over several years, a steady and continuous drain on resources must impair the ability of the enterprise to continue. The first impact of loss is on liquidity, but there is a limit to the extent to which it can be reduced and still allow the business to continue to operate, not only at the current but indeed at any level. Additional outside resources will be needed to fill the gap, but they will be harder or even impossible to obtain because of the very circumstances which make them necessary. It will be difficult, if losses have been heavy and sustained, to take advantage of the prospect of profit if it should emerge. Available resources may have been reduced to so low a level that they are no longer adequate for the job they are intended to do. Purchase of additional plant etc. that may be necessary to take advantage of any change in circumstances may be quite impossible, working capital may already be very small or even non-existent. The development of a situation such as this calls for closing down the business, or if the prospects of future profits are sufficiently real, for a reorganization or transfer of the business to a new group with available resources, but one which may be unwilling to commit them to the enterprise as it exists, or to the particular managerial group in control.

RETURN ON CAPITAL EMPLOYED

An enterprise is established to make profit by employing in a productive manner the assets committed to its charge. Profit is therefore the test of success; profit is needed to enable management to continue functioning and to fulfil the duty imposed on it of servicing the capital with which it has been endowed. An additional surplus, retained profit, is useful as a basis for development; indeed it is very nearly in the category of an imperative, and many members of both management and ownership groups would regard as unsound an enterprise unable to provide a reasonable amount of retained profit, enough at a minimum to act as a financial stabilizer against adverse conditions.

Some measure of the extent to which the profit is adequate for these objectives must be developed. Profit must be at least large enough to give a satisfactory rate of return on the invested capital, a basic figure below which it must not be allowed to fall, on average over a period of years, if the business is to continue in satisfactory competition with its rivals. Its ability to raise capital in future will depend, first, upon the extent to which the business continues to produce the minimum profit which will enable it to pay a dividend that satisfies investors on the basis of comparisons they are able to make with alternative investment possibilities and, second, because retained profit must act both as a stabilizer and as a basis for expansion, upon whether a sufficient surplus emerges to meet these requirements.

The figure of capital on which the expected return should be made includes not only subscribed capital but also retained profit, i.e. the ownership interest, the effective capital of the business at a particular date. It may be expected that retained profit will be capitalized from time to time and that the separate balance carried forward on profit and loss account will be kept at a low level. Capital employed may also be defined to include long-term loans or sometimes as total assets.

The amount of the expected profit, covering intended dividend and retention, may then be expressed as a percentage on capital employed, e.g. the ownership interest. This approach is widely used today as a method of assessing the adequacy of the profit in relation to the resources committed to producing it. The standard is reasonably objective, in the sense that it can quite easily be used as a base for a comparison to judge whether investment proposals are satisfactory, and subsequently how achievement measures up to estimate. It can also be used to compare results over time and with results achieved by other businesses, which can themselves be translated into the same language and so provide material for an assessment of the relative levels of the profit return. Care must be taken to define capital employed in the same sense for all elements in a particular comparison, i.e. as the interest of the ownership group, the interest of this group plus long-term loans or as the total assets. The definition chosen for capital employed will depend at least to some extent on the purpose for which the percentage return is needed and the type of assessment that is being made, and it is probably wise to be flexible in this matter.

The possibility of variations in the definition and interpretation of the term 'capital employed' must receive careful attention when the concept is to be used to make some assessment of progress. Adjustment to the recorded value of assets to allow for such facts as changes in the general level of prices is common practice today, but no generally agreed procedure has been adopted, and the calculations made by different enterprises will not necessarily be on the same basis; the effect of alternative choices would need to be examined in practice, before any conclusions are reached from a comparison of the rate of return on an inter-firm basis.

The significance of the definition of capital employed becomes apparent when it is related to the financial structure of the business. Development is often financed on the basis of long-term loans and if profit expressed as an average rate of return exceeds the interest payable to the lenders, there will be a surplus available for the ordinary shareholders. A substantial surplus may emerge in good times from such an element of gearing, and this will provide a valuable addition to the profit available to ownership; the reverse will be true in bad times and it may even be difficult to meet the interest payment to lenders. A business which is financed to any significant extent by means of long-term loans may produce a better return on capital employed, interpreted as the ownership interest, than another company which depends entirely on share capital and retained profit. The return produced by the first business may however be lower than that of the second if capital employed is defined to include long-term loans. There is probably a case for avoiding the rather narrower definition of capital employed as the ownership interest and accepting the rather wider one which includes long-term loans. The use of this definition of capital employed will help to eliminate the distorting effects of differences which result from the various mixtures of capital resources from which an enterprise can choose.

The problem of comparison may be further aggravated if a company depends very heavily on short-term credit to finance its work. A company which expands unilaterally the credit terms it gets from its suppliers because it pays no interest on such resources should be able to produce a larger return than another business which maintains a more normal credit situation. The fact is that a business which plays on its creditors in this way may be able to increase its profit without expanding the base for the return on capital calculation, and as a result may produce a more favourable rate of return than might have been expected, but financial stability will suffer. The excessive use of short-term credit, the extension of the normal credit terms, must produce financial instability; it is indeed one sign that this stage has already been reached, that a potentially dangerous financial situation has developed and the company may be forced to cut back its rate of activity.

The method of calculating the return on capital can of itself have no effect on the financial stability of the business, but it is not impossible that a base could be chosen that masks a very pedestrian out-turn, and perhaps one that is deteriorating. It could be argued, for this reason, that the total of the assets in use provides the most satisfactory basis on which to calculate the return; indeed it would be reasonable to go further and to call for a revaluation on a current price basis.

An additional factor must be borne in mind if an attempt is made to compare the trading results of one enterprise with those of another similar business. There is a surprising lack of exact comparability between the work of two apparently very similar enterprises. Most businesses operate on a mixed basis in the sense that each relies on a variety of different products, and the range of products on which A depends may differ substantially from those on B's list despite considerable overlapping. The differences between the two businesses may be on the fringe, and account for no more than say 20 per cent of total production, but there may be wide variability and significant differences in the profit returns from these marginal activities; these differences may be sufficient in their effect on the final return, on the average rate of return on total capital employed, to render comparisons of doubtful value, if they are used as the sole method of assessing relative efficiency in the use of resources. Variations in profit mix may have a similar effect, and it may be difficult for outsiders to identify such a change. The analysis of turnover and profit produced by different lines of product can be very useful to other managements attempting to make comparisons.

The use of return on capital as a good basis for inter-firm comparison is affected by the fact that both profit measurement and asset valuation are always to some extent a subjective process; the problem is discussed in the last section of this chapter.

CASH FLOW

The term cash flow is widely used today and refers to and includes all the cash that comes into the hands of management and is available for spending during a particular period of time. The concept of a rate of cash flow, the rate at which resources become available, is a relevant factor in any assessment of the current and expected financial stability of an enterprise. The significance of this concept is that management has control over the destination of liquid cash that comes into its hands, and if the flow is at a sufficiently high rate, management should be able to meet the commitments which it has accepted and which are judged to have a prior claim on the available resources.

Any failure to meet claims as they fall due is likely to damage the credit image of an enterprise and consequently its ability to fund its activities.

Much of the cash flow that comes under the control of management is earmarked to pay for raw materials, wages, salaries and other running expenses. It is a fact of economic life that if the enterprise is to remain in business it must continue selling and meet the consequent costs. There is thus a continuous flow of goods etc. into and out of the business, and because this movement is in both directions the cash flow which follows it is largely repetitive and the outward movement is in many ways mandatory. A management wishing to stay in business enjoys no effective right of decision over the disposal of that part of the inward cash flow that must be used to meet this repetitive demand for payment to cover the cost of its sales. Failure to meet such a demand on any significant scale must mean that the continuity of the business itself is in danger, although changes in the nature of its activities are not precluded.

The significant element of cash flow inwards that is relevant to managerial decision is the part that is free for disposal, in general the surplus that is not required to meet the repetitive demand for expenditure necessarily incurred to earn revenue. The basic constituent of such systems is profit which produces the increase in net assets, initially a surplus of liquid resources. Profit is a residue, an excess of revenue over costs and by definition it is not required to meet payment for expenses incurred in the earning process. These expenses have been deducted before the profit is measured. The cash received from sales has first been used to meet the total periodic cost, and the residue, the surplus, remains available in liquid form for spending.

There is however a second element in net cash flow measured on a periodic basis. The earlier discussion about the repetitive element in outwards cash flow assumed that such expenditure was met by the early payment of cash. There are, however, important exceptions, sometimes referred to as 'non-cash' expenses, because the payment does not take place during the period covered by the profit calculation. This non-cash element of expenditure covers all the depreciation charges together with the amounts written off any other item that has been capitalized, e.g. research costs.

A cash outflow to meet the total cost of the asset, a part of which is periodically charged against revenue, did of course take place, but at an earlier date and within an earlier accounting period. Management did exercise its prerogative to use resources to buy a long-term asset, such as new plant, but the cash, perhaps produced by retained profit, was spent in an earlier year. The immediate charge against revenue did not include the full cost as in the case of the repetitive payments; some part, e.g. 10 per cent or 20 per cent, was treated as a period cost and the surplus was carried forward to be charged against the revenue of each of those later years in which it was expected to make an effective contribution to production. The total cash outflow in this first year must have substantially exceeded the depreciation charge in that year. The position is reversed in the later years of the asset's life: the cash outflow is less than the total costs charged against revenue, and the net cash inflow available for managerial decision is the total of the net profit plus the non-cash expense, as defined above, charged against revenue.

Effectively the amount available to management is the net profit plus the depreciation charge. That charge of itself however does nothing to create inwards cash flow. The existence of this flow depends entirely upon whether enough goods are sold at a sufficiently high price to cover the cost of materials consumed, wages etc. as well as the non-cash expenses, and to leave a surplus or residue of profit. If a loss has been suffered the cash flow measured by the depreciation charge will of course be reduced by the amount of the loss and it may even disappear.

The projection of the future or expected cash flow is an important part of the procedure for forecasting and budgeting. The expected receipts for a given period and the rate of receipt will be estimated and compared with the anticipated payments and the rate of payment; any gap, particularly important if it is a deficit, will be estimated in advance. The ability to use a cash surplus to advantage and to take steps to ensure that a deficit is covered are important elements of financial management. Permanent capital should be invested profitably, but held at the lowest level consistent with permitting the business to develop unhampered by a shortage of resources. Short-term deficits should be anticipated and covered by arrangements for an overdraft to be available as the gap emerges. It will be easier to make the arrangements if there is reasonable anticipation of any shortage.

An advance calculation of profit is a second important element in the forecasting procedures but it does not provide all the data needed for the calculation of a cash surplus or deficit, partly because it makes no allowance for payments of a capital nature, and there may also be non-revenue receipts. There is the additional problem implicit in the profit calculation that expenditures incurred are not necessarily chargeable costs in the periodic income calculation. The cost of raw materials purchased is not the same as the cost of raw materials used; the point becomes very significant when finished goods, in which the raw materials and other costs are embodied, are the subject of valuation and particularly when totals of stocks vary substantially from one period to another. A case can be made for sticking to cash receipts and cash payments when advance calculations or forecasts are prepared because this avoids the contentious problem of stock valuation and the depreciation charge which necessarily intrude into the area of profit measurement. The calculations of cash flow are of a much more factual character and while forecasting always presents problems of valuation, the forecast of expected profit is more difficult than that of cash receipts and cash payments because of difficulties such as choosing the correct methods of valuation; in short these are additional problems which appear when profit measurement is attempted, but which are absent when cash flow is being calculated.

It must be accepted, however, that while calculations of cash flow and the measurement of profit overlap, they are essentially two distinct exercises, and the information provided by each has its own specific purpose. The calculations are complementary, not substitutional, and there are normally good reasons why both should be undertaken; the effect of the additional element of valuation on the profit calculation must however be understood when an appraisal of the expected results is being made, but there is no case for suggesting that because the two statements produce similar or overlapping information it is better to choose the one which may be the more accurate. The flow of funds statement as a method of communicating information of financial significance is widely used today and it has become an important accounting report in the area of *post facto* assessment, but it supplements rather than replaces the profit and loss account. The total amount of information available is expanded by the production of these two reports and they should both be used if a wide and critical analysis of business activity is to be undertaken.

Two different purposes are fulfilled by the documents. The profit and loss account, despite the problem of valuation, provides the information on facts that must decide whether a business is viable in the sense that it has provided, and is therefore likely to continue providing, a satisfactory expansion from internal sources. No other accounting report provides the data for the assessment of the probability of long-term viability, the most important element in the life of any business. The historical account cannot predict results over the long-term future, a feat which no accounting report or mathematical calculation is capable of doing: these long-term possibilities depend as much as anything on the quality of present and future management. A good current profit-making enterprise, however, provides by its existence a clear indication that there is a public interest in and demand for its product, that good management is there to produce it at a low enough cost and that the business therefore possesses the recipe for long-term success.

The cash flow statement, and especially its projection into the future, provides information that is not available in the profit and loss account, information of a different type which supplements what appears there. The statement is concerned basically with the need for financial resources, with their origin and with their use by a business in the context of the ability of the business to meet its commitments, short- and long-term, as they fall due; the emphasis is on the maintenance of, and on the expected maintenance of financial stability. The statement is used as a guide to the desirability of accepting further commitments on the basis of the financial resources currently available or, if this appears to be unreasonable, to the need for procuring additional financial resources before any fresh commitments are accepted.

The most satisfactory way of using such accounting reports and forecasts as profit statements and flow of funds statements is a joint use. Profit or the likelihood of profit in sufficient quantity is a justification for the use of financial resources. Reports on past activity will indicate the extent to which it has been possible to produce a profit with a balanced use of resources; estimates of future results will indicate the extent to which profitable activity is possible on the basis of the resources likely to be available or whether, because the level of activity is expected to exceed certain limits, more resources will be needed. Potential profitable use of resources is a justification for getting them, but provision of resources does not itself produce a profit. Consideration must be given to the prospect of existing resources proving adequate, to the prospect of resources expected from retained profit over a period meeting an existing or an emerging shortage, to the prospect of a temporary overdraft bridging a short-term gap and to the possible need for additional permanent capital. The absence of a hope of future additional profit provides no justification for seeking additional resources; decisions about the future can only be taken satisfactorily if, before they are made, both aspects of enterprise activity, profit and cash flow, are taken into account.

A reasonable profit in relation to the resources committed is one ingredient necessary to justify a decision to invest, and a cash flow that will permit the maintenance of financial stability is the second ingredient. The *post facto* assessment must pay attention to both factors and in both cases will review the extent to which expectation has been fulfilled.

REFERENCES AND FURTHER READING

Anthony, R., *Financial Accounting*, Irwin, 1980.

Goch, D., *Finance and Accounts for Management*, Kogan Page, 1985.

Magee, C.C., *Financial Accounting and Control*, Allen and Unwin, 1968.

Magee, C.C., *Framework of Accountancy*, Macdonald and Evans, 1979.

Magee, C.C., *Rowland and Magee's Accounting*, Gee, 1971.

Solomons, D., *Divisional Performance: Measurement and Control*, Irwin, 1968.

11

Cost Control

R.J. Brown

The preceding chapter considered the broader implications of the control system and attention is now directed to a specific aspect of the general subject, that of cost control. The author of the following chapter has had many years' experience organizing the cost control systems of a large manufacturing plant. He looks upon the subject as being of the nature of profit control which should be examined under each of the following headings: the production situation, the project situation and the lossmaking situation.

In the production situation the investigation of standard cost variances can be of some assistance so far as direct costs are concerned but the author regards standard costing as of little practical benefit in the control of overheads. He emphasizes the importance of constructing efficient procedures for the control of overheads because this classification of business expenditure is tending to increase as a proportion of total costs. He regards more direct methods of controlling overhead costs, such as by actual limitation of inputs, as being most effective.

Likewise there are limitations on the typical use of budgetary control in the project situation, and here the initial budget should be formulated on the basis of cost saving or profit enhancement elsewhere. The author thus sees severe limitations on the effectiveness of the traditional techniques of standard costing and budgetary control, but his criticism is constructive and he makes a number of other practical and specific suggestions for the control of costs and the improvement of profits.

The objective of commercial enterprise is the creation of profit. Profit is made when the revenue earned from the sale of a product or service exceeds the cost of its provision. Cost control can be considered as the process of minimizing the inputs necessary to achieve sales, and is thus a significant factor in the maximization of profits.

It should be understood that businesses incur costs not only in achieving current revenue, but also in servicing future activity.

The need to control both types of cost is important, but the techniques applicable to their control differ. In this chapter the distinction is drawn between:

1 the *production* situation – where the concern is to minimize the costs directly incurred in achieving current sales;
2 the *project* situation – where cost incurred cannot be directly associated with sales, or is being incurred today in the expectation that, in future, a profitable output will emerge. In this latter circumstance, the detail and dimensions of the result are largely uncertain. Research, development and advertising expenditure are included in this category, but in practice all items of overhead expenditure involving people, plant or services lend themselves to being controlled by this approach.

The techniques described in these situations are concerned with producing optimum efficiency, and assume a degree of confidence, certainty and stability about the current and future circumstances of the business. In practice, all businesses will encounter situations where for at least some part of their activities for some period of time, substantial difficulties are encountered in profitably supplying the market. In such situations, the need for retaining flexibility and reducing downside risk will be paramount, and may be inconsistent with achieving theoretical optimum cost efficiency. The techniques which may be applicable to these circumstances are described in this chapter as the 'lossmaker situation'.

The types of action which can be applied to all three of these situations fall into two categories.

1 physically limiting the inputs or expenditure incurred by the business;
2 maximizing the efficiency of the operations of the business. Within this, a major requirement of the process is the careful and accurate diagnosis of the problems in order that attention and

action can be centred on a proper remedy.

In either case, it is necessary to develop yardsticks on the basis of which appropriate action can be taken. Against the background of this general perspective on day-to-day cost control, it is now appropriate to consider the various specific techniques employed in dealing with these situations, and their suitability and limitations.

THE PRODUCTION SITUATION

The conventional technique used in controlling the profitability of production situations is standard costing. This rests on the basis that the standard cost is a predetermined yardstick of what output ought to cost, and actual costs are then related to this yardstick; the points of difference or 'variances' which emerge identify the areas of inefficiency and enable action to be centred on remedying them.

In practice, standard costs are established for each operation peformed on each component produced, building up in total to a standard cost for the final product. The standard cost normally comprises three separate elements:

1 *The material element.* Self-evidently, the standard material cost of an item is a function of the amount of material which ought to be used in the production of the item, and the price which ought to be paid for that material in whatever quantity it is purchased. Inevitably, some discretion has to be exercised in determining whether it is expedient or meaningful, in a particular situation, to attribute all material consumed in the production of an item specifically to that item, or whether to treat some as general overheads, e.g. cutting oils, paint, solder, electricity.
2 *The direct labour element.* This element relates to the cost of those people whose work should result in the direct and immediate creation of output. The time which such individuals ought to spend in the performance of a particular operation is determined, and this combined with the rates of pay they ought to receive, enables the direct labour element of the standard cost to be computed.
3 *The overhead element.* In essence, this is computed by taking all costs incurred by the business, other than material and direct labour costs, and attributing them to individual operations. The

total amount to be recovered is normally that defined in the annual budget or forecast. This total amount is often then apportioned between various cost centres within the production process, e.g. a type of machine or production department. The level of activity anticipated in the forecast for each cost centre is then expressed in an appropriate unit such as machine or direct labour hours or some dimension of material used. From this, a standard cost of overheads per hour (or whatever) for that cost centre is established. The overhead element of the standard cost of an operation is then derived by multiplying this overhead rate by the hours etc. which ought to be taken in the execution of that operation.

Provided that what has been produced in a given period is identified, that output can then be expressed in terms of what it ought to have cost in total, and also separately the labour, material and overhead elements of that total.

By comparing the actual expenditures under the same headings, the areas in which costs have been higher or lower than they ought to be can be identified. In addition:

1 If the difference between the price actually paid for material and the amount allowed in the standard is recorded, the cause of any variation in material costs can be further analysed into whether it is a function of the amount used or the price paid.
2 Similarly, if the actual hours worked by direct labour in a period are recorded, any variance in direct labour cost can be analysed into whether it is a function of the efficiency of labour or the hourly rate paid to that labour.
3 Finally, if actual overhead expenditure is related to the forecast, then any variance in overhead cost can be analysed into whether it is a function of the amount spent, or a difference in the level of activity (recovery).

This approach to analysing the causes of variances can be carried on virtually indefinitely. Provided that effort and expense are available to measure one variable, the other can always be deduced. Typically, a business may thus identify the effect of using non-standard materials and the creation of scrap on material variances; the effect of waiting time, scrap and higher than standard skilled labour on labour variances.

If the business is fairly large, it is obviously essential to ask the question not only 'what?' but 'who?' is the cause of these variances, since it is individuals who must take action to remedy the problems. A global result for the business as a whole does not help to resolve the problem since it cloaks a large number of varying items. It is probable that the analysis will need to be carried down at least to departmental level, and in the case of labour analysis, conceivably down to that of the individual operator.

On the basis that the objective of business is the earning of profit, standard costs are also applied in the analysis of the profit and loss account. By relating actual and forecast sales turnover to the actual and forecast standard cost of these sales, the extent to which sales volumes, sales prices and product mix have affected total actual profits relative to forecast profits can also be established.

Through the technique of standard costing a reasonably objective analysis of the historic performance of the business is obtained, although it should be recognized that the counting, evaluation and analysis required itself involves an on-cost to the business, and this on-cost will increase directly with the amount of analysis required.

Given that the information is available, it is perhaps worth considering its application in controlling rather than simply analysing profits. The following points can be made:

1   It needs to be recognized that the question relates to what has already happened, and assumes that if action is not taken, the problem will recur in the future. While this assumption may have some logical limitations, it is sound enough in practice to use as a working hypothesis.

   The essential requirement is that the information is produced as soon as possible after the event has occurred, thus minimizing the period over which the loss is occurring before action is taken.

   This comment is particularly appropriate to the material usage and labour efficiency types of variance which both reflect areas where performance can go 'off the rails' very quickly. With variances such as overhead recovery, gross profitability, sales volume and labour and material prices, the need for rapid reporting of actual results is perhaps less pressing, since the problem ought to have been foreseen and action taken accordingly. On this point more will be said later.

2   In the area of overhead control, standard costing, of itself, is of little practical benefit. Overhead expenditure variances are, in

fact, identified by the budgetary control process. So far as overhead recovery variances are concerned, it is feasible to evaluate factory output programmes, and in the event of an underrecovery to determine whether it is a function of low demand or inadequate achievement against that programme. As noted, however, it is suggested that the effect of a fall in demand on a factory's performance can, and should, be anticipated rather than measured in hindsight.

3   Increasing proportions of total costs are inevitably being incurred in the area classified as overheads. This has been brought about by two trends.

First, there is a trend towards the replacement of direct labour by the use of machines in virtually all spheres of industry.
Second, there has been a corresponding growth in the number of employees supporting the production process rather than being directly involved in it. The substitution of machines for workers has increased the requirement for production engineers and setters. The accelerating advance in technology has demanded the involvement of more people in research and development, since a company which produces an obsolete product very quickly becomes obsolete itself. The increased level of fixed overheads involved in both the mechanization and staff only indirectly involved in production makes the maintenance of sales volumes particularly critical, and thus yet more people have become involved in the process of marketing the products of the business.

Because of this trend, and because of the inadequacy of standard costing techniques as a mechanism for controlling overhead costs, it is suggested that standard costing is becoming less relevant as a technique in profit control than has previously been the case.

A final feature of the practical problems which can be encountered in the application of standard costs to overhead control is that the more remote an overhead is from the actual production process, the more arbitrary does any allocation of that cost to the product become, and the less meaningful the variances which are computed against the standard. The trend is for those overheads which are directly related to the production process to form a decreasing proportion of the whole.

4   In the area of direct labour costs, the increasing mechanization of the industrial process has resulted in the output of direct operators being determined not so much by their own efficiency and

effort, but by the 'cycle time' of the machines or the speed of the conveyor. As a result, the effort of the individual is likely to be a less significant factor in the creation of variances than has been the case previously, and in many situations factors such as attendance and industrial relations problems assume much greater significance. Since the identification of the remedial action in these cases does not rely on the application of standard costing, the technique itself is of less significance in profit control.

There is also, perhaps an inherent danger in the principle of standard costing which considers labour as being a variable cost where in practice the description 'hourly paid' no longer means that such employees can be dismissed at will. This is of more relevance in considering the lossmaker situation.

5   The process of increasingly sophisticated mechanization has made the usage of materials more predictable owing to quality becoming more consistent and usage being more carefully governed. This tends to minimize the size of variances, and thus the significance of standard costs in profit control.

6   A final point of concern is that the standard costing technique can result in a rather fatalistic approach being taken to profit control. If the price of material becomes more expensive, the standard cost of the material element is in turn revised. If the wage paid to direct labour is increased, the standard rate of the direct labour element is revised in step.

The standard costing approach does not immediately direct attention to the fundamental questions such as whether these increases are out of line with the general trend of cost increase or whether some alternative approach to the production of the product would not prove more cost effective, e.g. could an alternative type of material be employed, or could the method of manufacture be changed?

With overhead rates, the process is even more insidious, since by definition the standard overhead rate is that which has to be applied to recover what are expected to be the actual costs. It does not attempt to deal with the question as to whether those actual costs are reasonable.

Even in the field of labour efficiency and material usage variances, there is a tendency for this drift in standards to occur. In practice, a gap will nearly always occur between what an item ought to cost, and what in practice it does cost. This gap soon becomes recognized as normal, and thus attention ceases to be centred on it, as a result of which a less stringent yardstick is effectively created.

These features do not, of themselves, negate the value of the standard costing technique, but it does need to be recognized that the standard itself is by no means immutable, and that almost as much attention needs to be paid to the way standard costs inflate, as is paid to the variances which the standard costs reveal in analysing actual performance.

It must be stressed that the foregoing points do not argue for the abandonment of standard costing as a technique for profit control; they simply attempt to put its limitations in the modern business situation into perspective. The area of profit control quite apart, standard costing continues to fill a virtually indispensable role as a basis for stock accounting and the evaluation of output of multi-product concerns. It also is often the only practical starting point for price setting when a very wide range of products is handled, and where no clear market demand pattern can be established.

Owing to the increasing proportion of total costs that is represented by overheads in modern industry, the need to find approaches to deal with 'project situations' is becoming more urgent, while the conventional 'production situation' is one which is diminishing in significance.

The control of project situations is dealt with in the next section, but the techniques for dealing with the profit control of production situations are by no means limited to standard costing. Some supplementary approaches which can be taken are as follows:

1   Perhaps the most obvious control which can be exercised is by limiting the inputs into the 'production situation'. For example, the recruitment of labour can be limited to the level projected as capable of handling the factory programme; controls can be exercised on orders on suppliers for materials before they are released, so as to identify and query situations where an above-standard price is to be paid; controls can be applied to ensure that only sufficient material is issued from the stores as is required to produce the programmed output by the standard methods of efficiency. It can be argued that these controls are exceedingly crude in that, of themselves, they provide no assurance that the required output will be achieved. They are, however, highly effective in limiting the total costs that are incurred, and thereby directing attention to the efficient use of the inputs, having disposed of the problem of the inputs themselves being potentially too great.

2   As noted before, as far as possible an approach should be taken which prevents a variance occurring and initiates the right action to avoid or minimize the financial costs or maximize the opportunities. In this area, the data may not be 'financial' in the strictest sense of the word, but their consequences must be perceived in a financial way.

Given that in many industries there is a lead time, which is measurable in weeks rather than hours, between an order being received and a sale occurring, the most obvious area of attention should be the order intake. The volume of work which this represents should dictate the short-term policy of a business as to whether it engages additional labour, or replaces vacancies as they arise and whether overtime is worked or not. The unit selling price of each order should be vetted before it is accepted, and its impact on future trading results projected. The acceptance of substantial volumes of orders at lower than forecast rates of profitability signals a red light for the pricing policy of a business or for its original perception of the nature of the market. A buoyant state of incoming demand should direct the attention of a business to being selective in prices accepted, giving production priority to the higher-margin business, and considering which orders use the least of the scarcest resources, in so far as these options are open in a practical commercial sense.

The business must be alert to external influences affecting the order intake. In domestic markets, government fiscal policy and activities by competitors are areas which can affect demand in a relatively short period of time. In overseas markets the effects of movements in rates of exchange, and the political and economic stability of the countries concerned, are significant factors. The fact that these can rarely be quantified with any accuracy, and that the business can rarely influence the course they take, does not minimize the need to see them as significant inputs into the process of controlling profits and costs on a day-to-day basis.

Likewise, an industrial relations problem needs to be assessed in terms of its effect on future profits. Not only should a financial view have a bearing on the way the problem is resolved, but the action which needs to be taken to overcome the financial consequences of the dispute needs to be formulated as it occurs, not after its effect has been measured.

3   A final point is that all controls and systems within a business have a financial implication, even if they do not actually form part of

the accounting records of the business. As part of the process of profit control, it is not only reasonable, but almost imperative, that a financial view is taken on the adequacy of such activities as production control, stores recording systems, wages booking and buying office procedures. It is within these activities, after all, that many of the causes of the phenomena which are blandly described as cost variances actually occur.

PROJECT SITUATIONS

Project situations were earlier defined as being those where for a finite input of expenditure, a direct and immediate effect on output or sales would not be expected to occur, i.e. most items classified as fixed or semi-variable overheads. The classic technique for dealing with such situations is that of budgetary control.

Within this definition falls a tremendous variety of costs, ranging from those which could be considered unavoidable in the short term, such as rent and rates, through those which are fundamental to the production process, such as the cost of power, tooling, transport and stores, to those which are more concerned with the evolution and development of the business, such as costs of advertising, design and development, methods improvement and systems analysis.

Budgetary control is relatively straightforward and involves two stages. First, there is the establishment of the budget which determines the amount of money which a particular department or activity (with an individual identified as responsible) ought to incur over a period of time; and second there is the process of measuring and controlling actual expenditure in relation to the budgets.

The essence of the budgets is that they identify who is to be accountable for the item of expenditure. Where the item involves the cost of employees, the budget will be expressed both in terms of the numbers of individuals employed in a particular department, and in the sums of money which will be spent on the employment of those people, covering not only their salaries and associated costs, but also such incidentals as travelling, entertainment and stationery costs.

Costs such as plant and building maintenance, rents, rates, power, advertising, will be expressed in finite sums of money, but under each heading it is quite possible that major individual items of expenditure will be specifically identified.

Such budgets normally establish, in total, the limit of expenditure for a period of a year, and within that year an assessment of the proportion of that budget which is likely to be spent in each month, or quarter.

Sometimes these budgets are considered conditional on some other variable, such as sales, being as forecast, in which case the flexible budget technique is employed.

Businesses differ as to how managers should be accountable for their expenditure. Some firms consider it sufficient for a manager to contain overall expenditure within the total amount budgeted; others expect managers to contain expenditure on each individual item in the budget to within the amount allowed.

The practical control of actual expenditure within budget occurs in two ways:

1 Actual expenditure is recorded on a regular (normally monthly) basis, and is related to the expenditure which was budgeted to occur over the same period. Significant variances are identified as a result, and on the principle that problems which have occurred in the past are likely to occur in the future, attention is centred on particular areas in order that appropriate action can be taken.
2 A more direct impact is made by only allowing expenditure within the budgeted level. This involves the process of vetting decisions to engage employees or place purchase orders, to ensure that by taking a given course of action actual expenditure will not as a result exceed the amount forecast.

In practice, items of expenditure which occur frequently, but where each transaction is of small value (e.g. travelling expenses and cutting tools) are best controlled by the first method, while those of high value but restricted incidence (e.g. advertising expenses and plant overhaul expenses) can be controlled by the second process.

While the mechanism for controlling expenditure within a budget is largely self-evident, the actual process of deciding what items the budget should include presents far greater problems. In this process, there can be no absolute set of rules or neat formula, but the following represents some of the approaches which are, or can be, applied:

1 It is possible that a commitment to incur certain specific expenditure has emerged as part of the strategic planning process, the result of which is that the question is one of 'when' rather than

'whether' the item is to be included in the budget.

2   Such items apart, the most obvious and powerful objective criterion for determining budgets is to require evidence that a particular item of expenditure can be expected to be offset by an even greater level of cost savings elsewhere, or will generate a greater level of profit.

Given that a business is often presented with a number of alternative propositions, each competing for limited cash resources or limited amounts of managerial time, such an approach enables the business to rank these propositions in order of priority.

There is a tendency where this approach is being adopted for those proposing that the expenditure should be made to take a somewhat optimistic view of the savings. To guard against this, it is important that, wherever possible, the expected savings are not only expressed in bald profit terms, but also in terms of some tangible and quantifiable change which will take place, e.g. numbers of employees on a particular activity to be reduced from a to b, quantities sold to be increased from c to d, machine breakdowns to be reduced from d per cent to e per cent.

To ensure that a proper discipline is maintained in these projections, it is necessary subsequently to review whether these anticipated changes were actually achieved. By the same process, if the budgeted item involves expenditure in a series of stages, it is desirable to specify review points at which it can be considered whether the results and costs of the item to date have been as projected, before any further monies are spent.

A further need where, say, staff are being engaged or assigned to undertake a particular, rather than an ongoing task or project, is to identify the likely duration of the task, so that as the scheduled completion date approaches, proper steps are taken to ensure that the staff are deployed on to the next potentially most productive activity.

This profit-and-loss approach to establishing budgets ought to be applied wherever possible, but it is suggested that in practice the number of areas in which it can sensibly be applied is limited, and other, less objective approaches also need to be considered.

3   A basis which can be adopted in preparing budgets is to establish what level of overhead expenditure the business can afford. This process involves establishing the gross margin which it is projected will be earned in the coming period, determining the net

profit which ought to be earned and thereby deducing what can be spent on overheads. Strictly speaking, such an approach inherently assumes that overheads are a non-productive luxury, rather than fundamental in enabling profit to be generated in the short or long term. This approach tends on the one hand to neglect the reality that overhead expenditure will almost inevitably become an increasing part of a thriving business enterprise, while on the other hand, it can result in an attitude of considerable complacency regarding overhead expenditure in times of plenty.

The approach does have some validity if the constraint on overhead expenditure is seen as being one of cash availability rather than profit. After all, what is declared as profit in the short term is largely a product of some fairly rigid accounting conventions regarding the capitalization of expenditure, and a course of action which enables the maximum profits to be declared in one year may be quite the wrong course of action to ensure the long term prosperity and growth of the business. With cash, however, neglect of the short-term requirements can be extremely dangerous for the business.

While in theory the need to generate profit in a particular year need not be considered as a necessary constraint in establishing overhead budgets, in practice the performance of the management of virtually all major businesses is judged by shareholders on the basis of the half-yearly figures; which is a very sound pragmatic reason why this approach is adopted!

While the previous approach can be of assistance in defining the total overheads the business can afford, it does not answer how the money is to be allocated between the various activities of the business.

Individual managers of the business can be asked to state the amount of money they need to have included in the budget for their particular area of responsibility.

However, unless managers are made fully aware of the levels of business activity anticipated in the period of the budget, the answers provided may be consistent with the achievement of excellence for individual functions but be unaffordable for the business as a whole.

On the question of excellence, it should be stressed that in business this is a relative rather than an absolute issue. The objectives of the business need to be clearly stated. Thus, the resources which a warehouse manager would feel are needed to ensure despatch of all orders within twenty-four hours, are likely to be very different from those required for despatching all orders within fourteen days.

It is not proposed to consider the topic of management by objectives in any greater depth, but simply to suggest that it can be rationally considered as integral to the budgetary control process.

5   Determining budgets simply on the basis of what managers ask for is a technique which relies on subjective valuations, and on the integrity and competence of the individual managers which unfortunately are qualities never possessed in equal measure by all human beings. There is a need to have other more objective measurements. The simplest and most commonly applied of these is to base the budget on what was spent in the previous year, together with an appropriate provision for inflation. This historic approach can sometimes be made more sensitive by considering the criteria which determine the amount of overhead expenditure incurred on a particular activity. The number of people employed in a buying office might thus be considered as a function of the volume of productive materials purchased. The number of people and money budgeted for the buying department would, in this case, be varied according to the forecast increase or decrease in the value of production materials puchased in the coming year.

Such an approach has the obvious limitation that it is likely to perpetuate inefficiencies which have arisen in the past. In practice most businesses have a vast range of incidental expenses for which this is the only practical basis on which to compute a budget.

An approach which can sometimes be effective, provided those involved are willing to be committed, is quite arbitrarily to set a low budget for a given year for a particular item or items, to centre people's atention on actually reducing costs to keep within the budget.

6   In circumstances where a budget cannot be established on a logical profit-and-loss basis, it can often be very revealing to consider what would happen if an activity were not undertaken at all, and then work up to the point where the budget will provide for the minimum possible service, but at the same time involve the least resources.

Another approach is to consider what would be the cost if an activity were performed in another way, e.g. renting rather than buying office equipment, despatching goods by train rather than by post. Individually, the examples given are deliberately somewhat trivial, since the wider issues are areas which should receive exposure as part of the process of strategic planning. Cumulatively, consideration of a range of these smaller options can however lead to a significant improvement in operating costs.

The process of overhead cost control should not only be concerned with the establishment of budgets and containing expenditure within these budgets. Indeed, the budgets should be considered as guidelines, not tramlines.

Remember that when the budget is being compiled, there may be only the sketchiest view of the justification of incurring expenditure which represents an investment (e.g. in a new computer system) as opposed to expenditure which is largely inevitable (such as rent and rates). In the case of investment expenditures, the controlling management will not consider itself irrevocably committed to the expenditure simply because it has been included in the budget, but will formally review the case only when the fullest information has been assembled.

By the reverse process, during the period covered by a budget, it is quite likely that an opportunity to advance the prosperity of the business will emerge which had not been previously anticipated, but which would require overhead expenditure for which no provision had been made in the budget. It is important that the application of budgetary control does not result in a business operating in such an inflexible way that such opportunities are turned aside.

A further danger in operating budgetary control is that individuals feel committed to spending all money allocated in a budget in a given period (this is a particularly common problem when budgets are based on historic expenditures). This attitude tends to result in funds being squandered at the end of a budgetary period. The tendency seems to be particularly prevalent in local government but is by no means absent from many large commercial organizations. In practice it is suggested that budgetary control is not of itself sufficient to minimize overhead costs. There is also a requirement for perpetual alertness to prevent unnecessary expense being incurred. In general, a second opinion as to whether money should be spent is helpful.

Overhead items must be considered in the same way as attention is traditionlly concentrated on the production process, by regularly considering the value of a particular activity, considering whether it is being performed by the most effective means, and considering whether the least number of resources is being committed to that activity. It is suggested that business managers are traditionally orientated to think in this way about the direct production process, but often experience difficulty in adapting their thinking to the more abstract problem of overhead control, in spite of the fact that overheads are likely to increase while the direct costs of production are likely to contract.

THE LOSSMAKER SITUATION

The techniques of cost and profit control which have been discussed so far are really only appropriate when the circumstances in which a business finds itself are broadly as expected. In practice, even with the best planning and forecasting, every business will occasionally encounter situations which are substantially worse than would have been expected affecting, if not the business in its totality, at least individual product ranges. The types of problems which create these situations are: encountering greater difficulties in the production of a new product than was expected; encountering abnormal increases in the costs of one of the factors of production; finding that the demand for a new product was lower than expected; encountering a fall in demand owing to the activity of competitors; or experiencing abnormal difficulties as a result of government fiscal policy.

The main difficulty is that although the problem may be perceived very quickly, it is often difficult to know whether it represents a fundamental long-term problem which the business will be unable to overcome, or whether it is a short-term problem which will ultimately be resolved. The issue becomes one as to whether to 'ride out the storm', or to abandon the activity at an early juncture to minimize potential losses.

It follows that the tactics of profit control should be for the business to remain as flexible as possible for as long as possible, so that either option can be pursued.

This is likely to require decisions to be made which on a straight profit-and-loss basis are not necessarily the most attractive propositions. For example, it may be preferable to incur high maintenance costs on old machinery rather than replace it with new equipment; it may be preferable to increase overtime working rather than to engage staff to fill vacancies; it will nearly always be preferable to rent rather than to buy; and investment decisions will be based on which option provides the shortest payback period rather than that which provides theoretically the best discounted cash flow.

A further commercial reality which will need to be recognized in these situation is that inadequate liquidity is more likely to sink the ship than simply the absence of profits as computed on the conventional accounting basis. Attention may need to be centred on minimizing stock holdings, even at the expense of less than optimum production efficiency being achieved. It may well result in length of credit being a significant factor in the selection of suppliers and by the same process, payment terms will assume greater significance in the selling process. The liquidity requirement is also likely strongly to influence the rent or buy decision as much as the flexibility requirement.

A marginal cost approach to business decisions is likely to be far more appropriate in these circumstances than when the situation is close to that which has been expected.

So far as costs are concerned, making in is likely to be more attractive than buying out if the problem is one of demand. It is also likely that in practice so-called direct labour will prove to be very much of a fixed overhead, and in these circumstances it may be appropriate to use direct workers on jobs which generate some revenue although not recovering their full hourly cost.

Perhaps the most significant area of cost and profit control is that of selling price. Businesses are far less certain of the demand curve of price against volume for their products than is implied in conventional economic theory. In practice, businesses tend to establish a price level for their product, find that this results in their earning a reasonable profit, and are then extremely nervous about departing radically from that level for fear of finding themselves in a less advantageous position.

If a business is in the position that relatively high proportions of its costs are fixed, but it can accommodate a substantial increase in volume without incurring any increase in these fixed costs, then it may well gamble on facing an elastic demand curve and reduce its prices. Conversely, if variable costs constitute a high proportion of total costs, or if a substantial increase in fixed costs would be required to provide additional capacity, the business may as well gamble on an inelastic demand curve, and increase prices.

If it is possible to take those gambles in an individual discrete market, rather than across the entire range of business, then this is likely to minimize the risks involved. Thus, the decision to change prices might be tested in a particular self-contained territory, or an individual product out of the range.

All these courses of action are only appropriate as devices to play for time in the hope that the situation will take a turn for the better. What is absolutely fundamental is to make sure that if the situation does not improve, the activity is abandoned before losses put the whole business at risk.

To this end, the point of no return must be clearly predicted. The business must be quite specific about the duration and/or extent of the losses it is prepared to incur before it cuts out a lossmaker, and it should establish these principles as soon as possible once the losses are perceived as occurring.

How the lossmaker will be cut out will depend on the cash flow it generates. If it is a net user of cash the cut needs to be made as soon as possible, but in other situations it can be allowed to fade out until it reaches the stage where it ceases to be a positive generator of cash.

The lossmaker situation is one of the few areas in which business decisions must be considered as relatively intractable once made.

Concurrently with reaching a decision as to when to abandon a lossmaker, the business should also start to formulate policies as to whether alternative ventures should be pursued, and tactically, how the minimum loss can be incurred in disposing of the lossmaker and its associated resources and assets. In this latter respect, a marginal costing approach is again likely to be highly relevant.

THE HUMAN FACTOR

Clearly, most of the techniques outlined above are concerned with the process of analysis. They identify points of weakness and areas of opportunity. They do not stipulate the specific action which needs to be taken, nor do they, of themselves, result in action being taken. Costs and profits are actually controlled by people taking action, albeit in an informed manner.

Unfortunately, human beings behave in complex and somewhat unpredictable ways. With a machine, the pressing of an appropriate button will automatically result in its performing a prescribed operation – provide a human being with a financial analysis, and a state of inertia is just as likely to result! A vital aspect of cost and profit control is getting people to react to the information provided. Clearly, this is an extremely complex subject, and arguably practical experience is of more relevance in solving the problem than is academic theory. However, the factors which determine the way people react to financial data fall broadly into the following categories.

1. *Comprehension.* Whoever receives financial data and is expected to act on it should understand its meaning and significance. At foreman level, this may amount to an understanding of the concept and significance of measuring labour utilization and efficiency. At more senior levels, a more general appreciation of the derivation, construction and relevance of the profit and loss account, balance sheet and cash flow statement is probably called for. In a wider context, the overall performance of a business is dependent on the interrelated activities of the departments within it. However, the existence of a departmental structure presents a natural barrier to people perceiving this interrelationship, and encourages them to pursue narrow objectives associated only with the advancement of their particular specialism. There is thus a need for all managers to develop a general understanding of the problems and objectives of other functions in the business.

2. *Communication.* The clarity with which financial reports are presented is important in the process of communication. In addition, as has been mentioned previously, it is essential that the resolution of problems is identified as the responsibility of a specific individual, e.g. it is desirable that a problem of generally high tooling costs is identified as being specifically associated with the press shop, rather than the factory as a whole. However, the periodic formal report should represent only one level at which costs and profits are controlled. As a matter of normality, and on an informal basis, particular financial problems or opportunities should be perpetually in the process of being identified and discussed with a view to action being taken by those involved. It is essential for this process to take place if financial problems are to be avoided rather than tackled after the event.

It may be difficult for this process to occur in organizations with very rigid defined structures, and clearly it requires a generally high level of comprehension, and an even greater degree of commitment from the parties involved.

3. *Commitment.* As a starting point, the more committed the employees of a business are to making it successful, the more readily are they likely to react to information on cost and profit control. The

degree of this commitment will be determined by a combination of the financial rewards offered by the business, the significance of the threat of loss of security, the basic satisfaction which the job provides, and the sense of communion with fellow employees. While this general area is popularly regarded as the preserve of the personnel function, it is suggested that it would be naive of someone concerned with cost and profit control to ignore its relationship with profit maximization.

On a more specific level, it is one thing to agree upon seeking to meet the objectives of a business, but it is quite another to agree upon the means by which this objective should be reached. A budget or forecast which has been agreed will clearly receive a higher degree of personal commitment than one which has been imposed. Unfortunately, economic conditions are often such that the aspirations of all individuals in an organization cannot be fulfilled in establishing such budgets. In those situations, it is imperative that at least the overall position of the business which has created these constraints is fully understood by all involved. In addition, if the strategy of the business is clearly defined, then individuals may well be prepared to modify their natural aspirations if they perceive them either as fundamentally inconsistent with the strategic objectives, or simply tactically unattainable in the short term, but realizable in the long term.

THE STRATEGY OF COST CONTROL

Most businesses find the climate in which they are operating increasingly competitive. Developments in communications and transport have made the world a smaller place, enabling a wider range of suppliers to enter particular markets, with legislation promoting 'freer' trade facilitating this process. Other, traditional markets may have become closed as countries have sought to protect and develop their own industrial bases. Overlaying the whole process, the rate at which technology advances is increasing, with the consequence that competitors can steal a competitive edge by advancing the fundamental design of their products, or processes employed in their manufacture.

It needs to be recognized that the techniques of standard costing and budgetary control are concerned with businesses looking inwards at their affairs, and optimizing cost for a given situation. For the purpose of day-to-day control, such an approach is both necessary and appropriate. It does not of itself centre attention on what is happening in the outside world, with the risk that one may thus become the most efficient blacksmith or manufacturer of valve radios, only to find that the market has moved away.

The process of addressing this problem is a fundamental issue for the business as a whole, and requires clarity from the outset as to the product(s) and market(s) which the business is intending to supply, and the means by which it is to differentiate its product or service from that of the competition.

The focus of cost control becomes the necessity to match or improve upon the cost control achieved by competitors. In this regard 'cost' has many facets, representing the fundamental cost effectiveness of the design of the product and the methods employed in its production, through the source and price of the inputs used in production, and on to methods by which the product or service is marketed and distributed. Regard may also need to be taken to the way the business is organized and where it is located, relative to that of the competition.

This process is of assistance not only in identifying the areas for improvement within the business itself, but also in identifying areas of weakness in the competition. Nor should the process be considered one of slavish imitation: if a business has decided to differentiate itself on the basis of quality and service, and a competitor achieves lower 'cost' by sacrificing those, the business has little to gain by following the competitor in this regard, *unless* it decides to change its basic strategy.

The essence of cost control by comparison to competitors is consideration of cost *efficiency*. Put another way, 'does the competitor do it better?' While a business will never have access to the competitor's exact costs, reasonable estimates can be made by observation. In general terms, methods of production employed by the competitor are determinable by technical examination of the product, while market intelligence should reveal the principal sources of supply for materials. The competitor's route to market should be a known fact, and a fair assessment of the scale and disposition of the sales force can be made. The cost of premises and workforce can broadly be established on the basis of their size and location.

Where points of difference emerge between the circumstances of the business and its competitor, the business should challenge its own practice. For example, a competitor is using components from a proprietary manufacturer, while the business is manufacturing those itself. If the competitor's practice is 'wrong', why is that so? Nothing in this process should be presumed to be immutable since the concern is with strategy. For example, if the competitor benefits from operating in a lower labour cost area, by what means can the business match unit labour costs, or should it reconsider its own location? If a competitor benefits from economy of scale, how is this scale achieved and what steps can the business take to emulate that process? If there is a process by which the cost of the competitor can be matched, this must be incorporated into the operating development strategy of the business. If the competitor has an immutable cost advantage, then the business must ensure that its product or service is sufficiently differentiated from that of the competitor.

The process described above concerns the defensive aspects of a cost control strategy. The assumption must be made that the competitor is not going to stand still, and thus a process of emulation will always leave the business one step behind. Offensive aspects of a cost control strategy are concerned with being better than the competitor. The process described above should reveal the businesses' relative strengths, and exploit these. More positively, it is true that the world will beat a path to the door of the man who designs a better mousetrap. In practical terms, however, it is very difficult to cause wholly original ideas for cost reduction to be generated, and even more problematic and risky to develop them into a working reality. Businesses can, nevertheless, develop a competitive edge in their own industry, by considering the solutions adopted by companies with similar problems operating in other industries. For example, a business involved in mass-production of assemblies might refer to the practices adopted in the white goods industries; a business with a problem in distribution might refer to the retail sector for inspiration. The business will be looking at practices in a diverse range of industries, dependent on the particular area of operations where it is seeking to reduce cost.

The process of strategic cost control, as described above, is necessarily more a question of business orientation than of numeric technique. In summary, however, it possesses the following characteristics.

1 It provides a relatively specific focus on areas where the emphasis on cost ccontrol should be centred.
2 It can provide specific objectives for cost reduction, which are not simply academic, but necessary for the survival of the business,

and are, by definition, attainable.

3   It requires a specific attitude to be adopted by the business as a whole, consistent with the general philosophy that companies should be market led. It demands that every manager has accountability for cost in a strategic sense as well as in a tactical sense. The human factor as described in the previous section is vital to the process of strategic cost control.

FURTHER READING

Drury, C. *Management and Cost Accounting*, Van Nostrand, 1985.

Horngren, C.T. and Foster, G., *Cost Accounting: A Managerial Emphasis*, 6th edition, Prentice Hall, 1987.

Layne, W.A. and Rickwood, C., *Cost Accounting*, Macmillan, 1984.

Lock, D. (editor), *Project Management Handbook*, Gower, 1987.

Moriarty, S., *Cost Accounting*, Harper and Rowe, 1985.

Mott, G., *Management Accounting*, Gower, 1987.

Owler, L.W.J. and Brown, J.L., *Wheldon's Cost Accounting*, 1984.

Pizzey, A., *Principles of Cost Accountancy*, Cassell, 1987.

Taylor, A.H., *Costing for Managers*, Holt, Reinhart and Winston, 1984.

Wilson, R.M.S., *Cost Control Handbook*, Gower, 1982.

12

Controlling the Funds

R. Aitken Davies

This chapter is allied to the author's analysis of Cash Forecasting in Part 1. He now examines, from an essentially practical viewpoint, the methods by which the funds flowing through a business can be controlled and focuses on the control of working capital, especially stock, debtors and creditors. He emphasises that it is the efficient conversion of business inputs into cash which generates profits and maintains the solvency of the business.

INTRODUCTION

Like much of business terminology the word 'funds' can have a number of meanings. In the present context it means the money or money's worth which flows into and out of a business in the course of its operations. It embraces the assets which are held for conversion into money and the liabilities which are due to be paid in the near future, in other words the current assets (stock, debtors, cash and short-term investments) and the current liabilities (creditors and short-term indebtedness).

The difference between current assets and current liabilities is normally called 'net current assets' or 'net current liabilities', by accountants. Other titles are: 'Circulating Capital' and 'Working Capital'. Because the latter term is probably the most familiar, it will be used throughout this chapter. Its use does not, however, imply that other elements of business capital do not 'work'. Funds are invested in the business on a long term basis, as in fixed assets, and these assets are essential factors in generating the income which flows into working capital.

The existence of adequate working capital is a measure of the solvency of the business considered over a period of roughly a year. The most immediate indication of solvency is 'liquid capital' which comprises cash and assets realizable in the short-term, (such as short-term investments), less current liabilities.

The survival of a business depends on its remaining solvent, in other words its ability to pay its creditors. This simple fact makes the control of funds of such great importance. The focus of control must be on working capital. Managing the funds is usually regarded as the direct responsibility of the financial controller. However, the movement of funds is due basically to the business operations, and the ultimate responsibility for maintaining solvency must lie with the managers.

THE ELEMENTS OF WORKING CAPITAL CONTROL

The four ingredients

What, then, are the characteristics of working capital which make it so important to justify the continued and close attention of the financial controller?

The ingredients in the control activity may be characterized thus:

1 Servicing the business.
2 Minimizing the costs.
3 Security.
4 Liquidity.

These elements are not mutually exclusive but interact to create the nub of the control problem, which is simply to find the optimum level of working capital conducive to and supportive of the successful business.

Servicing the business

The items embraced by the term 'working capital' sustain the business by bridging the time lapse between the incurring of expenditure in the manufacture and supply of a product or service and the receipt of the consideration from the purchaser. Thus, working capital provides materials and labour for stock and the overhead activities to

Controlling the funds

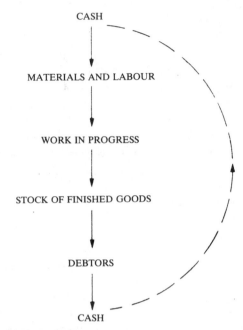

CASH

MATERIALS AND LABOUR

WORK IN PROGRESS

STOCK OF FINISHED GOODS

DEBTORS

CASH

Fig. 12.1 Working capital service cycle

support the production and selling functions of the business. There-after, it finances the debtors from whom further funds will be extracted, in due course, to pay for the next cycle of activity. In practical terms this means that the service function of working capital can be seen as a progression of cash, through the other forms of current asset, back into cash as illustrated in Fig. 12.1.

This figure also symbolizes the trading cycle and thereby serves to highlight a critical test of the success of an enterprise: which is that the cash at the end of the working capital service cycle should exceed the input at the beginning, the difference being realized profit before capital charges.

It is not always appreciated by non-financial managers that ad-equate cash flow and working capital can be at risk in periods of expansion as well as recession. Uncontrolled action to increase sales will tend to result in high levels of stocks and debtors, as well as possibly excessive credit given to customers. In turn, working capital will be depleted and rises are likely to occur in operating costs and probably in interest charges. In the end the survival of the business will be jeopardized by lack of funds.

Minimizing the costs

Business managers are usually aware of the costs associated with investment in working capital whether the funds are internally generated or are raised from external sources or are a mixture of both. This was not always the case, particularly where, in a well-established organization, funds which supported working capital levels were internally generated. If the funds are internally generated, the cost can be regarded as the higher one of the rate of interest which could be obtained by investing in the external money market, and the return on the enterprise's marginal investment opportunity which has to be foregone because of the resources tied up in net current assets. In the case of external funds, the cost is the higher one of the rewards they command by way of interest/dividend and, again, the return foregone from the marginal investment opportunity.

Inadequate stocks are likely to involve loss of sales and so will an unduly stringent credit policy. It may be worth while to invest in stocks in order to obtain discounts or bulk purchases or to prepare for a sales promotion campaign. Thus in the control of working capital cost minimization needs to be reconciled to profit maximization.

Security

The third element of working capital control is security. This encompasses many areas of concern in relation to the integrity of the current assets in which funds are employed by the organization. In the case of stock, the questions of theft, loss, deterioration and control of consumption must be considered and managed. In relation to debtors, their stability, inclination to pay and trading reputation must be considered if the organization's credit control function is to perform adequately. The security problems of cash are self-evident.

As a general rule, one would expect the security problem to increase as the level of current assets increases but, as is the case with so many general rules, a host of exceptions can be found in particular circumstances. Hence, one may experience no additional security difficulties from holding £1M in cash than those experienced in holding £0.5M; nor in storing 15 tonnes instead of 10 tonnes of copper in an adequately appointed building; nor of granting £50 000 rather than £40 000 credit to a solvent and reputable customer.

Liquidity

The essence of the liquidity problem could not be simpler, namely that an organization must always be in a position to meet its liabilities as they arise. Consequently, in this area, working capital control is especially concentrated on cash and the need to predict cash requirements so that potential surpluses and deficits are forecast well before they prove to be an embarrassment. Problems of cash forecasting are considered in Chapter 8. Suffice to say here that the conditions in which cash is useful to have in quantities exceeding what is necessary to meet immediate liabilities must be very rare indeed. It is therefore contended that hard cash is one element of working capital which should be consistently minimized, even if this means that periodic surpluses are invested in short-term money markets.

WORKING CAPITAL BUDGETING

If the process of constructing an organization's budget were to be viewed as consisting of a consecutive series of logical steps, then it should be apparent that the sales forecast would come first and the working capital budget last. Budgeting is, of course, an iterative process. Each element of the budget interacts with the others and modifications are made as the consequences of assumptions become apparent in the budgeting process. The working capital budget cannot be prepared until all the other budgets are available since, by definition, it must be a quantification of the current assets and liabilities needed to service the levels of activity implicit in those other budgets.

The interrelationships of the different components of what, when integrated, will become the organization's master budget are complex and in no case is this more true than in the case of the working capital and other budgets as Fig. 12.2 illustrates. Fortunately, the algorithms associated with the compilation of the master budget are well within the state of the art of modern computing technology and can be represented by a financial model. The obvious advantage of modelling the budget is that a range of sensitivities can be assessed and the effects on the business's working capital requirements quantified with relative ease.

It is customary, for monitoring and reporting purposes, to phase agreed budgets into review periods (usually of four weeks or a

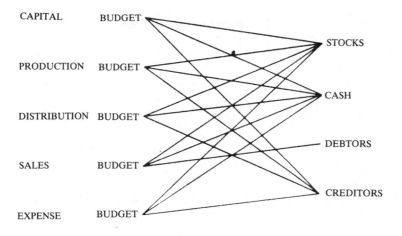

Fig. 12.2   Interrelationship of working capital and other budgets

calendar month each) and this practice is of particular benefit to the working capital budget because of the transitory nature of the items which it comprises. Indeed, in relation to the cash element of this budget, it may be desirable, or even necessary, to work on much shorter review periods for reasons of liquidity monitoring, perhaps of a week each or, in extreme circumstances, on a daily basis.

Stocks

The term 'stocks' is taken here in the broadest sense to cover:-

1   raw materials (which service the production function of the business);
2   work in progress (which also services the production function);
3   finished goods (which service the sales function);
4   stores (which service production in the form of bought out components and consumables and the overhead activities of the business such as in the maintenance and administration functions).

As indicated earlier in this chapter, the service function of working capital is but one of four elements in determining optimum levels, the others being cost, security and liquidity. In practice, these competing

Table 12.1
Budgeting for stocks
(A check list of factors to be considered in determining stock budget levels)

FACTOR	QUESTION
Business Activity	
1. Plans and budgets	Are increased/decreased stocks required to service expanding/contracting trading activity?
2. Periodicity	Are there seasonal or other factors affecting levels required in particular accounting periods?
3. Product mix	How are sales and production broken down between individual product lines?
4. Marketing	What confidence levels of immediate delivery are acceptable?
Physical Considerations	
5. Nature of stocks	How long and in what condition can they be stored?
6. Storage capacity	What are the physical limitations on storage from both security and space viewpoints?
7. Lead times	What are the time lapses between:
Supplier	(a) order to supplier and delivery to stock
Manufacture	(b) receipt of order for out of stock line and delivery to customer
Distribution	(c) receipt of order for an item not in stock locally and delivery to customer
Economic	
8. Forecasting sensitivity	What would be the effect of $\pm10\%$ (say) errors in budget assumptions for sales and production?
9. Contingencies	What, if any, buffers are desirable to allow for the effects of errors in forecasts, industrial action and other unpredictable events?
10. Economic order quantities	What benefits can be obtained from bulk discounts avoiding small order surcharges and similar factors?
11. Economic batch quantities	What are the economics of producing different batch sizes of the company's product lines? (e.g. tooling costs v. stockholding costs).
12. Storage costs	What is the capital cost of holding the proposed level of stocks? What are the revenue costs of storage? How do these compare with projected price movements in raw materials and labour inputs? What alternative uses for the funds thus employed are being foregone?

elements give rise to a wide range of questions which must be addressed by the financial controller in the budget compilation exercise and in monitoring the working capital budget during the budget implementation period. The check list in Table 12.1 identifies some of the main considerations that will apply.

Operational research has created a number of useful concepts and analytical techniques for the purpose of deriving theoretical optimum stock levels. These processes can be modelled and it would be negligent not to apply the rigours of scientific analysis to this area of an organization's activity. However, there is a danger of becoming too mechanistic in stock control policy and the financial controller must avoid an inflexible imposition of such controls as economic batch quantities and minimum re-order levels. These will depend on essentially subjective judgements of what will happen in the economy generally and in the specific markets in which the organization's suppliers operate. Again, it is now quite feasible and desirable for the stock control activity in most organizations to be computer modelled, thus facilitating sensitivity analysis and producing a sensible stocking policy for each of the company's raw materials, products and stores lines based on flexible optimum quantity levels.

Debtors

Debtors are a function of credit sales, the incidence of those sales in the budget period and the organization's credit policy. Inevitably the success of a credit control policy depends on the rigour with which it is applied. The degree of such rigour in turn depends upon the strength of the company's market as well as the motivation and direction of those concerned in selecting and applying the policy. But whatever the credit control policy and however effectively it is applied, there will always be an element of overdue debt unless the business is in the fortunate position of being cash only such as a high-street super-market.

It is possible to develop sophisticated debtors analysis by computerized models feeding from the sales budget, augmented by an analysis of the type of sales expected (cash, credit and extended credit for example) and the anticipated characteristics of the customers themselves. For example, payments for credit sales from large organizations may be regarded as fairly secure but, as anyone knows who has traded with a major UK company, there are delay mechanisms inherent in bureaucracy. On the other hand, trade with small jobbing builders is notoriously volatile and it would be inappropriate to apply the same assumptions to the rates of payment and default as one would to a multi-national giant.

A further factor which should be borne in mind when deriving the debtors budget is that there is an inclination on the part of those to whom credit facilities are extended to use payment of creditors as a short term instrument of cash flow management. In times of restricted credit in the money markets, it would be wise to assume, (though not necessarily to accept) that payments may be rather slower than in more relaxed financial conditions.

Again, however, there is good reason to avoid the pitfall of over-sophistication in deriving working capital budgets. The best indicator is often a reference to historical trends. Unless a change of policy is envisaged in the budget period (e.g. by introducing discounts for early settlement) debtors budgeting is best effected by reference to a percentage of sales, as analysed by relevant accounting periods, with the credit period determined in accordance with past experience.

In the absence of any historical information (for example, in a new market or for a new company) a forward looking assessment will be required, based on:

1 Credit policy to be adopted;
2 Type of custom expected (e.g. allowing plenty of time for payment from jobbing builders),
3 Strength of the company's market position (e.g. a monopoly supplier of an essential product can exert considerable pressure for timely settlement).

Creditors

Creditors budgeting is, in many ways, the antithesis of debtors budgeting. Instead of asking what credit should be allowed and what pressures can be exerted to secure timely payment for sales, the financial controller must ask what credit period can be negotiated or assumed before settling the company's debts and, the corollary, what pressures his or her company's creditors can apply to minimize the period of credit.

It may be helpful, in this connnection, to categorize creditors along the following lines:

1 statutory (e.g. tax, national insurance and licences) where legal sanctions may be applicable if payment is delayed;
2 essential: any interruption of deliveries may affect the company's performance quickly and adversely;

3 dependent: the suppliers rely on the company for a substantial proportion of their business and could not afford the loss of this. Extended credit may be negotiable with this category of supplier subject to their own liquidity problems and to any business ethics the company may wish to observe.

4 Discount: worthwhile financial advantages are offered in return for early settlement.

Such classification of creditors has a place particularly where liquidity problems are arising. However, for most budgetary purposes, it is sensible to assume, in the first instance, that payment of creditors will be effected by the due dates on the grounds that such an approach would be conducive to goodwill of the suppliers and, generally, to the reputation of the firm. On this basis, the creditors budget can be related directly to the budget for purchase of goods and services and the settlement terms agreed with the suppliers.

The financial controller must also be alert to obligations which do not arise in the normal course of trading activity, but which must be provided for in the creditors budget and consequently in the cash forecast.

Reference to the capital budget will be required to assess the timing and scale of settlement of capital creditors. In the case of existing commitments, this exercise should be a relatively straightforward one of extracting details from extant capital contracts. Cruder measures will, however, be needed for the uncommitted element of the capital budget since it is unlikely that detailed work programmes and contract terms covering aspects such as progress payments will be available at the time of budget compilation. A further complication is that provision must be made for the release of any retentions becoming due for payment against existing or completed contracts for capital expenditure in accordance with the terms of those contracts.

Appropriations of profit in the shape of dividends and taxation must also be accommodated in the creditors budget projections and the financial controller may have to construct a profit-and-loss appropriation budget if this has not already been done as part of the company's overall budget process. Table 12.2 below should serve as an aide memoire to the compilation of the creditors budget.

Cash

Detailed consideration of the problems of budgeting for cash, a key

Table 12.2
Calculating the creditors' budget

Category	Source of information	Common settlement terms
Purchases for stock	Stock budget	Monthly
Direct costs	Expense budgets	Monthly or quarterly[1]
Capital investment	Capital budget	Subject to contract
Statutory (UK)		
Value added tax	Sales/creditor's budgets	Quarterly[2]
Advance Corporation Tax/ Income Tax	P and L appropriation	Quarterly[3]
Corporation Tax	P and L appropriation	Annually[4]
Social security contributions	Expense budgets (wages and salaries)	Monthly
Appropriations of profit	P and L appropriation	Bi-annually[5]

[1] Direct costs in this sense implies that they are not charged through stores control procedures, e.g. services (electricity, gas, telephone), cleaning contracts, maintenance contracts.

[2] VAT represented by an excess of output tax (primarily on sales) over input tax (primarily on purchases) must be accounted for to the Customs and Excise on the fixed quarter days relevant to the particular company.

[3] Advance Corporation Tax on qualifying distributions (primarily dividends) and income tax retained on annual payments must be accounted for to the Inland Revenue on the calendar quarter days and, in addition, at the end of the company's accounting period if this does not fall on a quarter day.

[4] Corporation Tax is normally payable 9 months from the end of the company's accounting period.

[5] Appropriations of profit cover items such as dividends, capital distributions and financing costs (e.g. bank and debenture interest).

element in the working capital budget, is given in an earlier chapter.

The completed working capital budget

Derivation of the cash budget should complete the detailed construction of the working capital budget which can then be consolidated and presented in a suitable form. The particular circumstances of the organization will determine what constitutes a suitable form for presentation of the working capital budget but Table 12.3 should serve most purposes with the minimum of adaptation to individual requirements. With the initial derivation of the working capital budget in the organization's budgetary control process, it is likely that there will be unacceptable aspects which will necessitate further

Table 12.3
Format for working capital budget

ITEM	Review period	1	2	3	4	5	6	7	8	9	10	11	12
	WORKING CAPITAL BUDGET 19—										(+) = current asset (−) = current liability £000's		

DEBTORS

STOCK

Raw materials
Work in progress
Finished goods
Stores

SHORT-TERM INVESTMENTS

CASH

CURRENT ASSETS

CREDITORS

Trade
Statutory
Other

SHORT-TERM LIABILITIES

NET WORKING CAPITAL

BUDGET ACTION NOTES

235

iterations of the budget. These will be either for the purposes of eliminating the cause of the problem or for seeing that it is accommodated comfortably within the action plans which will derive from the budget. As has been said before, revisions of the budget should be easy given the present availability of cheap but effective microprocessing and software technology. Examples which will require budget revisions are cash shortfalls arising from stocking up to meet a sales surge; arrival of the due date for payment of the company's corporation tax bill; the declaration and payment of interim and final dividends; a contractual date for payment of a substantial capital creditor. All these can be smoothed when seen in the full context of the working capital budget and the actions which have been deemed necessary can be documented in the 'budget action notes' section of the form shown in Table 12.3.

WORKING CAPITAL MONITORING AND CONTROL

One confident assertion which can be made about budgetary control in general is that, whatever the quality of the budget compilation exercise, the effort will be rendered worthless unless first, there is a sound monitoring procedure and, second, the information available through that monitoring procedure is actually used by those in authority as a basis for making decisions. Here, one might note the ever present danger of confusing the words monitoring and control in relation to budgeting. Neither the compilation nor the monitoring of a budget provides any control intrinsically; the control must be exercised by those with the power and the perception to react effectively to the messages created by the budgetary control process.

The way budgetary control assists those in authority to manage their business is that it facilitates the comparison of performance against a series of pre-determined indicators (or budgets). The working capital budget differs from most other indicators in only one major respect; its constituents fluctuate rather than accumulate. In this sense, the phased working capital budgets can be regarded as being essentially self-contained within the accounting or review periods, in contrast to the other budgets where aggregation is necessary to reflect the company's progress towards its objectives.

This leads to the matter of presentation of the working capital monitoring data. As with all questions relating to the display of information, the matter is essentially subjective. It would be presumptuous to indicate any sort of standard format in such a context

Time	Component	Budget			Flexed Budget			Actual			Variation from Flexed Budget			Forecast −−/−−/−−			(−) liability (£000's) Note line below
		1	2	3	4	5	6	7	8	9	10	11	12	13	14	15	16
	DEBTORS																
1	Trade	X			X			X			X			X			1
2	Other	X	X		X	X		X	X		X	X		X	X		2
	STOCK																
3	Raw materials	X			X			X			X			X			3
4	Work in progress	X			X			X			X			X			4
5	Finished goods	X			X			X			X			X			5
6	Stores	X	X		X	X		X	X		X	X		X	X		6
7	SHORT-TERM INVESTMENTS		X			X			X			X			X		7
	CASH																
8	In hand	X			X			X			X			X			8
9	At bank	X	X		X	X		X	X		X	X		X	X		9
10	CURRENT ASSETS			X			X			X			X			X	
	CREDITORS																
11	Trade	X			X			X			X			X			11
12	Statutory	X			X			X			X			X			12
13	Other	X	X		X	X		X	X		X	X		X	X		13
14	SHORT-TERM LIABILITIES		X			X			X			X			X		14
15	CURRENT LIABILITIES			X			X			X			X			X	15
16	NET WORKING CAPITAL			X			X			X			X			X	16

Comments and Variance Analysis

Note no.

Include in this section:

(a) main factors in flexing of original budget;

(b) explanations of major variances from flexed budget;

(c) significant features of forecast for next review period;

(d) action and recommended action notes.

but Table 12.4 is included as a straightforward approach to monitoring the elements of a working capital budget.

It will be seen from Table 12.4 that provision is made for the 'flexing' of the working capital budget. The term 'flexing' is used here to indicate that the budget has been revised to take account of known variations in the original assumptions in order that time and effort is not expended in variance analysis and reporting of factors which have already been discerned and explained. Sceptics often claim budget flexing is merely a cosmetic exercise designed to conceal management shortcomings by adjusting budgets to coincide more closely with actual performance, when the real need is for strenuous efforts to raise actual performance to meet the objectives implicit in the original budget. However, there is considerable merit in flexing the working capital budget to reflect changing circumstances and thereby to preserve its value as a front-ranking performance indicator. For example, a shortfall in sales should reduce both the debtors and the stock requirements of the company, not to mention the inflow of cash from the proceeds of sales. Any criticism that the flexing hides shortcomings of performance elsewhere can be met by showing comparison of actual performance against both the original and flexed budgets, as indeed the sample format in Table 12.4 seeks to do.

A further valuable refinement in working capital monitoring is the use of forecasting by which means requirements can be regularly reviewed and updated independently of the budget. Such predictive reporting is particularly beneficial in the shorter term when the confidence levels in the predictions should be at their height and the company's liquidity considerations at their most immediate. Again, provision is made for such forecasts to be recorded in Table 12.4 and it is suggested that predictions should be for the end of the subsequent review period, although there is no reason why a longer forecasting cycle cannot be used where appropriate.

In the remaining paragraphs of this chapter, some more specific matters of interest are raised in relation to the monitoring and control of the components of the working capital budget.

Stock

Reference has been made earlier in this chapter to the advantages of a computerized stock control model. Such a model will enable any changes in the range of variables affecting stockholding to be introduced into the system and revised optima then computed at great speed. Thus, such factors as a drop in sales, change in sales mix, lengthening of delivery times for bought-out components or a change in prices can be assimilated rapidly into the stock control model and the stock budget flexed accordingly. In normal conditions, the use of the model in the monitoring process should facilitate quick decisions on stocking policy and enable positive direction to be given to the person concerned in good time to avoid adverse trends.

Whilst the algorithms for the stock control model are outside the scope of this overview, it should be appreciated that two critical inputs to the model for each line held in stock will be:

1 the anticipated stock consumption for each review period (the aggregate of which might generate optimism and trigger stock levels in that period) and
2 the economic re-order level at which those responsible for the physical control of stores should initiate a replenishment order.

The stock control model is not a complete answer to a company's inventory policy. The model (somewhat reassuringly) cannot replace the entrepreneurial nous, experience and business instinct required, for example, in executing successful commodity deals in spot markets, nor indicate when losses should be cut by disposal of obsolescent, slow moving or deteriorating stores. In these matters and others like them, commercial acumen must be brought into play, and the financial controller's role possibly limited to the provision of advice in the following areas:

1 marginal cost of storage;
2 net realizable values;
3 economic indicators in markets for stocks/stores concerned;
4 projected consumption based on latest sales forecast;
5 cost of capital;
6 effects of replacement costs on the organization's trading performance.

The compilation from scratch of delivery lead times, consumption rates and stocking costs for hundreds, or perhaps thousands, of stock and stores items is a lengthy exercise. It may be appropriate here to apply the 80/20 rule of thumb. In this context, the rule claims that 80 per cent of the stock value will be represented by 20 per cent of stock items and vice versa. Whilst one must be cautious with rules of thumb, the principle of concentrating initially on high value stocks and stores for a major exercise in developing input for a sophisticated stock control model is not a bad one. From this point, one can work through the items on a company's inventory gradually and parameters for each stock item can be reviewed on a regular cyclical basis to ensure that the optima are updated for changing circumstances. The length of the review cycle will depend upon the nature of the industry; engineering companies, for example, may find a three year cycle entirely adequate, whereas an organization involved in fashionable attire would be unlikely to benefit from anything longer than a quarterly review. The results of a continuous review can be regularly fed into the stock control model which will assist in flexing the stock budgets automatically as well as keeping the overall stock levels under permanent scrutiny. The main characteristics of each stock line which need to be included in the review are:

1 delivery lead times for bought out material/components;
2 manufacturing lead times for stock items made in-house;
3 distribution lead times for stock items kept in geographically de-centralized stores;
4 economic batch quantities for manufacture;
5 economic order quantities for purchase;
6 the need to maintain buffer stocks for contingencies;
7 rates of consumption;
8 marginal costs of storage.

Debtors

The mechanics of credit control, the first stage of debtors control, are fairly common to all organizations. There should be a procedure for obtaining credit references for each new customer and then establishing a credit limit based on the expected level of trade and the client's financial circumstances. Where, subsequently, the credit limit is on the verge of being exceeded, it is reviewed and an increase allowed or credit withdrawn pending payment against the existing debt, as deemed appropriate. Similarly, where debts are not settled within the laid down credit terms, suitable steps must be taken, with the option available of withdrawing or extending credit facilities and/or taking legal action to recover amounts overdue. Credit decisions are not purely mechanical matters: pragmatism is called for in the degree of control exercised in each case. For instance, if business is slow and the market weak, less stringent policies may be rewarded.

Conversely, buoyant sales may support a more rigid policy although, even in this happy position, it may pay to think of the future in relation to goodwill won or lost during times of plenty.

The level of debtors has a direct yet deferred relationship to credit sales based on average credit permitted. An extremely useful measure of debtors control is an 'age analysis' which can be compared with historic and budgeted trends to indicate the success or otherwise of current policy. This information can be incorporated into a regular debtors monitoring report such as is illustrated in Table 12.5. If the argument that debtors cannot be subject to the same scientific assessment as say stocks, is accepted, then there remains a gap in the budgetary control process. In practice, this gap will normally be filled by commercial and intuitive judgements on the part of the sales/ marketing management. Experienced management accountants will know that these managers are usually reluctant to quantify their business judgements. A useful stratagem is to delegate responsibility for accounts collection to the sales representative who secured the original purchase, once the debt becomes overdue. A further refinement of this policy is to reflect the degree of success in avoiding overdue debts in any schemes for calculating bonuses and commissions for the sales force, a concept fully vindicated by the fact that it is the payment for goods which realizes profit rather than the sale. Apart from the financial stimulus to the salespeople, it is well accepted that personal contact is the most effective means of collecting accounts, where the customer is still solvent.

Cash discounts can be used to encourage early payment of invoices but, in practice it is difficult to justify a rate which is significant enough to influence large organizations to settle more quickly than they would otherwise. For example two-and-a-half per cent is not an uncommon inducement for prompt settlement of accounts, but, whilst it represents an annual rate of 30 per cent, it does not generally seem to have the desired impact on large corporate debtors. There has to be a fairly serious liquidity problem, or, alternatively, a high return investment opportunity available to justify such a cash discount, and the organization must always be alert to the danger of unscrupulous creditors (and they certainly exist) who subtract cash discounts whether or not they pay by the contractual settlement date. On the other hand, industry and commerce is not receptive to the imposition of penalties for late payments in respect of regular credit trading and any attempt to operate such a policy is likely to be met with adverse commercial reactions except in an extremely strong

Table 12.5
Debtor's Monitoring Report

AGE ANALYSIS		Review period ended —				
		Under 28 days	28–56 days	56–84 days	Over 84 days	Bad
1 Current position	(£)	X	X	X	X	X
	(%)	X	X	X	X	X
2 Budget	(%)	X	X	X	X	X
3 Historic trend	(%)	X	X	X	X	X
4 Last review period	(%)	X	X	X	X	X
5 Next review period	(£)	X	X	X	X	X
(forecast)	(%)	X	X	X	X	X

ANALYSIS OVER 84 DAYS

Customer	Credit limit	Salesman responsible	Amount outstanding	Over 84 days	Action
1					
2					
3					
4					
5					
6					
7					
8					
9					
10					

sellers' market. The truth is that there is no substitute for vigorous credit control policies backed up by regular personal contacts with customers:

Dividends

There is some scope for manoeuvre in the dividend policy adopted by the company, although the financial controller's options are limited by what is acceptable to the Board, and ultimately, to the shareholders. Whilst it is usually most desirable that as much of the company's fixed and working capital requirement as possible is financed from retained profits, it is common to find deep-rooted prejudice amongst Board members in favour of recommending at least the maintenance of the previous level of dividend whatever the profit performance; what is more, this attitude is equally commonly reflected in the expectations of the shareholders. The financial controller may have to be satisfied with persuading his Board to limit any proposed increase where cash is tight.

However, apart from the size of the dividend, there is the possibility of synchronizing the timing of the payment with a good period in the company's cash flow profile. Thus, it may be an advantage for a retail company to pay its dividend in December when it should be enjoying the fruits of a seasonal upsurge in sales. In addition, it should be noted that, under UK tax law, Advance Corporation Tax (ACT) is payable on dividends at a level equivalent to the basic rate of income tax on the amount distributed as if that were a sum net of basic rate income tax. Thus, if the dividend were £150 000 and basic rate of tax 25 per cent ACT of £50 000 would be due (being $\frac{1}{3}$ of £150 000). ACT can be offset against the company's main corporation tax liability and, in addition, against equivalent ACT paid on any dividends it may receive from UK companies, but there may be substantial timing differences for cash budgeting purposes.

FUNDS FLOW STATEMENTS

The importance of a company's performance as measured by utilization of funds was recognized by the accountancy profession in October 1975 with the publication of Statement of Standard Accounting Practice (SSAP) 10 entitled *Statement of Sources and Applications of Funds*. This required the inclusion of a funds flow

Table 12.6
Statement of sources and applications of funds

SOURCES	This year		Next year	
	£k	£k	£k	£k
Profit before tax and extraordinary items	X		X	
Extraordinary items[1]	X		X	
Adjustments for items not involving movements of funds[2]	X̲		X̲	
Total generated from operations		X		X
Funds from other sources[3]		X̲		X̲
		X̲		X̲
APPLICATIONS				
Dividends	X		X	
Taxation	X		X	
Purchase of fixed assets	X		X	
Loans repaid	X̲		X̲	
		X		X
		X̲[4]		X̲[4]
CHANGES IN WORKING CAPITAL				
Increase/decrease in stocks	X			
Increase/decrease in debtors	X			
Increase/decrease in creditors excluding dividends and taxation	X			
Increase/decrease in cash	X			
Increase/decrease in short-term investments	X̲			
		X̲[4]		X̲[4]

[1] Extraordinary items would include, for example, profit on sale of investments.
[2] Adjustments would include, for example, depreciation.
[3] Other sources would include, for example, cash from issue of shares.
[4] These figures must equate.

statement with published accounts of enterprises with a turnover in excess of £25 000. The funds flow statement shows, as the name suggests, the sources of funds coming into the business and the use of funds by the business . The balance is reconciled to the change in net working capital in the period concerned. The form of this statement is given in Table 12.6.

Whilst the SSAP is limited to the presentation of historical information, there is no reason why the movement of funds cannot be budgeted and monitored in the same format as illustrated in Table 12.6. This represents an alternative approach to the cash budgeting and cash monitoring method which is discussed in Chapter 8 and demonstrated in Tables 8.1 and 8.2 of that chapter.

CONCLUSION

In acting in the capacity of financial controller, the accountant's responsibility is to represent the financial conscience of the organization in which she or he is employed. Arguably, the roles of entrepreneur and financial controller are not compatible and accountants are often held to be insensitive to the spirit of enterprise in their propriety and financial prudence. However, as has been contended in the preceding paragraphs, it is the efficient conversion of business inputs back into cash which generates profits and underwrites the continued existence of the company; and these are unshakably the prime aims of all enterprise.

FURTHER READING

Accounting Standards Committee, Statement of Standard Accounting Practice SSAP 10: Statements of Source and Application of Funds, 1975.

Bryant, J.W. (ed), *Financial Modelling in Corporate Management*, Wiley, 1982.

Firth, M., *Management of Working Capital,* MacMillan, 1976.

Franks, J. and Broyles, J., *Modern Managerial Finance*, Wiley. 1979.

Han Kang Kong, *Financial Management*, Butterworths, 1984.

Lee, T.A., *Cash Flow Accounting*, Van Nostrand Reinhold, 1984.

McLaney, E.J., *Business Finance*, McDonald and Evans, 1986.

Makridakis, Wheelwright and McGee, *Forecasting Methods and Application*, Wiley, 1983.

Taha, H., *Operations Research*, Collier Macmillan, 1982.

13

Internal Audit and Internal Control

P.C. Chidgey

The author of this contribution argues that systems of management accounting, whilst fulfilling essential roles in providing information for management, have certain defects in respect of the completeness, the timeliness and the objectivity of the data produced. All businesses, as a result, need systems of internal control and most need internal audit functions, particularly those of any size and where branches are involved. Whatever changes of emphasis or direction may await the external audit, it may be widely agreed that the internal audit function is now well established and must develop in parallel with the growth of computerized information systems. The potential of the internal audit is examined in detail and in depth by the author of this chapter, which covers not only the techniques and problems of the function but also defines the principles to be applied. The natural extension of the audit of records and systems towards an audit of management and the difficulties associated with such an audit, are carefully analysed. The chapter is concluded with some interesting observations on possible developments in the scope of the audit committee.

An audit is normally thought of as the annual independent verification of a company's accounts for the benefit of its shareholders. Because of the legal requirements for an audit of virtually all companies in the UK (and of large companies in most other countries) large amounts of money are spent on this type of auditing.

From the company managers' point of view such audits are not primarily directed to assist them achieve their goals and objectives. The external auditor's primary purpose is to report to the shareholders, not to report to management. Many will write management letters highlighting any areas of weakness they have encountered, but these often meet only some of management's needs.

Auditing, however, has many more uses than the verification of accounts. When employed internally it is a useful management tool which independently identifies departures from specified standards in any area and acts as a first stage in a programme of improvements. Internal auditing can help management to assess many aspects of a business's performance.

THE AUDIT PROCESS

To be effective the audit process should consist of:

1 Setting standards: choosing those standards by which the subject of the audit will be assessed. Examples are: existence of effective controls, performance and reporting standards (including accounting standards).
2 Investigation: collecting evidence about the matters which are subject to audit.
3 Reporting: feedback to independent interested parties comparing standards with actual practices.
4 Action: recommending follow-up procedures to correct reported departures from standards.

If these four stages are followed internal auditing can identify problem areas where departures from specified standards have occurred and be the first stage of action to improve those areas.

Main purpose of internal audit

In all types and sizes of business the management need to take steps to ensure that:

1 the financial records are accurate and up to date,
2 the company's assets are protected against fraud and misappropriation.

As a business grows both in size and complexity it must set up systems to ensure these objectives are met. In practice, the chief purpose of internal audit is to ensure the integrity of these systems by assessing whether they are operating to acceptable standards.

Other purposes

However, the internal audit process is used by many companies in further areas to assist management. It is extended to assess the information system with the objective of ensuring management are receiving relevant and reliable information on which to take decisions. In addition, internal audit is sometimes extended to cover performance itself. Here the aim is to measure whether performance has reached acceptable standards. The extension of audit into these areas raises a number of issues, amongst which is whether the reports should be disclosed more widely, and these issues are further discussed in the final part of this chapter.

INTERNAL CONTROL AND INTERNAL AUDIT

This section discusses the use of internal control systems and internal audit on the provision of credible accounting records and the protection of the company's assets.

Credible accounting records

Management needs to ensure the credibility of their accounting records for a number of reasons:

1 they form the basis of the annual published accounts,
2 they allow the production of reports for day-to-day decision-making which enable them to assess their company's present situation and analyse past performance,
3 they aid in the compilation of forecasts,
4 they allow comparisons between actual results and budgets, and the identification of reasons for variances.

In addition, where a business has geographically dispersed subsidiaries or branches where local management make their own decisions, central management will need credible information from all these areas to assess the effects of these decisions and to show them the overall position of the group.

Protection of assets

Management must also ensure that the assets of the business are protected against losses. There are two main aspects to this:

1 physical security of assets, and
2 control over transactions.

Physical security of assets covers not only protecting against the risk of theft by, for instance, ensuring cash is always kept securely and banked promptly, but also taking adequate physical precautions (and ensuring sufficient insurance cover exists) to guard against such disasters as fires, floods or computer breakdowns.

Losses of assets can also occur in the process of transactions. For example, losses can occur if credit sales orders are accepted from uncredit-worthy customers or purchase invoices are settled before proof has been given that they were bona fide purchases, and the goods received.

Internal Control Systems

The first step in achieving these objectives is to set up Internal Control Systems. These have traditionally been set up to ensure accurate and up to date records and to protect the company's assets. These systems are perceived to be of such importance that in certain types of business which hold money on behalf of clients there is a statutory obligation to have such systems.

Principles of internal control

To be effective, a system of internal controls should be based on certain fundamental principles:

1 Segregation of duties – accounting responsibilities are divided amongst employees in such a way that no single person is responsible for the whole of a transaction. The guiding principle here is that those who authorize a transaction must not also be in charge of the relevant assets, and that neither should be responsible for recording the transaction.
2 Authorization and approval – procedures should ensure all transactions are approved by a responsible official with a limit set on the amount each official can authorize. The principle is that as far as possible, each person's work is checked by another without any unnecessary duplication of effort.
3 Physical controls – these are controls over access to assets and records.

Such control systems may well be complex. To cope with this, management should draw up a plan of their organization. This plan should record clearly by means of charts and where necessary a manual of procedures, the responsibilities of the different officers. This should help to eliminate any indeterminate areas which may otherwise lead to confusion. Without such clarity, the result may be that controls are either not exercised or are unnecessarily duplicated. In addition to naming those responsible for individual controls, a detailed plan of the organization also helps to identify the way authority is delegated downwards through the levels of the business and the corresponding way that information should flow back up.

Importance of evidence

An essential part of a control system is evidence of performance. It is necessary for individuals to sign to indicate they have done a piece of work or performed a check and that whoever checks or approves or scrutinizes their work also signs to indicate they have done this. Without this evidence there is no means of knowing that the system has been functioning as set down.

Limitations of control system

Regardless of how effective an internal control system appears in theory there is no guarantee that it will function well in practice. Control systems depend on people and people are subject to such failings as fatigue, boredom and lack of understanding. Furthermore, most controls are not effective if there is fraudulent collusion between employees. Thus the best control systems are not proof against every failure, although the risk of such failures is reduced by the use of suitably qualified personnel, who are trained to perform their duties adequately.

In order to counteract the risk of systems failure, management should regularly examine the systems to ascertain how well they are operating and pinpoint and rectify weaknesses. In many larger businesses, however, their sheer size means that line management are unable to devote sufficient time to making adequate reviews. Here, the potential benefits from a regular examination of systems will often justify the costs of setting up an internal audit department to perform this function.

Internal audit

An internal audit to ensure compliance with control will follow the normal audit process of standard setting, investigation, reporting and action. The standard used is the existence and proper operation of controls which are sufficient to ensure adequate records and protection of assets. This can be further broken down into specific objectives for each area of the business. For example, one objective may be to ensure that all despatches are invoiced and the invoices properly recorded. Another may be to ensure that all fixed assets are physically secure. As with all other means of control internal audit costs money and it is necessary to choose which objectives to pursue based upon some criteria such as the size of likely loss should controls break down.

AUDIT METHODS

To meet these objectives, the internal auditor should initially review the internal control systems as laid down, taking into account how they meet the principles set out above e.g. segregation of duties. Weaknesses noted as a result of this review should form part of the final report. The auditor should then test the system as it operates in practice.

Evidence that controls have been exercised (in the form of signatures of the individuals carrying them out) will be sought. A second part of the testing is to re-perform the control to prove that where there is a signature indicating a control has been carried out, it has in fact been carried out. For example, the internal auditor could inspect invoices to ensure that there is evidence that controls, such as matching to goods received notes, have been carried out and then re-perform the control by checking to the appropriate goods received notes.

Not all testing needs to be this detailed and a less time consuming but just as effective procedure in some cases would be to scrutinize the results of exercising the control. For instance, the internal auditor may closely scrutinize the debtors' ledger to obtain some indication of whether credit control is functioning as efficiently as it should. A large number of overdue balances may mean that there is no effective check of credit-worthiness.

In some areas, such as physical controls, it may be necessary to observe the controls in action: perhaps inspecting the opening of the mail to see if all receipts are pre-listed, before being passed to the cashier for entry into the records; it will then be necessary to ascertain whether the control is fully implemented by ensuring that a check is made of cash book entries to the pre-lists. The control procedures operated within the warehouse can be checked to make sure that no item is withdrawn without an authorized requisition note.

Similarities to external auditor's work

In testing to ensure reliable records are kept and all assets are safeguarded, the internal auditor will conduct very similar checks to those of the external auditor, because they are both very much concerned with this area. However, the external auditor looks at the audit from a narrower point of view: that of ensuring the records are sufficiently reliable to form the basis for accounts which show a true and fair view. The internal auditor's concern will be whether the systems achieve the purposes, for example, protection of the company's assets, for which they were designed. Because of the similarities of their work it will often be cost effective to develop a joint plan which is suitable for the purposes of both and prevents duplication of work.

Small companies

The structure of some groups is such that there are a number of small divisions or subsidiaries. These raise special problems for those attempting to install controls and for the internal auditor. In many small entities, adequate segregation of duties is rendered impossible by lack of staff. In addition, control may be centred in the hands of one individual and there may well be little documentary proof that any control systems are functioning. Here the internal auditor should vouch the recorded transactions and make great use of comparisons either with budgets or past years' performance, attempting to identify reasons for any significant variances.

Regardless of size restrictions, certain controls should still be present. For example, cash and cheques should always be kept safely and banked promptly. In extreme cases where effective controls are impossible, it may be advisable to centralize certain procedures. Head office could be given charge of the sales ledger and credit control, with the subsidiary's responsibility finishing once the goods have been despatched. It could also control purchase orders, with area 'heads' only allowed to place orders up to a stated amount. Any in excess of this should be approved by 'head office'. This may, however, prove to be an expensive way of instituting control.

Reporting and action

Once the internal auditor has completed testing a particular area, a full report should be made on it. The report should always go to someone who is independent of the person in charge of the area reviewed. However, it is often useful to discuss the report with this person, before it is issued.

The report should generally cover:

1 weaknesses in the design of systems
2 deviations from the system which he has discovered
3 recommendations for improvements.

Management should always answer each point raised. This is particularly important where suggestions are not implemented. The internal auditor should not become involved in implementing recommendations as this will cause problems when subsequently assessing the improvements in practice.

COMPUTERIZED SYSTEMS

Problems of computerized systems

Advances in technology now mean that even the smallest companies can afford to use computers to process their accounting records. These present special problems both in the development of an internal control system and its audit. Although a computer often brings great benefits to a company from its ability to process large numbers of transactions at speed there are also new dangers to the validity of accounting records and of losses of assets from its use. The main problems which are characteristic of computers and which should concern an internal auditor when assessing systems are:

1 loss of audit trail,
2 over reliance on computer controls,
3 lack of adequate precautions to cover breakdowns,

4   the risk of numerous errors occurring as a result of inaccurate reference data,

5   too much dependence on a small number of computer experts.

Loss of audit trail

On a manual system, it is normally possible to follow a transaction through the system, by tracing from source documents, through the intervening stages to a final entry in the books of account. In a computer-based system the intervening stages are sometimes recorded only in machine-readable form and it is impossible to trace a transaction from beginning to end. In addition, the system may generate transactions itself of which there is no visible record; for example, interest charges may be calculated, and applied to certain accounts, entirely by computer program.

In some computer-based systems, printouts showing the results of processing are either not produced or are in summary form only. For example, a month's purchase invoices may be input to the computer with the resulting output merely consisting of a total figure for each type of purchase. To overcome these problems an internal auditor will often have to use special techniques (see below).

Computer controls

Computers can be used by a management to exercise a degree of control which is often more reliable than a manual system. Computers can be programmed to reject or list items which do not correspond with set criteria: if a customer's credit limit is exceeded, or if the amount of a purchase invoice is outside pre-set limits, the computer can be programmed to show these particular items in an exception report. Other examples are password controls to prevent unauthorized access, and programmed checks, such as 'run-to-run' control totals, to ensure accurate processing. A run-to-run control involves checking the sum of a number of items with another total before the program will continue, for instance agreeing the sum of the analysis of purchase invoices to the total figure of these invoices calculated by a separate operation of the computer.

Provided these programs have been designed to cope with all exceptional transactions or conditions which may arise, the system will always perform exactly as it is programmed. These controls are often more difficult to override than those in a manual system.

However, computer controls only operate effectively if they are used as part of an overall control system. There should always be adequate manual controls which follow up, investigate and where necessary rectify errors, exceptions and differences reported by the computer.

The internal auditor should not allow over reliance on the computer's procedural controls. When reviewing the systems the internal auditor must check that there are adequate manual controls backing up those computer controls which are used. In addition, there will be a need for manual controls to ensure that the computer captures all the data it should. One way of doing this is by pre-totalling batches of data before they are fed into the computer and then checking that the total output figure agrees. There are special techniques to test the controls are operating properly (see below).

Physical controls

An inherent problem with any accounting system is that a major failure of such systems could destroy the company's accounting records. Such failure could occur for reasons such as fires, floods, power failures or even deliberate destruction. Unfortunately, a computerized system is more susceptible to such hazards than a manual system. Fire, for example, is a risk in any mechanized area and fire-fighting equipment should always be at hand. A business must take adequate procedures against such failures. Above all there must be adequate backup in the event of such a breakdown. Copies of important files should be stored at another location, so that in the event of the destruction of the originals, these files may be used. There should also be adequate stand-by facilities to enable processing to continue in the event of a breakdown and to reconstruct the records. The internal auditor must pay careful attention to this area as the potential for loss is very large.

Errors in reference data

Because of the volumes of transactions processed by a computer an error in reference or standing data may have widespread effects. For example, where a computer produces invoices and a sales price is wrongly entered, it may be used on many invoices before the error is discovered. The systems should ensure that these errors do not occur by ensuring all reference data is checked when input and from time to time by printing out all such data and checking the manual records. It is a useful control for copies of amendments to standing data to go automatically to Internal Audit for subsequent verification.

Data banks

Another aspect of the same problem results from the use of data banks. Data banks use the same basic accounting information in many different ways. For example, the sales figures are used to analyse the sales by products, by geographical or customer distribution and also for costing, stock-level, credit-control and forecasting purposes. Thus the same basic information is capable of reclassification and use for completely different purposes and by departments other than those which originated the data. A mistake in the original data can thus invalidate all the subsequent analyses and so here also it is vital that the initial input data is correct. Where databases are used the internal auditor must pay particular attention to this part of the system.

Dependence on experts

As in a manual system there should be division of functions. However, the number of people involved in a computer system will often be considerably less than in an equivalent manual system. In large companies a small number of data processing personnel may be the only ones with a detailed knowledge of the sources, processing and distribution of data. Furthermore, they may be aware of any internal control weaknesses, and therefore able to manipulate the data being processed or stored.

Where a company develops its own systems the systems development personnel should therefore not operate the computer. To support this it is also important that access to live files and programs should be restricted to the operators and librarians. If program amendments need to be carried out, there should always be full authorization, and the internal auditor should check that this procedure is followed.

In smaller companies such division of responsibility may not always be possible as there is often one person who is responsible for all aspects of the computer system. Here segregation of duties will often either not be possible or be less effective. This may be less of a problem where, as often happens, a company purchases from an outside supplier a software package which cannot be altered.

With the growth in microcomputer systems physical controls over access to records have become more difficult to implement. The growth of terminals and on line systems means that a wide number of people can have access to the records of the company and have power to update them. Here some type of password control and access log are normally necessary to protect the records.

Special audit techniques for computerized systems

As explained above the internal auditor will need to direct attention towards the operation of the computer. When there is a loss of audit trail there must be a check that the program is operating accurately, for example, is there a correct analysis of purchases? Are the computer operated controls functioning correctly, for instance, the run-to-run control totals? Are the exception/rejection reports complete and accurate?

If the system produces adequate visible evidence, the internal auditor may be able to use this to obtain evidence about the operation of the computer. However, where there is a loss of audit trail and the auditor wishes to test the operation of programmed controls, manual tests will not produce sufficient evidence. Computer Assisted Audit Techniques supplement the usual tests. These fall into two main categories – audit interrogation software and test data.

Computer assisted audit techniques

Audit interrogation software refers to specially produced computer programs which can, amongst other things, perform the same computations or produce the same analyses as the main programs. The results of this are compared with the actual results to establish if the programs are operating correctly. They can also be used to produce information in a form not usually available from the computer. Test data is specially prepared data which can be processed by the main programs. The auditor knows what the results should be, and can therefore see whether the programs operate as anticipated. In particular, by choosing a wide variety of types of transactions, the ability of the controls, such as production of exception reports to deal with unusual cases, can be tested.

Some systems may include specific features designed to help the internal auditor. These may include 'resident programmes' which allow the internal auditor (or anyone else) periodically to obtain printouts of transactions, standing data (including amendments), and other items within specified limits which have been processed by the computer. The validity of a sample of these will then be checked.

Systems development

Where a company develops its own systems, the internal auditor should be involved. It must be ascertained whether there is sufficient control over the initial development; over the ensuing testing for effectiveness through the use of 'desk-testing' and 'pilot-runs'; over the subsequent amendments which must be authorized; and before the whole system is retested. It is best for controls to be incorporated in the systems from their inception. However, it is a common failing for computer experts to be more concerned with their programs than with security. The internal auditor can provide this important security viewpoint when the systems are in an embryonic form. Changes made when the systems are developed are extremely expensive and aggravating.

MANAGEMENT AUDITS

Extension towards audit of management

Internal auditing can go beyond the traditional area of identifying problems arising in the application of controls within a company, into those stemming from the operation and performance of the company itself. The use of auditing for these purposes has been termed 'operational' or 'management' audit.

This can be used to assess the adequacy of the information systems as an aid for management. Further, it can be used in the assessment of the various aspects of performance including the way that plans are made, the methods of implementing them, and adaptation to change.

Management information

The aim of management is to achieve certain business objectives. This they attempt to do by a constant process of making plans, implementing them, and adapting these plans and methods based on new information about their previous attempts, and about changes in the business environment. Throughout this process management need credible and useful information about the world in which they operate, about the resources available to them, and about the results of previous efforts. To satisfy these needs, they rely upon information systems, one of the most important aspects of which is the accounting system.

Performance will suffer if management does not receive and act upon sufficient relevant information. An audit of the information systems can assess whether they are receiving all the relevant information that they need and how well this information is used. The audit of information systems has been a natural role into which audit has developed. Traditionally, the accounting systems have been the focal point for testing within the objectives of protection of assets, and correctness of recording. The assessment of information systems concentrates on the same records, but with the emphasis in terms of the usefulness of the information.

Problems with accounting information

Traditionally, management accounting systems have not provided an adequate reflection of the results of performance because:

1   at best they only paint a partial picture of what has happened in the sense that a table of figures can never adequately describe a business;
2   they are liable to bias in the interests of those preparing and recording the information. This is particularly so in cases where the accountants are part of a local management team but are responsible for reporting to central management as well, or where large quantities of basic data come from production departments who will be paid bonuses on the basis of their results.

In small or medium-sized businesses these problems are not crucial as direct knowledge of the business from other sources can remedy any misleading impressions that accounting information gives.

However, as a business expands management can no longer have direct contact with all the areas for which they are ultimately responsible. They are therefore less able to complete the picture of the firm that the accounting systems give them and less able to identify those occasions when the accounting system is providing an erroneous or incomplete picture of what has happened.

Audit of management information

The auditor tests to a standard of 'usefulness'. Generally, to be useful, information should be accurate, relevant and timely. Accuracy should normally be guaranteed by adequate internal controls. The internal auditor must assess the needs of management which will depend on the type of decision which they are making. (Whether they should be making these decisions is a performance measure, which may also be subject to audit.)

Management will require specific reports, in order to make their decisions. For example, a work in progress report may be necessary to assess the stage reached on a contract, the costs to date, those still to be incurred and whether the total is within the estimated budget. If they are not obtaining this information, the standard is not being met. The internal auditor thus compares what information is received with what is needed and reports any inadequacies.

Audit of performance

An audit of performance aims to give management an independent view of events in the areas beyond direct contact, by reporting actual or potential problems which the system would not usually report, or would not report in time.

Audit fulfils two needs as far as examination of performance is concerned.

1 it provides an independent review of internal practices throughout the company (and the performance resulting from their use) based upon a standard of what practices should be followed;
2 it can also provide information on the results of those aspects of performance which are not provided because of the inadequacies in traditional management information systems.

The performance audit must go through the four stages of establishment of standards, investigation, reporting and recommendations.

Standards

The development of a standard is a far more difficult exercise when auditing performance. At the basic level of routine and repetitive tasks, set procedures can be used as a standard and the auditor reports on degree of compliance. However, many parts of management's function do not lend themselves easily to the issue of guidelines and in these cases some other standard must be used.

A general answer to this problem may be obtained by looking at different aspects of performance in the light of how they contribute to the company's objectives. This is obviously much easier in companies which adopt a 'management by objectives' style. It is far more difficult, however, where formal objectives are not stated. Indeed, one of the advantages of using auditing in the management area is that it frequently leads to a more formal examination of objectives. In some areas the auditor will need to use standards derived from apparent best practice outside the company or based on the performance of the functions at an ideal level. This type of exercise will require knowledge and experience of the area under audit.

There are problems with most of the approaches. A too ready acceptance of internal standards may lead to their adoption even when they result in inefficiency. So it is always useful to use some sort of outside reference point.

Additionally, there are some potential pitfalls which the internal auditor must be aware of and, where possible, avoid. One instance of this is where a standard set to promote the efficiency of one function harms another. For example, a decision which improves purchasing efficiency may lead to increased stockholding and may harm production where extra costs will be incurred. Another potential pitfall is that the operations may be subject to controls from bodies outside the company. For example, government controls over pollution levels may prevent management from operating processes at peak efficiency. Any standards set should take this into account.

Investigation

The investigation stage will use the methods and techniques which have been developed in the traditional field of auditing. The auditor will become familiar with the area under review and then by means of questionnaires, tracing of records and direct observation obtain evidence about performance in that area. A review of purchasing, for instance, may consist of questioning responsible officials about their methods, observing the methods in practice over several days and tracing records of past performance to check that what has been investigated is representative of what is normally done in the department.

The evidence that an auditor can collect in respect of performance is less conclusive and reliable than in other areas such as correctness of accounting entries. When assessing the evidence the auditor will use much more subjective judgement. Accordingly it is necessary for the auditor to evaluate sceptically the significance of this evidence.

Reporting and action

The report is often more detailed than the usual internal audit report. It should describe the standards used to assess performance, the methods of investigation and the opinion on the area under review, indicating the degree of assurance.

A crucial use of the audit findings is to improve performance. If this is not done there will be little benefit from the audit. Ideally, it should provide the basis of decisions made by the managers of the departments concerned and their superiors about improvements in future performance. This can range from adjustments of routine procedures to the installation of new systems.

Problem areas

Objections are sometimes made to using internal auditors for performance audits on the following grounds:

1 lack of knowledge,
2 lack of independence,
3 restriction of size.

Lack of knowledge

The auditor carrying out a performance or management audit may not be skilled in the particular area he is auditing. As the work of the internal audit department develops into these areas, it calls for a correspondingly greater breadth of vision from the auditors involved. There are still, however, advantages in an independent investigation even by someone not skilled in a particular area, so long as she or he can apply properly the evidence-gathering techniques of auditing. Techniques such as standardized questionnaires and checklists have proved very useful in ensuring that internal audits are of a high standard despite the lack of specialist knowledge on the part of those carrying them out.

Independence

Often the auditor is used not only to discover problems but also to make recommendations and assist in the introduction of improvements. This is a dangerous course because the internal auditor will inevitably suffer a lack of independence in a subsequent review of the system that he or she is in part responsible for. There will be occasions, however, when just by stating the problem the remedy will become apparent and other occasions when the most cost-effective course will be for the auditor to recommend small changes. It is also normally accepted that an auditor should be consulted about the appropriate levels of control to be incorporated in for example, a new information system. However, the risk of loss of independence must always be recognized as a major disadvantage in using the internal audit department in anything but a small way outside its usual function.

There is an additional disadvantage in that the organization will not be receiving as much benefit from the internal audit department as it should. This is because internal auditors are specialist auditors and are of most value to the organization when performing that role. They are thus more likely to be economically employed in auditing further areas rather than implementing improvements to existing areas.

Restrictions of size

The desire to limit costs may also have a significant effect on internal audit departments. Any control system is only efficient when the benefits exceed the costs. Where costs are restricted, the audit work should be concentrated on those areas with the greatest effect on company performance, and those least susceptible to management control. Some small or medium-sized companies may find that it is simply not cost-effective to maintain a permanent internal management audit department. The same tasks could be carried out by means of informal management review, but this may not be satisfactory as discussed earlier in this chapter. An alternative is to use either the external auditors or management consultants on a sub-contract basis.

External auditors

The proposal for 'management' or 'operational' audits by external auditors has the attraction of cost savings as the external auditor is involved in the company's systems anyway. However, this also raises problems of auditor independence.

The primary role of the external auditor is to establish for the benefit of the shareholders of a company that a set of financial statements prepared by the management of that company give a true and fair reflection of company performance in the last accounting period and its position at the date to which the accounts are prepared. In this context the external auditors are acting for the shareholders, and should be independent of the management of the company.

To extend the external auditor's function to report to management on information systems and performance while still continuing to report to shareholders on the accounting statements could, however, cause conflicts of interest. The auditor here would be responsible to management and at the same time responsible to the shareholders to perform an audit of statements prepared by management.

REPORTING

Extension of reporting function

It is argued that the external publication of reports on company performance and systems by auditors has two advantages. The knowledge that such a report is to be prepared should induce more efficient behaviour among certain companies and the reports themselves should be a useful source of information for judging the relative efficiency of different managements. This would result in corrective pressures or decisions to re-allocate resources to more efficient areas. In particular, proposals have been made to disclose reports to external third parties, as part of an extended external audit which also covers internal controls, management information and performance.

However, there are inherent problems with this in the areas of

1 standards,
2 competence,
3 evidence and

4 confidentiality.

Standards

Auditing is a process during which the subject of the audit is independently assessed and reported on, in terms of a standard. Information systems and performance are capable of being judged in accordance with many different standards each of which may be perfectly valid given the purpose for which the audit is undertaken, and none of which can lay claim to universal application. In the absence of a single well-defined standard, however, comparability between reports on different companies will be difficult to achieve and the reports could even be misleading if it is assumed that they are in terms of a common standard.

Competence

It is doubtful whether the external auditor, although presently qualified to undertake reviews of internal controls and possibly management information systems, would have the necessary skills to perform 'management' or 'operational' audits. Suitably qualified individuals would have to be employed to fulfil this role, and this would significantly increase the cost of these audits.

Evidence

Because of the subjective assessments which are required during a management audit, the final report may not be given with a level of assurance significant enough to be of much use to external users. An internal audit reports problems in departments which management can investigate further if they are unhappy with the degree of subjective judgement involved in identifying them. External parties would not have this option.

Confidentiality

The publication of certain details may harm individual companies. Competitors could take advantage of reports or weaknesses in different production areas or unscrupulous employees would take advantage of disclosed weak controls. Even in the context of a national requirement for such audits there would still be the problem of international competitors.

Audit committees – a possible solution

An alternative is the use of audit committees which provide a channel of communication between the authors of the audit report and the management of the company. This idea originally developed in the USA, and they are now a Securities Exchange Commission requirement.

An audit committee for these purposes would be composed of representatives from various interest groups which would receive audit reports on all aspects of the company's affairs and would be able to commission further work if required. This would allow confidentiality to be maintained and also ease the problems relating to standards and evidence.

The proposal would however, result in a different role for the audit committee than is presently conceived in the UK where its chief purpose is seen as providing a link between external auditors and the company. The proposed role would be as a body independent of management perhaps comprising non-executive directors which could apply pressure on them to perform in an efficient manner, with the ultimate sanction of publication of the results of the auditors' investigation. Such a committee would provide a useful force for more efficient performance.

This proposal would, however, be costly and would only be appropriate for larger businesses where there is a significant divergence between management and owners or long-term loan creditors. Each business considering the adoption of such a committee in the absence of a national requirement must weigh the costs against the anticipated benefits as in all other aspects of the use of audit for management purposes.

CONCLUSION

Initially, auditing was restricted to ensuring that a set of financial statements showed a true and fair view. Its use was extended to ensure compliance with internal controls which attempted to protect the business against loss of assets and incorrect financial records. Techniques have developed to take into account growing computerization of a company's systems. It has further developed so as to encompass an assessment of the factors which affect performance itself; so far these uses have been almost primarily for the benefit of

management. However, the increasing demands for greater accountability within society, may in the future result in the use of audits to
report on an infinite range of topics for the benefit of a much wider
range of external interested parties.

REFERENCES AND FURTHER READING

Courtemanche, C, *The New Internal Auditing*, Wiley, New York,
    1986.
Internal Auditing (Journal of the Institute of Internal Auditors), UK.
Spronck, L.H., *Managing Coordinated External and Internal Audits*,
    Wiley, New York, 1983.
The Internal Auditor (Journal of the Institute of Internal Auditors),
    USA.
Venables and Impey, *Internal Audit*, Butterworth, 1985.

14

Planning and Control of Research and Development

A.W. Pearson

As pointed out by Avison Wormald in an earlier chapter, a significant aspect of the change which is continually affecting business operations lies in changes in technology. In the following chapter Alan Pearson, of the Manchester Business School, who has specialized for many years in the problems associated with research and development, examines the factors involved in the successful planning and control of this business expense.

He insists that, as with any other business investment, the benefits derived from research and development should exceed the costs. The obvious problem in the case of this kind of expense is that the benefits likely to be derived from a particular project, or of a number of associated projects, are uncertain, and may not materialize at all. For this reason monitoring and control processes must quickly recognize when significant changes occur and point to the necessary corrective action, which might, in the extreme case, be the cancellation of the project.

In monitoring the expenditure the major need is to control the timescale of the work in relation to the output; the cost will be largely controlled by the number of people assigned to the work. The total funds to be allocated to R and D need to be based on identified organizational requirements as a result of 'top-down planning'; while at the same time the planning and control of individual projects will be based on 'bottom-up planning', for which the charting of key decision points or milestones will be helpful. The communication of information will be immensely aided by the computer, and it is noteworthy that most writers in this book refer to the immense potential available to business in the modern developments of electronic data processing.

The author of this chapter reiterates the warnings of other contributors of the danger of incurring large cash outflows with benefits far into the future but the inevitable long time period involved in many projects emphasizes the need for close monitoring of progress. His long experience of the research and development area leads him to conclude that 'most attempts to impose standardised systems seem to have met with little success', and this thought again reflects the opinion of other writers dealing with other aspects of business expense. So far as R and D is concerned Alan Pearson suggests that financial planning and control should be motivational rather than penalizing and the process should secure the involvement of the research teams.

Investment in research and development must be looked at in the same way as any other investment in the business – the benefits it produces must exceed the costs. However, it is by no means easy to ensure that the practice lines up with the theory. The available evidence from a wide range of companies suggests that the costs incurred in the R and D phase of well-managed projects can be reasonably controlled, but that the time to completion is often significantly underestimated. Problems are also frequently encountered in the implementation phase and this causes further delays. Lengthening of the timescale to completion can have adverse effects upon the benefit stream which may not only be delayed but may be significantly altered due to external influences, for example, competitive activity and changes in economic, social, political and environmental factors. It is also clear that assessing benefits is a very difficult task which must take into account a wide range of effects and compare the anticipated future position with the likely situation if the research and development work had not been undertaken.

Financial planning must recognize these uncertainties, particularly with respect to longer-term work, and appropriate monitoring or control procedures must be instituted which are capable of recognizing significant changes and indicating corrective action as early as possible.

In practice it has been found to be useful to approach the problem from two directions: first, to consider the overall allocation of funds to R and D based on identified organizational needs, and second, to consider the planning and monitoring of individual projects. The evidence is that attention to the former has a significant influence upon the success of the latter, allowing individual initiatives to be encouraged and managed within an agreed overall framework. The two approaches are complementary and in most organizations both will be used as starting points, with links becoming apparent at a very early stage, as the next two sections aim to show.

TOP-DOWN PLANNING

In the late 1960s the word 'relevance' was frequently heard in discussions about the allocation of funds to R and D. Very simply this was meant to direct attention to the need to support R and D work which if successful would be put to effective use by the organization. In the late 1970s the phrase 'top-down planning' was used very frequently. This refers to an approach which systematically questions where the organization is going, and examines the structure of the organization in terms of its size, the nature of the component parts, their growth, profitability and their strengths and weaknesses in relation to competitive and other environmental forces. The purpose of this exercise is to identify where the organization is likely to end up if it continues in the way it has done in the past, and where it may need to change in order to improve its viability in the future.

Such an analysis will usually be undertaken by individuals or groups of people who are responsible for, and knowledgeable about, a specific area of activity and will often follow organizational lines, for example, focused on products or areas of like characteristics. Within the analysis a 'technological audit' should be undertaken and this will reveal both the level and type of R and D activity which can be directly related to the support of specific areas of the organization. Such information then forms the necessary background to detailed discussion about the relationship (or 'relevance') of the R and D expenditures to the needs of the organization, with emphasis being placed on the longer- as well as the short-term needs.

The time orientation of the people involved in such discussions may be different, with R and D tending to look further ahead than, say, production or marketing people. This must be accepted. The purpose of top-down planning is to focus attention on the organization needs and each function should have an opportunity to make its view clear about these needs, bearing in mind the specialist knowledge it can contribute to the discussion. Differences of opinion are best brought out into the open at this stage, and it must be accepted that there is no certainty about the future. All opinions must be listened to. Where wide differences arise more information may need to be collected, and more views canvassed. However, it may well be that such differences still persist, and in this case it may be necessary to consider the variation of views as being a good representation of the actual situation, i.e. to accept that a high level of uncertainty exists about the future. In this case a decision may have to be taken to authorize a programme of work which will cover the different views and hence allow flexibility. This will almost certainly require the allocation of more resources to the area, with a consequent reduction in the risk. If this is the accepted strategy efforts must be focused on identifying those features of the situation which can be monitored to indicate at the earliest possible time which areas should be given priority.

Top-down planning is therefore a way of focusing management attention on the needs of the organization. It forces people to ask questions about the relationship between the expenditures on the different functional areas and the alternative futures which the organization may encounter. In this process the R and D people should have every opportunity to put their own views forward about, for example, potential new technologies which may be seen as threats or opportunities. A thorough discussion of all these issues will reveal areas for attention and will generate commitment to a project, by the organization and by the project leader and the team. Such a commitment is a necessary condition for success.

It is not, however, also a sufficient condition, as many champions of 'non-successful' projects know to their disappointment. Many other factors need to be taken into account and as some of these change over time, for example legislation, it is important to have a planning and monitoring procedure which will provide useful information to all parties. Such a procedure can form an important part of the 'bottom-up' form of planning.

BOTTOM-UP PLANNING

This approach implies that individual activities or projects are the starting point for analysis. In many areas this is indeed the case. Ideas arise in a variety of ways: from discussions, casual meetings, problems, etc., and they often form the basis for a request for funds to develop the idea into a proposal backing a request for a larger allocation of resources. Requests for small amounts of funds for developing ideas should always be encouraged and seriously considered. In general such ideas will lie within areas which will be of potential relevance, simply because they will utilize the skills of people who have been recruited in line with the organization's needs. The major cost of encouraging such requests is in fact the 'opportunity' one of not applying the same resources to other ongoing or preselected projects. However, the positive side of this is the increased motivation which can be generated by allowing some freedom for individuals to pursue their own ideas, and to convert them into projects which they can 'champion'. In most organizations the decision as to how much of this type of activity to encourage, and in which direction, is left to the R and D director, whose responsibility it is to develop and maintain an exciting and creative environment which will be a positive asset to the organization. Many R and D directors report a lack of initiative on the part of their scientists and technologists in bringing forward new ideas, rather than any excessive demand. In some organizations this is partly due to pressure from projects of a more immediate concern to the organization's needs, which itself can be due to lack of an adequate planning and monitoring system.

The important point about the bottom-up planning approach is that it focuses attention on the level of resources which will be required to service all the projects which have been accepted into the R and D portfolio. If these projects are to be progressed well they cannot command in total more resources than are available, at any one time. This may sound an obvious statement, but the evidence is that many organizations consistently fail to complete projects on time due to the pressure on resources. If this is the case, corrective action must be taken either to reduce the number of projects which are being progressed simultaneously, or to bring in assistance from outside agencies, for example contract research organizations. Both of these are essentially short-term measures. In the long term serious consideration needs to be given either to reducing the number of projects which are accepted into the portfolio or to increasing the level of in-house resources in areas which are causing delays. If the first of these alternatives is chosen it will be necessary to examine carefully all the projects and to assess their relative importance to the organization, so that any trimming down can be done in areas which are likely to have less significant effects. This can only be done after due consideration of the plans produced by the approach discussed in the previous section, and hence the top-down and bottom-up approach will come together when questions of direction and priority are raised. An important point to note is that unless this trimming down is well managed there will be a continuing scramble for resources which will lead to the not uncommon situation in which progress meetings end up as being primarily concerned with establishing priorities. The inevitable consequence is a lowering of motivation of the people involved in low-priority projects and a reduction in financial return when compared with that planned.

Project evaluation and selection

This is an area fraught with difficulty. The literature is full of methods which have been designed to be helpful. These range from simple cash flow models, the use of net present value and internal rate of return accounting procedures, checklists, various forms of decision analysis incorporating probabilities of technical and commercial success, and the more analytical approaches based on mathematical programming techniques. In practice the evidence suggests that the simpler approaches are the ones most commonly used; this being often justified because of the lack of adequate data for the more mathematically-based models. The simple cash flow models and weighted checklists are therefore much in evidence. More recently emphasis has been placed on the behavioural aspects of decision making and a number of multicriteria approaches – some using the facilities of the microcomputer – have been described. These look to be very promising, and it is expected that they will become increasingly accepted as valuable aids to decision making.

PLANNING AND MONITORING

The success of the approaches outlined in the previous two sections wil depend upon the degree to which the performance on individual projects matches up to the expectations. The purpose of a good planning and monitoring procedure is to ensure that any differences can be quickly identified and appropriate action taken. A number of methods are available for doing this, and the choice should be made in the light of the organization's needs, with one point being emphasized: the simplest and most flexible approach should be adopted. Many people still consider that the introduction of formal planning and control procedures into R and D will stifle creativity and initiative. Most attempts to impose standardized systems seem to have met with little success. It is comparatively easy for an individual or group to get around a system they do not see as useful and which takes up time they feel could be better allocated to their scientific and technical activities.

Planning and monitoring must be seen as a positve aid to the individual, the project group and the organization. Any techniques which are used should be seen as valuable aids to the team-building and leadership needs of a project. They should help focus attention on both the task and the people aspects of management, and they should take into account the variables which are specific to the situation – for example, the development level of the team members – as well as the technical and organizational complexity of the project. This leads to a variety of methods being used for the planning of individual projects, the choice depending upon the type of work and the management style of the project leader. However, there is a need for a reporting and monitoring procedure which will provide common information across the whole of an R and D establishment and which places emphasis on obtaining and presenting information in a form which is useful for management purposes. Some approaches which have been found useful in practice are discussed in the following sections.

Project planning

Several methods have been described in the literature and further information can be obtained from the articles listed in the bibliography. Briefly they fall into the following categories.

The bar chart

This is probably the oldest and yet still the most commonly used method in many R and D establishments. The chart is really a calendar planner on which individual activities are identified and the time over which they are expected to be progressed indicated by a bar. The degree to which a particular activity has been completed is often indicated by a dotted line under the main bar. The advantages of this approach are its simplicity and its visual impact. It is not, however, always easy to update, and not so easy to show dependencies between activities. Although both these disadvantages can be overcome, more complicated projects are often planned using a form of network diagram.

The network diagram

This can take a variety of forms. Until recently the most commonly met was the simple form of PERT or activity on arrow diagram. Standard computer programs are available which allow easy presentation and analysis of such networks and also easy updating. In most cases the same programmes allow for the printing out of a standard bar chart for any section or all of the network. They also include facilities for multi-project scheduling and for resource levelling which can be very useful. Networks of this type are most commonly encountered in larger projects of a more development type and particularly where external inputs are required, and external deadlines have to be met. They are used also where standard practices must be followed to satisfy, for example, government and legislative requirements.

Alternative forms of network diagrams are available, notably the activity on node, or activity in box method sometimes referred to as the metra potential method (MPM). As the name implies, the activities are written inside the boxes or nodes and these are linked by arrows which show the dependencies. The variation is claimed to provide more flexibility at the initial project design stage and is more closely related to the engineering flow diagrams with which many scientists and technologists are already familiar.

Arguments against the use of networks have, however, been put forward by many people who believe they are too structured and inflexible and not capable of handling the uncertainties associated with R and D projects. Some of these arguments have been countered by the further development of the methods, for example, to allow alternative outcomes to be considered at any node or activity completion point. At such points allowance can also be made for recycling by incorporating feedback loops into the diagram.

Research planning diagrams (RPDs)

A further development of the network diagram, essentially following on from the activity in box approach, specifically calls for the incorporation of decision nodes. This is a very valuable addition in an

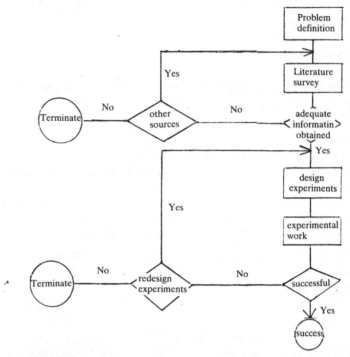

Fig. 14.1   The research planning diagram (RPD) format

area like R and D and the approach has been found most useful. Another point in its favour is the similarity to the commonly accepted logic or flow diagram which is used in other areas of business activity. A very simple example showing the basic format is shown in Fig. 14.1.

The milestone chart

This is perhaps the simplest of all approaches and is generally used to provide a summary of the information which has been spelled out in more detail using one or more of the previously outlined methods. As will be seen later, it can form the basis of a very effective reporting and monitoring system. The basic characteristic of the approach is the identification of milestones, or key events, which can be readily identified in advance and recognized when they occur in time. In the case of R and D projects these may be defined in terms of, for example, technical specifications which have to be met, tests which must be completed, pilot plants built, production facilities designed, or specific market research information gathered, etc. The dates by which these activities should be completed then become the milestones. These will often be associated with specific review meetings.

The milestone chart is used in many organizations and expanded versions often include a breakdown of the activities by function or by individual, so that the responsibility for actions can be clearly identified. For this reason the name 'activity matrix' has been used to describe this form of presentation.

Monitoring

The purpose of outlining some of the approaches to planning individual projects was to illustrate the variety. As stated earlier, the preference for a particular method will depend upon the type of project, and the management style of the team leader. Any method must be seen as an aid to, and not as a substitute for, management. The project leader is responsible for planning, or agreeing the plans, and for progressing the project. However, it must be accepted that many things can change during the course of the work, and corrective action may need to be taken during the life of a project. The first person to recognize this is likely to be the project leader who is responsible for taking the necessary initiatives. The purpose of a good monitoring procedure is to record progress and to report actions which have been taken which were not originally planned and which might have consequences for the organization. In addition it should highlight, if necessary, where actions are not being taken at the correct time.

The monitoring procedure should be essentially a communication system which adds to, but does not replace, the direct contact which is always necessary between the various parties interested in a particular project. It will almost certainly provide some historical information, but its value will be significantly increased if it also focuses attention on future expectations.

Historical analysis

Most organizations require all people involved in project work to record on a standard form information about the allocation of their time on different activities. Such forms are usually completed weekly and relate to the actual expenditure of time over the immediately preceding time period. Breakdown of time may be in half-hour intervals, half or whole days. This is converted into cost information by the use of simple factors based on the salaries of different categories of individuals with overheads being added in many cases. Sometimes the accumulated costs form the basis for direct charging to customers or departments within the organization. In most cases they are presented so as to show the actual expenditure on the project alongside that originally agreed. Such information may be given in the form of a cumulative expenditure chart, but it is obvious that such information is of little value unless one can be clear about how much progress has actually been made on the scientific and technical work. That is why it is essential to have some form of plan, along the lines discussed earlier, set out in such a way that the actual work progress can be assessed at regular intervals against identifiable and agreed criteria.

An important point to note is that it is the exception rather than the rule for the individuals to be working on only one project at any given time. If this is the case, it must be accepted that information about time, and hence cost, allocation to individual projects cannot be accurately assessed. Experience therefore suggests that although it is usually thought necessary to collect historical information on project costs it is not of very great practical use for management purposes. Clearly it can be used as an indicator of how much effort is being applied to a project, but its value is diminished if it cannot be directly related to the expected technical progress as set out in the original plan. One way of doing this is through the milestone chart. As defined earlier, a milestone is a point at which agreed and recognizable criteria have to be met. The actual cost of reaching a given milestone can therefore be compared with the original estimate and a simple chart can be used to illustrate progress (see Fig. 14.2). This diagram can show both cost and time slippage.

This figure shows that milestone 1 was reached on time, but at lower cost, 2 on time but at higher cost, and 3 again on time, but with cost exceeding expectation. However, such a chart only indicates actual achievement against milestones and information about progress between these key points cannot be easily gained without a more detailed breakdown of the project into smaller activities. It is possible to do this and at the extreme every activity can be individually monitored and progress of cost and time against expectation almost continuously assessed. This is often referred to as the work breakdown approach. In this case computer analysis of a network-based

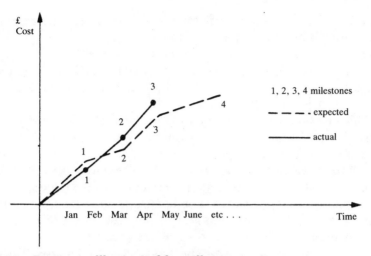

Fig. 14.2   Progress illustrated by milestone chart

plan is useful, but in general the amount of information required and generated becomes too much to handle effectively, and if often leads to an adverse reaction from scientists and technologists who think too much of their time is taken up in what they see as unnecessary administration. This is particularly so in projects with a relatively high degree of uncertainty, where they feel they may require to take initiatives which were not specifically planned but which will ultimately be of advantage in steering the project to a successful conclusion. Such initiatives should be encouraged in R and D and it has been found possible to allow a reasonable degree of flexibility by staying with the broad milestone approach but calling for information about future expectations as well as accounting for past expenditures as outlined in the following section.

Progress charts

When a project is selected and a project leader identified a plan is drawn up and agreed. This plan may be based on any of the approaches outlined earlier, for example, bracket network, RPD, but the key point is that it should highlight important decision points or milestones. The number of these will depend upon the type and size of project and the anticipated ability of the team to manage the work, including expected variations within the agreed plan. The milestones need not be very close together, but they should not be so far apart that the opportunity for taking corrective action is delayed too long. They may coincide with review points, and estimates of both time and cost to reach them should be made however uncertain these may appear to be at the outset. Such estimates can be updated as more information becomes available and as such the learning of the project is more clearly indicated.

This information could be added to the simple historical analysis chart described earlier, but this would very quickly become confusing if many changes occurred in the estimates of the time and cost required to reach future milestones. An alternative is to consider the time and cost variables separately and it has proved to be most useful to emphasize the time variable in the first instance partly because this can be more accurately monitored but also because time delays usually indicated the need for corrective action which if not taken is likely to reduce considerably the financial return on a project.

The simplest of the time-based charts in use has been referred to as a 'slip-chart, because it very clearly shows when progress is slipping (see Table 14.1).

The numbers refer to key stages or milestones in the project, and the chart acts as a historical record of how the estimates of the time required to reach a particular stage have changed as the project is progressed. In this respect it provides future-oriented information which is extremely valuable for planning purposes. Anticipated slippage is clearly shown as a movement to the right in the number associated with the milestone, and commands the attention of all interested parties. The chart therefore acts as an extremely powerful communication device. The information contained in the graphical

Table 14.1
Example of a slip chart

		Calendar time					
		Jan	Feb	Mar	Apr	May	June	etc.
	Jan	1	2	3	4	5	6
	Feb	1	2	3	4	5	
Review	Mar	1	2		3	4	5
time	Apr	1	2		3	4	
	May	1	2		3		4
	Jun						
	etc.						

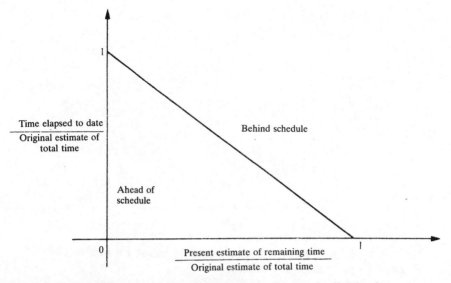

Fig. 14.3   Progress against expectations for an individual project using time dimensions

presentation can quite easily be put on to a computer. Print-outs can then be obtained as required of the progress of any individual project or of groups of projects associated, for example, with one area of activity or under a single management, or relevant to and perhaps supported by a particular client.

Other forms of presentation can also be of value. For example, progress against expectations for an individual project can be portrayed graphically (see Fig. 14.3).

A plot of the progress of a project on these two dimensions will show up deviations from plans as overruns above the line and ahead of schedule below the line. Both these methods are simple to use and are visually very easy to understand. They clearly indicate deviations from plan, not only those that have occurred, but also any that are expected in future periods. This is most important if corrective action is to be taken.

The reason for choosing time as the major variable on which to focus was discussed earlier. Overruns on time are more frequent and often much larger, and the effects of such overruns on the financial return can be very large.

However, this does not mean that cost can be ignored. Historical methods of accounting were discussed earlier, and these can be extended to include future projections in a number of ways. Many

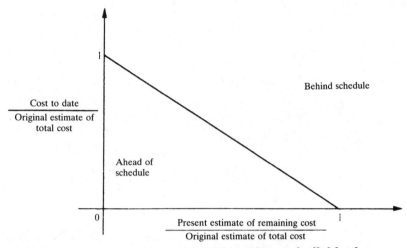

Fig. 14.4 Progress against expectations for an individual project using cost dimensions

organizations now require a cost to completion figure at major review times. This information should be provided by the project leader and based on best possible estimates of the cost of the work outstanding, including any originally unforeseen requirements. Estimates can be derived by extrapolation from the information to date of actual against planned expenditures, and in some cases this is not an unrealistic approach, as past problems frequently indicate future difficulties. The work breakdown method lends itself neatly to this approach through the identification of performance 'efficiency' factors. Care must be taken, however, to ensure that such an approach is not applied mechanistically. The aim of a good monitoring and reporting procedure should be to identify problem areas as quickly as possible and to take corrective action to improve performance in the future.

Future cost estimates can be incorporated directly into the simple type of monitoring chart as shown in Fig. 14.2, or they can be presented as a cost slip chart (see Fig. 14.4).

An organization may choose to emphasize time or cost reporting as its needs dictate. However, it is obvious that both can be useful and taken together will often provide additional information. For example, keeping time and cost progress charts side-by-side will enable slippage in either or both of these parameters to be considered at the same time. Some conclusions which might then be drawn are as follows:

1 time overruns but not cost overruns suggest a lack of effort on the project;
2 cost overruns but not time overruns suggest problems are being encountered but extra effort is being allocated which looks like overcoming them;
3 cost overruns and time overruns suggest there are problems which are proving more difficult to handle.

Each of these alternatives will require a different type of management action and the value of the reporting system is the simple indication which is given of the possible area for attention.

PORTFOLIO ANALYSIS

The approaches described above are essentially designed for assisting in the management of individual projects. The project leader and team are the people who supply the information and as such are the first people to identify deviations from the plan. They are therefore able to take corrective action if this is within their terms of reference, or to suggest alternative courses of action if they require additional resources and/or support from other key people in the organization. The value of the approaches must therefore be that they do not take away the responsibility for managing a project from those most closely concerned with its progress. Essentially what they do is recognize the uncertainty associated with research and development and encourage project leaders to provide regular position reports in the light of the progress made.

The individual planning methods focus attention on key decision points, milestones or review points. At these times the project leader will be expected to make a more detailed report on the project. Such review points will normally be agreed in advance. The progress chart, by its very nature, provides much more up-to-date information about the state of a project but without requiring this information in a detailed form. If milestones are not going to be met then the sooner this is recognized the better. In some cases this can lead to more rapid corrective action being taken; in others it may lead to an earlier decision to terminate a project which would otherwise become a cash drain with little prospect of providing an adequate financial return.

An important point about the progress chart approach is that it is clearly first and foremost an information system, with the project leader at the centre of the information network and primarily responsible for any necessary actions. It is possible to go further than this and provide some information to management on a more general basis by presenting the information in alternative forms. For example, the basic information already provided for the progress charts can be converted into ratio terms as follows:

$$\frac{1 - \dfrac{\text{Cost to date}}{\text{Original estimate of total cost}}}{\dfrac{\text{Present estimate of remaining cost}}{\text{Original estimate of total cost}}}$$

becomes $\dfrac{\text{Original estimate of total cost} - \text{cost to date}}{\text{Present estimate of remaining cost}}$

A ratio of

1 then indicates a project is on schedule for cost (but not necessarily time)

<1 indicates a project on which overspending is likely

They can be used in conjunction with other information, e.g. expenditure to date, but they must be treated with some caution. They can clearly form part of a management by exception system but here there is a danger that they will take away the main feature of the progress chart which is its value as a communication device. Management by exception systems can too easily become the tools of people who know little about either the technical side of the work or the needs of the organization in respect of the output. Some projects may need urgent attention when only very small exceptions are reported; others can tolerate much larger variations without causing undue alarm. The people who should be most concerned are those closely concerned with the project and outside interference should only be required if they are not taking the necessary actions. The use of ratios must therefore be seen essentially as a back-up mechanism, used mostly for senior management to monitor key projects. Their value will be diminished if an attempt is made to use them as the main control mechanism.

However, it is useful to consider whether additional information of a more general nature might be obtained about the overall performance of an R and D establishment which could be put to good use. There are two particular approaches which should be given serious consideration. The first focuses on the factors which cause delays to projects and the second on the outputs from projects in relation to the expectations. Obviously these two are interrelated, but can be usefully examined separately.

Constraints on individual projects

The progress chart is built up from information supplied by the project leader. Deviations from the original plan will be due to a variety of causes. A simple request for information about the nature of factors causing delays can be very illuminating. In practice these usually fall into a few categories, for example lack of resources, external factors, technical problems.

An analysis of all the projects in the R and D establishment may also reveal a significant number of delays due to the same factor. If so, corrective action should be taken, which will reinforce the value of the planning and monitoring system, as people will see that the information they are providing is being used to their advantage. For example, if lack of resources is a common constraint then action to increase the level of resources or to reduce the number of projects will be much appreciated. It will also be of considerable motivational value to project leaders who will have to spend less of their time fighting for priority and working with inadequate support facilities. The advantage of the progress chart is that it focuses attention on any likely changes in future resource requirements on individual projects owing to changes in expectations about the achievement of particular milestones. Taken over the R and D establishment as a whole this information is of great value from the resource allocation point of view.

Output assessment

At the beginning of the chapter the potential value of top-down planning was discussed. The actual value of this approach will be partly determined by the ability of the R and D establishment to complete the projects which are agreed to be relevant to the different needs of the organization. A coding system can be developed which shows the relationship of an individual project to a particular need, e.g. business area, short or long term, product or process development, etc. Projects can then be identified readily and at appropriate intervals, say quarterly or annually; all projects related to a given need can be examined and their progress noted. This analysis may well reveal areas for concern, for example, that short-term projects are being progressed more effectively than long-term ones, etc. From the financial planning point of view, it will provide a simple breakdown of the expenditures and the progress which has been made against the expectation in each area. Deviations between these two can then be examined to see whether corrective action needs to be taken.

It must also be remembered that an R and D establishment will have activities which cover a wide range of uncertainties. The proportion of low to high probability of success projects will depend upon the needs of the organization at a particular point in time as well as the attitudes to risk of the key decision makers. This balance must be reviewed at regular intervals and the monitoring procedure should highlight those projects in which the uncertainty is not decreasing over time at the expected rate. Again, the project leader will be the first to recognize the lack of uncertainty reduction, but this will also be highlighted through the lack of progress towards meeting defined milestones within the agreed timescales and cost. Decisions on whether to continue with such projects are not easy to make, as many major innovations have come about after sustained effort over many years with success always looking possible but always appearing to be just out of reach. In such cases the size of the potential benefits will usually be the deciding factor in obtaining further backing, but this must be balanced against the potential losses of not being successful, or of being beaten by competitive activity. There are many examples of organizations falling into difficulties through backing innovations requiring excessively large cash outflows with benefits appearing very far in the future.

CONCLUSIONS

A financial planning and control system is just as necessary in research and development as in any other area. However, it must take into account the uncertainty surrounding the activity. It must be flexible and it does not need to be complicated. It must be motivational rather than penalizing and the responsibility for management has to remain at the level at which the work is being done.

There is considerable evidence that the internal evaluation of projects is very compatible with external evaluations where the goals are agreed and accepted. The aim therefore is to provide the right environment in which the project leader and team are motivated to be honest with themselves and with the organization in the reporting of progress. The monitoring system can then be oriented towards signalling deviations about which other people might express different concerns than those most closely connected with the work. Such signals will encourage communication and agreement on actions which will be of benefit to all interested parties. The emphasis is on the positive aspects of monitoring which are too often hidden by disagreements about the reasons for deviations and the implied blame which often leads to the adoption of defensive positions by the different parties. The value of good feedback which can be provided through a simple planning and monitoring system cannot be over-emphasized.

Planning methods can be allowed to vary within the organization, although there may be some advantage in agreeing the type of approach which is likely to be most suitable for different types of projects. Monitoring is more useful if there is a high degree of standardization, so that comparative analysis can be done and attention paid to those factors which will improve the overall management of the R and D establishment.

In looking at possible approaches more emphasis is placed on forward than on historical analysis, with time being considered of prime importance. It must be remembered that the largest part of the cost of an R and D establishment is in the people, and unless significant amounts of outside work can be rapidly commissioned it is not easy to overspend significantly on the overall budget. The evidence is that many organizations fail to live up to their expectations in respect of completed projects in any given time period. It must therefore be more sensible to develop a monitoring system which focuses on outputs and the approaches outlined in the previous sections are of assistance in this respect.

The basic characteristics of the suggested approaches should be carefully examined before any new system is considered, as experience suggests that the imposition of formal planning and control systems on R and D has not met with a great deal of success. Any system which is likely to be accepted and effectively used will be one which can be seen to be helpful to all parties. In this respect a monitoring of the system itself is also necessary, so that adaptations can be made in the light of experience, to ensure that the maximum use continues to be made of the information generated.

REFERENCES AND FURTHER READING

Beastall, H., 'The relevance tree in Post Office R & D', *R & D Management*, **1**, no. 2, February 1971.

Brooke, D.G., 'The use of slip charts to review research projects', *R & D Management*, **4**, no. 1, October 1973.

Costello, D., A practical approach to R & D Project Selection, *Technological Forecasting and Social Change*, **23**, 1983.

Davies, D.G.S., 'Research planning diagrams', *R & D Management*, **1**, no. 1, October 1970.

Davies, G.B. and Pearson, A.W., The application of some group problem solving approaches to project selection in research and development, *IEEE Transactions in Engineering Management*, **EM–27**, August, 1980.

Dunne, E.J., How six management techniques are used, *Research Management*, March-April, 1983.

Fishlock, D., *The Business of Science*, Associated Business Programmes, London, 1975.

Hardingham, R.P., 'A simple model approach to multi-project monitoring', *R & D Management*, **1**, no. 1, October 1970.

Lanford, H.W. and McCann, T.M., Effective planning and control of large projects – using work breakdown structures. *Long Range Planning*, **16**, no. 2, 1983.

Liberatore, M.J. and Titus, G.J., The practice of management science in R & D project management. *Management Science*, **29**, no. 8, August, 1983.

Mansfield, E. How economists see R & D. *Harvard Business Review*, Nov–Dec. pp. 98–106, 1981.

Parker, R.C. and Sabberwal, A.J.P., 'Controlling R & D projects by networks', *R & D Management*, **1**, no. 3, June 1971.

Pearson, A.W., Planning and monitoring in research and development – a 12-year review of papers in R & D Management, *R & D Management*, **13**, no. 2, 1983.

Pearson, A.W. and Davies, G.B., Leadership styles and planning and monitoring in R & D, *R & D Management*, **11**, no. 3, 1981.

Souder, W.E., A system for using R & D project selection methods. *Research Management*, **21**, no. 5, pp. 29–37, 1978.

15

Development Overseas

Avison Wormald

*The justification for the inclusion of a chapter on development over-
seas is that a number of concerns are multinational in their operations
and, as Elwood Miller points out in the next chapter, this category in
strictness covers both a few large and many small businesses. Others
which do not fall within the generally accepted notion of 'multinational' engage as a matter of course in worldwide activities through
branches, subsidiaries and associate companies; and for an even larger
number exporting is an integral part of the business. However, it is
when a company first extends its operations into overseas markets that
a fundamental change occurs in the nature of the business. Furthermore, as the author of this chapter points out, any form of international
activity is fraught with continual change, much of it unpredictable, in
political, economic and monetary aspects.*

*The author, who has held top level appointments in international
companies, lists the main problems of development overseas as:
communications, complexity and risk. These factors are especially
prominent in connection with questions of credit, foreign exchange
and finance. The chapter contains a great deal of practical advice for
dealing with these questions and also refers to the vexed problems
associated with transfer pricing and the minimization of taxation. The
chapter ends with a reference to the different bases available for
consolidating the accounts of parent and subsidiary where different
currencies are involved. Many of the specialized accounting problems
introduced by the author are developed in the next chapter in relation to
multinational companies.*

Since the time of Adam Smith and the publication of *The Wealth of Nations* it had been increasingly accepted that international trade was advantageous to most countries. Then rather more than a century ago Ricardo showed that even when nations could be self-sufficient, there was generally an advantage in exchanging goods where there was a comparative advantage in the production of the same goods. If the advanced countries have sometimes retreated into protectionism it has not been so much from conviction as from disequilibria and pressures.

The individual trader or company follows this trend perhaps not because of economic conviction but because of government encouragement to take up such opportunities. There are, however, special problems in three main areas, namely communication, complexity and risk (Wormald, *International Business*, Pan Books, 1973). These problems affect all aspects of business, and perhaps the financial area more than most.

THE ROLE OF THE CHIEF FINANCIAL OFFICER

To a very large extent it depends on the chief financial officer whether business can be done at all in the international field, and if it is done, whether it is continuously and consistently profitable.

In the first place, the ability and willingness to extend credit to the overseas buyer is often critical in making a sale. There is, particularly in major capital equipment transactions, a good deal of open or disguised credit competition, although attempts are constantly made to limit some features of it by international agreement.

Credit has to be financed, so that the ability to finance it in the cheapest way is crucial. Moreover, credit represents risk, possibly of non-payment and frequently of exchange, so that the ability to assess the risk and to use the most appropriate means to limit it is also very important. Both these factors are reflected in some form in price, so that financial decisions are those which determine whether the business is profitable or not at prices which are competitive enough to obtain it.

The raising of local capital, the protection of the company's assets in foreign countries, taxation and the remittance of profits are further areas where the chief financial officer has a key role to play.

For every country currency is one of the most important manifestations of sovereignty and every country has its own fiscal and economic policies. Even where these are liberal and even favourable to the foreign business, they have to be studied and taken into account.

FOREIGN EXCHANGE

The simplest external transaction leads to problems of pricing and payment where the financial manager is involved. The price to the foreign buyer can be in the seller's currency, the buyer's or a third 'international' currency such as the US dollar. For the seller, the domestic currency has the advantage that the exact amount due will be known, although that seller or that government may prefer another currency if the national currency is depreciating rapidly in value or if it is desired to make payments abroad.

The buyer, on the other hand, will have to purchase the necessary foreign currency, and in most cases the rate of exchange between domestic and foreign currency will not be fixed. So at least between the time of the quotation and the acceptance there may be a change, favourable or unfavourable. The buyer may well prefer a quotation in his or her own currency or in a third, such as the US dollar, which may be more familiar than the seller's.

The fact that the foreign exchange transaction offers both sides the opportunity for gain as well as loss is generally immaterial, since buyer or seller will generally prefer not to have to bother about the speculative element. That is for the professional risk taker in currencies.

In the first place, the buyer can merely purchase the necessary foreign exchange to pay for the goods at the time of accepting the offer made. In this way it is known exactly how much the goods cost. The foreign exchange can be deposited in a bank and will earn interest. The rate of interest, however, even on a time deposit, will frequently be below that obtainable by some alternative use of the funds. But in this way virtually all the risk has been covered, although if the exchange rate moves in favour of the buyer's own currency there will obviously have been a *'manque à gagner'* or a lost opportunity, since he would now be able to buy the currency cheaper.

It will not always be convenient to immobilize funds in this way, a long time ahead perhaps of the payment which has to be made, or the rate of interest which can be earned may not be considered sufficient. In this case there exists the alternative of the forward exchange market. This may be of advantage to the seller also, in the contrary case where the quotation is in the buyer's currency, or in a third currency; it may be necessary to know at the time of concluding the transaction how much will be received in her or his own currency.

The forward exchange market, to which access may be obtained through any major commercial bank, will provide a quotation for a contract to buy or sell a wide range of currencies for delivery up to (normally) six months ahead. Contracts for longer periods are possible but can be very expensive.

According to the view the international money market takes of the two currencies involved, the price of the currency purchased may be higher or lower than the present price. Equally, when the contract matures and the currency is delivered it may be found that the contract price may be higher or lower than the then prevailing price. The rates for the principal currencies against the pound sterling are quoted daily in the London *Financial Times* for one month and three months.

If the forward exchange contract is made through the buyer's normal bank it may involve no down-payment at all, and therefore the funds are available for different uses. In other cases it may involve the payment of 5–10 per cent of the value, according to the credit status of the buyer and the risk involved in the particular currency. The buyer of the 'forward exchange' now knows exactly how much it will eventually be necessary to pay, as the buyer of the goods, or to receive as the seller. Funds wil not have been appropriated and the judgement of the market can be taken as regards the future relationship between the two currencies concerned.

These two arrangements can be combined in some cases (and dependent on exchange control regulations that may be in force) to produce a *foreign currency swap*. In this case the foreign currency is purchased in the 'spot' market and simultaneously a forward contract is arranged to sell the same amount of the currency at a future specified date. This is to cover the case when, for example, funds have to be advanced but will later be repaid in the same currency. There are also credit 'swaps' available in some countries: a bank in the foreign country makes a loan to a local borrower, for example a subsidiary of a foreign multinational, accepting the foreign exchange risk but of course charging interest on this loan. The foreign company then grants a loan to the bank outside the country, and normally this loan will be larger than the first so that the bank is compensated for the exchange risk and expenses.

All the foregoing arrangements are 'hedging' or safety devices to limit the risks implied in handling transactions involving foreign currencies. (In the strictly technical sense these measures are used to eliminate or reduce 'uncertainty', which is distinct from 'risk' in that it is possible to assign probability values to the latter.) It should be noted that normally it will be considered that the domestic currency is 'safer' than the foreign currency, since in effect the main part of the business of the buyer or seller is in any case inextricably involved in its own currency, good or bad. To take a 'bear' view of one's own currency and to hold funds in foreign currencies is normally considered to be speculative and, of course, may even be illegal.

This discussion was predicated on the requirements arising from the purchase and sale of goods but of course the arrangements mentioned are widely used in other cases where there has to be a transfer of funds across the exchanges.

PAYMENT AND CREDIT

The question of payment arises in the simplest international transaction and it is therefore natural that there should be a wide range of instruments to deal with it and the related problem of credit. These arrangements also cover the important aspect of 'bridging' finance, that is to say financing the exporter's outlay over the frequently long period between the despatch of the goods and the receipt of payment.

The letter of credit

The normal risks of commercial transactions are greatly increased in international trading, frequently because there is less knowledge on the part of one or both parties to a transaction about the other. Commercial practices differ greatly from country to country and there may be difficulties, imaginary as well as real, in obtaining recourse in the courts against one of the parties. The exchange risks already discussed also affect the arrangements in most cases.

The letter of credit has an important place in the list of arrangements designed to reduce risk. It consists essentially of an undertaking given by a bank, on behalf of its client, to a third party to the effect that it will honour its drafts on it provided that they comply in every respect with the requirements specified in the letter itself.

Since it constitutes an obligation to pay, the bank will require that it be backed by the necessary funds or that the bank should have control, partial or complete, over the goods involved in the transaction. Normally the credit will be irrevocable; if it is 'revocable' in very rare instances, then the conditions under which it can be revoked will obviously have to be precisely spelled out, otherwise the credit is valueless as a guarantee.

Letters of credit have value to both buyer and seller and the initiative to use them may come from either party to a transaction. To the seller it guarantees that the funds for payment are available; if it provides that payment may be made in his own currency it eliminates the exchange risk. If the credit is 'confirmed' through a branch or correspondent bank in the seller's country the guarantee obviously extends to payment as distinct from the availability of funds and then becomes virtually total. To the buyer also the letter of credit may have value since it immediately establishes unimpeachable credit-worthiness normally at very little cost, while it removes any risk there might have been in advance payment, if such were required by the seller.

The form of letters of credit, the legal situation, the costs and extent of discounting facilities differ from country to country so that both sides should obtain detailed information from their banks on these points.

The choice of payment method

Briefly the choices are between an irrevocable credit opened by the buyer in a bank in the name of the supplier and other methods mentioned above. The irrevocable letter of credit gives total security of payment, as far as both buyer and seller at least are concerned, but the seller may not obtain the funds until the goods are delivered. It is also mainly used where the seller has some doubt at least about the creditworthiness of the buyer.

Broadly speaking the choice of other methods will be between bank loans, or overdraft facilities (especially in the UK), and commercial paper which can be discounted or sold outright in the bill market. The value of commercial paper depends essentially on the credit standing of the parties concerned, and on whether it has been 'accepted' (see below) by a recognized financial institution, in the UK a major commercial bank or an 'accepting house' or merchant banker. When the paper is graded first-class it is the cheapest available source of funds, normally being at least 0.25 per cent cheaper than bank loans, and in times of tight money this spread can be up to 2.0 per cent. This method also has the advantage that it does not affect the general debt structure of the business, since it is self-liquidating. It should be clear that it can be used independently of shipping documents; in other words the sale can be on 'open account' if the relations between buyer and seller make this preferable, while the financing arrangements are made in parallel but independently of particular shipments.

Documentary credits, in the form of bills of exchange payable for example at 30, 60 or 90 days are generally preferred since they can be discounted in the bill market through the seller's bank and enable him to obtain his money much earlier. In most countries banks themselves will advance loans on bills of exchange, where the credit of the supplier is sufficiently good. A frequently used form of bank credit is the time draft which is drawn on the bank at the same time as the bill of exchange. Whichever method is used depends on the credit standing of buyer and seller, which in turn will affect the cost of the transaction, and the extent to which the seller at least can finance the transaction himself.

The residual risk in these transactions is covered partially at least as far as the bank is concerned by insurance of the goods, sometimes material proof that the goods exist in the form of warehouse receipts, frequently stipulations as to the nature of the goods, e.g. that they should be readily saleable in the event of default, and finally credit insurance.

Use of statistical methods

With a variety of sources of finance available statistical methods may be used to determine the lower-cost 'mix'. If the sums are large and there are several methods available it may justify the use of linear-programming techniques, the uses and limitations of which are explained in the standard treatises on mathematical techniques applied to financial problems.[1]

Credit insurance

This originated some sixty years ago and has increased steadily in volume and scope. It can confidently be said that the bulk of trade with the communist countries would not have been possible without it

---

[1] For example, Van Horne, (1977).

because of the lack of experience of most firms in the West in dealing with these countries, the very stringent requirements laid upon them by the buyers and the long credit terms frequently required.

The manner of operation of the British Export Credits Guarantee Department (ECGD) is typical of the many institutions, government and private, which now provide these services in all the principal trading countries of the West.

Medium- and long-term financing

The problems of medium- and long-term financing are different from those of ordinary commercial transactions, financed largely by documentary credits and discounting. They arise in connection with the sale of capital equipment or with the financing of direct investment in the foreign country. Whereas the terms of everyday commercial transactions do not normally involve complex financial packages, this is more likely than not to be the case with capital equipment sales. Medium-term finance is generally taken to be six months to five years, and long-term from about this period to very long periods indeed, perhaps exceeding 20 years.

The possibilities here are chiefly: loans to the buyer, which may be quite separate from payment for the goods; loans raised by the seller to allow credit to be given and payment in kind from production facilities to be established.

In most countries the commercial banks remain the major providers of funds, but their attitudes vary widely from country to country, and are constantly evolving within the country. British banks have traditionally regarded themselves as providers of working capital, either for seasonal peaks or to bridge periods of expanding business before more permanent arrangements could be made. This attitude has now virtually disappeared, although many bankers would agree that it colours their basic thinking. German banks on the other hand have made little difference between short- and long-term finance providing that the terms were satisfactory.

In the UK, the ECGD has proved indispensable in bridging the middle-term gap, by insuring the credit risk and thereby enabling the debt itself to be used as collateral, rather than the assets of the company making the sale.

The ECGD operates normally by a comprehensive cover of the seller's business, not merely the more doubtful areas. There are also 'tailor-made' policies for large capital goods and similar transactions. The ECGD guarantees can be used as security against bank loans and thus greatly facilitate the financing of longer-term projects. Normally of course a proportion of the risk, sometimes quite small, must be assumed by the seller.

These facilities, although increasingly used, are likely to be rather expensive so that other alternatives may be considered. Either the seller or the buyer, for example, can raise money through an issue of debt either in the national or the international money market, the terms being geared to the length of the repayment period, long-term rates tending to be higher than short-term.

Both the buyer and the seller may also seek funds from official sources, particularly the World Bank or its affiliates. Such loans are available for major projects which contribute to the economy of the country concerned, generally a less developed one. In the case of the UK there may also be the possibility of a government-to-government loan for a particular project, while in the USA the Agency for International Development (AID) is the main official channel for such loans.

The European Investment Bank

In the EEC the European Investment Bank, founded in 1958, has become a major supplier of long-term funds for large projects, particularly those concerned with the restructuring of industry and problems created by the integration of markets. It administers the resources of the European Development Fund and has therefore a special role in connection with the associated territories of the EEC.

Like a number of development institutions it seeks to avoid propositions which can be financed through ordinary private channels, although this is of course not a clearly defined concept; it depends a good deal on circumstances. It does not take equity positions and the project for which funds are required must be approved, though not necessarily guaranteed, by the government of the country concerned. Typically loans are for a period of around ten years, with a grace period of at least two years during which interest is not payable.

In general, in the case of large projects, there is great advantage in close collaboration between buyer and seller in regard to finance, thereby taking advantage of the credit status of both parties and the financial resources which may be available to one side and not the other. In particular, the exchange risk is something of major importance in regard to which close collaboration may be essential. There have been many cases of loans raised in foreign currencies which have had to be repaid at very unfavourable exchange rates (e.g. in the worst days of the pound sterling).

Finally, the Japanese have assisted the buyers of complete plants by offering to take at least part-payment in the form of the product, fertilizers or plastics, for example. Of course such arrangements have been facilitated by the fact that in the majority of these cases the plant contractor concerned has been associated with one of the great banking and trading houses and has been able to use their international selling organization to dispose of the product. Such arrangements can be very attractive to the buyer since it may take him some time to absorb the full production from the plant.

CAPITAL INVESTMENT ABROAD

So far the subject has been chiefly the payment and financing of commercial transactions, including large and long-term ones. Many of the considerations apply to the most long-term and hazardous transactions of all, that is to say where investment in a foreign country is made in fixed assets and the associated working capital.

The decision to invest in a foreign country may arise from a variety of reasons: exports may have attained a level where they justify local manufacture; there may be pressure from the local government, who may eventually close the market to imports; there may be resources to exploit of labour, materials, or geographic position, so that local investment appears attractive in itself. These are largely commercial and manufacturing decisions, but at many points in the feasibility study and inevitably before a decision to proceed is taken, a variety of financial considerations has to be taken into account. These are, principally, the financial climate of the country concerned; its relations with the investor's country; the availability of capital; taxation; the ability to remit funds in either direction, including dividends; the financial structure of a local company; requirements as to local participation; detailed capital and operating budgets. Direct foreign investment may take several forms, that is to say investment in a foreign company, acquisition of such a company, or a 'grass-roots' project to trade and manufacture. In all these situations, all or most of the foregoing considerations apply.

The financial climate

At the very outset of any economic feasibility study a view will be taken about the desirability of the prospective host country as a place for long-term investment, if only to screen it out in favour of more promising candidates. Such studies are expensive in money and labour.

The criteria most used relate to political and economic stability and a number of other factors which may be subsumed under the heading of 'integration in the international economic and financial community'.

Although a great deal has been written about this subject in general, something like second sight is needed to be right over the long term. Purely impressionistic judgements are however greatly to be deprecated; they have for example excluded from the purview of many British companies countries which have an excellent record and most promising future, such as Venezuela. The best that can be said about this immense topic is that a detailed checklist of points for investigation should be made, using inter alia material published in the standard works and periodicals such as the *Columbia Journal of World Business* and the *Economist*. There should then be exhaustive on-the-spot interviews with local politicians, businessmen and notables. The views of the local embassy are always valuable but it has to be remembered that all the senior staff are changed every few years, many of them have no detailed knowledge of the country and draw their information from quite restricted sources. The value of their views is largely that they are able to bring a wide perspective and experience, as well as trained judgement, to bear on the problem. What they certainly will know is the attitude of the country concerned to the UK or the USA, for example, which may be reflected in such matters as reciprocal tax treaties and trade agreements.

In discussions on the desirability of countries as places to invest the security of capital against expropriation is generally prominent. Expropriation is rather rare (although the case of Peru is fairly recent); what is more to be feared is nationalization or the forced sale of a majority interest. Looked at in this way few countries have been guiltless. The target for this type of action is more likely to be basic industry, such as has been nationalized in the UK, so that it has been the policy of some major companies, such as the RTZ Corporation, to bring in local capital from the outset. This is indeed now mandatory in certain countries, such as those of the Andean Pact (Venezuela, Columbia, Peru, Ecuador and Bolivia) and in most other countries the extractive industries, for example, will be reserved at least partially to the state. If therefore the project concerned is of the basic type, the most careful soundings will have to be taken in official circles. Of course, in many cases foreign companies have enjoyed freedom for sufficiently long to make the venture financially attractive, even though this freedom may have been curtailed later. A writer has aptly referred to capital investment of this kind as 'an investment with a fixed maturity'.

The other major risk factor of a general character is inflation. With rising levels of inflation in both the UK and the USA in the decade of the 70's the nature and importance of this factor is better appreciated. Inflation may affect the proposed investment in several ways: by erosion of working capital; by erosion of fixed assets, unless depreciation is allowed on a 'present-value' basis; indirectly, by price control which will probably be used by government in an attempt to restrain inflation. On the other hand, an attempt has to be made to assess what are considered as 'normal' profit margins, and in some cases it will be found that these offset the factors mentioned. The propensity to inflation in a given country is a factor which can be forecast, at least in a general way, for quite long periods ahead, since it depends largely on deep-seated structural and social factors; Brazil for example, uses controlled inflation as an instrument of policy Venezuela has had historically a low rate of inflation; US foreign, political and economic policy made inflation virtually inevitable.

Availability of capital

It will only be in very rare cases that the investor will wish to provide all the capital, both fixed and working, himself. Apart from offering a participation to local investors and using credit from commercial banks, he can frequently obtain grants and aid in kind from national and local authorities anxious to attract investment (not necessarily foreign) and in addition in many countries he will find an industrial development bank using government funds and frequently acting as an executive agent to promote enterprises identified as desirable by government planners. These frequently make available long-term loan capital at lower than commercial rates, with a grace period of several years before interest or repayment starts. In some cases there may even be equity participation. The fact that the Development

Bank is involved may also help in getting tax concessions. External development agencies, such as the World Bank or the European Investment Bank, already mentioned, may also be sources of funds for major projects.

It may be the policy of the foreign investor to make the minimum possible fixed investment, deriving his profit from the sale of goods and services to the company, and in this case he may provide funds through the current account, supplying on extended credit, so that in effect they are part of the capital of the business. This has two advantages: the interest and profit on the investment is self-liquidating; and the capital itself can be increased or reduced according to the view which is taken of the situation at any one time.

This policy raises the difficult question of 'transfer' prices. In many cases a foreign subsidiary will be looked on by the parent as a vehicle for selling goods produced elsewhere by the same company or group. The fact that a commercial relationship of this kind exists obviously provides tempting opportunities for extracting profits, and thus avoiding or evading local taxation and perhaps also exchange control, where it exists. This subject has become in recent years one of the principal arguments used against the multinational corporation. Undoubtedly it is possible to transfer profits by this means to areas of lower taxation and, by obvious subterfuges such as invoicing through an address of convenience in a tax haven, to avoid (or evade) taxation in *any* country, including the domicile of the parent company. The legality and advisability of any such arrangement is a matter on which expert advice should be taken in each case, but it should be remembered that in many countries the price of goods will be closely scrutinized to see whether there is a likelihood of such methods being used, and inter-company transactions may be scrutinized by the tax authorities.

Taxation

The case mentioned is one important aspect of taxation in foreign markets. In this case it is a potential advantage enjoyed by foreign companies. There are disadvantages also. In particular, the foreign company will generally consider that it should conform to the law, even if it takes advantage of legitimate loopholes. In many countries the native company will not feel this compulsion, and may only pay a fraction of the taxes it should. This may give it a strong commercial advantage, and this aspect should be looked at closely when setting up the foreign operation, to see whether a company paying taxes as prescribed can compete pricewise with others who do not.

The most serious concern of foreign companies is generally double taxation, that is to say taxation at the source and taxation where the profits are received. In a large number of cases both the UK and the USA have tax treaties, or double taxation agreements, which provide for the offsetting of the foreign tax against domestic tax. However, if the foreign tax is higher, then the effective rate will be the higher of the two.

By no means all countries are included in these arrangements, and then it is likely that profits remitted will be taxed in two places. It is these cases which give rise to many arrangements involving tax havens. It should be borne in mind that even the non-remittance of dividends may not exempt the parent company from taxation in all cases, and dividend policy in the subsidiary should be carefully considered from this angle. It may also be possible to remit some profits in the form of management fees or royalties, which may be allowed as business expenses in the foreign company.

Many countries have adopted withholding taxes on the remittance of dividends and profits, additional to the local income taxes. This of course makes it even more desirable to find other means of transferring funds. In some countries which have no tax treaty, the parent company may have to make a tax declaration on its local earnings, and in this case the withholding tax will be offset against any tax held to be due. In these cases the expenses of visiting directors and personnel can be included as business expenses. This form of treatment arises where the country concerned takes no cognisance of the fact that the local company has a foreign parent or shareholder.

The financial structure of the affiliate will also be affected by the taxation question, since it may be considered preferable to provide a substantial part of the capital as a loan. In all probability the interest on this loan will be allowable as a business expense, and therefore taxable only in the hands of the recipient. The repayment of the loan itself will not be taxable in the hands of the recipient, although in this case it may have to be made out of taxed profits. If depreciation allowances are generous, it may of course be repaid from *untaxed* cash flow in this way.

In each case, consideration should be given to all these possibilities namely transfer pricing, royalties and management fees and loan capital, and the optimum mix chosen with a view to the present and future tax liability. Few companies, it may safely be said, give sufficient thought to this aspect; frequently however it is a key factor in the profitability of the operation.

Transfer of funds

The number of countries where there is complete freedom to remit funds is very few, although the trend towards the creation of larger economic units, such as the EEC, the Andean Pact and the Latin America Free Trade area is providing a partial solution.

Difficulties in remitting funds may affect the ability to pay for essential raw materials as well as dividends and repayment of debt. The difficulties may be of two kinds: the need for permits, and the exchange rate at which funds can be officially transferred. The situation will obviously be affected by the view taken by government of the country as to the essential nature of the operations, so that if they are of any considerable size a specific commitment should be sought from the government. It will not amount to a guarantee but will establish a negotiating base at the least.

Equally it should be borne in mind that there are frequently restrictions on local borrowing by foreign companies, so that it is not always possible to respond to a policy of control of remittances by borrowing locally. There may well be a situation where owing to the growth of the business and or inflation, a continuous flow of capital will be required from the parent company, without always the assurance that it can be repatriated.

It may be noted that in some countries, including the UK and the USA, it is possible to insure at least against the ability to repatriate capital owing to political action.

Frequently legislation will include a requirement to have local capital and also directors and staff. In this case the freedom of manoeuvre in regard to remittances may well be affected, as the nationals of the country concerned may not identify their interests with those of the foreign company.

Financial reporting

Since different currencies are involved the question of the consolidation of subsidiary companies' overseas earnings is extremely complex. Should the parent company's accounts show what is believed to be the real business situation (sometimes called the 'economic' position), that is taking into account the longer-term earnings position, exchange and remittances, or merely translate into the national currency the performance of the subsidiary, using the most convenient rate of exchange? In some countries there are mandatory requirements, while in the UK the public accounting bodies have made recommendations, which however are not binding on the company.

Where earnings are not consolidated the problem also exists, and there may be a temptation to present the situation in the best light, changing the basis of reporting accordingly. For example, where the foreign currency has not actually been converted into the domestic currency, there may nevertheless be an 'unrealized' exchange loss. This need not necessarily be reported but, of course, unless the situation improves it will eventually have to be reported when the loss is actually 'realized'. Even more than in domestic accounting it is important to take a conservative view of earnings, asset values and potential tax liabilities in overseas operations.

REFERENCES AND FURTHER READING

Eiteman, D.K. and Stonehill, A.I., *Multinational Business Finance*, 2nd edition, Addison Wesley, 1979.

Van Horne, *Financial Management and Policy*, 4th edition, Prentice-Hall, 1977.

Wormald, A., *International Business,* Pan Books, 1973.

16

Accounting Problems of Multinational Business

Elwood L. Miller

In this chapter Elwood Miller extends the theme of overseas develop-ment, introduced by Avison Wormald in the preceding chapter, by considering the specific problems of the multinational corporation from a financial viewpoint.

The difficulty of defining a multinational business is solved by the adoption of the simple description of an enterprise that conducts operations in more than one country. The author acknowledges the fact that such a definition embraces very small companies as well as the immensely large organizations with which he is principally concerned. He demonstrates that the turnover of any one of the few larges multinational companies exceeds the gross national product of many individual nations. In spite of, or perhaps because of, their size, power and resources, there is evidence that these companies can have a beneficial influence on competition, consumer choice and the flow of capital. 'Multinational businesses', according to the author, 'accept the environmental challenge as problems waiting to be converted into opportuntiies'.

The central problem of the multinationals is one of co-ordination of operations, and the heart of the process of co-ordination lies in the accounting information systems. These systems can be greatly aided by developments in computerization, provided that the computerized system is installed with the direct participation of management. This advice is strongly supported by P.V. Jones in his chapter on Computer-isation. However, financial reporting is complicated by the need for it to fulfil both local and parent company purposes. Another accounting problem, particularly related to the consolidation of the results of all the member companies of the group, is to decide whether the company is represented by the proprietary entity or the parent company concept. In this connection the author holds that 'reporting all transactions as if they were conducted in the parent company domain can only produce economic nonsense'. The only present remedy is the use of supplemental data to the accounts.

Reiterating the message of Avison Wormald in the previous chapter, the author says: 'Since economic conditions are not static, the ability to adapt and respond to change . . . is of major importance'. The quoted statement is made in particular relation to the need for multinationals to 'manage and co-ordinate resources on a global scale'.

The problem of establishing 'fair' transfer pricing policies is examined in relation to the interests of the business and to those of the countries concerned, with the conclusion that multinationals must not be too greedy. The author also discusses the need for performance evaluation by units and within units. This activity should be the product of forms of responsibility accounting which should 'prohibit the arbitrary allocation of expenses among units'. The much used measure of the return on investment is regarded with considerable qualifications as an evaluator of performance or as a motivator. The author ends with a plea for commonsense explanations in multinational accounts.

Some wise man once mused that the only constant was change. Few people like change. It often requires adjustments to familiar habits. Sometimes it forces people to accept ways of thinking that seem totally alien. Perhaps the attribute of change that makes it most uncomfortable is timing. This might also be the reason why many governments and individuals seem uncomfortable with multinational businesses. Not only do multinational firms beget change out of necessity but they transmit it rapidly across national boundaries.

For simplicity, a multinational business or company (MNC) may be defined as an enterprise that conducts operations in more than one country. This definition includes tiny companies as well as industrial giants. Each faces similar accounting problems; the differences are mainly in degree.

Multinational companies have begun to outgrow countries. If the 100 largest economic entities in the world were listed – countries, by gross national products, and industrial companies, by annual sales – the listing would contain 50 countries and 50 companies. Annual sales of the world's *largest* industrial company (either Exxon or

General Motors in recent years) exceed the individual GNPs of 87 per cent of the free-world nations (106 out of 122) and are larger than the GNPs of the smallest 54 nations combined. The *smallest* MNC on the list will have generated sales in excess of $5 thousand million – larger than the GNPs of 72 individual countries and larger than the GNP of the smallest 18 nations combined (Miller, 1979).

Virtually all the attributes of MNCs are a function of size. MNCs are considered to be: efficient, powerful, stable, oligopolistic, dynamic, and flexible. Although these characteristics are relative, the larger MNCs face only two effective challenges: a government (either home or host) and another competing MNC.

Multinational businesses are the first economic organisms engaged in the management of resources on a global scale. While feared in some quarters because of the options they have available, MNCs are reported to have, on balance: (a) increased competition; (b) increased consumer choice; and (c) directed capital and other resources where needs and opportunities existed.

Most of the MNCs (95 per cent) are headquartered in eight countries: France, West Germany, Japan, the Netherlands, Sweden, Switzerland, the UK and the USA. Lacking an effective system of international law, MNCs must depend upon themselves to exist and function in a host of different environments: social, cultural, legal, and economic. Multinational businesses accept the environmental challenges as problems awaiting to be converted into opportunities. Most MNCs strive to purchase, produce, and assemble wherever they can at the lowest net costs, and to market their outputs where they command the most attractive prices. The central problem, then, is co-ordination of operations. Accounting and information systems constitute the heart of the co-ordination process.

At the risk of perpetuating the mythical dichotomy of accounting, this chapter will be divided into financial and managerial segments, followed by some concluding remarks on the states of the international accounting arts.

FINANCIAL ACCOUNTING PROBLEMS

Financial accounting is considered to represent the portion of management information shared with external users. Two financial accounting dilemmas are unique to multinational businesses: multiple accountings and foreign currency translations. For each topic, the backgrounds, available alternatives, and the approaches suggested will be addressed.

Multiple accountings, reportings, and disclosures

Accounting is said to be the language of business. Unfortunately, there is no international language of business as yet. Multinational operations are conducted in many dialects, both in the languages of people and of business.

In many instances, the first 'foreign' operations of multinational businesses were established as branches. Accounting and reporting systems represented duplications, in miniature, of those used by the headquarters supplemented by whatever reporting requirements (usually minor) were imposed by the host governments. In effect, these fledgling activities were not considered as foreign but were operated as if they existed in Liverpool or Manchester (for a London company) or in Chicago or New Orleans (for a New York firm).

Over time, branches and agencies were supplemented by subsidiaries and affiliates. Home-country oriented (ethnocentric) attitudes and systems were no longer feasible. Instead of mere appendages of the parent, foreign operations assumed the roles of strategic linkages in a transnational network (or TNN). Stockholders evolved into 'stakeholders', including influential interests such as trade unions and governments (Perlmutter, 1969a and 1976b).

Accounting systems also evolved. Differences in statutory and other reporting requirements of parent and host countries were usually overcome by the maintenance of multiple records. It is not at all uncommon today to find: (a) the official set required by the host country; (b) the set specified by the parent; (c) a set maintained to satisfy local tax regulations; and (d) a mini-set devised by local management for decision-making purposes.

MNCs place priority upon accounting information needed to operate. External financial reportings are (and have been) a nuisance: compliance reports bearing costs but few real benefits. Consequently, managements often regard external financial reportings as appendages of their internal information networks.

Consolidated reports

In less than three decades, consolidated financial reports of large multinational companies have completed their full circle of usefulness as far as most external users are concerned. Complexities inherent in modern business, aided by myopic accounting approaches (particularly in the USA and Canada), have enabled consolidated statements to conceal more than they reveal. In the two countries cited above, consolidated statements have evolved from general-purpose to single-purpose reportings having limited usefulness, and then only to shareholders of the parent company. There are several underlying problems and causes.

Preparers of consolidated reports are faced with several dilemmas:

1 How should the structure of the business be reflected?
2 How should the differences in accounting standards and tax regulations of the several component legal entities be reconciled?
3 How are the various national currencies to be translated into a common denominator?
4 Are the relative inflation rates between and among various host countries represented by differences in exchange rates? If not, what other means can be employed without double-counting the effects?

The answer, it seems, to each question is 'it all depends'.

Company structures

In most countries, the structure of the business may be represented by the proprietary, entity, or parent-company concepts, alone or in combination.

The *proprietary* concept does not commingle parent-company and minority interests. The investor takes up only the proportion of the assets of the investee that are owned; the assets may either be combined or reported as a one-liner investment, depending on the compatibility of the operations of the businesses. Historically, the advent of the conglomerate company rendered proprietary theory obsolete. Today, proprietary concepts are usually employed only in those cases in which no single investor company has ownership control.

Under the *entity* concept, both parent and minority shareholders are credited with their proportionate equities in the combined assets, tangible and intangible (including any differential or goodwill).

The *parent-company* concept emphasizes the ownership interest of the dominant or parent company; the minority interest in net assets (excluding goodwill) is disclosed almost as an 'outsider' interest rather than as a segment of equity.

Although the problem of structure also confronts domestic consolidations, considerations are more complicated for transnational businesses that operate within multiple legal and tax environments. In such cases, attempts to combine legal entites into a single economic entity, however it may be structured, face many conceptual hurdles in an effort to present economic reality fairly. While generalizations are always difficult, some can be offered. Practices in the USA[1] generally follow the parent-company approach for controlled subsidiaries, and the entity concept for associated companies (those in which 'significant influence', but less than majority control, exists).

The EEC seventh directive, adopted June 1983, basically requires consolidated financial statements of EEC-based undertakings where the parent company holds the majority of voting rights in a subsidiary, has a majority on the governing board, or exercises a dominant influence over the subsidiary pursuant to a contract. Where the parent company is outside the EEC, member states have the option of accepting the parent's worldwide consolidated statements, prepared in a manner equivalent to the seventh directive, in lieu of the EEC sub-consolidation. France and the Netherlands have partially adopted the directive; Germany implemented the legislation at the end of 1985. All member states must conform by January 1, 1990.

In this writer's opinion, the consolidation problems concerning company structures, like most accounting issues, cannot be resolved by specifying the use of any single, normative method. Standard-setting bodies, it seems, might be well advised to specify what methods are to be used in what circumstances, and require appropriate disclosures of the methods employed.

Another quite useful requirement would be the prominent listing of all companies related to the parent and the extent of ownership. The list should be divided into one part containing those companies which were included in the consolidated reports and a second part listing those reflected in the typical one-line disclosure 'investments in unconsolidated companies'. Many European countries are far ahead of the United States in providing this information.

---

[1] Except for 100 per cent elimination of intercompany profits (an entity concept) as a matter of convenience.

Accounting standards and tax laws

The labyrinth of various accounting standards and tax regulations poses particular consolidation problems for multinational businesses.

As mentioned earlier, consolidated statements have become single-purpose reports furnishing a macro view of a multinational business to its parent shareholders. Consequently, it has become standard practice to adjust all transactions that occurred in different host country environments to conform with the accounting standards and tax laws of the parent's country. Naturally, these adjustments are well-intentioned; i.e. to report all transactions within accounting and tax frameworks familiar to the parent stock holders. Nonetheless, reporting all transactions as if they were conducted in the parent domain produces economic nonsense more often than not. Many multinationals are induced to operate in other economic environments because of business and tax incentives that are more favourable than those afforded by the parent country. To repudiate these benefits in the consolidation process is to ignore economic reality, particularly for those multinationals that consider foreign operations as long-run growth areas and that deploy and redeploy foreign assets at will, rather than seek a one-way flow of profit repatriations. For such companies, the home-country domicile of the parent is largely incidental. The tax incentives are, of course, much more of a problem for parent companies in countries, such as the USA, that function within worldwide, rather than territorial, frameworks of taxation.

As the process of harmonization of accounting standards and tax laws moves forward gradually (such as in the EEC), some of the problems mentioned (as well as many of the existing incentives) will be removed. In the interim, however, managements can only adopt a situational approach in order to assure that financial reports, taken as a whole, coincide with economic reality. Given the inflexibility of the financial statements themselves, management must resort to devices such as supplemental data sections and president's or directors' messages in order to provide fair and useful information. Such approaches should be encouraged.

Segmented disclosures

In October 1975, Price Waterhouse issued its edition of *A Survey in 46 Countries: Accounting Principles and Reporting Practices*. Of the

246 topics in the survey, nearly forty were related to consolidated and/or segmented reportings. The survey included fourteen leading industrial countries and thirty-two developing and/or emerging nations. An interesting continuum was discovered. In six of the forty-six nations surveyed, only consolidated statements were issued to shareholders (Canada and the USA were the only industrial countries in this group; ten others had prohibited this practice). At the other end of the reporting continuum, in eighteen countries (including five industrial nations) only parent-company statements were supplied to users.

A two-dimensional problem was depicted. Some countries were still moving toward consolidated statements. Others provided nothing else. Still others (such as the UK) required firms to file financial statements of all companies (subsidiaries, parent, and consolidated) with a government agency or registrar.

Consolidated statements provide a macro glimpse of the total economic entity, and this still picture of a moving scene is necessary. However, consolidated reports are threaded with aggregate information and can conceal more than they reveal. Adequate micro (segmented) disclosures by multinationals (as well as domestic conglomerates) are necessary to enable users to examine the weft and warp as well as the entire fabric.

Small wonder, then, that the OECD specified essential segmented data, as well as information for the enterprise as a whole, in the disclosure guidelines for multinationals contained in its 'Declaration on International Investment and Multinational Enterprises' adopted on 21 June 1976 (see Fig. 16.1). On the heels of the OECD guideline, the European Parliament called for 'binding rules' to give the weight of law to the guideline. Instead, the fourth company law directive of the EEC implemented the segmented requirements: notes analysing turnover by category of activity and geographical market.[1] Consolidated reportings were the topic of the seventh directive now in its advanced stages of implementation.

---

[1] The OECD *Declaration* was implemented by the US government in Public Law 94–472 (International Investment Survey Act), and by the Financial Accounting Standards Board in its *Statement of Financial Accounting Standards No. 14*, 'Financial Reporting for Segments of a Business Enterprise', December 1976.

Fig. 16.1

OECD Guidelines for Disclosure of Information

Annex to the Declaration of 21st June 1976 by Governments of OECD Member Countries on International Investment and Multinational Enterprises

GUIDELINES FOR MULTINATIONAL ENTERPRISES

Disclosure of Information

Enterprises should, having due regard to their nature and relative size in the economic context of their operations and to requirements of business confidentiality and to cost, publish in a form suited to improve public understanding a sufficient body of factual information on the structure, activities and policies of the enterprise as a whole, as a supplement, insofar as necessary for this purpose, to information to be disclosed under the national law of the individual countries in which they operate. To this end, they should publish within reasonable time limits, on a regular basis, but at least annually, financial statements, and other pertinent information relating to the enterprise as a whole, comprising in particular:

   i)   the structure of the enterprise, showing the name and location of the parent company, its main affiliates, its percentage ownership, direct and indirect, in these affiliates, including shareholdings between them;
  ii)   the geographical areas* where operations are carried out and the principal activities carried on therein by the parent company and the main affiliates;
 iii)   the operating results and sales by geographical area and the sales in the major lines of business for the enterprise as a whole;
  iv)   significant new capital investment by geographical area and, as far as practicable, by major lines of business for the enterprise as a whole;

---

* For the purposes of the guideline on disclosure of information the term 'geographical area' means groups of countries or individual countries as each enterprise determines is appropriate in its particular circumstances.

v) a statement of the sources and uses of funds by the enterprise as a whole;

vi) the average number of employees in each geographical area;

vii) research and development expenditure for the enterprise as a whole;

viii) the policies followed in respect of intra-group pricing;

ix) the accounting policies, including those on consolidation, observed in compiling the published information.

Both directives, like most laws, specify only minimum reporting standards. For fair presentations, product or category-of-activity reports should be carried to segment margins – sales or turnover, less all directly traceable expenses (without any arbitrary allocations of home office expenses or income taxes). Geographical area results should also reflect segment margins but, where practicable, also reflect estimates of local income taxes. Together with disclosures of assets employed in each of the segmentations, users will at long last be able to glean some idea of the relative risks and profitabilities of the important parts of complex organizations. Managements of most well-managed companies have these data at hand and work with them regularly; segmented reporting merely stipulates that the data, in a condensed format, be shared with interested stakeholders.

Foreign currency translations

The translation of foreign currency transactions is as old as record-keeping itself, and was cited in the works of Pacioli (see Brown, 1905). Modern theorists hold that a transaction is *measured* in a foreign currency if it is expressed in a monetary unit other than that of the local domicile. A transaction is *denominated* in a foreign currency if settlement is to be made by a specific sum in a foreign currency, regardless of the exchange rate existing at the time of settlement. In the course of trade, one participant will face neither problem; the other will be confronted by both.

The affected firm can treat the transaction and settlement as one event or two. If one event, the purchase (or selling) price would simply be adjusted for any difference (the conversion gain or loss) upon settlement. If the purchase (or sale) and subsequent settlement are considered to be two transactions, the conversion gain or loss would be treated as a separate, interim event: the result of a change in money prices. Naturally, the net result is the same regardless of treatment. Those who have engaged in international trade have learned to reckon with and accept changes in money prices as one of the costs of doing business. However, the transaction described assumed two separate entities, legal and economic. The advent of multinational businesses complicated otherwise simple events.

Suppose, now, a different circumstance in which a US parent firm has a wholly-owned subsidiary in the UK. The subsidiary obtains a long-lived asset here by means of a long-term debt denominated in pounds sterling. The subsidiary has no problem since the transaction is measured and denominated in its local currency. The parent, however, will report different results upon translation and consolidation of the subsidiary statements, depending upon whether the event is considered to be one or two transactions. If one transaction, the exchange rate at acquisition of the asset would also be applied to translate the debt over time. No imbalances (gains or losses) would be reported while the debt was held or upon payment in sterling by the subsidiary. Translation would simply express the amounts in their dollar equivalents at the time of acquisition. If two transactions are assumed, the acquisition would be translated at the rate existing on the date acquired (at a point in time), but the outstanding debt would be translated at the current rates (over a period of time). The imbalances would be reported as translation gains/losses (while the debt was held) and conversion gains/losses (upon settlement). This method measures and denominates the transaction in the parent's currency, as if the transaction were conducted by the parent, in the USA, and in dollars. Unfortunately, this unrealistic, if not mythical, approach was adopted by the American FASB (1975).

Typically, today, operations are undertaken in other domiciles in response to existing inducements, whether strategic, legal, tax, financial, etc. Methods of consolidating financial statements (as used in the USA) that: (a) recast foreign transactions to conform with US accounting standards, and then (b) translate them as if they occurred in the USA, are worse than useless. The resulting reports were not only unrealistic and far cries from fair presentations, they were misleading to the extent that users (external and internal) were induced to take uneconomic actions. Internally, managements were induced to incur the real, economic costs of hedgings in order to protect against paper, translation 'losses'. Multilateral netting pools were established at considerable cost by large companies, yet the operating costs involved were not related to the real savings alone (the conversion expenses saved), the mythical translation gains and losses were considered as well. The economic benefits of profitable foreign investments were commingled with those of other operations; only the translation effects were separately disclosed for all to see. Consequently, some otherwise desirable undertakings may well have been foregone, for who keeps an account of opportunity costs? Externally, investors may well be encouraged to change their portfolios in face of the yo-yo earnings effects upon reporting companies.

Attempts to seek out and document the uneconomic actions mentioned are futile and irrelevant. The fact that an accounting practice induces such uneconomic action is prima facie cause for concern.

Economic sense can only be portrayed by retaining the essence of transactions as made in foreign domiciles, then translating them using the current rate (that existing on the balance sheet date), often called the European method. Imbalances would still occur wherever foreign investments are accounted for by use of the equity method. Such temporary imbalances should be recognized for what they are – translation differences – and recorded simply as deferrals or reserves. Gains and losses on foreign exchange should be recorded only when realized through the process of conversion – the actual exchange of one currency for another.

Fortunately, reason finally prevailed in the USA, and the FASB (1981) permitted the use of the current-rate method of translation so long as the sub-units were basically independent and operated in economies that were not hyper-inflationary (less than 100 per cent cumulative inflation over the most recent 3-year period).

MANAGERIAL ASPECTS

The preceding accounting problems of multinationals pertain to external financial reporting and, as a consequence, arise primarily because reporting practices must conform with standards devised to protect external users. Managerial, or internal, accounting is not governed by externally imposed constraints. Managements are free to develop and use data internally as they see fit. As a result, managerial accounting or information problems arise from the scope and complexity related to the co-ordination of widespread operations.

Decentralization – the process of delegating decision-making authority as far down the managerial hierarchy as possible – has been credited with the creation of domestic industrial giants, such as General Motors. Hindsight indicates that decentralization was appropriate for the efficient management of business segments that were, in fact, miniature businesses having acquired unique niches in the economy as well as the requisite economies of scale. Multinationals, on the other hand, must manage and co-ordinate resources on a global scale: buying, producing, marketing, and financing wherever the most favourable conditions exist. Since economic conditions are not static, the ability to adapt and respond to change (or to manage change) is of major importance. Decentralization is the antithesis of multinational operations; instead, co-ordination has become the theme.

Co-ordination explicitly requires centralized information and control of the main aspects of multinational operations. Four of the most troublesome aspects will be mentioned briefly and separately, although all are interdependent.

Information systems

In a business context, an information system should furnish the right information, to the right people, at the right time. A good information system is one that does this at the lowest possible cost. Consequently, much as resources are viewed by economists, good information systems do not exist but are 'becoming'. As a result, managements must be content to make do.

Information systems of most multinationals evolved much as the companies themselves. Domestic systems were transplanted, then adjusted for local differences. Over time, a rather disjointed network of different components had grown in a random manner. Today, many multinationals are attempting to integrate the collage of systems one function at a time in order to disrupt operations as little as possible.

Multinationals might have evolved without information networks. However, they would certainly have been less efficient.

As with domestic networks, information systems of multinationals are constructed upon and around the accounting system in order to comply with legal and tax requirements. Problems of volume have been tempered by the use of computers and standardized reporting formats. Timeframes and privacy have been aided by the use of coded Telex transmissions and satellite telecommunications.

The remaining hurdles are people-oriented (political, social, economic, and cultural) and not easily resolved. Experience indicates that a single monolithic information system cannot serve the diverse needs of local managers and the coordination needs of central management. At best, multinational systems can attempt to supply the information needed by local managers to make decisions within their scope of authority, and to transmit the parallel but different information needed laterally (by sister units) and vertically (by the headquarters for centralized planning and co-ordination). The connecting loop, of course, relates to downward feedback from the headquarters. Most of this information is quantitative and structured; it is often called the formal information network.

Of at least equal import for global operations is the informal or strategic information system involving changes, actual or anticipated, in the local environments, e.g. laws, regulations, government policies, labour relations, consumer tastes, and the like. Such information does not lend itself to structuring in content or timing but, instead, depends upon the astuteness of management.

Two generalizations can be made. First, monies wasted on false starts have convinced managements that the computer is no more a system, in itself, than is an adding machine. Companies increasingly will not consider computerized systems without the direct participation of management in order to preclude the systems serving the whims of computer departments instead of the needs of managements. Second, effective information systems can only be developed over time, based upon the considered needs and inputs of all levels of management.

Transfer prices

There is a consensus that, within the domestic milieu, the function of transfer prices strives to assure equity and goal congruence among the segments of decentralized firms. There is also a growing (yet long overdue) consensus that, in the international sphere, transfer prices are used to achieve a great diversity of goals and purposes, often interrelated and/or conflicting (see, for example, Sharav, 1974). Examples abound, as well as allegations, indicating that transfer prices can be (and have been) used to circumvent almost any type of control imposed by a host government.

As mentioned earlier, multinational businesses attempt to deploy and redeploy resources wherever they can be used to best advantage. Transfer prices are those amounts assigned to the movements of goods and services between and among related subunits of an organization. In the realm of international business, the organization considers itself a single, economic entity: the transfers are often viewed as internal transactions to be priced as management sees fit. The sub-units, however, are considered as separate, legal entities by the host governments concerned; the transfers across national boundaries represent external transactions subject to valuation by 'arm's-length' criteria, as if the transactions were consummated by unrelated parties.

These two concepts of transfer prices represent the extremes of a continuum of methods found in practice. Arm's-length prices tend to be inoperable for a variety of reasons. On the other hand, multinational manipulators soon find themselves confronted by a maze of variables, often conflicting and posing a myriad of trade-offs. Unsuccessful manipulators soon learn to compromise; those that are successful are soon branded as undesirable citizens by host (and often home) governments and sanctioned accordingly.

Because of the need to adapt to changing events, multinationals cannot be expected to employ a uniform 'policy' of transfer pricing. Neither can multinationals be expected to transfer the same good to a single recipient from various sources at the same price – that expectation conflicts with economic reality. Transfers will be expected to be made at fair prices, with 'fair' being determined *ex post facto* by the host government and the multinational. Since fair prices connote amounts in excess of cost, most multinationals have developed dual systems of transfer prices: the fair price, for external use; a cost-based price for internal decision making. In sum, multinational businesses should avoid becoming too greedy. Host governments will tend to be satisfied with a reasonable share of tax and other economic benefits.

Performance evaluations

Responsibility accounting is the process that attempts to trace and compare the inputs and outputs of definable segments of an enterprise, whether domestic or multinational. Over time, these segments or responsibility centres have been labelled as cost, expense, revenue, profit, and investment centres, dependent upon the inputs and outputs controllable by the segment. Much like transfer prices, responsibility accounting concepts were products of decentralization. Delegations of authority carried with them the responsibility to make periodic reckonings of accomplishments. These periodic reckonings are called performance evaluations.

Unfortunately, while performance evaluations are widely used, they are not as widely understood and often are misused. Domestic ramifications will be examined first, since they are transferred to and permeate international practice; then the peculiar aspects affecting foreign operations will be addressed.

Domestic operations

In the domestic context, insufficient attention is directed to what is being measured, the meanings of the measurements themselves, and the controllability of the inputs and outputs by the levels being evaluated. Frequently, activities that produce entirely for distribution to affiliated units are converted into profit centres. Pseudo profits are added to the prices of internal transfers, thus obscuring realities. Production activities are basically cost centres. Attention should be directed primarily towards the control and use of resources employed, usually by means of standard cost and budget systems. This cardinal error stems from the recognition that profit is an inclusive denominator and a powerful motivator. However, few levels below the top executive echelon are really responsible for profits. Consideration must be applied to the meanings of measurements (Wilkinson, 1975) as well as the attributes measured. For example, monetary measures are products of units and prices. In times of rising prices, monetary measures used alone often confuse accomplishments and circumstances. Focusing upon quantities of units (goods or services) is an excellent way of eliminating the uncontrollable effects of changing price levels. In all cases, evaluations should focus upon those operating aspects that are controllable at the particular levels. This last observation prohibits the arbitrary allocations of expenses among units. The above tenets are so frequently violated in practice that one can only believe that they have come to be ignored completely.

Two additional fallacies are interrelated. First, the duality of performance evaluations is often not recognized. Rarely can the same criteria and measurements be applied to operations and the personnel involved – overall functions and responsibilities seldom coincide. A second common fallacy is the misplaced reliance upon the data in routine, financial accounting reports as the basis for performance evaluations. Financial accounting reports are designed to, at best, report on the accountability or stewardship of the company as a whole (a macro viewpoint). Applications to segments are unwise.

The ill-placed emphases upon profit as an evaluator also afflict other profit-based criteria such as return-on-investment (ROI) and residual income (RI). The literature over the years has been replete with the inherent shortcomings of both measures as evaluating mechanisms so these faults will not be addressed here. Suffice it to say that such uni-dimensional measures are used today by those who, for whatever reasons, do not care to devote the time necessary to make reasoned assessments of operating results.

While ROI has defects as an evaluator, it may be even more suspect as a motivator – and for the most profitable segments. For example, the manager of a segment reflecting an ROI of, say, 30 per cent would not be motivated to undertake a venture expected to yield 20 per cent, thereby lowering his performance (and bonus). However, if the other segments of the company are earning returns of only 10 to 15 per cent, the company as a whole will have missed a desirable opportunity. This defect may be remedied by a refinement of the ROI method (residual income) that considers returns in monetary terms as well as percentages. Here a threshold rate of return is applied to the resources employed and the resultant amount is deducted from reported profits reflecting a residual (or deficiency) amount. Also, various threshold rates can be applied to different resources (or operations) bearing different degrees of risk. Thus, the refinements mentioned make residual income a more flexible and logical approach than ROI. Nonetheless, both methods suffer from the remaining defects cited and should be approached with due caution.

Foreign operations

The foregoing problems are common to evaluations of domestic operations and managers. Evaluations of foreign activities are fraught with all those mentioned plus several others. Domestic operations benefit from a common set of environmental factors, whereas foreign operations are often conducted in circumstances that defy standardized measurements. Furthermore, it is common for some overseas activities to perform strategic roles that are not profit producing at all. Headquarters' decisions concerning co-ordination and deployment of resources (including the multiple approaches to transfer pricing) directly impact the operating results of individual units. Whose decisions are being evaluated? Should the evaluations be made in the currency of the parent or of those of the foreign domiciles? How are relative inflations and exchange-rate fluctuations (two related but dissimilar matters) to be taken into account? Such questions do not lend themselves to simple solutions.

Regardless of the defects related with profit-based measures, studies recurringly indicate that ROI (or some variant method) is employed almost universally (Persen and Lessig, 1979). Executives acknowledge the weaknesses mentioned yet contend that ROI is the best method available. That borders on nonsense.

Most executives will also admit that ROI and similar measurements based on financial accounting reports are used because they are routinely available and are easy to calculate and compare. Moreover, top executives are evaluated by ROI methods, why should it not be applicable to others? While the demands on executive time are often tremendous, it should be recognized that the results being evaluated usually represent the fruits of a year's efforts by other parties. Surely performance evaluations warrant more time and thought than perusal of lines on a graph or an array of numbers on a list.

Realism and equity suggest a process similar to the following:

1 define the purposes of the various units;
2 determine the roles of the units and their managers;
3 select appropriate criteria to measure efficiency (doing something right) and effectiveness (doing the right something);
4 establish standards to evaluate the above performances;
5 select the timings of evaluations;
6 establish a process to communicate the results.

If nothing else, the above process will tend to create a better understanding of the company as a whole as well as the interrelationships between and among segments, domestic and foreign. Past results and future prospects will, more often than not, be seen as the products of a melange of factors: past decisions made by managers at the headquarters and unit levels, the effects of subsequent events (planned and otherwise), all coloured by future expectations.

Furthermore, increased reliance upon multi-dimensional tools, such as flexible budgets, as motivators and evaluators would effectively cure the disease attributed to uni-dimensional measures: management myopia. Far too many American firms have been accused, and rightly so, of overemphasis upon short-term results: the next quarter's or year's ROI or EPS. Consequently, American firms have lost their willingness to take risks, to compete for promising markets, and, in fact, have surrendered markets to foreign competitors. Sadly, many of these allegations are true. However, if change is to occur, managements and accountants will have to change not only their ways of thinking but also those of the members of the investing communities. More relevant methods of performance evaluations will have to be adopted and publicized.

Normative measures will be found difficult to construct. Subjectivity will be found equally difficult to avoid. Such tends to be the nature (as well as the source of the challenge and satisfaction) of the multi-dimensional art of multinational business.

Taxation

The intricacies of international taxation are addressed elsewhere in this book. This section will examine briefly some of the aspects of accounting for the infinite forms of international taxation that vex most businessmen (and accountants as well). Some cautions are in order. Few accountants can lift, much less comprehend, the more than 68 000 pages comprising the current manuals of the US Internal Revenue Service alone, not to mention the directives employed in other countries. Also, the US system of taxation is without parallel as far as complexity is concerned: it is unwieldy. Unfortunately, more countries seem to be gravitating toward US methods and the problems of tax accounting will tend to become even more complex.

Tax accounting procedures should serve three needs of managers of headquarters and foreign companies:

1   to comply with statutory requirements;
2   to reflect fairly the amount of taxes paid or payable;
3   to assist in tax planning.

Compliance with statutory requirements is simplified in those countries (such as France and Sweden) which require conformity between financial and tax accountings. Most countries, however, recognize that tax accounting (serving a macro purpose) should be separated from financial accounting (servicing the needs of micro units or firms). In the latter cases, supplementary tax records must be maintained, the accountant's function being to reduce redundancy and cost as much as possible.

Difficulties in accounting for some local taxes paid usually concern the volumes of transactions, such as those related to border, sales, and value-added taxes. These are best resolved by standardized or computerized handling. Documentation supporting other local taxes paid, such as on business incomes, is typically a non-recurring yet important matter. The standard advice encourages firms to understand the statutes and, where interpretations can vary, take the most favourable avenue that can be supported by documentary evidence.

At the headquarters level, accounting for taxes paid by foreign units is relatively straightforward if the headquarters' domicile taxes incomes earned solely within its borders (the territorial principle of tax domain).

On the other hand, if the headquarters is located in a country (such as the USA) that exercises taxing authority on incomes wherever earned (the worldwide principle), significant accounting problems result. To avoid double taxation of foreign-based company incomes, the USA employs complex systems of tax treaties and foreign tax credits. Both systems mandate accurate, supplementary accountings be maintained.

Close co-operation is required between accounting and tax departments, as well as mutual understanding of the peculiar needs of each. For instance, tax departments need detailed operating statements for each foreign location; consolidated statements are of no value at all. Natures and sources of revenues and expenses must be clearly described. Foreign tax receipts, translated copies of returns, and detailed information often prove to be difficult to obtain where there is no control of foreign entities.

International tax planning is a process that draws on accounting, tax, and other projections of data to determine whether, where, how, and with whom to conduct operations in order to achieve the desired business objectives with the minimum total tax burden. Considerations of proposed new ventures offer a wide range of alternatives. Tax planning of ongoing foreign operations soon becomes a maze of trade-offs resulting from change, both in frequency and magnitude. Experience indicates that, on an ongoing basis, planning of the sources and timing of dividend repatriations furnish the greatest benefits. Tax planning, much like all forms of forward thinking, also provides a better understanding of the complex multinational organism. Manipulations of other tax trade-offs, while important, should not be allowed to relegate otherwise sound business strategies to minor roles.

ACCOUNTING FULL CIRCLE

Accounting enjoyed an international genesis or birthright. The Babylonians, Greeks, Romans, Turks, and Italians contributed and combined ideas and practices that led to the invention of bookkeeping. The invention of movable type by Gutenberg, a German, enabled a Franciscan monk to describe double-entry bookkeeping for use by the rest of the existing world.

In the outpouring that followed, bookkeeping travelled in the wake of business to Holland, Scotland, England and eventually, to America. In the process, bookkeeping was transformed into a profession known as accountancy, or the language of business.

Over time, the influences of different environments led to the crystallization of national accounting practices. Today, there is US accounting, UK accounting, German accounting, and so on. The result is a language of business consisting of many dialects.

The present situation is also something of a paradox. International accounting organizations are pressing for greater uniformity of national accounting and reporting standards. On the other hand, multinational and other complex companies are being required to employ local approaches to accountings of international operations. The solution, of course, lies in the middle ground, in reaching agreement, initially by regions or spheres of influence, eventually worldwide. In the process, international accounting will develop and mature while serving the needs of an interdependent world community. Accounting will have come full circle.

During the interim, standard-setting bodies must realize that time and circumstance have precluded reliance on normative applications if economic sense is to be reflected in financial reports. The situational approach must be recognized. This means that standard setters should seek to identify those cases that are alike, then prescribe the accounting practices most appropriate. More responsibility and reliance will need to be placed upon the judgements of managements and auditors: the former to match situations and accountings, as well as to explain the methods used; the latter to attest to the appropriateness of the methods selected as well as the fairness of the reported results.

Examples of useful management explanations are:

1 the structure of the firm – organizationally and geographically;
2 differences between the home and host environments – economic, legal, tax, and accounting;
3 the effects, good and bad, of the above differences upon the financial reports;
4 the effects, good and bad, of changing price levels and how management is planning to keep the stockholder whole (Miller, 1978);
5 the nature of foreign operations: whether they are short- or long-run ventures, considered as dependent or independent activities and, consequently, the perceived extents and effects of foreign exchange exposure, segmented as considered necessary.

These examples may seem to be radical suggestions. Nonetheless, they are compatible with the fact that accounting, financial reporting, and auditing are adaptive arts, rather than rigid sciences.

Furthermore, the suggestions for commonsense explanations threaded throughout this chapter can be implemented internationally today, regardless of the differences existing in the languages of people or the languages of business. We should get on with it.

REFERENCES AND FURTHER READING

Brown, R. (ed.), *A History of Accounting and Accountants*, Jack, 1905.

Financial Accounting Standards Board, *Statement of Financial Accounting Standards No. 8*, 'Accounting for the Translation of Foreign Currency Transactions and Foreign Currency Financial Statements', FASB, October 1975.

Financial Accounting Standards Board, *Statement of Financial Accounting Standards No. 52*, 'Foreign Currency Translation', FASB, December 1981.

Knickerbocker, Frederick T., *Proceedings: First Annual International Business Conference*, Saint Louis University, 1 December 1975.

Miller, E.L., 'What's Wrong with Price-Level Accounting', *Harvard Business Review*, Nov.–Dec. 1978.

Miller, E.L., *Accounting Problems of Multinational Enterprises*, Lexington Books D.C. Heath, 1979.

Miller, E.L., *Inflation Accounting*, Van Nostrand Reinhold, 1980.

Perlmutter, Howard V., 'The Tortuous Evolution of the Multinational Corporation', *Columbia Journal of World Business*, January–February, 1969 (a).

Perlmutter, Howard V., 'Alternative Futures for the Multinational', *Proceedings: Second Annual International Business Conference*, Saint Louis University, 16 December 1976 (b).

Persen, William, and Lessig, Van, *Evaluating the Financial Performance of Overseas Operations*, Financial Executives Research Foundation, 1979.

Sharav, I., 'Transfer Pricing – Diversity of Goals and Practices', *Journal of Accountancy*, April 1974.

Wilkinson, J.W., 'The Meanings of Measurements', *Management Accounting*, July 1975.

17

Financial Control in the Public Sector

John Lloyd

The object of the following chapter is to examine present and potential developments in financial control techniques for the public sector of the economy. Because of the immense and varied range of undertakings in that sector the author focuses on the health services, but the principles he derives are of equal validity to other public sector organizations, as well as to profit-making enterprises. The chapter therefore stands in its own right in a volume devoted to financial planning and control, not only because of the immense resources which are applied to public services, but also because of their consequent influence on business. Many commercial enterprises are, for example, virtually dependent on contracts from central or local government.

Of direct relevance to business are the analogies, expressed and implicit in the chapter, between the public and private sectors so far as financial control is concerned. Where there are differences they are largely matters of degree and not fundamental. The absence of a profit motive in no way limits the need for cost control. Indeed, the private sector could learn many lessons from John Lloyd's discussion of the defects of too rigid budgeting procedures; the virtue of establishing output criteria; the conflict between control by volume of activity rather than quality of performance; the need for delegation of responsibility for costs; the evaluation of options; and the use of performance indicators. His theme, which is applicable to all organizations, is the need to obtain the most effective use of the resources available.

The author emphasizes that essential to the management of any kind of activity is the existence of a multidisciplinary team for the planning and monitoring of performance. In the health service that team will include consultants and medical staff as well as members from financial and administrative functions. Likewise, in the field of commerce and industry, that team must embrace operating managers as well as accountants and administrators. The problem of management is to resolve differences of viewpoint and approach amongst the professions represented on the team, and to ensure that a commonly understood language is used.

The economic reality of limited resources is increasingly producing a sharper, more commercial approach to management in the public sector. The Ward Sister still dispenses love and care in abundance but is also likely to be a budget holder in a decentralized management system. Teachers face pressure for some form of appraisal and performance-linked remuneration. At the same time the drive for efficiency and the pursuit of value for money provide opportunities for enhancing the status and role of financial management in such areas. For too long financial accountability was viewed as simply ensuring that spending did not exceed the approved allocation and that no fraudulent use was made of the funds. In the current environment real managers, rather than administrative facilitators, have a key role to play in providing relevant information and 'quantifying' situations. In many ways the social objectives of much public expenditure, and the absence of any market test, increase the need for rigorous evaluation, and the continuous examination of operational costs and activity.

Although it is easy to go too far in emphasizing the similarities between the activities of private and public sector organizations, the sensitive manager can recognize the common ground. Lessons of common usefulness can be learnt from either sector. Nevertheless, the financial manager of any organization should first seek to understand the underlying culture and specialized institutional arrangements which exist in the unit under control. Any failure to do so can result in anomalies due to the nature of the activity. Payment by results in an American Police Force led to greater activity in the form of more arrests – but more wrongful arrests.

The public sector covers an extremely wide field, but in order to narrow the discussion and give it a practical emphasis, this chapter concentrates primarily on the health service, especially performance evaluation and monitoring in that service. It is particularly in this area that the new breed of general manager, equipped with the sharp management techniques of the private sector, seeks to evaluate organizational performance. They are themselves stimulated by short term contracts and performance reviews, and their power is increased by the greater independence and flexibility now given to the individual hospital or other unit.

The movement to introduce a more commercial approach, and to highlight problem areas with discretionary slices of financial information, is not without its critics. Many perceive a danger that a cost-efficient approach could edge out health care effectiveness, with consequent damage to both patients and staff. For example, with workstudy and detailed costing it is possible to reduce the length of stay for in-patients, and consequently to increase the total throughput of the hospital. Output rises, average cost per case declines, the waiting list is reduced and ministers applaud! However, the temptation to win the quantity battle may have sinister repercussions on the quality goal, and lead to an increase in readmissions, like new cars returning for further attention under a warranty scheme. Such a process is frustrating for the patient and any cost savings can prove to be illusory.

In such a situation the family and the community services must step in to provide accommodation, care and attention. The hospital finds itself running harder to stand still, and the increased work load demands more funds to service the higher level of activity. The excellently organized pathology department, providing an efficient and fast service, will quickly find that its reputation leads to increasing demands for more sophisticated tests of a more expensive nature.

Comparisons with the private sector

The manager within the health service faces certain dilemmas not suffered by a private sector counterpart. The objectives of commercial undertakings are clear, namely to cover total costs and to generate funds and prospects for continued survival. The health service has many, often not very well-defined objectives some of which are in conflict with each other. The clinician is determined to maximize care for individual patients; the manager's perspective is to improve care for a specified population.

In organizational terms the hospital manager can be viewed in parallel with the commercial executive counterpart, in the sense that she or he controls an independent unit which is, however, in turn controlled by a 'holding company', represented by a district or regional health authority. Head Office sets out the strategy, provides the funds, and allows the individual unit managers operating discretion in whatever way best suits the particular conditions. However, the special environment in which the health service manager operates imposes a more difficult and tortuous task in imposing financial controls. Questions of financial viability and laid-down procedures can be relegated to the rank of minor matters in a situation dominated by life-and-death decisions. Medical power and influence is strong, and there still exists a mystique which renders even limited evaluation of procedures a matter of difficulty. An analogy can be found in education where teachers resent any interference in their academic freedom, or the idea of any form of performance evaluation, whether by students or others. Likewise in industry salesmen frequently maintain that their effectiveness and flair must not be inhibited by rigid procedures; and the research engineer is traditionally antagonistic to cost control.

As in industry, the skill of the financial manager in the public service must be supplemented by a high level of ability in political and human relation abilities. Nevertheless, medical professionals, constantly grappling with the strain of tightened budgets, and consultants managing their surgical and medical teams, are showing signs of welcoming financial information systems which assist them in their management role.

A system which provides accurate and detailed information on the cost implications of different levels of activity, and how costs vary with changes in case-mix and treatments, is a positive aid to better decision making. Financial managers must try to remove the suspicion that their function is only to enforce cuts. They should build incentives into the system, so that genuine and successful efforts to be more efficient are rewarded by some claim on the savings, and are not penalized by reduced budgets.

A budgeting system, even if based on sound principles of accountability and delegation, can be frustrating if the quality of the data provided is inadequate. Understandable resentment and disillusion is felt by clinicians who, given timely warnings of overspending their budgets, cannot derive enough information to know what to do about it. It is not very useful to provide information on average cost per in-patient day when the consultant wishes to know how total costs will change if the length of stay of patients in a particular ward varies, or if the treatment approach is changed. Moreover, slavish subjection to budget limits can be misguided where the marginal cost of extra activity is really quite low and the benefit of such activity is high. In the same way in industry overspending on the budget can be quite justified where it is due to increased activity which produces more sales and more profit.

In many public services the absence of accurate information has led to a vacuum where decisions are often based on convention and subjective evaluation. Information technology is breaking down these imprecise procedures, but there is an obvious danger that by focusing on the more obvious measures of performance, such as costs, the exercise will assume the limited role of good housekeeping rather than opening up a chapter of efficient and dynamic management.

USING SCARCE RESOURCES

Public services, like any other form of economic activity, use up scarce resources which could have been used beneficially elsewhere. Planning and control in the public sector must then serve two aims: to ensure that organizations are engaged in activities of significant benefit to consumers; and that this is being done with minimum cost. In business, this is understood only too well: the need to produce the right product at the right price. What is more difficult to ascertain in time is just what is the right price and the right product. In business the market will ultimately and inevitably produce the information one way or the other.

The effective planning and use of resources in the public sector require the application of techniques to allow, indeed to force, an organization to evaluate its own performance in relation to set criteria, and ultimately in relation to benefits achieved. It is a soul searching exercise, designed to ask awkward, fundamental questions, but as an approach to problem solving has much to recommend its more general use.

The health service, like the police and the education system, is faced by many competing and emotional demands on its finances. One way forward for the planner/manager is to establish a framework of outcome-related budgeting, and to consider expenditure plans in the light of both the cost and the effectiveness of different priorities.

The police force is having to consider its objectives and priorities very carefully as competing claims are advanced; and some, at least implicit, recognition seems to have been given to public safety and the prevention of disorder, as being more important than the solving of personal crime.

The calculation of cost-effectiveness in health is extremely complicated. One measure, for example, is Quality Adjusted Life Years (QALY). This concept tries to capture both the quantity (years) of life delivered by different medical interventions, and the quality or comfort of such years. Using patients' assessments of the quality of their survival, allows an all-embracing measure of outcome. Certain procedures may prevent premature death, but permit a life pattern of some pain and disability, so its QALY score might be exceeded by an intervention generating a similar life extension, but of a higher quality. Such calculations are controversial and difficult but the need to make the calculation forces planners to recognize the true nature of the choices available and to make explicit their reasoning. By comparing the cost and the success of different medical interventions we can spell out the consequences of devoting resources to one rather than another and focus attention on patients and their health. The allocation of resources so as to produce maximum benefits is a more complex exercise than simply counting the number of out-patient attendances, and involves the concerted effort of clinicians, financial staff and economists. It is the approach commonly used by business in maximizing profits.

OUTPUT BUDGETING AND OPTION APPRAISAL

Output or programme budgeting can provide the crucial information for planning purposes. Moving away from the traditional and conventional input budgeting approach means relating budgets to various programmes, e.g., surgical, or to particular client groups, e.g., the elderly. The approach demonstrates the extent to which the expenditure is appropriate to the priorities and choices of programme adopted. Within the hospital context, a financial presentation linking expenditure over a number of years to the activity levels of individual programmes can be of great value. Studies using these principles have managed to allocate the vast majority of total spending to specific programmes and consequently to monitor them on cost per bed day and per discharge. This form of budget analysis helps to reveal which programmes merit more serious examination. Thus in one case the expenditure on maternity cases continued to rise whilst the number of patients was falling. The reason could have been inertia and inefficiency, but in this instance was a genuine effort to improve the quality of the service. The point is that budgeting by programme focuses attention on such issues, enabling managers to bring the costs and activity of individual programmes under the same microscope.

Of equal importance to programme budgeting is the evaluation of the different options available to meet the objectives of the organization. A typical example might be the various options available for improving the quality and quantity of health services to the elderly, an area in which research reveals a severe deficiency. Although the mention of option appraisal may alarm some health service personnel, there is a pressing need for the financial officer to play a major role in the collection and evaluation of information, financial and otherwise, for such appraisals. In this exercise the financial officer should become an influential member of a multi-disciplinary team, making the basis of decisions less opaque to fellow professionals and to the general public, but for this purpose it is necessary to take a wide view to include the non-financial repercussions of the various options. An enlightened view of the nature of efficiency shows that simple cost minimization is only one part of the choice, and that anyway costs borne by those outside the service, including patients, should play some role in the equation. Option appraisal often means that, by rigorous comparisons of the alternative costs and benefits, a more radical solution than the immediate favourite can be the most feasible and economical.

The above points are illustrated by the following case study.

A case study

A hospital needed to save money and saw some salvation in closing two wards at weekends, operating them on a five-day-week basis. The wards provided a valuable service by concentrating on short-term elective cases needing both medical and surgical treatment in one area, thus giving specialized and efficient care. However, as time went on it became obvious that the new system involved considerable changes in admission arrangements, nurse training and other organizational factors. Staff regarded the scheme as yet another ill-conceived, money-saving operation. They resented the change as they felt that their work loads had increased and they lost many of their less dependent patients. Those on the five-day wards were considered to be in a privileged position, but they became quickly disillusioned by the increased burden of paper work. With patients coming and going more quickly, they felt that their work required greater communicative and clerical skills, for which they had not been adequately prepared.

Large financial savings were expected because the wards concerned were closed for three nights and two days each week. However, the high overheads showed only marginal reductions. The saving in lighting and heating was small and portering costs had already been reduced to the weekend minimum. The fixed cost of catering remained high, and the apparently variable cost of food did not decrease significantly for the small change in the demand. The saving in nursing wages was partly offset by the need for additional nursing aid to cope with the resultant pressures elsewhere in the system, and the need to provide cover for patients who could not be sent home during the weekend. Expensive treatments, such as operations, X-rays and medication, had to be carried out in fewer days and, as a result, the cost per patient per day rose. Community services were hard pressed to deal with the Friday night exodus. Meanwhile valuable facilities were left unused for two days a week.

The failure of the scheme was due to lack of rigorous initial analysis and pre-planning by a team which should have consisted of representatives of all the interests involved, not only financial management.

CAPITAL PROJECTS

Financial techniques for the appraisal of capital expenditure in business are dealt with in detail elsewhere in this book. These techniques are equally applicable to the health service when appropriately adapted. It is again important, however, that the projects shall be appraised by those who will be responsible for managing and operating the facility when it is acquired.

An obviously important example of a major project in the health service is a proposal to build a new hospital, usually as a replacement for one or more older buildings.

Pressure to do so is likely to be exerted by politicians, health authorities, medical staff and local interests, and the capital may not be unduly difficult to obtain. However, the new facility will determine the nature of the service to be provided for many years and the capital expenditure is soon likely to be exceeded by the operating costs. The capital cost can, therefore, be over-emphasized; more important factors in the appraisal are the ensuing revenue expenditures and benefits. The project will, accordingly, need rigorous assessment not only on financial but also on operational grounds.

The first and obvious question to be considered by the appraising team is whether a new hospital is really necessary, bearing in mind that a number of hospitals and other health facilities are working at less than full capacity. This may be due less to lack of demand than to over-stringent cost control programmes. Nevertheless, one new hospital replacing, say, two old establishments may be designed to meet the full demand and at the same time effect cost savings. There is, however, always a danger of over-estimating cost savings when activities are concentrated on fewer but newer sites. The expected savings may fail to materialize, not through any conspiracy on the part of the staff, but simply because they seize the opportunity of improving the service in the changed situation.

The essence of capital budgeting techniques is to consider the alternatives: one is the 'no change' situation. This may be justified for good reasons other than inertia. To achieve comparable results in new premises may take many years and much good fortune.

On the other hand the opportunity cost of the large areas of land occupied by many hospital sites may be decisive. Some of the old Victorian mental institutions, for instance, occupied enormous areas of land. The market value of this land is the opportunity cost of continuing to operate the present establishment on that site, where a smaller site would do equally well. In this and other ways the possible generation of funds on a commercial basis can well be included in the appraisal of a project for resiting an existing hospital.

Indeed, with the increased independence now being given to individual units, income generation might with advantage be included in the tasks of hospital management, much in the style of fund raising college principals in the US. Apart from realizing the opportunity cost of land, income can be generated by hospital management by more effective pricing, administration and collection of monies from facilities privately used.

Performance indicators

It is impossible to capture and reveal the full multi-dimensional nature of performance in the public sector by simple statistical measures. However, the attempt should be made despite the well recognized dangers of drawing too many implications from such measures; the absence of a sound information base can provide a cloak for inefficiency, confusion and self-interest.

Performance indicators are used in business to compare the efficiency of one factory with another and, by a system of inter-firm comparisons, of one company with the average performance in the industry concerned. These figures require careful interpretation in the light of the particular circumstances of each unit subject to comparison. In the same way perfectly plausible explanations may account for discrepancies between hospitals in the cost of providing support services, medical and paramedical, per in-patient case. However substantial differences should not be dismissed as necessarily owing to special local conditions but should be seen as evidence to warrant further investigation. Apart from comparisons with other units, the trend of the indicators represents an important element in the management information system and can act as an incentive to improve performance.

The object of developing performance indicators is ultimately to improve the standard of the service. The mere publication of figures demonstrating, for instance, that a hospital has a particularly high average length of stay per in-patient will not improve the situation. Managers must first have confidence in the figures, must be motivated to influence them and be sensitive to those which genuinely reflect good or poor performance.

There are, however, considerable difficulties in measuring performance in the public sector. The high cost of treatment per case may be cause for alarm for the financial team but may be viewed with satisfaction by the clinicians as evidence of quality service. How does one judge the performance of medical practitioners? The views of the patients are likely to be haphazard, with one favouring the 'pill dispenser' and the other the more thoughtful counselling approach.

In the health service, where the objectives are many, including care, cure and prevention, it is impossible to compare with precision the achievements of different institutions. Only on a broad front by deciding priorities between the principal alternative programmes, can some form of output budgeting be fully effective. For the more limited purpose of assessing and comparing current operation, performance is viewed in terms of activity such as number of patients, number of consultations, average cost per patient, and numbers of nursing staff in relation to patients. The statistics of course need interpretation: very high resources do not necessarily mean good performance nor do low resources mean poor performance. The indicator should act as a signal for further investigation. This is especially so when a whole set of indicators is considered, relating to clinical, financial and manpower factors, and when due account is taken of different case mixes.

Despite assurances that the statistics are meant as indicators rather than standards of performance, the presentation of the figures tends to create a defensive attitude on the part of the staff. The imputation that the figures reflect on the quality of the work is resented, and staff feel that their time could be better employed than in the exercise of collecting information. They become suspicious of the figures, especially when simple errors are disclosed, or when the main objective of the information appears to be to improve the position of the organization in some league table. Similar human reactions occur in the business environment.

Consider, by way of illustration, figures of discharges from hospital. The staff are aware that efforts to reduce lengths of stay could be at the expense of patient satisfaction and of community services. If the community services are unable to cope with the increased work, clinicians will be frustrated by their inability to influence the figures. The indicators must, in consequence, be made more sensitive, perhaps by incorporating rates of readmission augmented by measures of patient satisfaction.

With increasing decentralization of authority in the public sector more clinicians and managers become budget holders and are expected to participate in the management system. A similar trend is apparent in other areas of public service, such as the police force and education, and is comparable to divisionalization in business organizations. As a result many public health officers are closely involved in the establishment of performance indicators and their interpretation. It is necessary to encourage the clinician, already pre-occupied with the care of patients, to make a positive response to the management role; that it is not simply a matter of reducing budgets or of accepting the blame for over-spending must be made clear. One way to do this is to incorporate incentives into the system so that, for example, savings effected by a budget holder can in part be retained for improving the service. In any event a more cost conscious attitude is encouraged if individuals are aware of the real cost of the services they consume.

However, in certain circumstances, it may be impossible to keep expenditure within the limits set in a particular budget. The paramedical budget holder may, for example, be required to provide expensive additional services to the clinical divisions, above the level envisaged when the budget was formulated. In such circumstances the financial team must ensure that individual budgets contain an element of flexibility related to activity, comparable with a flexible budgetary system in a commercial organization. They must also ensure that all divisions are aware of the cost implications of their actions on other budgets. The surgeon needs advice on cost structures of alternative procedures and approaches. More fundamentally the planning and monitoring of expenditure needs joint debate at a high level of authority within the organization.

The growing sophistication of computerized information systems is revolutionizing the collection and hence the quality of the data available to decision makers. Small private hospitals now have the ability to cost out items relating to patient care and treatment in great detail. The techniques and approaches outlined in this chapter demonstrate means by which measurement and interpretation of data can provide sound management approaches both in the public and private sector. A more extensive application of such principles, combined with the widening information base, can produce radical changes enabling financial information to play a much wider role than merely serving the needs of good housekeeping.

FURTHER READING

Birch, S. and Maynard, A., 'Performance Indicators and Performance Assessment in the UK National Health Service', *International Journal of Health Planning and Management,* **I** 1986.

Devlin, B., 'Why all the sweat about budgeting?' *The Health Service Journal*, 6th March 1986.

Edmonstone, J.D., *Problems of Managing the NHS*, Health Services Manpower Review, November 1986.

Flynn, N., 'Performance Measurement in the Public Sector', *Policy and Politics,* **14**, No. 3, 1986.

Foster, H.T., 'Involving Clinicians in Operational Management', *Hospital and Health Services Review*, May 1986.

West, P., 'Outcome Measures and Health Care Planning', *Hospital and Health Services Review,* September 1984.

Yates, J., *Pig in The Middle,* The Health Services, October 1982.
Yates, J., 'When Will The Players Get Involved?' *Health and Social Services Journal,* 15th September 1983.

18

Financial Control in the Smaller Business

J.R. Small

Small businesses constitute an important sector of the economy and are rightly the subject of governmental encouragement in the form of advice, information services, financial assistance and a reduced rate of corporation tax. They are said to be a major source of innovation and many grow into large companies, although they are unlikely to do so without sound systems of financial control.

They are often closely associated, as suppliers and sub-contactors, with large companies, by which they are sometimes funded and may eventually be taken over. For these reasons the financial managers of large undertakings need to be aware of the particular attributes and problems of the smaller business.

The author of this chapter makes the important point that the sophisticated control techniques which may be operated by a large company are quite inapplicable to the smaller business. He insists, nevertheless, that a financial control system of a simple and realistic nature must be applied in the small business if it is to be viable.

The typical feature of the small business is that it has few, if any, levels of management between the directors and the shop floor. Thus the flow of information becomes more topical and more accurate. The disadvantage is that without adequate support staff, the manager's time and effort tends to be diverted to paper-work and accounting functions for which he may have no great skill, and little inclination.

This chapter suggests that financial planning and control in the smaller business is not fundamentally different from the systems applied in the large business, except in the degree of complexity. The starting point should be a business plan. This plan should include a statement of objectives and a review of resources, of which the key personnel will be an important element. The business plan should become a basis for the preparation of a rolling budget of two to five years, expressed in financial terms. In this connection emphasis is given to flexible budgeting and marginal costing techniques, the latter leading to the calculation of break-even levels. Cash forecasting and cash control are regarded as vital elements in the planning and control process.

Examples are provided showing how variances between budget and actual result can be analysed into their basic elements of price and quantity. The effect on profit of changes in price and cost is shown to be amenable to a simple form of sensitivity analysis. The chapter sets out the essential financial ratios which assist managers in interpreting the financial position and the trading results. Finally the author stresses the need for a logical approach to the appraisal and control of projects of capital expenditure, and indicates how this can be achieved.

This section of the book is concerned with financial planning and control in the smaller businesses. Of course, the principles of planning and control as dealt with in other chapters are equally applicable to all businesses no matter what their size and complexity; however, the practical implementation of these will vary from business to business. The smaller business will need to be selective about what techniques are chosen and how these are applied and will be guided in this by the management system which is in operation, the factors which are critical to the achievement of its objectives, and how regularly these factors have to be monitored. There will be both a need to avoid the 'sledgehammer to crack a walnut' syndrome (or in more contemporary language – information overload) and the 'flying by the seat of your pants' syndrome (or, again in other words, a zero information situation). Someone once described management as, 'the art of making irrevocable decisions on the basis of inadequate information' and the purpose of financial planning and control in the smaller business is to make this information less inadequate than it might have been and to direct management's attention to areas where decisions are required. It is not to convert the business from a 'no information' to a 'too much information' situation.

WHAT IS A SMALL BUSINESS?

We should perhaps start off by defining what we mean by a small business given that the business size spectrum ranges from the self-employed with low turnover at one end to the trans-national corporation at the other, often employing more people and having a greater income that many national governments. Governments and other agencies will often designate size as a function of annual turnover (sales income) for company reporting, grant awarding, cheap loan agreements etc. For other purposes, the number of employees may be the determining factor. There is little point here in seeking to arrive at some quantitative factor which will separate the small business from a not so small business. There is no neat dividing line and in any event most managers will know if they are working in a smaller business. The more important question is whether or not the planning and control system which is being applied is suitable given the nature of the business operation. This will take into consideration many factors such as number of employees, sales income, geographical and number of locations of production, distribution and selling, asset and liability values and so on. Perhaps the most critical size factor is the number of levels of management between those responsible for directing the organization and the shopfloor operatives. Typically in some owner/manager businesses there are no levels between top management and the shop floor and consequently communication should be easier. Indeed many management specialists in large organizations are continually trying to reduce the number of levels of management in order to create a system which will give them the potential benefits of a small business i.e. quick, reliable and relevant information, a more responsive and faster reaction, and better communication. Information is often a substitute for personal contact and the filtering of information through successive layers of management necessary in most organizations, can lead to distorted representations of the true situation.

MANAGEMENT TIME AND INFORMATION REQUIREMENTS

We said earlier 'potential benefits' because there is considerable evidence that many small businesses do not achieve these and it is worth looking briefly at some of the planning and control problems which adversely affect some small businesses. The most significant of these, which is not really a financial planning and control factor but which has a severe impact on it, is how managers, particularly entrepreneurial and/or owner/managers spend their time. Often the business has originated because a person(s) had an idea for a potentially profitable product or service which could fill a gap in the market or create a market if one did not exist at present. This idea will initially be the raison d'etre of the business: the embryo which eventually develops. This is where managerial skills should be directed, not only in the initial stages but also during development. Unfortunately, because of the small size, management gets over-involved in other areas where they have no particular skills or expertise. One of these is often doing paperwork, filling in forms and other accounting functions.

One of the scarcest resources in any organization is the time of key personnel and this has to be utilized in the most effective way just like any other resource. Why should this be a particular, but not unique, problem for the smaller business? A fairly obvious answer is that in small organizations there will be a shortage of managerial resources and these must be spread over a large number of functions. This is not helped by the business's market power or perhaps more appropriately, lack of it. Customers, once they are billed – and that may not be done very promptly – will take extended credit from them while suppliers may cut off supplies if their own accounts are not paid in due time. This may force the business into expensive overdraft or other loan arrangements.

A lot of management time will, therefore, be spent on chasing up old accounts or in pacifying creditors, which time, had it been available, might have been more productively spent in developing new business. The situation is not helped when the system tends to be managed on the 'fire-fighting' or 'squeaky-wheel' basis or, again to use more conventional terminology, a crisis management approach is in operation. Bank statements and the information they contain are often the main planning and control mechanism. If the statement is in credit attention is paid to business development; if it is debit then panic stations are taken to find the cash needed to get the business solvent again. This can be especially time consuming if dealing with a powerful client or government agency. VAT authorities, for example, enforce very strict controls for their own interests and require small businesses to comply with them. This may often exhaust time and resources, which could have been directed to other financial controls: the VAT man won't wait but other demands will, including management accounts and other management information. Similarly, grant awarding agencies often expect the same flow of information and returns for a £10 000 loan as they do for a £1 million loan.

If an adequate financial control system is to operate – and this is what this section will be discussing – then a certain minimum information is required. While the benefits of operating a simple system, for which many programmes operate on most relatively cheap PC computers, may be clear there are obviously set-up costs. When management resources are thinly spread and managers are required to be engaged in more than one task and have more than one responsibility then management time, which is one of the most significant sets of costs, takes on even greater weight. Information, therefore, has to be meaningful to managers and has to make some contribution to managerial activities. The information requirements of a parent company may be inappropriate for local management. Knowing the stock position for the sake of it is not much of an improvement over not knowing it at all. Information should lead to action and if it doesn't the benefit is not worth the cost. This question should always be asked in a small business, 'is the benefit worth the cost?' If the answer is 'No' then a second question has to be asked, 'is it because the system is inappropriate or is it because management are not making use of it?' In considering this latter question it should always be remembered that the big problem of poor financial controls in a small business is that the margin for error is smaller than for large businesses. Generally speaking smaller businesses have lower reserves to draw on and while a large business can cover even a big loss and can take a steady drain of smaller losses this is not so for the smaller business. This is why there is a basic minimum system of financial planning and control which is a necessary condition for the survival and development of the smaller business.

THE BUSINESS PLAN

The starting-off point for planning and control in an organization of any size is the business plan. While absolutely necessary when the business is looking for additional funds from the market it is also a necessary prerequisite for the establishment of both a meaningful budget and a strategic analysis of the actual results achieved when compared with it. The budget is the key management tool for planning and control for the immediate future: probably the current financial year rolling into the next. It will set out in financial terms what the business expects to happen. Thus the budget should be an integral part of the overall management strategy for the business. Too often in the smaller business there is an apparent discrepancy between the overall plan (even if this is very informal and merely a statement of aspirations) and the budget, and also between the budget and what is really taking place. There is an inability to reconcile even if this is just a simple attempt to explain why they all apparently differ. The budget should flow out of the rolling business plan and not the other way around.

A plan for the smaller business need not be complex but even in its simplified form it will contain all the essential ingredients of planning. Initially there will be a statement of the business objectives and with the smaller business these may be closely linked with the personal objectives of management. Following on from this will be historical information about the business as it stands today and how it got to that position. This will contain not only financial information but also information about the real things which underlie this like premises, plant and equipment, and so on. The product(s) will also have to be described in a non-technical manner even if it is a highly technical product, as also will the market.

It is perhaps unlikely that a sophisticated market research study will have been done but it is essential that it is demonstrated that the market has been researched and that the business has some idea of market size and potential, who are the competitors, how and where do they compete (on price and/or quality and/or specification and/or delivery and/or service). The same sort of analysis will be done for suppliers so that there is a clear understanding of the inputs, trans- formation, and outputs. In essence the plan will contain information on the organization, on its products, on its market and on its finances.

The information on finance will form much of the rest of this section, but before leaving the business plan the importance of people, particularly in the smaller business plan, cannot be over- emphasized. Most of the specialist skills, including managerial, will be restricted to a few people with each taking on more than one responsibility both on an ongoing as well as on a contingency basis. Success or failure in matching business plans and budgets with actual achievements will often depend on the availability of these key personnel. A knowledge of strength and weaknesses here is absolute- ly essential but equally important, of course, is the ability to identify who really are the key people. There are countless examples where in the smaller business the loss of a person – managing director, salesman, bookkeeper, storekeeper – who had not been identified as key has proved almost fatal.

THE BUDGET

The most powerful tool of planning and control will be the budget: planning because it will reflect what is expected to happen; control because control is exercised through action brought about by comparing an actual result against some yardstick. If we say, for example, that the price of something – a meal, a product, a haircut – is cheap or expensive we use these words because we are comparing the price with something else, for example, what we paid last time, what someone has paid for apparently the same product or service, what we expected to pay, how much cash in total we have. The most common tool of control is comparison with the budget.

The financial content of the business plan will contain forecasts of possibly from two to five years of the most critical financial information. There is no correct time period; it will all depend on the nature of the business. This will focus on the three prime financial problems, liquidity, profitability and asset/capital structure.

(1) *Liquidity*. The cash and other liquid resources needed to survive in the short term will be detailed in a forecast of cash in and cash out as explained in a previous chapter. The smaller the business the simpler this will be, and the closer one gets to the present the shorter the time period this will cover, for example, monthly for the first year, quarterly for the second year and annually for the third and so on. Even if nothing else is planned and controlled cash must be. This is the life-blood of the business inadequate control of which has been the single most important contributory factor to failure.

(2) *Profitability*. A forecast is required to assess the prospects of long-term survival and to see whether the rewards justify the capital invested and the efforts required. A forecast profit and loss statement for the appropriate time periods therefore will also be required. Although many smaller businesses have objectives other than profit e.g. independence, satisfaction, these have to be judged against profitability.

A form of profit and loss forecast for a small business is shown below in Fig. 18.1.

	Last year actual £	Budget/ forecast this year Total £	Monthly analysis				
			Jan	Feb		Nov	Dec
SALES							
COST OF SALES Materials Labour Factory Overheads Stock and WIP Adjustment Other Production Costs							
Total Gross Margin							
OTHER OVERHEAD EXPENSES Selling & Distribution Admin Research and Development							
Total							
Operating Profit Other Profit or Expenses							
Profit before Tax							

Fig. 18.1   Profit forecast budget

(3) *Asset/Capital Structure.* The third financial problem of any organization is to match its long term assets (fixed assets) with the long term capital needed to fund these. Therefore, forecast balance sheets (statements of assets, liabilities and owner's funding) as in Fig. 18.2 will also be required. There is a simple rule which has stood the test of time which is that short-term assets (debtors, stocks) should be funded by short-term capital (bank overdraft); and long-term assets (buildings, plant) should be funded by long-term capital (owner's capital, long-term loans). A proper relationship has to be struck between fixed (long-term) and current (short-term) assets, and how these are funded. Running a business profitably when it involves borrowing money, on which interest has to be paid, in order to extend the factory or to buy more equipment to generate even more profit, can lead to over-trading. Because of the time-lag between investing and getting the hoped-for return in terms of cash as well as profit, businesses can find they have lots of bricks and mortar but no working capital. A careful check over time will be needed then on the ratios:

Balance sheet forecast budget at at	Last year £	Budget/Forecast £
FIXED ASSETS		
CURRENT ASSETS Stock & work in progress Debtors Cash Other Total Current Assets		
Less:		
CURRENT LIABILITIES Creditors Accruals Tax Overdraft Other Net Current Assets Net Assets		
Financed by:		
Share Capital Retained profits Deferred tax Loans		
TOTAL		

Each main heading will be further analysed as required

Fig. 18.2 Forecast balance sheet

$\dfrac{\text{fixed assets}}{\text{current assets}}$ − If the trend is up or down then ask the question, 'why, and what are the implications?'

$\dfrac{\text{profit before interest}}{\text{interest on loans}}$ − If the trend is up or down (particularly down) then ask the question, 'why, and what are the implications?'

The annual forecast/budget broken down, into weeks, months or quarters (whichever is the most useful) should, therefore, flow out of the business plan and will demonstrate what is expected to be

	Last year actual	Budget fore-cast this year	Budget to date	Actual to date	Differ-ence to date	Budget month	Actual month	Differ-ence month
SALES								
COST OF SALES Materials Labour Factory overheads Stock and WIP Adjustment Other production costs								
Total								
Gross margin								
OTHER OVER-HEAD EXPENSES Selling and distribution Administration Research and development								
Total								
Operating profit Other income or expenses								
Profit before tax								

Fig. 18.3   Monthly Reporting Analysis

achieved by the business in terms of cash inflow and outflow, income and expenditure, asset and liability positions.

Budgetary control

The three essential elements of any effective budgetary planning and control system are:

1 current position;
2 desired position (business plan);
3 estimated position (first budget).

If the desired position is realistic in terms of the current position, but the estimated position is out of line with the current position, then appropriate thought can be given as to what action might be taken to attempt to reconcile them with perhaps changes in both estimated and desired positions, but eventually leading to changes in the budget for the ensuing period. Detail of the budget will depend not only on what information is desirable, but also on what actual results the financial accounting and/or cost accounting system can provide. The monitoring system will be based on control through feedback i.e. deviations from budgets will be highlighted and the most significant of these investigated and appropriate action taken.

A form of monthly reporting analysis is shown in Fig. 18.3 above.

Investigation of differences

There are only two reasons why an actual result can deviate from a budgeted result – either more or less physical resources have been used or sold and/or the price paid or received has been higher or lower. In a sophisticated budgeting system with detailed technical specifications underlying product costs, and technical forecasts underlying sales budgets then many different descriptions will be used to designate these differences, (usually called variances) such as material usage variance or labour rate variance. In essence they all relate to the same two factors: price and quantity. If it is planned to sell 100 units of a product at £5 per unit but 110 are sold at £4.90 per unit then the position will be:

Budget sales – £500
Actual sales – £539
Difference   – £ 39

The £39 increase in sales income over budget can be analysed as:-

Quantity. Increase in income due to increased sales quantity 10 units (110 instead of 100) at £5 = £50

Price. Decrease in income due to reduction in selling price per unit of 10p (£4.90 instead of £5) at 110 units = −£11.00.

Net increase £39

There is an accepted convention that quantity differences are priced at budgeted prices whereas price differences are evaluated on actual quantities. The same principles can be applied to the usage and cost of raw materials and labour and so on. With many types of expenditure, for example, rent, total differences will be used because it is not convenient to sub-divide them into, for example, the number of square metres at so much per square metre although it could be done if this were felt necessary. This type of analysis is at its most technically sophisticated in a full standard costing system. Even if, and this is likely, the smaller business does not have a technical and accounting system which will generate the information and/or it does not need it, the basic question which should be asked when any item of income and expenditure is different from what is expected is 'was the difference due to price factors and/or quantity factors?' Seeking to answer that question is an integral part of the financial planning and control system.

The second significant reason why an actual result may differ from a budget is that what has actually been achieved differs substantially in substance from what was budgeted for and this may not be immediately apparent from the financial figures. To take an extreme example, supposing it is planned to build a school annexe with four rooms and a small gymnasium for £1 million, but the £1 million is actually spent on constructing a swimming pool. Although there is no deviation in budget in terms of expenditure there is a substantial deviation in terms of what has actually been achieved. While this illustration is obvious and no one would be unaware of what had taken place there are many occasions when it is not so obvious. The approach here is to look at the actual results in comparison with two sets of figures. The first is the original budget (fixed budget) when you are answering the question, 'is this what I planned to spend and is this what I actually spent'; the second is to take the actual achievement and then compute what the budget (flexible or revised budget) would have been had you known that this was actually going to happen when the budget was originally set. The question you are now answering is, 'this is what I actually did, what should it have cost and how does this compare to actual cost?' This revised budget is then compared with the actual results. Suppose, for example, a company budgets its material expenditure, including waste and spillage, for the forthcoming period at £7000 as follows:-

1000 units of Product A at 10 lbs per unit priced at 30p per lb	£3000
800 units of Product B at 5 lbs per unit priced at £1 per lb	4000
	£7 000

What is actually produced is as follows:-

800 units of Product A at 10 lbs per unit priced at 32p per lb	£2560
600 units of Product B at 4.50 lbs per unit priced at 90p per lb	2430
500 units of Product C at 5 lbs per unit priced at £1 per lb	2500
	£7490

Comparison with the initial budget will show a difference in material spent of £490 as follows:-

	Budget	Actual	Difference
Product A	£3000	£2560	−£ 440
Product B	£4000	£2430	−£1570
Product C	–	£2500	+£2500
	£7000	£7490	£ 490

For control purposes however a more realistic comparison should have been made – and we shall assume it was forecast that a unit of Product C would require 4 lbs of raw material at 90p per lb – between what was actually achieved at budget cost and what was actually achieved at actual cost. The position now becomes:

Revised budget

800 units of Product A at 10 lbs per unit at 30p per lb	£2400
600 units of Product B at 5 lbs per unit at £1 per lb	3000
500 units of Product C at 4 lbs per unit at 90p per lb	1800
	£7200

and the comparison now becomes

	Revised budget	Actual	Difference
Product A	£2400	£2560	+£ 160
Product B	£3000	£2430	−£ 570
Product C	£1800	£2500	+£ 700
	£7200	£7490	£ 290

The individual differences can be further analysed in terms of quantities and prices as previously discussed but the important point is that for planning and, particularly, control purposes it is much more realistic to compare the actual spend of £7490 with the revised budget of £7200 than to compare it with the original budget of £7000. In a large business with many and complex products a formal system is necessary to achieve this. This may not be required in a smaller business, and is one of its advantages provided the questions 'Why did we differ from plan?' and 'Given that we did differ how well did we do in any event?' are able to be asked, and answered.

KEY RATIOS

The regular reporting and investigation of deviations from budget will form the basis of the planning and control system. The importance of the management of cash, profitability, assets and liabilities cannot be over-emphasized and this can only be done by prompt action. It will, therefore, be useful to seek to identify some key indicators or ratios which will act as signals to trigger further action.

The following have been found useful in practice.

$$\frac{profit}{total\ assets}$$ = prime measure of profitability and helps answer the questions as to how well the business is doing and would the money be better off invested elsewhere?

$$\frac{profit}{sales}$$ = final net profit margin and helps answer questions about prices in relation to costs, particularly overheads, and whether sales volumes and margins are sufficient,

$$\frac{sales}{assets}$$ = asset turnover and measures whether the total investment in assets is generating a sufficient level of sales or whether the level of sales being achieved justifies the

amount invested in assets such as plant and stock,

$$\frac{\text{sales (or purchases)}}{\text{creditors}}$$ = credit turnover and helps answer questions about the credit which is being taken and whether consideration should be given to paying quicker and getting better service or discounts.

All of these ratios are interlinked as demonstrated in the following graph which highlights that profitability is a function of profit margins and the speed of turnover (usage) of assets.

Suppose a firm's budget shows the following:-

Sales		£1000
Cost of sales		900
Profit		£ 100
Fixed assets		£ 500
Current assets:-		
Cash	£ 25	
Debtors	150	
Stock	200	
Creditors	(75)	
		300
		£ 800

It is therefore budgeted to earn a return on assets of 12.5 per cent by achieving a net profit margin of 10 per cent and turning over assets 1.25 times ie 1.25 × 10 per cent = 12.5 per cent.
   If the actual results are:-

Sales	£1000
Cost of sales	900
Profit	£ 100

Fixed assets		£500
Current assets:-		
Cash	£ 25	
Debtors	150	
Stock	400	
Creditors	(75)	
		500
		£1000

The firm will only have achieved a return of 10 per cent not because of a reduction in profit margins, these are still 10 per cent, but because it turned over its assets only once through over-investment in stocks which were turned over 2.5 times instead of 5 times as budgeted.

SENSITIVITY ANALYSIS

In addition the budget should highlight the importance of variations in important elements e.g. in selling prices, labour rates etc on profit so that management are immediately aware of the likely impact of changes in these. The impact of a 5 per cent increase or decrease in selling prices, assuming all other factors stayed the same, would increase or decrease budget profit in the previous illustration by 50 per cent.

Budget

Sales	£1000
Cost of sales	900
Profit	100

Impact on profit of variation

5% on sales price	$\pm$ 50 = 50% profit
1p per lb on raw materials used	$\pm$ 10 = 10% profit
25p on wage rates	$\pm$ 15 = 15% profit
1% in £1 v $1	$\pm$ 5 = 5% profit

It should be relatively easy for the manager to answer the question, 'What are the revenue or cost components in my business and where would a variation in prices have a significant impact on our profit?' and once answered then regular monitoring must take place.

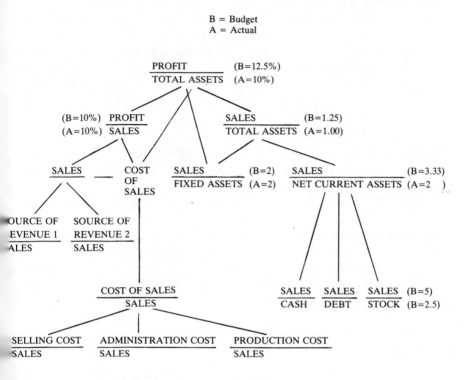

Fig. 18.4   Interlinking of key ratios

PROFIT AND OUTPUT

While the budget is the general monitoring tool there will be other day-to-day decisions with which management is faced and which will require a knowledge of the relationship between prices-costs-output. The accounting system will require to go beyond the normal financial accounting analysis and extend into cost accounting. In the smaller business a fully detailed cost accounting system may not be feasible but at least managers should know the major components of cost and how they relate to each other. It should indeed be easier to know the overhead rates in a small business i.e. how much do overheads increase everytime we take on more work and/or employ more people, or decrease as the case may be. Ideally a cost accounting system should be integrated with the financial accounting system but this may not be feasible. Nevertheless, whatever cost classification is done, even if it is on an ad hoc one-off basis, some attempt should be made to judge the credibility of these figures against the actual financial results when these are available.

Every manager knows that some costs vary directly with variations in activity (production or sales) while others remain constant, and others change but not directly. In coping with day-to-day decisions such as –, 'is it worth giving a 10 per cent discount to get this special order?' – 'should we buy-in this component rather than make it ourselves?' – 'how much extra will we have to sell to cover the increased costs of the new wage agreement?, and so on, requires some knowledge and assumptions about cost classifications and cost behaviour. Although not completely accurate and only true for restricted time period and within a narrow range over present output levels it has been found convenient to classify costs as either fixed, i.e. do not move with changes in output, or variable, i.e. move directly with changes in output. Such an identification is the basis of many areas of financial control and planning, such as marginal costing, profit volume analysis, and breakeven analysis. It enables the profit equation to be defined as follows:

sales income – variable (marginal) costs = contribution*
contribution – fixed costs = profit.

*contribution to cover other expenses and profit

This equation highlights that in order to make a profit the business has to generate, from its sales, income enough to cover its out-of-pocket costs and all these other expenses such as research, development, advertising, marketing which go under the generic phrase of fixed overheads before you can make a profit. There are many people who would argue that the most critical cost control required for a smaller business is the control of overheads. If, for example, the contributory margin is 20 per cent, i.e. for every £1 of sales the out-of-pocket costs are 80p then every additional £1 of overheads requires an additional £5 of sales to cover them.

A variation in profit will require a variation in one or other of these four factors. Suppose that the selling price per unit is £5 the variable cost per unit £2 giving a contribution margin of £3 i.e. 60 per cent and fixed costs are £10 000. In these circumstances the business requires to sell 3333 (£10 000 ÷ £3) units in order to break even, and 10 000 (£10 000 + £20 000 ÷ £3) units if, for example, it has a target profit of

£20 000. Similarly if there is a planned or forced reduction in selling price of 10 per cent the business will have to sell an additional 2000 units in order to make the same profit as before i.e. an increase in sales of 20 per cent. Similar calculations can be done for projected increases or decreases in volume and costs. This identification of the key profit factors as quantity sales, selling price per unit, variable cost per unit, fixed cost in total, is critical not only for planning what to do but also in controlling costs, particularly overheads.

Over the last fifty years there has been undoubtedly a shift in the type of cost incurred by businesses as more and more costs move from the variable to the fixed category through government legislation, convention, increased impact of administration, research and development and marketing. As a result the profit of most firms is now much more sensitive to variations in output. The greater the fixed costs the greater is profit sensitive to change in the level of activity. Unless a small business controls overheads it will not control profit or cash.

CAPITAL EXPENDITURE

In addition to day-to-day operating decisions, management will also be faced periodically with capital expenditure decisions. There are three stages in the appraisal of these:

1 *identification* – the need or the opportunity for capital expenditure, for example, in new plant and equipment, buildings etc, has to be identified,
2 *evaluation* – the apparent capital project has to be evaluated both in terms of profitability and cash flow;
3 *control* – once the capital expenditure decision is approved and implemented then it has to be monitored and controlled.

With step 1 (identification), other than perhaps systematic replacement, financial techniques have little to offer. With step 3 (control) this will be exercised through the normal budgetary techniques. Step 2 (evaluation) is one where other financial techniques come into play. There are many sophisticated ways of analysing investment opportunities most of which are based on the Discounted Cash Flow Principle (see also Chap. 6). This seeks to calculate a rate of return on investment comparable to a market borrowing rate so that the profitability of a proposed investment can be properly evaluated. The more advanced of these techniques will incorporate allowances for inflation and risk although, of course, risk has ultimately to be judged and no amount of processing data can eliminate it. Most small PC computers have off the shelf packages which will do this evaluation so the techniques are now available to even the smallest business. However, here again care must be exercised not to use the proverbial sledge hammer. Irrespective of the technique used, nevertheless, the underlying data requirement from the largest to the smallest project is the same and is of fundamental importance to all businesses. The starting point is a cash profile of the proposed capital expenditure i.e. a statement of cash inflows and outflows over the life of the investment. This cash flow profile will not only enable the business to calculate the profitability of the investment but it will also provide information on its effect on the overall cash budget. In assessing and evaluating this cash profile there are four key investment factors:

1 *Capital outflows and inflows* – this will cover all the capital costs involved in the initial purchase and set-up of the various fixed assets, plant, buildings, etc. It is likely that the bulk of these will appear right at the beginning or in the early years of the project. In assessing the capital expenditure required one must not forget the increased investment in working capital. New plant which will generate greater output which will lead to greater sales will require additional funds for stock, debtors and even cash itself.

2 *Operating cash flows* – these are the cash inflows and outflows which are expected to be achieved as a result of the investment – increased sales revenues less increased operating costs, or re-duced operating costs if it is a cost reduction investment and so on. Taxation benefits gained and liabilities incurred are important here. One of the most common causes of lower than estimated profits is faulty timing of cash flows. The estimated figures for both capital and revenue may be correct but if it takes longer to get the investment operational with a consequent delay in gener-ating positive cash flows then profits will be lower. Timing of cash flows is critical to profitability.

3 *The cost of capital* – this is either the borrowing rate or the desired rate of return the firm wishes to achieve. There is no point in borrowing money at 25 per cent to achieve a return of 10 per cent and if it is your own money there is no financial point in achieving a return of 10 per cent if you can invest the money outside and earn 12.5 per cent.

4   *The economic life of the investment* – this is not necessarily the physical life of the equipment, but is the length of time it is felt that the equipment can be operated profitably before it either wears out in physical or obsolescence terms.

Techniques of investment appraisal are dealt with elsewhere in the book, but in addition to knowing how profitable is the investment, it is almost as crucial to the smaller business to know when the cash invested will be repaid; the cash profile provides this information. Suppose a capital expenditure proposal has the following cash profile:-

Cash profile

Years	Fixed capital investment	Working capital investment	Sales income	Operating costs	Net cash flow
0	£80 000	£20 000	–	–	£100 000
1			75 000	35 000	40 000
2			75 000	35 000	40 000
3			75 000	35 000	40 000
4			75 000	35 000	40 000
5			75 000	35 000	40 000

This gives an apparently good return of 28.5 per cent. However, even if the borrowing rate is only 10 per cent it will be just over three years before cash outlays are recovered which is more than halfway through the project's life viz:-

Capital outstanding at beginning of year 1	£100 000
Notional interest at 10%	10 000
	110 000
Capital repaid	40 000
Capital outstanding at beginning of year 2	70 000
Notional interest at 10%	7 000
	77 000
Capital repaid	40 000
Capital outstanding at beginning of year 3	37 000
Notional interest at 10%	3 700
	40 700
Capital repaid	40 000
	700

Therefore just over three years are required to break-even in cash terms.

CONCLUSION

There is no simple panacea which will provide all that is required to solve the problems of financial planning and control in the smaller business. Nevertheless a necessary, if not sufficient, condition is management action. Purposeful action can only take place if information to point the way is available. Priorities have to be established as to what information should be monitored for control purposes; in the smaller business that relating to cash and overheads must be first.

FURTHER READING

Bank of England, *Money for Business*, 1987.
(Note: Most of major banks produce their own publications on financial planning for the smaller business, as do other private funding and government agencies).
Dewhurst. J. and Burns, P., *Small Business Finance and Control*, Macmillan, 1983.
Goch, D., 'Financial Management Control for Smaller Businesses', Certified Bulletin of Chartered Association of Certified Accountants, 1986.
Sizer, J., *Insight into Management Accounting*, Pelican, 1987.

Part III
Special Aspects

19

Systems and the Computer

P.V. Jones

The computerization of a large variety of financial records is now commonplace for most substantial companies and many small organizations. Nevertheless, as the author of this contribution indicates, there is evidence for the belief that the modern developments in computer technology are by no means fully appreciated or utilized by many financial officers. The former constraint of expense on the wider use of computerization has now been alleviated, particularly so far as hardware is concerned, and the advent of the mini and microcomputers, as well as developments in computer packages, have given a greatly enhanced availability to computer systems.

This chapter, which is firmly based on the realities of business financial operations, first discusses the potential uses of a computer in dealing with the simpler accounting routines. At the same time the dangers and illusions associated with such installations are clearly stated. The author emphasizes the vital importance of user participation in the design stage of the installation and refers to unfulfilled expectations arising from misconceptions as to the nature of the computer. He acknowledges that often systems are developed for the wrong reasons. He explains, on the other hand, how computerized systems may add immensely to the efficiency of financial data processing and reporting, not only for standardized clerical functions but also for the more sophisticated financial planning and control applications.

The chapter discusses the costs, both apparent and hidden, of installing a computerized system; the various schemes available for the purpose; training requirements; adaptation problems; and the essen-

tial prerequisite of management and staff acceptance. It concludes with some cautious forecasts with regard to data-based management information systems, networks of computerized systems; and the potential for the elimination of paperwork and routine manual operations.

In the short time since its appearance in the mid-1940s, the general-purpose computer has been widely used in business. Ambitious claims have been made for the capabilities of computers and their users. Some have been realized, some surpassed; others have been shown to be unreasonable or ill-considered. A realistic approach to current computer applications must begin by investigating the nature of this tool and its potential usefulness.

A BRIEF OVERVIEW OF BUSINESS COMPUTER SYSTEMS

For many people computers appear to have mysterious, even limitless, capabilities, an attitude often difficult to remove and one which will inhibit a full understanding of the usefulness of this tool.

The true effectiveness of a computer may be best explained by considering its limitations. The main requirement is that the computer must be programmed to do whatever task is planned. The computer has no capability of its own but its inherent usefulness can only be realized by using detailed instructions or programs, which we know as software.

Programming a computer is a lengthy and error-prone task. This is not because of any problem with the computer itself, but to the difficulty that human beings will always have in defining with 100 per cent accuracy any task that is to be performed. The sequence of events in producing a program is to define precisely the task that is to be carried out, to analyse all aspects of it including any minor variations and errors that could occur in that process and then to describe that set of activities in the program.

Much emphasis is placed on the task of describing the process in a program but this is not so critical as the initial tasks of defining the processes before programming. It is for many an unpalatable truth that the 100 per cent accurate description of the process is almost impossible to achieve at the first attempt. The logical outcome of this statement is that the full and final development of software will be achieved by the user of that software in the actual work place. This has many implications for new software and makes evident the benefits of software that has been in use by many users, preferably for a period of time.

In most cases the development of computer programs through the specification and design process will, in itself, contribute considerable benefits to an organization. The computer as a machine will simply add speed, accuracy and complete repeatability of operations; the enforced rigour of procedures and all apsects of the use of the computer, though often difficult to accept, will be seen, in themselves, as major components in the successful operation of a business. The enforcing role that the computer system plays by defining the work processes may often be seen as at least as important as the actual task it carries out.

Some of the many benefits of using a computer will include the compilation of many sets of records from entry of one piece of information, easy and fast retrieval of information from simple or complex sets of records, and the production of documentation as an integral part of the data collection process. In these processes records are created from which reports may be produced on all aspects of the business to assist management in decision making.

Full effectiveness of a computer system is achieved through a full and accurate specification of the requirements of all users of the programs. When designing such systems there are dangers that the design can be either over-complicated or over-simplified.

The over-complicated design attempts to take into account every single aspect of the business and its interface with the outside world. This is unlikely to permit the production of appropriate programs in any reasonable space of time.

The over-simplified program ignores important aspects which could be added as by-products of the current operation without too much extra difficulty. A good example of such additional information which is absolutely vital and not too complex to add, is the interface that accounting software requires with information for the auditor. It is very easy for an accounting system to perform its activities in such a way that no trace of the process may be easily seen by the auditor, who will then need to re-process the accounts completely to perform the audit. A small addition to the programs could make sure that sufficient information is generated to show each task as it occurs and so provide the records that the auditor needs.

The above rationale will suggest that the most effective and obvious uses for computers are in areas where business tasks contain a high component of repetitive and definable operations. Those tasks requiring human logic, experience and intuition are not most suited to computer operations since defining them is not only very difficult but, in some cases, quite impossible.

The aspects of each task that are most suited to the computer and those that are most suited to the human being can be effectively divided to produce optimum performance of machine and human being. Such design should be the aim of system producers. The current state of the art in systems production should take the view that computer systems and their users are all part of one complete process. Ideas about computers taking over the role of people or about computers being totally inadequate to the task in hand should be seen in the context of using human beings and machines for the task to which each is best suited, given the state of systems technology at the time.

Since many accounting tasks are suitable for computerization, the development of computers in business has largely stemmed from finance departments. A very high proportion of all computer systems in business use deals with the accounting operations of the organization.

In recent years software has been developed with consideration for ease of use by non-computer personnel. This has largely arisen from the availability of low-cost desk-top computers and the easy access which many users now have to considerable computing power. Only a few years ago the principal tool found on the accountant's desk was the spreadsheet. The spreadsheet allows tabulations of data to be manipulated and modified readily and so is able to satisfy many of the accountant's needs. It is, for some accountants, crucial to their daily work and their decision-making processes rely almost entirely upon the results of using such programs. (See also Ch. 7, Financial Modelling.)

The advertised image of computers makes it easy to forget that many organizations are still, and will continue to be, co-ordinated in their daily accounting tasks by centralized, and in some cases quite large, computer systems. There may be variations in the nature of the centralized systems and in some cases we may see centralization broken down into systems which, though together they make one large central system are, in fact, distributed locally. The principle remains, however, that such systems may be the backbone of the company's operation and we must not allow ourselves to think only of the popular notion of using spreadsheets and the small computer that an individual may have on the desk. Consideration of the operation of these 'centralized activities' is integral to a well rounded view of computers in the accountancy function.

Examples of ways in which the computer acts as assistant to the accountant spring readily to mind. Costing, particularly material costing, is a field in which the potential of the computer can easily be seen. In a manual system, the time delay in collecting and processing information about stocks received and stocks used for any given product often makes costing a process which relates to long outdated information. A system which is based upon the computer can provide cost information in advance of material usage. Such a report may be used for control purposes as manufacturing and sales activities proceed. Real cost control and accurate cost reporting become immensely more effective with instantaneous provision of data. For such a system, the main feature would be a stock-recording facility that identifies quantities and prices of stock, and books them against specific manufacturing tasks. This would take place not only as stock is issued from the stores but also when material requirements are being planned. Many other costing applications have been developed to provide similarly useful facilities.

One important function of the accountant in industry is to appraise alternative proposals for investment and other courses of action. For this purpose it is necessary to construct budgets, models and projections to seek the optimum choice. The calculations may not be difficult but are often tedious. The computer is an ideal tool for the accountant in providing the answers quickly without tiresome clerical labour. In some cases where a trial and error approach is appropriate, performance of a larger number of trials, which the speed of the computer permits without delay, means that the results produced are more soundly based than would normally be achieved manually. In this case, access to a simple computer input terminal could provide the service required. Alternatively, the request for the optimum or a range of variables to be used in calculation could be specified and the computer left to provide a printout as requested.

In both of these examples the computer acts as an assistant to accountants, thus making them more efficient. This is a much more effective role for the computer than that of simply replacing people. The cost-effectiveness of the accountant using this powerful aid is often of far greater significance than savings made by the 'number-crunching' activity of many machines. When considering the computer as an accountant's assistant, the possibility of the computer 'taking-over' can be ignored. The computer is not, at present, a 'thinking' machine and will not, in the foreseeable future, usurp the person using it.

These examples lead naturally to a discussion of some of the wide variety of possibilities offered to the accountant with regard to the main problem areas and control needs.

Representation in numerical form of the financial status of a company may be regarded as a model of its operation. The production of these data, in sets of accounts, is a major part of the accountant's role. From such a model, reports may be given upon status, or, analytically, upon specified operation conditions. By forward projection an estimate of future status may be provided. Such a model can ideally be kept by a computer either in part, e.g. the payroll system, or more extensively as a series of interrelated systems to make one integrated system. In this latter case, systems are subject to continuous further development, but they already provide the output of all required accounts from input of the relevant raw data. These systems may also be linked with various other functions of the business to produce an industry specific suite of programs.

The purchasing system, which may often be responsible for more than 50 per cent of the outgoing cash in an organization, is a useful function to consider as an integrated company model. Many of the decisions regarding replacement of consumables and so on are based solely on stock levels. The computer program can check goods issued and receipts, compare them with stock levels and initiate the issue of a purchase order. Other activities of purchase procedures can be handled by the computer, such as chasing receipt of goods and ensuring that payment is made at the correct time.

The spin-off from linkage into such a system is that all documents, such as purchase orders or payment cheques, may be printed by the computer from the data held. Such information, now held by the accountant's model, provides instant access to details of committed and available funds, either at the present time or at some given future time. While this is only one aspect of cash flow, it is evident that similar linkages with, for example, payroll and sales systems could provide a very accurate picture of cash flow from moment to moment. Within such a system, automatic checking takes place to perform tasks of maximizing cost-effectiveness in such matters as ensuring payments where discounts are given or chasing selected debtors. A well-designed operation of this type may completely change the cash flow and profitability characteristic of a company.

Such a set of interrelated systems offers opportunities for accounting for inflation and for rapid update as circumstances change and the business of the company is transacted.

The reporting opportunities are such that either actual current status or future situations may be reported including possible changes in costs, inflation, etc. Variances may be calculated automatically, i.e. reporting against budget and progress against budget limits or usage rates.

Many aspects of the operation of a company can be related to the accounts model; this would then more nearly represent the total activity of the organization. The computer would not perform manually impossible tasks but would make possible the speedy performance of tasks that would otherwise employ an army of manual operatives. The cost of these operatives may not be justified and their coordination would be very difficult; they would not have been employed for such work and therefore the computer based system is supplying a service that otherwise would not be supplied at all.

This brief picture of the accountant's organization model is not exhaustive but it indicates the potential of the flexible model approach that can add a powerful and cost-effective tool to the finance operation. While the former high price of computers tended to limit their use to the larger organizations, the great reductions in price now occurring are changing this restriction. Further aspects of this change are discussed in the final section of this chapter.

AVAILABILITY OF SYSTEMS

An earlier section of this chapter suggested that when considering the provision of a computer system one must first carefully define the application, next consider how the programs are to be obtained and finally look at the provision of the computer hardware to perform the task. There is, unfortunately, a great deal of evidence that many applications are considered from the other point of view, in that commercial and advertising pressures persuade potential users to buy a computer, to add some software and then to attempt to use it. This is a recipe for disaster unless the user is willing to accept the many artificial constraints and impracticalities that usually follow.

The starting point of the production of any system should be careful definition of the task to be performed, followed by a survey of the means of obtaining software to perform that task. The software may be made to order or be ready-made. The main differences are

371

that software made to order will take a long time to produce and to perfect, it will require a period of operation to ensure that all errors have been removed and will necessarily cost a considerable sum of money. The ready-made software will be much cheaper, as its development cost is spead over the many users who purchase it. The main constraint, is that this software will impose its own design features upon the organization using it. Whilst these design features may have many inherent variabilities and flexibilities to offer the user, there will certainly be some compromises to be made in fitting readymade software to an organization.

Having taken the steps of defining the task and investigating the availability of software, we are now at the last stage of obtaining suitable hardware upon which this software will function. Modern computers from many different manufacturers and of many different types will provide similar reliability and speed of operation. If some passing consideration has been given to the hardware whilst reviewing software availability, it can be expected that this final stage of obtaining hardware will, in fact, be the minor part of the task and the easiest to complete. Much of the software produced will run on a large number of different computers and even though developed for a special purpose can benefit from the large amount of standardization that now exists. This changes the view that the manufacturers of computers would have us accept, which is, first find your computer and then decide how to use it.

THE EFFECT OF SYSTEMS ON AN ORGANIZATION

This description of computer systems has so far omitted one very important aspect – the effects of their operation on the structure of the organization and on the people involved. The basic premise must be that the computer provides for the needs of the organization. We must not, however, expect it to fulfil all the requirements without some structural and procedural alterations to that organization.

To achieve the balance between organizational change and tailoring of the system to provide the ideal design to suit the application, consideration must be given to the personnel in the system. In many cases, the ideal solution will require a number of changes in responsibilities and administrative groupings which in turn may mean that the structure upon which the accountant bases activities will need modification. The computer system and organization structure interact and must be carefully blended. This is particularly so when the computer is used to provide information intended to guide processes of control within and outside the organization. The natural resistance to change which characterizes most organizations can make such changes very difficult to introduce at a stroke. The preparation of personnel and phasing of system implementation are, therefore, as important as the systems design. In finance operations, which are often the longest established activities of an organization, this is particularly relevant. Any approach to people which in any way threatens their livelihood must, inevitably, produce resistance. Yet it is often the co-operation of these people which will ensure the effective design and use of the computer application. In the early stages of analysis of existing manual operations and design of computer systems, the current operator is a vital information resource. Reference was made above to the role of the computer as assistant and to the fact that in most cases the individual will not become redundant as a result of the introduction of the computer system. But the nature of the work may be radically changed. Clerical functions may, perhaps, disappear because the computer will perform the mundane tasks.

It is important to consider not only those parts of the organization and those users who are directly affected by the computer system design, but also those outside the direct domain of the computer who will be affected by its operation. This may include suppliers and customers who will see documentation presented by the computer printout. An opportunity is thus presented to improve the image of the organization and to be more helpful to customers and suppliers by including more useful information on the documents.

Within the oganization there may be many individuals and departments whose work will be affected by the flow of fresh data and availability of reports which will result from the introduction of the computer system. The output from the computer may assist them in the performance of their daily tasks without excessive extra demands being made on the system design. The co-operation of other users outside those immediately involved may be secured and enhanced by its careful design and introduction. The financial planning and control that is inherent in the computer system is made most effective by that co-operation.

The system user must have a full appreciation of the role that the computer will play and the value and benefit that this will be to the individual and to the organization: from the earliest days of system design, the user should be consulted and involved. Alienation should be avoided by removal of threats to job security and by the provision of full information to prevent unhelpful rumours. The first task of sytem analysis may be a feasibility study. This could result in a decision that a computer is, or is not, suitable. Rumours of an unhelpful nature will spread rapidly unless authoritative information and full consultation are provided.

A system imposed upon the members of an organization may suffer from one or more of the dangers of the authoritarian approach. These can be summarized as follows:

1   The system does not take into account the real needs of the user and often generates more work for the user.
2   The output from a system does not present information in a way that may be either easy or possible to use. This will mean that the intended user may not use the reports at all, may have extra work to do in order to use the reports or may not receive full benefit from them.
3   The user does not understand the function of the system and is unable to use it effectively through failing to carry out the procedures required. Such a problem often renders the system practically useless.
4   The users will see the computer system as an alien force or a weapon to be used against them. The result of such an attitude is that the system and its equipment will be abused or not used at all.

To ensure that these problems are avoided, a number of precautions must be taken in the development and implementation of a system. First and foremost the user must be involved in the design of the system from the earliest possible moment. This may be organizationally satisfied by forming a small committee of a representative number of the users and of the computer system development team. Practically, user involvement will be satisfied when the user really contributes to the design. This may be in the form of providing information on local terminology, document layout, report style or procedure required. These are simple examples of the type of involvement that will encourage the users to see the system as their own and not as being imposed by some outside agency. A design developed in this way is more likely to be acceptable to the user. It is necessary to maintain this attitude throughout all stages of development of the design.

During the early days of investigation by the systems staff of current manual, semi-automated or computer-based systems, most of the work will be by interview of personnel and review of past documents. It is clear that the co-operation of the user is of paramount importance if the correct perception of system needs is to be gathered by the systems designers. Such co-operation must extend throughout the next stages of verifying that design perception is correct, developing the programs and procedures and implementing the finished product.

Many attitudes must be accommodated but, so far, only the users' attitudes have been considered. Those personnel indirectly associated with the system must also be considered, for example, the manager or supervisor of an accounting section, since the power and control which was once theirs will increasingly be handed over to the computer. The mystique which many people develop in performance of their daily work is often destroyed by the systems and procedures that accompany a computer system. For many people, a sense of personal achievement and job satisfaction are derived from their own job mystique and if they are deprived of this satisfaction then they must be given an alternative motivating force, e.g. the opportunity to work successfully with a powerful computer system and develop new skills. All these factors underline how very important it is that the system user is effectively included if a computer system is to be the appropriate tool for the job. Otherwise, the system will be the product of the computer department alone. With the best of intentions, such a system is unlikely to satisfy the needs of many of its likely users.

Throughout the design of the system it is essential that the total accuracy and security of the data are considered. The potential for erroneous data owing to user error can be very high if the system design does not recognize this possibility. As far as possible the design must, therefore, check data that is entered and provide information about that data so that errors may be quickly located and corrected.

It is essential that the system be secured against deliberate data corruption and fraud. Computer fraud is a growing, major concern for many organizations. The breakdown of barriers between the many users who were previously necessary in the process of performing a task, such as making a payment, can leave a computer system very vulnerable to fraud. The designer of a computer system must take a good deal of the responsibility for ensuring that, by observing simple principles in the way the system is designed, such fraudulent activities cannot be performed. Points to consider are that no one individual is allowed to have total control of an important series of activities, such as those involved in setting up a supplier account and subsequently making payments to that account. If large scale collaboration is required for fraud to be effectively executed; if users are excluded from parts of the system to which they need not have access; and if tasks can be spread over a number of different users, then dishonesty will be less likely. The designer must be constantly aware of the possibility of fraud and must seek to minimize the risk wherever possible.

From this brief appraisal, it may be seen that the personnel element of a system could be the single most important feature dictating success or failure. There is certainly evidence of this in many installations where loss of user goodwill or the imposition of staff and union resistance have destroyed all chance of efficient computer usage.

FACTORS TO BE CONSIDERED BY THE USER BEFORE INSTALLATION OF A COMPUTER SYSTEM

The membership of the user steering committee usually comprises a representative selection of both users and computer system designers. Considering the factors that should be noted when installing and operating a computer system, accountants would often be essential members of such a committee.

It can be a simple matter to make advance financial provision for necessary activities or expenditure, but often a computer system apparently costs more to install or to operate than originally anticipated. While cost inflation must take some of the blame, too often excess costs arise from an initial lack of understanding of the true costs to be incurred.

In addition to hardware and software requirements, many potentially expensive and sometimes long lead-time aspects of a system may be important. While many of these matters are the responsibility of the systems staff, in most cases accountants or their departmental activity will be affected by them.

The location of the computer and the type of room in which to house it will, in practice, affect the ease with which the user may have access to it. A mini- or micro-computer may readily be used in an office environment with little or no special preparation of the area, but the larger mainframe computer, which has some magnetic backing store equipment, will require an area which is dust-free and environmentally controlled.

The time taken to transmit documents and data for processing and subsequently to receive results is an important consideration. Where a computer is sited at a distance, the availability of vehicles to transmit documents, as against preparation and transmission of data locally, is an important determinant in the effective use of a system.

Every system user will need some training in providing data and in making effective use of the results. Insufficient attention to training may render the user unable or unwilling to use the system to its full potential. A well-organized training programme under the supervision of an adviser may seem costly and time-consuming but it will avoid the high cost of operating a system badly.

As a system is implemented, a number of processes must take place, for instance file conversion: converting all the data that a manual system user would require and transferring them to a form that the computer can read. The machine-readable form is usually based upon magnetic media. The process of extracting such data from records held, entering them on a form to be keyed in by an operator and carefully checking their accuracy, is a very lengthy operation. It can also be very expensive in systems where many thousands or millions of pieces of data are to be converted.

The testing of programs during development raises problems which may affect the accountant. For a system of reasonable size, the time required for program testing will be very long. Unless this testing takes place outside normal working times or the computer has great spare capacity, any existing systems on the computer may be slowed down. The task of testing programs is often seen as solely the work of system staff. This ignores the invaluable help that the user could give in defining test conditions. Sets of likely data should be solicited from users and finally used to prove the system.

The difficulty in program testing is in ensuring that all likely activities and conditions are adequately treated. The precise nature of these test specifications can be much more effectively defined if the accountant is involved in producing them.

Finally, during the implementation stage, the computer system should be run in parallel with a manual operation so that back-up services are available. It is reasonable to assume that some problems will arise to be dealt with. The parallel run will show that the system works and will effectively provide the final test of system capability.

In many cases, the time for parallel run operations will be shortened by introducing the computer system in phases. The temptation to shorten the parallel run time to save costs must be weighed against the cost of launching a system before it is ready for use: the complete loss of a service could result if the computer system should stop without some back-up provision. The cost, in loss of user goodwill, difficulties during the period without the computer and problems in restarting, can be very high.

When the system is in use consideration must be given to an important and too often neglected aspect of the use of a business system, that is securing the data against loss. However reliable the computer may be there is always the possibility that breakdown could damage the data stored, or that a power supply failure or some action of the computer operator could corrupt the integrity of the data. This often bedevils very small computer systems where nobody is officially assigned the task of administering the system. To minimize this risk the data should be periodically copied to some form of magnetic media which can be stored in a safe place, preferably away from the computer premises. In the event of some corruption or loss of data the copy may be used to restore the data to a previous operational state. Clearly such a method provides data security far superior to that offered by manual systems. Should a disaster such as fire or flood damage the computer systems the computer may be replaced and brought quickly to a full operational state with the data on the secured copy. If a manual system were damaged by similar circumstances the data would be irretrievable. The data held by an organization is a most valuable and potentially irreplaceable resource and every attempt to secure it should be made. The loss of such data has many times been the cause of a subsequent bankruptcy.

THE FUTURE OF COMPUTERS IN FINANCIAL APPLICATIONS

Vital to the future of computers in finance operations is the availability of cheap hardware. Until recently, for many tasks a computer could not be considered because the capital costs were too high. The equipment which can now be purchased for the price of several electric typewriters, offers great potential for many accountancy tasks.

In the past, the lack of suitable software has inhibited the use of computers. The development of cheap hardware has opened new markets, provided higher sales potential and, therefore, greater motivation to develop software. In recent years the production of suitable software has been considerable. Potential for selling many thousands or hundreds of thousands of copies of software has created a commercial environment in which very high quality software is a commercially viable proposition, since price has fallen to a very small fraction of development costs.

Amongst the most important types of software that have been made available in recent years we must include the spreadsheet program and the word processor. In the very large market for small computers, a considerable proportion of the sales is attributed to these two types of software alone. The spreadsheet provides instant access to calculated tabulations of data; the word processor is a convenient means to reproduce a very good copy of the information that it is wished to transmit. Some of the most successful aspects of this software are embraced by those programs that are commonly called integrated packages which include the facilities of a spreadsheet, word processor and data handling system together with, in some cases, a means of graphical representation, communication with other computers and on-screen diary and time-management systems.

For many business users of computers the use of integrated packages radically affected their business lives. Linking such packages into the main computer systems within the organization will further integrate the entire organization.

The future of computers has been radically altered by new methods of programming. While programming aids have developed over the years, the means by which a computer is made to respond to the user's needs requires adjustment. Two developments in the state of the art make useful contributions. One is the availability of database management systems which provide access to a potentially vast data resource as defined and entered by the user, in any way specified by the user. Such systems have been combined with ever more powerful programming languages which contribute to making the development of new applications very much faster and very much more accurate in the result. This encourages the production of standard software which can easily be modified to suit individual user requirements. It also allows those special user requirements which previously would have been very expensive to meet owing to the time taken for their production, to be satisfied in a relatively short space of time and therefore at a reasonable cost.

The other development is the simplification of the relationship between the user and the machine. This has been accomplished through devices to make keyboard entry easier, touch sensitive screens to allow direct indication of those items on the screen that are required, ball track devices to allow the user to point to facilities on screen, and voice recognition devices to allow spoken communication.

Voice recognition has now found its way into a number of systems both for entry of data and for computer output of information. This is a very difficult field and one which should not be too optimistically regarded in terms of the speed with which it will become generally and commercially available. It is likely, however, to be an important future refinement.

All the developments discussed in this chapter are likely to make considerable demands upon the accountant. The reaction to computers by the finance departments of organizations has been variable and often, justifiably, very cautious. To realize some of the potential that has been mentioned in this chapter, the accountant will be faced with choosing between wide-ranging computer-based systems. Some will undoubtedly be 'gadgets and toys', others will offer great effectiveness in accountancy tasks. The profession should seek positive evidence of the usefulness of these tools. The best results will be achieved with a sound balance between caution and willingness to take a lmited risk, where a need can be satisfied by the use of a computer.

The closer relationship that the accountant is likely to have with the computer owing to its falling cost and ready availability will improve his or her knowledge of systems. In setting out tasks for programming and for developing procedures, the attitudes which were previously the domain of the systems designer must play a considerable part in all aspects of accountancy activities. The future for the accountant will be in dealing with more locally available computers to provide local services. These computers will be linked to a central computer to deal with centralized issues and to other computers to transfer information. Such networks are already in various stages of development. The term 'distributed processing' is used to describe the large number of computer systems based on a central computer with a number of remote local stations. In such areas as the transfer of money between computers in banks and associated systems, this has been happening for some years.

The logical conclusion is to remove the paperwork from within and between organizations. This will have a profound effect on the work in finance departments. Major problems remain to be overcome in the areas of social acceptability but the ultimate result of all these developments will be to eliminate routine labours and leave the accountant as the intelligent decision-making component of a system. The nature of the work will continue to make the accountant a pioneer in the use of computers.

FURTHER READING

Audit Commission, *Computer Fraud Survey*, HMSO, 1985.

Carter, R. and Martin, J., *Systems, Management and Change*, Open University, 1984.

Certified Bulletin, *The Data Protection Act*, Certified Accountants Publications Ltd, 1985.

Drew, R. and Smith, J. *Microcomputers for Financial Planning*, 2nd edition, Gower, 1987.

Edwards, C. and Bryant, N., *Developing Business Systems Applications*, Prentice Hall, 1987.

Long, L., *Computers in Business*, Prentice Hall, 1987.

Sanders, M., *Computer-aided Management*, Woodhead–Faulkner, 1985.

Travis, B.J., *Auditing the Development of Computing Systems* Butterworth, 1987.

20

Social Accounting

Richard Dobbins and Stephen Witt

The authors of this chapter point out that although financial texts often postulate that the objective of the firm is to maximize its market value, that is not a view which is universally accepted. It is considered that a company has many obligations to the community and to the environment, and even the traditional profit and loss account reflects in some degree the interests of various groups other than investors.

Social accounting is defined in the chapter as 'the measurement and reporting of information concerning the impact of an entity and its activities on society'. The chapter specifically categorizes the activities which are covered by this definition and the authors maintain that what has become known as human resource accounting is also embraced by the general subject.

The quantification in monetary terms of the social responsibilities of business is difficult and rarely attempted; it involves experimentation and adaptability to the business concerned; but it has promise of considerable value to those interested in the industrial and commercial world. 'The traditional leavening of discretion exercised in conventional financial accounts', the authors consider, 'may be successfully transferred to social accounting'. They provide examples and a model of how this can be done.

Modern financial texts postulate that the objective of the firm is to maximize its market value (see, for example, Dobbins and Witt, 1988). Acceptance of this single objective should lead managers to maximize the anticipated level of net operational cash flows and minimize the perceived level of risk associated with those cash flows. The value of the firm is its discounted anticipated net operational cash flows, and acceptance of projects with positive net present values will increase the market value of the firm. The firm's market value can be expressed as follows:

$$V = \sum_{t=1}^{n} \frac{1}{(1 + r)^t}[R - W - I]_t = \frac{x}{\rho_k} = \sum_{t=1}^{n} \frac{A_t}{(1 + r)^t}$$

where:

V	=	the market value of the firm,
r	=	the required rate of return,
R	=	the firm's anticipated operational receipts,
W	=	the firm's anticipated operational expenditure,
I	=	the anticipated level of new investment,
x	=	the firm's net operational cash flows, i.e. $R - W - I$,
ρ_k	=	the overall market capitalization rate depending upon the firm's operational risk class, i.e. k, and
A_t	=	the firm's anticipated net operational cash flow in each future time period t, i.e. $R - W - I$, or x if constant.

The above equations demonstrate the equivalence of modern approaches to the value of the firm which is the discounted future operational receipts less operational expenditure and new investment, or the capitalized future (constant) net operational cash flows, or the discounted net operational cash flows receivable in all future periods. In operational terms the objective of the firm is to maximize anticipated net cash flows, and minimize risk (which results in a lower discount rate or capitalization rate). The trade-off between risk and return ensures that two companies with the same anticipated net operational cash flows will have different market values, depending upon their overall risk classes: the greater the risk, the higher the discount rate and the lower the market value.

The single financial objective of maximization of the market value of the firm has not been universally accepted. Even a cursory glance at the conventional profit-and-loss account suggests that companies have responsibilities to various interest groups, in addition to the providers of funds. Table 20.1 can be interpreted as suggesting that corporate managers have responsibilities to consumers, managers of international payments, suppliers, employees including managers, local communities, and managers of government finances as well as shareholders and providers of loan capital. Other interest groups might include competitors, females, non-whites, the disabled, sports

Table 20.1
Companies' responsibilities to various
interest groups

Profit-and-loss account for the year ended 31 December

Conventional			Interest groups
UK sales	100		UK consumers
Export sales	60	160	Foreign states, treasury
Less: cost of sales		40	Suppliers
		120	
Less: wages	70		Employees
salaries	20		Directors, managers
expenses	10	100	Local community
		20	
Less: interest payments		4	Debenture holders, bank
		16	
Less: taxation		6	UK government
		10	
Less: dividend		5	Shareholders
Retentions		5	Shareholders, managers,
			employees, government

and charity sponsors, and all those concerned with conservation of the environment.

Managers of industrial enterprises have been called upon both to recognize the interests of various groups when making decisions and to make periodic reports to interested parties, in addition to the providers of funds who have rights to receive information under the Companies Acts. The provision of information for interest groups other than that information regarded as being of considerable importance to the providers of funds, is generally referred to as social accounting. (In fact, political and societal pressure for increased social accounting mounted considerably during the 1960s and 1970s but then lessened dramatically as a result of the recession during the early 1980s.) Applied social accounting tends to be little more than additional corporate reporting whereby information relating to employment, energy utilization, charitable donations, exports and product safety is disclosed. Social accounting is not cost-benefit analysis. Many advocates of social responsibility would like corporate managers to take social costs and social benefits into account when making decisions, and indeed the net present value formula can be adjusted for social costs and benefits, although the monetary measurement of these items is extremely difficult.

As a result of pressure for corporations to report their social performance, there has developed the concept of social accounting, which may be defined as the measurement and reporting, to management, investors, and a firm's public, of information concerning the impact of an entity and its activities on society. It is worthwhile emphasizing the relationship between social accounting (or socio-economic accounting, or social audit or social responsibility accounting) and conventional accounting measures. While many of the social effects and impacts of a modern corporation cannot be assessed by the financial and economic mechanisms of traditional accounting information, social accounting not only includes but extends many of the procedures and statements present in established financial accounting practices. The social significance of profit and its distribution, of capital investment, of employment opportunities, and so on, have to be considered before dealing with other categories of social performance. Human resource accounting can also have beneficial and valuable attributes as an effective component in a company's overall social accounting machinery.

SIGNIFICANT AREAS OF SOCIAL PERFORMANCE

A useful categorization of the variables present in social accounting measurement has been advanced by the Canadian National Association of Accountants. Social concerns are divided into the following four major components:

1 community involvement;
2 human resources stewardship;
3 physical resources and environmental stewardship;
4 product or service contributions.

Community involvement includes those socially oriented activities which tend primarily to benefit (or disadvantage in some cases) the general public, e.g. philanthropic programmes, community

Table 20.2
Categories of social concern

Community involvement	Human resources stewardship
1 General philanthropy	1 Employment practices
2 Transportation	2 Training programmes
3 Health services	3 Promotion policies
4 Housing	4 Employment security
5 Aid in personal and business problems	5 Remuneration and retirement benefits
6 Community planning and improvement	6 Working conditions
7 Volunteer community activities	7 Health and safety
8 Specialised food and welfare programmes	8 Job satisfaction
9 Education	9 Communications and participation

Physical resources and environmental stewardship	Product or service contributions
1 Air	1 Labelling and packaging
2 Water	2 Marketing representations and product claims
3 Sound	3 Guarantee and warranty provisions
4 Waste creation and disposal	4 Consumer satisfaction and complaints procedure
5 Scarce resources usage and conservation	5 Consumer education
6 Aesthetic considerations of design and presence	6 Product quality and suitability
	7 Product safety
	8 Constructive research and development
	9 Advertising and promotion

involvement by employees, corporate community services. 'Community' in this sense means more than just the specific geographical location of company offices and plants. Human resources stewardship covers activities directed to the well being of employees, e.g. hiring practices, pension and retirement benefits, working conditions, training and promotion policies, job enrichment and satisfaction. Physical resources and environment stewardship includes corporate activities directed towards the conservation of resources and the protection of the environment. Product or service contributions of a social nature deal with the impact of a company's products and services on society and its relations with consumers, e.g. product quality and innovation, advertising and packaging, product safety, guarantees and warranties, customer satisfaction and consumerism.

The checklist of items under each of these four main headings (Table 20.2) identifies typical examples of social performance. The list is neither all-inclusive nor ranked by importance, but it serves as an initial framework for social reporting.

Within these areas, the modern corporation will identify standards and objectives, whether from governmental legislation and regulation or from societal pressure and demand or from internally perceived norms of 'good behaviour'.

REPORTING PROGRESS

Even when an organization has developed a presentation format for its social accounting report, there are two other basic dimensions which will affect the final published report: specificity of disclosure, and focus of disclosure. Current social reports employ at least three different degrees of specificity. The descriptive format provides a purely qualitative commentary on the firm's social activities. The quantitative format depends on the use of specific data to summarize performance. The monetary format requires the conversion of activities to monetary amounts and accounting statements reflecting the social costs and benefits of a company's activities. For example, the social balance sheet and income statement of a company may quantify such social costs as pollution from automobile commuting by its employees and inequality of opportunity. On current performance, the descriptive format is the most commonly used, often supplemented by illustrations and sporadic quantitative data. The monetary format is a rare and still experimental phenomenon. The overriding problem of course, is that of quantification.

There is the additional factor of the focus of social performance reports. While sophisticated analysis and reporting exists within organizations for internal social accounting purposes, it will be some considerable time before externally directed reports are similarly sophisticated. Companies tend to experiment with social performance accounting before publicly disclosing the results, and disclosure usually follows a non-objective pattern. The focus of disclosure will be either input-oriented, in which case the report will concentrate on the firm's efforts and expenditures in specific areas, or performance-oriented, in which case it will attempt to measure the output of social activities and their impact on society. Comparison with explicitly defined company objectives is obviously easier than comparison with general societal goals, and most social accounting statements issued so far have generally taken the easier alternative.

There is no consensus as to the correct format for social reports and a number of options is available in each of the three dimensions: categorization, specificity, and focus.

MONEY VALUES IN SOCIAL ACCOUNTING REPORTS

There are considerable difficulties involved in the quantification of social objectives, but accountants and financial managers should possess the necessary skills for the task. The measurement of the net profit of a major industrial undertaking calls for many calculations relating to stock valuation, cost of research and development, depreciation charges, etc. Furthermore, accountants have faced many of the problems of income measurement for a considerable period. The traditional leavening of discretion exercised in conventional financial accounts when valuing mineral reserves or goodwill may be transferred successfully to social accounting.

If it is decided that the process of assigning monetary values to social inputs and outputs, however difficult it may prove in practice, is capable of being carried out in some meaningful way, it is then possible to move to a social accounting income statement. If the reasonable convention that all production is socially desirable is adopted, then it is possible to arrive at the form of social income statement shown in Table 20.3. The category 'socially desirable

Table 20.3
Social value-added statements

	£
'Conventional' value added	XXX
Socially desirable outputs not sold	XXX
	XXX
Socially undesirable effects not paid for	(XXX)
Net social profit	XXX

outputs not sold' would include such items as job training, minority employment, health and safety at work, and leisure and environmental contributions. On the 'socially undesirable effects not paid for' register might be entered such items as air and water pollution, increased demands on public transportation systems, and usage of dwindling resources. The resultant social 'profit' or 'loss' might well be a more potent measure of an enterprise's role in and effect on society than conventional financial accounting measures of value added.

HUMAN RESOURCE ACCOUNTING

Advocates of human resource accounting (HRA) stress the importance of the human element in organizations and the failure of conventional accounting in dealing with it as an asset. In its simplest form HRA involves the identification of the costs of recruitment, training, and maintenance of an entity's human assets. Five widely documented methods of valuation can be identified: historical costs, replacement cost, opportunity cost, value measurement, and non-monetary measurement.

Historical costs

The total cost of the investment includes those quantifiable expenditures associated with recruitment, selection, hiring, training, placement, familiarization and development. This method simply capitalizes human resource costs and does not seek to value people. It is similar to the approach followed when valuing fixed assets and writing-off their cost over their useful life. The cost is capitalized, not being charged against current income, and a deferred taxation charge is made on the notional increase in profit.

Replacement cost

This method is based on current value or replacement cost. Under this system, an organization values an employee at the estimated cost of replacement with a new employee of equivalent ability. The application of such a method, however, is made difficult by the problems of defining and measuring replacement costs.

Special aspects

Opportunity cost

This is a largely artificial method involving the concept of the competitive bidding process. Under this system, profit-centre managers are encouraged to bid for scarce employees, the successful bid being included in the organization's human investment calculations. Employee abilities are related to profit generation, and may lead to a more efficient allocation of human resources.

Value measurement

Under this method, established capital budgeting techniques are applied to people, the argument being that the value of a firm's employees is their discounted future earnings. Value methods try to measure economic value rather than simply record investment in human resources at historic or replacement cost. An alternative approach to value measurement is that of estimating the contribution of human resources to the economic value of the firm. Valuation is determined by allocating to human resources a portion of the firm's present value (this being defined as discounted future earnings).

Non-monetary measurement

This method is fundamentally different from the other four. Basically, the alternative approaches which have been proposed have centred on social and psychological determinants or what have been labelled causal and intervening variables which combine to affect end result variables. Briefly, leadership skills and policies influence employee attitudes, motivations, behaviour and goals, which in turn affect sales, costs, cash flow and profit.

The benefits of HRA include the important influence on management's attitudes towards employees and the proper consideration of human assets when preparing strategic and budgetary plans. The influence of human variables on a firm's performance and profitability may be better understood, and human resources may be allocated more efficiently. From a cosmetic viewpoint, the realization by a firm's public of its strong commitment to its employees may enhance its image and standing. Against this must be set the reluctance of financial accountants to bring the process of valuation on the basis of future earnings into records of accounting transactions. Additionally, there is a widespread antipathy amongst employees and others to the whole concept of human resources being either owned by or even made profitable use of by firms. Not to be overlooked is the fact that an increase in the firm's capital base and reported profit will lead to changes in the rate of return on capital employed and other financial ratios.

A SOCIAL REPORTING MODEL

Table 20.4 shows the format and constituents of a proposed social accounting statement, based on the conventional profit and loss or income statement.

Taking the social benefits side of the equation first, the individual constituents can be defined and quantified as follows:

1   products and services provided (the present value of the entity's output, together with the value of facilities or services provided to other elements of society);
2   payments to other elements of society;
3   additional employee benefits (the value of fringe benefits, training programmes, recreational or social benefits – this should be the value to the employee, *not* the cost to the company, which is shown separately);
4   donations to the community (both money sums, whether by direct gift or sponsorship, and gifts in kind – the loan of an executive, for example, or the granting of time off for local council or voluntary duties);
5   environmental improvements (landscaping a gravel pit, for example, or providing a company bus service);
6   ancillary benefits (factory crèches or public education programmes, for instance).

Matching these benefits will be the categories of social cost, defined broadly as follows:

1   goods and materials acquired;
2   fixed asset purchases;
3   labour and services used;
4   public services and facilities used (the entity's share of the cost of the police and fire services, or the use of roads, parks, sewers and so on);

Table 20.4
Social reporting model

Responsible Undertaking Limited – social account

		£
Social benefits		
Products and services provided		XXX
Payments to other elements of society:		
Wages and salaries	XXX	
Payments to suppliers	XXX	
Taxes and rates, etc	XXX	
Dividends and interest	XXX	
	——	XXX
Additional employee benefits		XXX
Donations to the community		XXX
Environmental improvements		XXX
Ancillary benefits		XXX
Total social benefits		XXX
Social costs		
Goods and materials acquired		XXX
Fixed asset purchases		XXX
Labour and services used		XXX
Public services and facilities used		XXX
Payments from other elements of society:		
Customers	XXX	
Investors	XXX	
Lenders	XXX	
	——	XXX
Work-related injuries or illnesses		XXX
Discrimination and disadvantage		XXX
Environmental damage		XXX
Other costs		XXX
	——	(XXX)
Social profit (or deficit)		XXX

---

5 payments from other elements of society (customers, investors, lenders);

6 work-related injuries and illnesses (the present value of lost income);

7 discrimination and disadvantage (the present value of lost income, in cases of discrimination, and the extra cost caused by disadvantageous treatment);

8   environmental damage;
9   other costs (product shortcomings, for example, or undesirable
    attitude formation).

Much of the information needed for the compilation of a social
account in this recommended format will already be available to
management in conventional financial accounts. For the rest, most
can be gathered with relatively little effort and minor modifications in
the entity's information processing systems. Some of the information
will be difficult to obtain and even harder to translate into monetary
values. This may prove expensive for the organization. However, the
essence of this system is that the information network will need to be
established only once. Replication of the process annually or regularly will reduce the unit costs considerably. The criteria to be adopted
will vary according to the reporting firm's understanding of its social
responsibility and its intentions: whether to report to the public its
effect on society, or to produce an internal account of its overall effect
on society. Finally, with any social account there is obviously room
for, and a need for, descriptive analysis of items which cannot be
quantified or of items which reflect social concerns or changing public
standards.

REFERENCES AND FURTHER READING

Belkaoui, A., *Socio-economic Accounting*, Quorum Books, 1984.
Booth, P., Moores, K. and McNamara, R., 'Researching the in-
    formation content of social responsibility disclosure', *British
    Accounting Review*, **19**, No. 1, pp. 35–51, April 1987.
Dierkes, M. and Antal, A.B., 'The usefulness and use of social
    reporting information', *Accounting, Organizations and Society*,
    10, No. 1, pp. 29–34, 1985.
Dobbins, R. and Witt, S.F., *Practical Financial Management*, Black-
    well, 1988.
Gray, R.H. and Perks, R.W., 'How desirable is social accounting?',
    Accountancy, pp. 101–103, April 1982.
Lewis, N.R., Parker, L.D. and Sutcliffe, P., 'Financial reporting to
    employees – the pattern of development 1919 to 1979', *Account-
    ing, Organizations and Society, **2/3** pp. 275–289, 1984.
Owen, D.L., 'Europe leads on social reporting', *Certified Accoun-
    tant*, pp. 39–40, January 1985.

Teoh, H.Y. and Thong, G., 'Another look at corporate social responsibility and reporting – an empirical study in a developing country', *Accounting, Organizations and Society*, **9**, No. 2, pp. 189–206, 1984.

Tinker, A. (ed.), *Social Accounting for Corporations*, Manchester University Press, 1984.

21

Mergers and Acquisitions

Richard Dobbins and Christine Parkinson

A firm can grow in two ways.

1   Internal growth results from the successful development of the firm's own investment schedule.

2   External growth is achieved by the acquisition of other companies. In addition, external growth involves the establishment of a purchase price, negotiation and tactical skills and quantification of merger benefits.

The evidence suggests that internal growth is a slower process than growth through acquisitions. However, growth by merger is subject to numerous regulatory controls. In theory, any merger which does not increase the economic value of the combined entities is not worthwhile. The evidence of recent merger activity suggests either the existence of significant non-quantifiable advantages or that bidding companies are taking an extraordinary long-term view of future economic benefits.

The main topic of this chapter is the merger investment decision, including motives for mergers and an appraisal of methods for valuing acquisition candidates. Brief comment is made on trends in merger activity over the last century, the regulatory framework in operation in the UK, and tactics available for defending against an unwanted takeover approach. One chapter cannot of course cover all aspects of mergers and acquisitions, nor any aspect in depth, and a final section offers a selection of books and articles for further reading on the subject.

Mergers began to occur with some frequency in the 1880s, much encouraged by the introduction of limited liability for firms in the 1862 Companies Act. The trend then was essentially for rationalization and concentration and was marked by the first 'wave' of mainly horizontal mergers, which lasted until just before the First World War. This first wave of merger activity was followed by a second which lasted from the mid-1920s until 1939, and which was characterized by vertical mergers. A third wave, in the late 1960s, was brought about by the perceived need for diversification as well as the need for concentration. The number and values of mergers in the UK in 1967 and 1968 were much greater than had been previously observed. According to Newbould, 70 per cent of the UK's top 100 firms and over £6bn were involved in takeover activity.

It is suggested that we are now in a fourth merger wave which began in the early 1980s, and appeared to peak in 1985/1986. An important difference between the boom of 1985/6 and previous merger boom years is that it was characterized by a few, large mergers. The top five mergers accounted for 59 per cent of the value of all acquisitions in 1986. One suggested reason for this latest wave is that it is 'strategic', which often means the merger is defensive. A defensive merger is undertaken to avoid being taken over oneself, or in order to acquire key personnel or technology. A second reason is that it is 'managerial'. Managers prefer to manage larger rather than smaller organizations, as they tend to be rewarded on the basis of span of control over employees, assets, sales, budget, etc. This managerial objective does not necessarily result in the creation of additional wealth and may therefore be regarded as economically undesirable.

THE REGULATORY FRAMEWORK

Merger activity in the UK was not subject to any form of statutory regulation until the introduction of the Monopolies and Mergers Act in 1965. There has, however, been a competition policy since the inception of the Monopolies Commission in 1948. The basis of modern British monopolies policy has in the main been concerned with the prevention of the abuse of a dominant market position, and not with the prevention of market power *per se*.

Workings of the MMC

An investigation of a merger under the Act is conducted by the Monopolies and Mergers Commission only on the reference of the Secretary of State for Trade and Industry. To be referred, relevant, non-newspaper, mergers must satisfy one of the two criteria. The proposed market share of the combined group will be more than 25 per cent of the market and/or the assets of the combined enterprise will exceed £30m. Nevertheless, proposed mergers which do not meet one or both of these criteria can be investigated if the Secretary of State believes there are wider social or economic issues at stake. The Director General of the Office of Fair Trading (OFT) can recommend an investigation to the Secretary of State but cannot make a reference direct to the Commission.

There is no legal requirement for a company to notify the Director General of a proposed merger, even if the Directors are aware that one or both of the criteria will apply. The Director General has a duty to keep informed of all mergers which may qualify for possible reference. If the merger is contested, the defending company, or competing bidder, may attempt to gain a reference as a defence. A reference to the Monopolies Commission is often enough to thwart any unwanted bid, owing to the heavy costs involved in complying with the commission's requests for information, and the delay of up to six months and occasionally longer.

Companies may ask for confidential guidance from the OFT before mounting a bid. Statistics on such cases are not generally available, although a high level of usage of this informal advice network is believed to exist. However, a word of caution: the OFT is not bound to honour its informal advice and a bid may be referred or not, as the case may be, contrary to previous indications.

In response to a reference the Commission is required to investigate and report on whether the merger so referred would operate against the public interest. In determining 'public interest' the Commission may consider any matters it thinks relevant including the promotion of competition, consumer interests, industrial efficiency and technological innovation, maintenance of regional balances in employment and the potential for increasing exports.

The City Code on Takeovers and Mergers

The City Code is issued on the authority of the Council for the

Securities Industry. The Code is administered by the Panel on Takeovers and Mergers and covers takeovers involving public companies, whether listed or unlisted, but not private companies. It is not enforceable by statutory powers, but by an understanding that, if it is not observed, the facilities of the Stock Market will be withdrawn. The Code was substantially revised in 1985 and is now published in two parts. One part contains a set of general principles of operation and the second more detailed rules on the procedures to be followed before and during a takeover bid. The rules apply to all parties concerned in a merger including advisors, the boards, and managements of the participating companies.

In 1986 the Takeover Panel introduced new rules in an attempt to stop the campaign of denigration and use of selective statistics in takeover battles which had become evident in 1985. The new rules prohibited the publication of advertisements connected with an offer or potential offer unless the advertisement falls into an exempt category (defined in the Takeover Code), which permits advertisements such as those required by the Stock Exchange, or normal corporate advertising.

Merger accounting methods

In the UK the two accounting methods which are acceptable are acquisition accounting and merger accounting. In this context the terms 'mergers' and 'acquisitions' are deemed to be separate issues. Although the terms have theoretically different meanings, in practice they are used synonymously.

Using merger accounting, the acquiring company would record the cost of investment in the offeree company at the nominal value of the shares issued in exchange. Using acquisition accounting the acquiring company would record the cost of the subsidiary at the fair value of the consideration given. Any excess of fair value over the nominal value of the shares issued is taken to a share premium account. The fair value is assigned to the assets acquired and any excess of purchase consideration over fair value is treated as goodwill. In this case pre-acquisition distributable reserves of the offeree company are frozen. Under merger accounting they are available for distribution in that cash distributions can be charged against pre-acquisition distributable reserves.

From a manager's point of view there are three advantages of merger accounting:

1 return on capital employed is greater because assets continue to be stated at cost;
2 reserves are available for distribution;
3 future reported profits will be higher as depreciation continues to be charged on original cost and there is no goodwill to be written off to the profit-and-loss account.

In SSAP 23, the Accounting Standards Committee takes the view that the two methods should not be alternatives. The circumstances when each method is used should be determined. The situation may be affected by a forthcoming EEC directive concerning the preparation and presentation of consolidated accounts, and by a recent announcement that SSAP 23 (Accounting for Mergers and Acquisitions), and SSAP 22 (Goodwill), are to be re-examined.

Tax implications

For the shareholders in the acquiree company, a disposal of shares for cash represents a chargeable event. For this reason, if an offer is for cash, it is considered prudent to offer a share on loan stock alternative. This may not always be possible where the bidder is an individual or a foreign registered company. Furthermore the existing shareholders may object to a dilution of their control by the issue of a large block of new shares. Research suggests that the reverse situation is more likely to deter shareholders in the target company from accepting an offer, i.e. shares of the bidding company may be considered 'poor quality'. Capital Gains Tax may be payable on a cash offer.

THE MERGER INVESTMENT DECISION

The merger or acquisition decision is an investment decision. As such it competes with any type of investment for use of a company's capital expenditure budget and can therefore be evaluated using traditional capital budgeting techniques, including net present value. Mergers and acquisitions are only worthwhile if the combined enterprise is worth more than the value of the two independent entities.

This section first examines the motives for merger, assesses the most appropriate method of valuing a potential acquisition and mentions the advantages and disadvantages of the various methods of financing.

Motives for merger

Two competing theories of merger activity have been offered. One view is that the firm is a value maximizer. This is the 'neo-classical' profit maximizing approach. A second theory relates to the maximization of management utility.

Value maximizing approach

In the value maximizing approach, the bidder makes a decision on the basis of economic return on the investment and the expected economic gain must, therefore, be positive for the bid to be undertaken. The gain can arise from a number of factors.

1 *Synergy* arises where the combined enterprise is expected to be worth more than the independent component organizations as a result of economies of scale, increased market power and shared resources.
2 *Greater efficiency* may be expected when the bidder expects to utilize the assets of the target, including managerial assets, more efficiently than the existing management. There is some empirical support for this belief, although in many cases the acquisition has resulted in the identification of surplus assets which have been sold.
3 *Information Assymetries* can arise when the bidder has non-proprietary knowledge about the target firm which is not available to the market in general. The theory is that the bidder will be able to obtain the assets at a discount from their true value. However, in an efficient market there are no bargains and we should not therefore expect to see cheap acquisitions.

Managerial motives

Managerial motives refer to behavioural theories of the firm which generally contend that the divorce of ownership and control has enabled managers to pursue their own objectives including maximization of the size of the firm measured in terms of sales, assets, number of employees and even expenditure. The assumption behind such motivations is that many managers are remunerated on the basis of the budget, assets they control, sales, or the number of employees under their command, i.e. the span of control.

Acquisitions to increase sales or assets

Managerial rewards tend to be related to span of control, which can be measured in various ways. Growth in assets and sales is often stated as an acceptable objective for industrial organizations. This should be regarded as a managerial objective which does not necessarily result in the creation of additional wealth. If the achievement of increased sales or assets are considered valid criteria for merger, all acquisitions would make sense, regardless of commercial logic or the price paid for the acquisition. Increasing market share in the same industry can make sense. Horizontal mergers are believed to be the most successful as they can result in genuine economies of scale. They should still be evaluated on the basis of NPV of future cash flows as discussed later.

Acquisitions for diversification

The urge to diversify reached almost epidemic proportions with the wave of conglomerate mergers in the late 1960s. It sometimes appears that directors and managers are trying to turn their companies into widely diversified unit trusts. Survival of the company is, of course, a top managerial priority and it should be possible to reduce the probability of liquidation by corporate diversification. Nevertheless such diversification is not necessary for shareholders, as investors can and do diversify their holdings across a number of companies without assistance from corporate managers. Corporate diversification does achieve improved stability of employment for management and employees but may not necessarily provide incremental wealth for shareholders.

Valuation of target companies

Two traditional approaches to valuation have been suggested for takeover. These are effect on earnings per share (EPS) and net present value of future cash flows (NPV). Adding companies together makes economic sense only if the market value of the combined enterprise is greater than the sum of the market values of the independent firms. This suggests that the appropriate method is NPV. However we shall examine both methods.

The net present value approach

The economic gain from merger is the NPV of the anticipated cash benefits resulting from the merger:

$$V_A^B = V_A + V_B + X$$

where:

$V_A^B=$ value of combined enterprise,
$V_A=$ value of acquiring firm, independent of the merger or acquisition,
$V_B=$ value of target company, independent of merger,
$X =$ present value of cash benefits resulting from the merger.

When the X-factor is positive, the merger makes economic sense. The merger is a viable economic proposition when the value of the two firms combined is greater than the two independent firms. Where the target company is a quoted company, the Efficient Market Hypothesis (EMH) suggests that the share price reflects all known information. If the possibility of an acquisition has not been detected by the market and therefore is not reflected in the share price, the potential target should be valued as follows:

1 forecast the post-merger cash flows and required rates of return;
2 use net present value method to estimate the value of the enterprise after merger or acquisition;
3 split the X-factor, which must be positive for the merger proposals to continue, between the shareholders of company A and Company B;
4 negotiate the merger terms from this basis.

If the market has detected a possibility of takeover, the share price will already reflect this and the acquiring company's managers should value the target company independently of its existing share price. The X-factor should be allocated between the shareholders in the acquiring company and the shareholders in the target company before the anticipated merger is reflected in share prices. To the extent that the merger is already reflected in the share price of both companies, this should be taken into account when negotiating an acquisition price. The ultimate allocation of merger gains between the two companies will depend on their individual bargaining powers and the influence on the share price of market perceptions of the future cash flow potential of the combined enterprise.

Mergers can also be valued using other capital budgeting techniques including internal rate of return, the profitability index, payback period, discounted payback period, effect on return on capital employed, and effect on EPS. Our preference is for the NPV technique which indicates whether or not the merger will create wealth and is easier to handle than IRR or PI, and which does not suffer from the inadequacies of payback, discounted payback, return on capital employed effect and effect on earnings per share.

Effect on earnings per share (EPS)

Many mergers have been justified in terms of the effect on EPS, and companies are often valued on some multiple of historic profits. The effect on EPS does not indicate whether or not a merger is wealth creating and is an unsatisfactory objective as it ignores cash flows and risk. It is an historic number based on past accounting profit, which is subject to the vagaries of accounting policies, particularly relating to stock valuation, depreciation, bad debt provision, currency depreciation. Accounting profit is taken from the previous year's profit and loss account and is thus an historic measure. Share prices reflect anticipated cash flows. EPS is essentially a payback period, and as suggested above, payback is an inappropriate method of valuing mergers as it takes no account of future cash flows and risk.

A dilution of EPS may not imply that the merger is undesirable. Such a conclusion is usually the result of a myopic preoccupation with the merger's initial impact on EPS and fails to take account of:

1   the long-term benefits;
2   the possibility that by merging with a higher P/E ratio company, the combined earnings of the two firms may be valued at a higher multiplier than were the earnings of the acquired firm alone;
3   the time value of money.

The only aspects of the merger investment decision which set it apart from other capital budgeting decisions are the possibility of the existence of the benefits of synergy and the allocation of these benefits between the shareholders of the merging companies.

An example will demonstrate the fallacy of using EPS as a basis of valuation.

Example 1

Firm A is considering the acquisition of firm B, a Company in an unrelated industry. Fill in the spaces below assuming that there are no merger benefits, and that A intends to acquire B by offering shares for shares. Two shares in A will be given for fives shares in B.

	Firm A	Firm B	A + B
EPS (Earnings per share) (£)	1.00	1.00	
PPS (Price per share) (£)	50	20	
P/E ratio	50	20	
Number of shares	100 000	250 000	
Total earnings (historic) (£)	100 000	250 000	
Total market value (£)	5 000 000	5 000 000	

What is the effect on earnings per share?
Has wealth been created?
Do we believe in financial illusions?

If Firm A acquires firm B without merger benefits, the X-factor is zero, and the total market value of A + B is £10 000 000. Historic earnings are £350 000, the number of shares increases to 200 000, the price per share becomes £50, the price-earnings ratio becomes 28.57, and earnings per share increase to £1.75. In fact, earnings per share increase by 75 per cent for both companies. If we make decisions on the basis of increasing earnings per share, then this is indeed a very profitable merger. However, wealth has not been created because the market value of A + B is exactly the same after the merger as before the merger. Furthermore, the wealth of each shareholder is unchanged. This is a conglomerate merger, and conglomerates are not popular with financial theorists. Shareholders can achieve diversification without assistance from corporate managers.

	Firm A	Firm B	A + B
EPS (£)	1.00	1.00	1.75
PPS (£)	50	20	50
P/E ratio	50	20	28.57
Number of shares	100 000	250 000	200 000
Total earnings (historic) (£)	100 000	250 000	350 000
Total market value (£)	5 000 000	5 000 000	10 000 000

The example illustrates that the merger could be justified in terms of increasing earnings per share, although only an illusion of wealth is created. The following example illustrates that earnings per share can still give the wrong answer, even when the X-factor is positive

Example 2

Firm A is considering the acquisition of firm B. The X-factor is estimated at £6000, and in the first instance A offers B shares in A at fourteen times B's historic earnings. Alternatively, a reverse take-over could be arranged whereby B would offer A shares in B at twenty-two times A's historic earnings. Examine the earnings per share effect. Which merger makes most sense, A + B or B + A?

	Firm A	Firm B	A + B (i)	B + A (ii)
EPS (£)	1.0	1.0		
PPS (£)	20	10		
P/E ratio	20	10		
Number of shares	1000	1000		
Total earnings (historic) (£)	1000	1000		
Total market value (£)	20 000	10 000	36 000	

If A acquires B, the X-factor is split on the basis of £2000 for A shareholders and £4000 for B shareholders. After the merger the value of the combined firm to the original shareholders in A will be £22 000, and the price per share £22. The shareholders in B will receive shares in the new company, A + B, valued at £14 000. It will therefore be necessary to issue 636 shares at £22 per share. Clearly, the merger makes economic sense, the shareholders in Firm A and in Firm B being better off after the merger. Furthermore, earnings per share increase by 22 per cent for both companies to £1.22.

If the reverse take-over is organized, the total market value of B + A will also be £36 000. The split of the X-factor remains exactly as before. Company A shareholders will receive £2000, and company B shareholders will receive £4000. After the merger the 1000 shares owned by the B shareholders will be worth £14 each. At £14 it will be necessary to issue 1571 shares to the shareholders in firm A. Unfortunately, earnings per share in the combined enterprise fall to 78p, a decrease of 22 per cent. If we make economic decisions on the basis of EPS effect, this merger appears not to make economic sense. This is clearly wrong. Shareholders in firm A and in firm B are wealthier. The fact that earnings per share have fallen is of no consequence to shareholders in efficient capital markets. If we did base our decisions on EPS effect, we would have to argue that A + B is a good idea, whereas B + A is a bad idea. Such an argument is clearly inadmissible.

	Firm A	Firm B	A + B (i)	B + A (ii)
EPS (£)	1.0	1.0	1.22	0.78
PPS (£)	20	10	22	14
P/E ratio	20	10	18	18
Number of shares	1000	1000	1636	2571
Total earnings (historic) (£)	1000	1000	2000	2000
Total market value (£)	20 000	10 000	36 000	36 000

POST MERGER PERFORMANCE: THE EMPIRICAL EVIDENCE

Academic studies in this area generally aim either to assess the gain or loss from a merger to particular groups of shareholders, or to assess the impact of merger on economic efficiency. The assessment of success or failure in merger activity can be accomplished, in broad terms, by two methods, either accounting based performance measures, or rates of return to shareholders based on share price movements. Most studies apply themselves to one or the other of these methods.

Accounting rates of return

The use of accounting ratios as a measure of profitability has a number of disadvantages. It is based on figures included in published accounts which, although prepared within the broad context of company law and Standard Statements of Accounting Practice (SSAP's), still allow considerable scope for a manipulative approach in the treatment of depreciation and stock valuation. Studies using accounting data are seriously compromised owing to the absence of information relating to long run impacts of the acquisition on the participants.

Returns to shareholders

Studies of stock market returns to shareholders are, typically, based on event-date methodology using the Market Model, or Capital Asset Pricing Model. Basically, these methods examine share price movements before and after an event-date, in this case a merger announcement. These attempt to measure the abnormal returns to shareholders in relation to returns which would be expected from an investment in the market as a whole.

A large number of studies have been conducted in the USA using such methodology, but similar research using UK data is extremely limited. The evidence appears consistent with the Efficient Market Hypothesis (EMH) that capital market prices fully reflect relevant information. The UK capital market seems to anticipate mergers in the industry (on average) at least three months prior to the merger announcement.

Research in the UK suggests that the main, if not only, beneficiaries in merger activity are the shareholders in the acquired company, and that on the whole mergers are not economically successful. References to the major studies on the success/failure of merger activity are given in the section on further reading at the end of this Chapter. It should be noted that research in this field is directed at public companies and that the success rates for mergers between smaller, private companies have not been empirically tested.

METHOD OF FINANCING

The merger decision is an investment decision as we have already emphasized. The value of the firm depends primarily on its investment schedule. Also, as we have shown, increasing earnings per share is not an acceptable objective in the merger decision. If this were so all mergers would be financed by cash. This is not the case, and in a period of rising stock market prices, it may often be advantageous for the bidder to finance the bid with his or her own, ordinary shares. However, the use of shares as an exchange medium is often viewed unfavourably by existing shareholders in the bidding company, particularly the large and/or institutional investors who may not wish to see their percentage holdings diluted.

Cash may be favoured as its value is known. It is independent of the future growth and profitability of the new entity. In short, it is risk free. Acquisitions for cash may give rise to a capital gains tax liability. There may be a conflict of interest between target and bidder regarding the relative merits of cash versus share exchange. Cash may be preferred by target shareholders but share exchange may suit the bidder.

A vendor placing may satisfy these apparently opposing interests. The bidder issues shares in exchange for the target company but arranges for the shares to be passed to a merchant bank which then arranges to place the shares with institutions. The cash so received is paid to the target shareholders. Such deals however are circumscribed by quite stringent Stock Exchange rules. The Stock Exchange places a limit on the size of an equity 'placing' and gives existing shareholders a pre-emptive right of first refusal.

The issue of fixed interest securities may be advantageous in certain circumstances and interest paid on such stock is allowable as a tax deduction. Since the Finance Act of 1984, convertible loan stock (CLS) is exempt from Capital Gains Tax, as are Government securities, providing certain conditions are met. The stock may be convertible into equity on specified terms and dates. Such an issue will ultimately dilute the equity base if the conversion options are exercised and under the requirements of SSAP 3, an earnings per share statistic must be stated on a fully-diluted basis. CLS may be a suitable option when the stock market is depressed. A disadvantage which may be cited is that issue of debt beyond a certain level may raise the company's capital gearing to what may be considered an unacceptable level of financial risk.

DEFENCES AGAINST MERGER

One feature of the merger wave of the 1980s has been the prominence of hostile or defended bids. The attitudes of managers, academics and business journalists to such bids are varied. Some see them as useful motivators to complacent management – the 'kick in the pants' theory. Others take the view that they are a drain on valuable managerial resources and may retard company performance for years after the bid. The emergence of the hostile bid as an acceptable method of growth has led to the use of an increasing number and variety of defence tactics by target company managements. In summarizing the more common tactics which have been observed the authors make no value judgement on them. Some are of dubious respectability, may be illegal and may offend the Take-over Code. They therefore require cautious prior consideration and be subject to legal and other appropriate professional advice.

Defensive strategies and tactics can be classified as either pro-active or re-active. Pro-active strategies are those which can be put in place by a company's management well in advance of any potential bid, although some may need prior approval of the shareholders. The best bid defences are often those which have been in operation for a long period before a bid is received, e.g. good communications with shareholders.

Pro-active strategies

1 Cross-shareholdings can be arranged between 'friendly' companies.
2 Company management may issue new shares to 'friendly' shareholders. Vendor placings are strictly controlled in the UK by the Stock Exchange and existing shareholders are given right of first refusal.
3 Companies may issue voteless shares and shares having special voting rights. This practice is frowned upon by the Stock Exchange and the few public companies which continue to operate special classes of shares are frequently criticized for the practice. However, the issue of such shares is not illegal.
4 'Golden Parachutes' may be arranged by companies. This is an American term for the agreement of substantial termination pay-offs for executives should the company be taken over by a predator.
5 Assets may be placed outside the control of shareholders. This can only be done with prior permission of the shareholders in an extraordinary general meeting.
6 Company rules may stipulate super-majority voting requirements for specified proposals including mergers and takeovers.
7 Directors may arrange a 'Buy-Op'. This is a scheduled repurchase of a corporation's own shares over a period of time in the open market.
8 Companies can maintain regular and informative communications with shareholders as a matter of company policy rather than as a 'fire-fighting' tactic.
9 Directors may seek a potential 'white knight' who will be prepared to make a 'friendly' bid in the event of a hostile one arising.

Re-active tactics

10 Directors may criticize the bid on as many grounds as possible,

including inadequate terms, lack of commercial logic, bidder's motives, and the quality of the attacker's shares.

11   Directors can issue an immediate appeal to shareholders not to sell their shares and not to accept the offer. A statement simply asking shareholders not to act until further notice may not be sufficiently positive.

12   The board may sell assets. The Takeover Code requires shareholder approval for sales of significant assets during a bid.

13   Directors may raise the dividend. The information content of higher dividends may affect the share price sufficiently to defeat the bid on its original terms.

14   A capital reconstruction can be organized, which may include a scrip issue or more shares or debt. This may affect the capital gearing to an extent which makes the bid a less attractive proposition for the bidder. Again, the Takeover Code rules against such behaviour unless the shareholders approve in an EGM.

15   A board under attack may make an acquisition of a third party to complicate bid proceedings and possibly make the target company too big for the bidder to acquire.

16   The 'Pac-Man' tactic is another American term for the situation where a firm subject to a bid has in turn bid for the bidder. However, if it is used, it will rule out many other defences such as an appeal to the MMC or EEC.

17   The directors may approach a 'White Knight'. This is an appeal to a friendly company to make a competing offer.

18   Share dealings might help to fight off an aggressor. There are two main strategies. One may buy the target's shares, or sell the bidder's. Purchasing the target's shares will reduce the number of shares available to the bidder and tend to support or raise the share price. It is important that the price be kept up to the offer price otherwise the bidder may purchase shares in the market. Alternatively, a target company's merchant bank might sell from its funds its holdings of the bidding company in an attempt to depress that company's share price to make the terms of a share offer less attractive. This may not please the shareholders of the Merchant Bank.

19   Directors may use business, social and political contacts. A company may stress its importance to the local community, local unemployment, local business prospects. The board may get the trade union to lobby for the incumbent management, and ask

customers and suppliers to suggest that they would end their relationship with the company if the management is changed.

20   Directors may threaten resignation. This threat will be most powerful in firms where a few key individuals are disproportionately important, e.g. in high technology or fashion, especially if there is a chance that they will set up directly competitive enterprises. The threat of resignation by top management has sometimes affected the MMC's decision. However, in such cases the bidder is likely to withdraw irrespective of MMC decisions.

21   Companies may appeal to the courts. In the UK few attempts to involve the courts have been made. The best chance for using this defence is by using the US courts against a bidder, if a suitable action can be found.

22   Directors can lobby the OFT for a reference to the Monopolies and Mergers Commission. This may be sufficient in itself to deter the bidder owing to the cost of the investigations. If the bidder persists, the time gained by a reference may enable the target to construct other defences.

23   Companies can appeal to the European Economic Community. Article 86 of the Treaty of Rome prohibits abuse of a dominant position. If a merger is prohibited by the Commission under Article 86, it cannot be authorized in the UK.

24   Directors could disclose new information relating to asset values, prospective profits, prospective dividends, new developments, management changes, asset sales, new inventions and other new developments.

25   A company may take a 'Poison Pill' which is the reallocation of the company's assets in undesirable ways, or the making of agreements which come into effect should the company be taken over which will make it a less desirable acquisition. This can also be used as a pro-active measure.

26   Boards may accelerate or launch corporate PR, e.g. use of press advertising (within rules of the Takeover Code), or produce and circulate a video tape to major shareholders with details of the company's arguments and its potential as an independent company.

27   A company may purchase its own shares if permitted by the articles, either in the market or by tender offer.

28   If the target company can demerge the subsidiary which operates the particular business in which the acquiring company is most

interested, the bidder may go after the ex-subsidiary and leave the former parent alone.

29   Directors may disclose damaging information relating either to the target or to the bidder. The Takeover Code now prohibits 'knocking copy' against the bidder. Caution is needed. Issuing damaging information about your own company in order to deter the bidder may be counter-productive in the longer term.

Such re-active tactics are usually adopted to defend the target company in the short run, ignoring profit considerations. They should be used with caution and with a view to potential legal action by shareholders after the event.

FURTHER READING

The literature on mergers and acquisitions is now extensive, although much has an academic bias which may not appeal to the practitioner. Two good books for the general reader, which can be recommended are *Mergers and Acquisitions*, by Terence E. Cooke published by Blackwell, and *Corporate Acquisitions and Mergers: A practical guide to the legal, financial and administrative implications*, by P.F.C. Begg. In particular, the former contains a good review of accounting problems and the latter provides comprehensive advice on planning and strategy considerations.

The standard text on the legal implications of mergers and acquisitions is by Weinberg and Blank; *Takeovers and Mergers* is published by Sweet and Maxwell, although the latest edition was published in 1979 and is now a little dated.

References to Newbould, Franks, Broyles and Hecht, Firth and Meeks are concerned with the success or failure of merger activity, mainly related to the merger wave of the late 1960s, early 1970s.

Most literature on defence tactics originates in the USA, e.g. *Merger Mania* by Michel and Shaked, but the references to Lofthouse, Wooldridge, Pickering and Danziger relate to UK defences.

A thorough examination of the theoretical background to mergers and acquisitions as well as finance theory in general is provided by Copeland and Weston in *Financial Theory and Corporate Policy*. The latest edition of the Takeover Code, extensively revised in 1985, is much improved in format and ease of use and is an essential reference.

Lastly, there are two useful, informative (if expensive) monthly publications dedicated to mergers and acquisitions: *The Financial Times' Mergers & Acquisitions* published by FT Publications, and *Acquisitions Monthly* published by Tudor Publications.

REFERENCES

Begg, P.F.C., *Mergers and Acquisitions: a practical guide to the legal, financial and administrative implications*, Graham and Trotwood, 1984.

City Code on Takeover and Mergers.

Companies Act 1985.

Cooke, Terence, E., *Mergers and acquisitions*, Basil Blackwell, 1986.

Copeland, Tomas E. and Weston J. Fred, *Financial Theory and Corporate Policy*, 2nd edition, Addison Wesley, 1983.

Danziger, Yoram F., 'Remedial defensive tactics against takeovers', *The Company Lawyer'* **4**, pp. 3–13, 1983.

Firth, Michael, *Share Prices and Mergers*, Saxon House, D.C. Heath, England 1976.

Franks, J.R., Broyles, J.E., and Hecht, M.E., 'An industry study of the profitability of mergers in the UK', *Journal of Finance*, **32**, no 5, pp. 1513–1525, Dec. 1977.

Lofthouse, S., 'Strategy and tactics for resisting takeover', *Long Range Planning*, **17**, No.4, pp. 38–50, 1984.

Meeks, G, *Disappointing Marriage: A study of the gains from merger* Cambridge University Press, 1977.

Michel, A. and Shaked, I., *Takeover Madness*, John Wiley, 1986.

Newbould, G.D., *Management and Merger Activity*, Guthstead, 1970.

Pickering, J.F., 'The causes and consequences of abandoned mergers', *Journal of Industrial Economics*, **31**, No. 3, pp. 267–281.

Pike, R. and Dobbins, R., *Investment Decisions and Financial Strategy*, ch. 10, Philip Allan, 1986.

Wooldridge, F., 'Some defences to takeover bids', *Journal of Business Law*, pp. 202–211, 1974.

22

Inflation Accounting

Raymond Brockington

The author underlines the importance of inflation accounting in relation to financial planning and control by his statement that its introduction is 'one of the biggest responsibilities which the accounting profession has ever undertaken'. This chapter carefully examines the nature of inflation and critically reviews discussion on the subject and the numerous reports, exposure drafts and statements of standard accounting practice issued by accountancy bodies.

Inflation is an effect of relative values which change even in a barter economy. In a money economy they are changing 'in a fashion to which a particular perception is imparted by our insistence on the adoption of a specific unit of account'. Inflation, maintains the author, is essentially an accounting problem and in the absence of explicit accounting adjustments an individual's assessment of the effect of inflation can be incomplete and highly subjective. The chapter cites the illusory pictures of growth and prosperity presented by accounts based on the historical cost convention and acclaimed with pride by company chairmen. It indicates how the holding of current assets causes loss but credit creates gain.

The doctrines of the two schools of thought, current purchasing power and current cost accounting, are examined and contrasted, and particular attention is given to the principles outlined in the Sandilands Report. The author finds much to approve in both these schools and concludes that 'the profession is right to move with all the caution and conservatism which its friends and critics alike are prone to impute to it.'

The reader will not have come this far without encountering, in many forms, manifestations of the problems in accounting caused by inflation. Although business management is concerned with the organization and optimum use of real scarce resources, it can plan, control and report on these things only after translating them into financial terms. This chapter is largely concerned with the reporting problems caused by inflation and hence with a consideration of relevant accounting standards and proposed standards. These are applied to the published accounts and are therefore a primary responsibility of the financial accountant and of the auditor. No financial manager dare, however, regard this as being outside his field. For one thing, any variation in the method of accounting used in external reporting is bound to spread backwards into the records on which it is based and hence to those on which also is based planning and control information. For another, the financial manager's ability to raise external finance, the planning of financial structure and the determination of the cost of capital, amongst many other things, are closely bound up with the information provided to external decision makers.

The chapter is organized as follows. First a general outline establishes what inflation is and puts the view that it is much more of an accounting problem than an economic problem. If the former could be resolved so that the reality of the underlying situation could be precisely conveyed then, it is argued, the economic consequences of inflation would largely cease to exist. Then some of the more important distortions in reporting which arise when the conventional historical cost (henceforth HC) method of accounting is used against an inflationary background are examined. This is to establish that the problem has quite profound consequences and that its solution is not merely a matter of pedantic nicety. Third, the two main schools of thought concerning inflation accounting, those of current purchasing power (CPP) and current cost accounting (CCA) will be considered in theoretical terms. Finally there is a review of practical developments to date from early Recommendations on Accounting Principles to the Accounting Standards Committee's SSAP 16 and its subsequent demise.

INFLATION – AN ACCOUNTING OR ECONOMIC PROBLEM?

An elementary text on economics will say that money has several important functions. It acts as a medium of exchange, as a store of value and as a unit of account. In such an elementary treatment there is unlikely to be discussed the very important issue of *how good* money is at performing these functions. It is in its deficiencies that the problems which inflation accounting seeks to resolve are created and, before consideration of that resolution, there should be careful attention to the precise nature of the problem.

It may charitably be assumed that if modern man wished for the first time to create money, people would be able to design something which fulfilled the purpose wholly perfectly. This, however, is not what happened. Money, once invented, has always been used for the same reasons and in the same way as any other commodity and has carried with it the congenital condition common to them all but which in money becomes a disease. Value in economic terms is determined by an interplay of a commodity's scarcity and of its desirability. Even in a barter economy relative values are constantly changing. A cow may cost three sheep one day but may exchange for only two on the following day. Where all commodities are of equal standing this relative change will be seen for what it is. It will be no more meaningful to say that cows have fallen in value than to say that sheep have risen in price.

A change in the analogy may make the point plainer. If one car travelling at 40 m.p.h. is overtaken by another travelling at 45 m.p.h. both drivers will recognize that each continues to make progress but at different speeds. The first driver will fall neither into the error of believing that the other is travelling at only 5 m.p.h. nor, still less, that of believing that he himself is moving backwards at that speed. If one or other car were arbitrarily designated and accepted as a new standard of rest, however, the perception would be quite changed.

In economic terms, once more, if sheep be designated as the commodity which henceforth is to act as money, the standard of value, it will then be declared unequivocally that the price of cows has fallen. The problem starts, then, when one point in a turmoil of confused motion is arbitrarily selected as the datum from which all other movements are to be measured. The possibility that the datum itself moves is thereafter precluded from consideration. The creation of money in the way described did not, of course, occur in an instant but there was a gradual development over a very long period. During this time certain commodities, usually the uncommon, durable and attractive metals, came to be desired for their usefulness as money above their usefulness in the direct satisfaction of human demands.

With one or two relatively shortlived reversals of the secular trend, inflation, the constant relative decline in the value of money or, as it is observed, the constant upwards movement of all prices, has persisted ever since. Why the movement is generally in one direction is a question beyond our present scope. It might be fair to suggest, however, that an impetus to this is that money (whether it be gold or banknotes) is a durable commodity of which, therefore, the available supply gradually increases over time as more is created than is consumed. Moreover, once such a trend has been established, expectations that it will continue must be a very powerful influence towards ensuring that in fact it does so.

The bearing of all this on the work of the accountant is that it will lead to a definition of inflation which is crucial to the formulation and understanding of processes designed to account for its effects. Inflation is not merely that prices are rising or that the purchasing power of money is falling. It is that relative values are changing in a fashion to which a particular perception is imparted by our insistence on the adoption of a specific universal unit of account. This gives rise to what is often termed the 'money illusion'.

Inflation is thus quite uniquely an accounting problem. It is because of the discrepancy it creates between perception and reality that it has such undesirable effects and for no other reason. If it were possible to account for inflation adequately, there would be no need to cure it although, as will be seen, the former is not necessarily the easier of the two to achieve.

The stock argument used in the past against making adjustment for inflation has been that it is unnecessary because inflation is so well understood a phenomenon that people automatically make their own mental adjustment for it and read figures in that light. To some extent this is demonstrably true. If a man goes into a shop to buy a pair of shoes and he is quoted a price which is double what he paid for similar shoes five years previously, he does not immediately assume that he is being overcharged. He looks at prices around him and makes appropriate allowance for the inflation of the five years. Again, people do not refuse to buy food because they now spend in a day what their parents used to spend in a week. Some adjustments are routinely made. On the other hand a unit trust management company is able proudly to advertise that the value of its units has doubled in the last ten years without at the same time pointing out that this actually represents a loss to the investor in real terms. Again, the houseowner is able to continue to complain about the struggle to meet her mortgage repayments even though inflation is rapidly lifting the real burden of the charge from her shoulders. The problem is that, in the absence of carefully designed explicit accounting adjustments, those adjustments which are made are incomplete, highly subjective and selective.

Consider how people might cope if there were inflation in the units of length rather than in those of currency. A glazier measuring up a window frame for a pane of glass would find that the glass supplied in the centimetres of today would not fit the frame measured in the centimetres of yesterday. In this situation no vague understanding that inflation was taking place followed by a rough and ready mental adjustment to allow for it would serve. Nothing less than a very precise knowledge of the extent of the change and a careful evaluation of its full effect would do. Clearly, then, there is a prima facie case which says that inflation will cause accounting statements to distort our understanding of the real situation and that we need some formal rectification of this to avoid that problem.

DISTORTIONS IN REPORTING

It will be helpful now to present a rather fuller case by giving some important specific examples of distortions caused in HC accounts where no subjective judgment can be expected to give any adequate adjustment. The importance of these examples is that they arise in a situation which is commonly met and which commonly leads to errors of interpretation of accounting statements. Company chairmen are very fond of calling the attention of shareholders to an impressive growth record which they will frequently exemplify by reference to figures drawn from successive accounts over a period of time.

The following table and chairman's statement relates to the imaginary company, Avocado PLC.

Year	1977	1978	1979	1980	1981	1982	1983	1984	1985	1986
Capital employed (£ million)	20.0	20.6	21.6	22.3	23.3	24.5	25.6	24.4	25.0	26.1
Profit (£ million)	2.2	2.3	2.6	2.7	3.0	3.4	3.9	4.0	4.3	4.7
Dividend per share	5p	5p	5p	6p	6p	6p	6p	7.5p	7.5p	7.5p

In the last decade we have seen a most encouraging growth in our business. In that time our capital employed, a measure of the total resources over which we have control, has increased steadily until it now stands at 1.3 times what it did in 1977. As might be expected this has brought a steady increase in our total profit. What is particularly gratifying, however, is that this has grown faster than capital, implying a substantially improving profitability as we have grown in size. Our profit represented a return on capital of 11 per cent in 1977 but by the year just past it had risen to 18 per cent. Whilst making appropriate retentions out of profit to finance our growth we have passed on a substantial part of the benefit to our members who now, after three increases in their dividend over the decade, enjoy an income which has increased by 50 per cent.

Such figures supporting such statements are a commonplace in the financial world and yet, where the figures have been prepared by conventional accounting methods, every one of the chairman's statements is completely invalid as will be shown.

The official Index of Retail Prices, used here as a convenient measure of inflation, averaged 182.0 in 1977 (January 1974 = 100) and it rose every year subsequently to a level of 385.9 in 1986. In order to retain its purchasing power of 1977, therefore, the company's profit would need to increase to £2.2 $\times \frac{385.9}{182.0}$ million by 1986. This gives a figure of £4.7 million which was, in fact, just achieved. Thus, we would argue, the chairman should have said 'Profit has remained stationary for the past ten years.'

Applying the same calculation to the dividend, this, in order to maintain its purchasing power, should have risen to 5 $\times \frac{385.9}{182.0}$ p by 1986, i.e. a level of 10.6p. The actual dividend is only about 70 per cent of this and the chairman might therefore have said, 'Because inflation has placed a considerable strain on our cash resources we have found it necessary to curtail dividends by 30 per cent during this difficult decade.'

The imaginary chairman made an approving comment on the company's return on capital and here the position is even more confused. The discrepancies caused within a conventional accounting system by inflation arise fundamentally because the unit of currency has a value here and now determined by its current market rating but accounts are dominated by a principle in which money is deemed to retain a value determined by some past market rating. This is the more complicated in that, although there is only one present moment, there is an infinity of past moments and different ones of these condition different parts of the accounts.

It may be supposed that the amount of the inflationary effect is related to the time elapsed since the historical moment when the recorded value was determined. Because fixed assets are relatively long lived the average time elapsed since the values in that account were determined will be relatively long. The profit-and-loss account contains one item, depreciation, which is as old as fixed assets but other figures are much newer. For this reason, in an inflationary period, reported profits might be expected to respond more quickly to the upward pressure of prices than do most of the assets. The lag of asset valuations behind profit-and-loss valuations will lead to an observed increase in the rate of return on capital – precisely the effect commented on by the chairman. The distortion cannot be quantified by a simple transformation of the figures given. It can, however, be said that the chairman has certainly overstated the position. Nor, it should be noted, is doubt being thrown merely on the trend which he has observed. The absolute level of the rate of return which may be used in, for example, evaluating alternative forms of investment, is also subject to distortion.

There is an equally important phenomenon where the facts themselves are influenced by inflation. Because some money values are free to float in a market and others are fixed by contract or by law, inflation will lead to arbitrary redistributions of wealth. The market value of a company's stock or of its fixed assets are free to rise in money value so that, other things being equal, there are no inflationary consequences of such investment in real terms. The value of debtors, bank balances and cash, however, are fixed in money terms and will, therefore, decline in real value causing the company an actual loss. By a similar argument a company under inflation will gain in real terms at the expense of its creditors and its suppliers of loan capital both of which will again have fixed money values.

Consider the following simple balance sheet for Mango PLC at 30 June 1978.

Share capital	£1 000 000	Physical assets	£1 500 000
Loan capital	1 000 000	Cash at bank	500 000
	£2 000 000		£2 000 000

Suppose that, for the sake of simplicity, the physical assets are non-depreciating, that all loan interest is promptly paid, that all profits are distributed as earned and that there are no debtors or creditors. The balance sheet, on conventional HC principles, will remain unchanged over time. We will look at the position at the end of December 1986 by which time the general level of retail prices had doubled. A balance sheet based on a fresh valuation of Mango's position at that time would appear as follows:

Share capital and reserves*	£2 500 000	Physical assets†	£3 000 000
Loan capital	1 000 000	Cash at bank	500 000
	£3 500 000		£3 500 000

* including revaluation reserve   † estimated current value

Note that the inflation-adjusted balance sheet shows a dramatically different picture from the HC balance sheet. The equity share in the business is up from 50 per cent to over 70 per cent. Overall solvency is greatly improved but liquidity is down. These improvements in the position have been *concealed* by a failure to account for inflation in the balance sheet and *caused* by a failure to account for inflation in dealings with the outside world.

Thus the existence of inflation where a conventional HC-based system of accounting is in use will have two effects. It will cause redistribution of interests between equity holders and debt holders and between goods owners and cash owners and it will distort the perception of reality so as to invalidate almost any observation which might be made in the interpretation of accounts. This is why the point was made earlier that inflation is wholly an accounting problem. If it were resolved then the distortions in the interpretation of data would be avoided. It is also impossible to believe that the massive capricious redistributions of income and wealth which occur now would be tolerated once they were revealed clearly for what they were. A satisfactory solution to the problem is not, however, easy to find, as the story of practical attempts to do so, to be told later, confirms.

TWO SCHOOLS OF THOUGHT

At a theoretical level, however, the argument can conveniently be divided between two main schools of thought illustrating the main consequences of the use of each.

Current purchasing power

The first, that associated with the current purchasing power (CPP) concept, argues that the relationship between a 1986 pound (say) and a 1977 pound (say) is not unlike the relationship between a pound and a dollar. They differ, that is, in terms of their purchasing power and can be converted one into another by means of an appropriate factor. Just as, on a particular day, we can accurately say that £1 = $2 so, it is argued, we can equally accurately say that

since $\dfrac{182.0}{385.9} = 0.47$ then $£_{1986}1 = £_{1977}0.47$

There is, however, one important reservation to make. Whereas there is a market which says that £1 = $2, there is no market as between £1986 and £1977. The rate of exchange is imputed from a consideration of index numbers as a measure of purchasing power. The selection of some specific index for this purpose carries an unavoidable implication as to how the uses to which the money will be put are seen. Use of a retail price index, as here, for example, implies an interest in purchasing power as applied to the range of goods and services offered in the retail market. Had the interest been in money as used for stock market investment (arguably more appropriate in the context of company finance) a share price index (of which there are several – not all in agreement) might have been used. Had the concern been with the use of money to purchase business fixed assets an index of freehold buildings or of plant and machinery prices might have been selected. Had the focus been on ability to finance stock an index based on raw material prices would have seemed appropriate. It is thus a practical flaw in the CPP concept, though not necessarily a destructive one, that there is no universal measure of purchasing power which is free of all implication about the specific use to which money might be put.

Look now at Mango's balance sheet as it would appear in December 1986 if prepared on CPP principles.

Some important points should be noted. All amounts not fixed by contract or by law, i.e. all monetary amounts, are indexed according to the selected measure of general inflation. The fact that 'Physical assets' now stands at £3 million, therefore, does not mean that these are deemed to have a market value of that figure. It means that at some historic time the acquisition of these assets absorbed a quantity of purchasing power assessed in terms of alternative goods and services which assessed now in terms of those same alternative goods and services would have a money valuation of £3 million. The physical assets *may* have a market value of this figure but this will be merely fortuitous and not a universal experience with CPP.

Share capital	£2 000 000	Physical assets	£3 000 000
Profit due to inflation	500 000	Cash at bank	500 000
Loan capital	1 000 000		
	£3 500 000		£3 500 000

* Profit from loan capital finance	£1 000 000
Less loss from holding cash	500 000
Profit due to inflation	£500 000

Monetary items, e.g. loan capital, creditors, debtors and cash, are not indexed and this leads to a 'difference' in the balance sheet identifiable as net profit or loss due to inflationary movements. This is shown on the balance sheet and an analysis of it follows. It is useful in emphasizing the consequences during a period of inflation of holding idle cash balances, which lose value, and of debt financing, which gives rise to inflationary gains.

CPP accounting is in many ways an attractive and logical extension of HC accounting. The so-called capital maintenance concept has always been at the heart of the latter in that profits are so computed that, after all have been distributed, including any on realization, liquidation would enable the repayment to the investor of his original cash subscribed. Obviously when inflation has taken place this repayment will be less valuable in terms of other goods and services which it will command than was the original amount invested. Under CPP when all reported profits have been distributed, including inflationary gains and, again, those on realization, liquidation would enable a repayment to the investor of the same amount of purchasing power, though more money, as the investor forwent when making the original subscription. It should be emphasized that the investor is not better off in aggregate by these manipulations. Under CPP lower profits would be reported and this retention would be the source of the higher money payout on liquidation. The concern here, however, is with accurate reporting and the contention is that historical cost, by ignoring inflation, has overstated profits.

Here is an example which contrasts HC and CPP. Satsuma PLC started in business on 1 January with a share capital, fully subscribed, of £500 000 and loan capital of £200 000. It immediately purchased stock for £600 000. On 31 December the stock was sold for £1 000 000, interest at the rate of 25 per cent for the year was paid on loan capital and the whole of the net profit was distributed as a dividend. The company was then wound up. Prices, as measured by a general index, had risen by 20 per cent during the year.

Satsuma PLC – Profit and loss account for the year ended 31 December

	HC	CPP
Sales	£1 000 000	£1 000 000
Less cost of sales	600 000	720 000
Gross profit	400 000	280 000
Less interest on loan capital	50 000	50 000
Net profit on trading	£350 000	£230 000
Inflationary gain on loan capital		£40 000
Less inflationary loss on cash		20 000
		£20 000
Total profit distributed as dividend	£350 000	£250 000
Realisation at 31 December		
Cash available after payment of		
dividend and interest	£700 000	£800 000
Paid to holders of loan capital	£200 000	£200 000
Paid to shareholders	500 000	600 000
	£700 000	£800 000

Current cost accounting

CPP's main rival is current cost accounting, CCA. The basic argument underlying this is that inflation causes reporting problems because of the multitude of valuation occasions used under HC. The way to deal with this is to maintain all accounting values at up-to-date figures. For historical cost, the amount that was paid for assets is substituted current cost, the money amount which would now have to be paid for them. An advantage which is claimed for this method is that the balance sheet becomes a statement of true values rather than a mere list of unexpired balances and that this makes it of real use in determining the relative merits of alternative uses of funds. One point should be made quite clear, however, CCA is more than a means of accounting for inflation. It is a different system of accounting based on a quite different principle from HC. It deals with inflation almost incidentally and cannot distinguish between general inflation and market price fluctuations.

Suppose there is a period of price stability and that a business is operating at a constant level of activity, HC, CPP and CCA will all report similar profits and will show constant financing. Then comes a period of general inflation. Under HC enhanced profits will be reported (because selling prices will rise in advance of historically based costs) but increased finance will be seen to be required (whether this be acquired by new issues of capital or by voluntary retention of profit). Under CPP and CCA lower profits will be reported and, given the constant level of activity, no extra finance will be shown to be required. CPP and CCA thus (broadly) agree with one another and disagree with HC. Suppose now that, instead of general inflation, there are specific price rises owing to relative scarcity in the assets in which the company deals. Now HC and CPP will agree with one another that additional finance is required, although they may not agree on the precise extent of it. CCA will, however, show constant financing but lower profits. It is a matter of argument as to which is right but there is some intuitive appeal to an argument which says that a pocket of scarcity in an otherwise inflation-free economy would require extra finance in its exploitation. If this is correct then CCA is wrong in denying it.

Now look at Satsuma PLC again to see what its accounts would look like under CCA. For this is needed one new price of information. The replacement cost of the stock had risen to £690 000 by 31 December. The HC figures are repeated for purposes of comparison.

The two ideas explored can fairly be characterized as follows. CPP is investor-centred and seeks to preserve the investor's capital in all its alternative uses. It seems ultimately, therefore, to envisage the

Satsuma PLC – Profit and loss account for the year ended 31 December

	HC	CCA
Sales	£1 000 000	£1 000 000
Less cost of sales	600 000	690 000
Gross profit	400 000	310 000
Less interest on loan capital	50 000	50 000
Net profit distributed as dividend	£350 000	£260 000
Realisation at 31 December		
Cash available after payment of dividend and interest	£700 000	£790 000
Paid to holders of loan capital	£200 000	£200 000
Paid to shareholders	500 000	590 000
	£700 000	£790 000

liquidation of the company, the antithesis, that is, of the going concern concept. CCA, on the other hand is company-centred. It values resources in their existing uses and capital is maintained in the sense of being able to support the current level of real resources actually employed.

CCA, in the pure form illustrated here, has an important weakness where general inflation exists. Although it recognizes that the increased prices of non-monetary assets require an increased money capital, it does not recognize that this is also true of monetary assets. If prices have doubled so that physical assets have doubled in money value, the company will certainly also need to maintain a doubled cash balance and allow its debtors to double as well. CPP allows for this by computing the loss due to holding cash and debtor balances but CCA, in its basic form, does not.

ACCOUNTING FOR INFLATION IN THE REAL WORLD

It has already been said that the solution is not a simple one and the story of attempts to formulate it reflects this. It is a story which is not yet ended and which is likely to continue for some time.

The problem found quite early recognition in recommendations issued by the Institute of Chartered Accountants in England and Wales. Recommendation 12 (1949) and Recommendation 15 (1952) referred to it but ended by endorsing the HC method. Not until January 1973 were any forceful proposals for action placed before the accountancy profession. Then the Accounting Standards Committee issued. Exposure Draft (ED) 8, 'Accounting for changes in the purchasing power of money'. Before ED 8 could crystallize into a standard the government had announced the establishment of its own committee to look into inflation accounting under the chairmanship of Sir Francis Sandilands. The standard based on ED8 was, therefore, pending the report of that committee, issued as a provisional standard only. Professional Statement of Standard Accounting Practice 7, as it was numbered, was issued in May 1974.

The important provisions of this standard can be summarized quite shortly. Historic cost accounts were to continue to be prepared as heretofore and inflation-adjusted statements were to be produced as supplementary statements to those accounts. The method of adjustment was to be CPP using the general index of retail prices. All non-monetary assets and the share capital and reserves were to be revalued by reference to changes in the index since acquisition or issue and the difference was to be interpreted as the gain or loss due to inflation. The virtues of (P)SSAP 7 would appear to be that if offered a very rapid and easily calculated adjustment for inflation and that it retained the well-understood system of HC at its base. A weakness seemed to be that by producing in effect two sets of accounts each purporting to present a true and fair view it seemed likely that confusion would be caused.

In the event (P)SSAP 7 became a back number before it had been implemented by more than a handful of companies. The Sandilands Committee reported in September 1975 and with recommendations quite contrary to the proposals of the Accounting Standards Committee. The report envisaged the replacement of the HC method of accounting entirely by a CCA method. The concept of current cost which it proposed was that of value to the business or deprival value. This is a somewhat difficult concept to put into practice involving, as it does, the selection of the appropriate measure of value for each asset from a choice of economic value, realizable value and replacement cost.

An example will make this principle clear or, at least, highlight the complexity of it. Value to the business can usefully be thought of as the amount which would be needed exactly to compensate for the loss of the asset. If an item had a replacement cost of £4000, an economic value (discounted expected cash flow) of £2000 and a realizable value of £3000 then the value to the business would be £3000. The argument is that a rational company would be seeking to sell rather than use such an asset and would certainly not replace it. Therefore the proceeds of realization is the relevant measure of value. If the figures had been replacement cost £1000, economic value £2000 and realizable value £3000, value to the business is only £1000 since replacement can be effected at that figure and would be worthwhile. Generally value to the business is the *lower* of two values. One of these values is replacement cost and the other is the higher of economic value and realizable value. The report, it should be added, after establishing the principle of value to the business, accepts that in a very large proportion of cases replacement cost will be the only figure which can feasibly be determined and that this would generally be used.

It is, in any case, reasonable to suppose that assets offered by the market generally have economic values in excess of their price (otherwise none would be sold).

The Sandilands report proposals began to take practical shape when the Accounting Standards Committee issued ED 18 in November 1976. Its main feature was the adoption of value to the business as a basis of valuation in accounts to replace historic cost completely. Revaluation was to take place annually on the date of the balance sheet and the surplus thereby created was to be taken to a revaluation account. The depreciation and cost of sales figures used in the profit-and-loss account were to be the value to the business of the resources used at the time they were used. The revaluation account would notionally represent the necessary augmentation of money capital to enable the current level of investment in physical resources to be maintained. The surplus was then to be taken to an appropriation account where a transfer to permanent reserve would be made of an amount determined at the discretion of the directors. Under ED 18 no provision was made for increased requirements of net monetary resources.

In the calm words of the Accounting Standards Committee (ED 24, paragraph 6), 'It became clear that the Sandilands recommendations, and ED 18 which stemmed from them, were not acceptable.' It is perhaps inappropriate that more than this should be said about the events which led to a vote by the members of the Institute of Chartered Accountants in England and Wales massively rejecting.

against strong advice to the contrary from the Council, the abandonment of HC. There were several important objections to ED 18. One was that it was dangerous to replace HC with the untried CCA without some experimentation and research to test its utility. Another was that the ED 18 proposals were very complicated and thus difficult and expensive to put into operation (ED 18 ran to 332 paragraphs as against (P)SSAP 7's 44 paragraphs). Yet again the omission of any adjustment in respect of net monetary items was seen by many as a basic weakness.

The collapse of ED 18 was followed by the introduction of the stopgap 'Hyde' proposals which were then themselves displaced by ED 24. This exposure draft experienced a relatively easy transition into a definitive standard, SSAP 16 (issued in March 1980). Under SSAP 16 CCA information was to be given in a supplementary statement and not embodied in the primary accounts which would still appear in HC form. In the supplementary statement three adjustments to the HC profit were to be made. These were a charge to allow for the greater current cost of sales over historic cost of sales; a charge to allow for the excess of current cost depreciation over historic cost depreciation; and an adjustment in respect of monetary working capital. Monetary working capital is defined in the Standard as trade debtors less trade creditors but may also include cash and bank balances where their exclusion is likely to be misleading. The intention of this adjustment is to allow for the necessarily increased money investment in working capital occasioned by rising prices. These adjustments lead to what is termed the current cost operating profit.

It is then further recognized that to the extent that finance is by means of loans fixed in money terms there is an additional benefit to equity holders. This is represented by a gearing adjustment which, in effect, writes back that proportion of the previous adjustments which would have been attributable to debt holders had their investment been index-linked. All surpluses relating to these adjustments are credited to a capital maintenance reserve.

SSAP 16 had a brief and sad life. It quickly had to be acknowledged that it could serve as an interim measure only and three years was set as a trial period after which it would be reviewed. From the beginning there was widespread non-compliance with the standard and it only just survived an attempt (through a narrowly defeated motion set before the members of the English Institute) to terminate it before the end of the trial period. Subsequent attempts to replace SSAP 16 with an acceptable successor failed to gain sufficient support even within the membership of the ASC. The current position is that we have in place no standard or other regulation concerning the production of inflation adjusted figures. It is, however, interesting to note that current company legislation, as embodied in the Companies Act, 1985, permits, without requiring, the use of current cost valuations and the prescribed balance sheet formats contain a heading for revaluation reserve.

What ultimately emerges as the definitive way of dealing with, or of avoiding, the problem of inflation in accounts will be a consequence of historical processes which can now probably not be greatly influenced by any single individual. Perhaps the ideal method could be approached more nearly by an amalgam of the CCA and CPP principles which might exhibit the hybrid vigour which is the characteristic of a successful union. The suggestion is of a system of CCA with the incorporation of a careful segregation of gains and losses attributable to a background of general inflation. The figures for Satsuma PLC will once again serve for illustration.

It is contended that there are several elements in this company's activities each with its own separate outcome. It carried on a trading activity. This led to a profit which can be appropriately evaluated in CCA terms. It held cash. Inflation meant that a loss was caused by this activity and CPP provides a convenient way of evaluating this. The company owed money. Inflation makes this a profit-making

Satsuma PLC – Profit and loss account for the year ended 31 December

Sales		£1 000 000	
Less current cost of sales		690 000	
		310 000	
Less interest on loan		50 000	
Trading profit		260 000	(as per CCA)
Gain on borrowing		40 000	
Less loss on holding cash	£20 000		
Loss on holding stock	30 000	50 000	
Net loss due to inflation		(10 000)	(as per CPP)
Available for distribution		£250 000	

activity. Finally it held stock. This is a neutral activity where stock price rises are exactly in line with general inflation but either a profit- or loss-causing activity where this is not the case. The profit or loss can be determined by comparing CCA and CPP figures.

On these principles Satsuma's accounts look as shown above. The realization at 31 December is as for CPP.

The essence of the method can be seen by looking at a comparison of the treatment of stock by four methods. This was bought on 1 January for £600 000 and had a replacement cost on 31 December of £690 000 by which time the general price level had increased by 20 per cent. There is a money gain of £90 000 on the stock holding which is treated by the various conventions as follows:

	HC	CCA	CPP	Hybrid
Not segregated, appears as increase (decrease) in trading profit	£90 000	–	(£30 000)	
Augmentation of money capital to preserve purchasing power		£90 000	£120 000	£120 000
Segregated as specific inflationary profit (loss)				(£30 000)
	£90 000	£90 000	£90 000	£90 000

The introduction of inflation accounting is one of the biggest responsibilities which the accountancy profession has ever undertaken. Historical cost accounts were in origin statements of stewardship, that is they were a straightforward account of how entrusted funds had been deployed. If the world chose to use them for other purposes, including valuations and assessments of economic performance, then it did so at its peril and it was a fair defence for any shortcomings that the accounts had never claimed to have been designed to bear that load. Inflation accounting is to be introduced, however, specifically to remedy the defects of HC in satisfying users' current needs for information. It has to be accepted that any new system carries an implicit warranty of fitness for this purpose. The accountant cannot thereafter shelter behind the principle of *caveat emptor*. In these circumstances the profession is right to move with all the caution and conservatism which its friends and critics alike are prone to impute to it, and it may ultimately be right not to undertake the responsibility at all.

FURTHER READING

Allen, D., *Dynamic Management Accountancy*, Butterworth, 1987.

International Accounting Standards Committee. Financial Reporting in Hyperinflationary Economies. Exposure Draft (ED31). 1987.

Joint UK Accountancy Bodies, *Current Cost Accounting*, (SSAP 16). 1980, amended 1985.

Kirkman, R.A., *Inflation Accounting in Major English-speaking Countries*, Prentice Hall, 1985.

Miller, E.L., *Inflation Accounting*, Van Nostrand, 1980.

23

Tax Planning

John Chown

As the author of this chapter points out, tax strategy should be a principal element in financial management. Tax planning is concerned with future tax liabilities, that is, with the fiscal implications of current decisions, not with the past. Because of the complexity of the subject the chapter concentrates on two aspects of current importance: international operations and the small business, thus having relevance to earlier chapters in this book. On international operations the author considers in particular: the tax effects of group structure in the case of multinational companies; the tax traps involved in foreign currency transactions; and the relative merits of borrowing by the parent company or the foreign subsidiary. In the section on the small business, much practical advice is provided on methods of distributing profit, capital gains and the advantages of incorporation. Special attention is given to the raising of finance under the Business Expansion Scheme.

This chapter cannot attempt a comprehensive treatment of the UK tax system, or even of those tax factors which affect corporate financial decisions. It concentrates on two groups of topics where many businesses could benefit from more information. These are international operations and the small business.

Tax strategy should be a principal element in financial planning, although only too often it is not. The genuine tax planner should be concerned, not with arguing the tax computations of a trading period now past, but with the consequences for bottom line after-tax profits of decisions now being taken. The tax planner has to look behind the often misleading conventions of traditional accounting practice to the real economic and cash flow effects of the decisions involved.

These future tax liabilities will involve the tax system, not as it is now, but as it will be when new projects currently at the planning stage are actively generating profits. It is a measure of the speed of change that of the seven topics covered in the equivalent chapter in the 1981 edition of this book, four – inflation, stock relief, capital investment and leasing – are now for practical purposes superseded, and no longer particularly important.

The United Kingdom Corporation Tax reform of 1984 reduced the rate of Corporation Tax from 52% to 35%, but by phasing out first year allowances and by abolishing stock relief the yield of Corporation Tax has actually increased. The United States Tax Reform Act, which became fully operational in 1988, has much the same effect on the taxation of companies, and goes much further than anything that has yet been attempted in the UK in the reform of personal tax. Other countries seem likely to follow these examples. The ground rules have changed considerably and many companies, particularly those with international activities, have had to rethink completely their tax strategy.

This chapter deals only with taxes which fall on company profits. Readers will hardly need reminding of the substantial increase in recent years of the burden of national insurance contributions and local rates, nor of the problems of remunerating employees at all levels.

The central message of this chapter is that tax is too important to be left to the tax specialists. Taxation is an important component in cash flow and has to be treated as a principal (but by no means the only) factor is general tax planning.

INTERNATIONAL OPERATIONS

Group structure

Should a company with a number of foreign subsidiaries group some or all of these subsidiaries under an intermediate holding company in a third country? There may be management advantages in doing this as it may be a good method for paving the way for the future flotation of parts of the business. There is seldom a dramatic tax saving and normally the decision stands or falls on commercial or management considerations. There are some tax traps, mostly minor, and these should be watched.

Sometimes, the traps can be serious. In two cases in the author's experience the companies may have been saved from expensive consequences by a matter of weeks. Each of the companies had trading activities in the UK, and also substantial overseas income which had been taxed in the country of source and on which full credit for overseas tax was available. This produced no problems as long as the UK company continued to be profitable. In one particular year the UK company had a trading loss of £1 million. In the normal way this would be available to be carried forward against future profits, and a return to profitability was confidently (and, as it turned out, correctly) expected. Overseas income of £1 million gross, £500 000 after tax, was received in the same company. There would be little or no UK tax liability on this because of credit relief for the foreign tax. However, the rules require that the gross foreign income be first offset against the loss, eliminating the carry-forward. The credit relief would be wasted. When profits resumed the UK company's profits would be unnecessarily increased by £500 000! There was just time to save the situation and to arrange that the foreign income was received in a separate subsidiary. This subsidiary then itself paid no tax because of credit relief, but the parent UK company could then carry forward its own loss against future profits. Although a loss in one group company can be (and in normal circumstances is) offset against the profits of other group companies, this treatment is optional and requires a positive election by the companies. Simple – but it saved £500 000.

Another common type of case is where a company has two subsidiaries, A and B, in another country. Because there is no common parent in the country, A and B are not a 'group' for tax purposes. This fact is only recognized, too late, when A makes a profit and B makes a loss and it is discovered that they cannot be offset. This has happened in the author's recent experience to large companies in the UK, the USA and Germany.

INTERNATIONAL FINANCING

The international management of debt can be a powerful source of profit and, as many UK companies have found to their cost, a dangerous source of loss. A company needing to borrow to finance an overseas venture can arrange for the foreign subsidiary to borrow locally, or can borrow at parent company level and transfer the funds to the subsidiary by interest free loans, loans carrying interest or equity shares. It can choose between short, medium and long-term debt and, significantly, between the two currencies to be borrowed.

The abolition of exchange control, the Big Bang in the City of London, and the rapid development of global financial markets now offers a wide range of financing and hedging techniques to the corporate treasurer, who can now raise money and manage her or his exposure to exchange rate and interest rate risks. The bad news (on this front) is that many of these techniques have been packaged as financial products and aggressively sold by bankers who have, only too often, not thought through the tax consequences. The serious tax traps in options have now typically been removed. Swaps treated by banks as the greatest financial innovation ever made are still viewed with some scepticism by international tax specialists.

The central problem in the UK remains tax fragmentation. Over the years British companies have lost several billion pounds by borrowing a foreign currency at a low interest rate only to find that sterling being weak they will have incurred substantial losses on repayment which were then proved not to be tax deductible. Virtually all these losses could have been avoided had the problem been recognized or had specialist professional advice been taken. Following the Marine Midland case and several discussion drafts the UK Revenue published a 'Statement of Practice' in February 1987. This was intended to be their interpretation of the existing law but it was quickly made clear to them that there was no substitute for change in the law itself. A Working Group is now considering the problem and it is hoped that new legislation will be introduced in 1988. Meanwhile treasurers should be on their guard and look carefully at any proposals involving transactions in foreign currency.

SMALL COMPANIES

We have come a long way from the dark days of 1965 when to be a 'close company' meant being subject to fearsome fiscal penalties. There was another bad patch in 1975 when Capital Transfer Tax threatened the survival of a family business. Now, fortunately, small business is actually encouraged by a reformed tax system. The key measure in Nigel Lawson's 1984 Budget was a proposal to phase out 100 per cent first year allowances while reducing (in three stages, now completed) the rate of Corporation Tax from 52 per cent to 35 per cent. On balance, the combined effect is slightly to increase the effective tax burden on capital-intense manufacturing companies while usefully reducing it on service businesses.

The position of the smaller company is somewhat different. The rate of tax on profits up to £100 000 was 30 per cent before the change. It has since been reduced, in line with the basic rate of income tax, to 25 per cent (1988–89).

The reduced 25 per cent rate applies to profits up to £100 000. Profits in excess of £500 000 will be subject to the full Corporation Tax rate with a catching-up rate in between. This (now small) penalty can be avoided by bringing forward fixed capital expenditure (*not* financed by leasing) or by other methods of tax postponement.

The profit figure is struck after deducting directors' fees and related expenditure. A closely owned company can apply its flow of profits in several different ways. Profits can be paid as director's fees or other remuneration when it will be subject to tax at personal rates but will, of course, be available for personal expenditure. Profits can be retained in the company when they will be subject to Corporation Tax. Such profits are not directly available, and it is as well to remember that, in principle, the growth in value resulting from these accumulations will be subject to Capital Gains Tax on the scale of the company. There are useful reliefs from Capital Gains Tax on retirement. Capital Gains Tax is also now indexed for inflation. Even where the business was started up with a nominal capital of, say, £100 there can still be some relief as indexation is based on 5th April 1982 values.

Profits can also be distributed as dividends. In this case tax will be payable but the individual recipient will enjoy an imputation credit. Now that the investment income surcharge has been removed there is, in fact, no 'corporate' penalty on paying dividends instead of directors' fees. Indeed, dividends may now be preferable as no national insurance contributions will be payable. A point to watch here is the adverse effect of paying dividends and prejudicing pension entitlement under the company scheme or under a retirement annuity.

Directors' fees and salaries (unlike dividends) can be used as the basis for the calculation of pension fund entitlements and contributions. Every owner of a private company should consider taking maximum advantage of the rules permitting profits to be appropriated tax free into a private pension fund. The investments of a pension fund are exempt from almost all taxes. Until recently a private fund had been feasible only for large schemes but it is now possible for a private pension fund to be set up for the controlling directors and key executives of a company.

A perhaps unintentional side effect of the 1984 Corporation Tax package is that it adversely affected unincorporated businesses. They suffer from the elimination of first year allowances without the owners receiving any corresponding reduction in their personal tax rates. It is quite possible that this point may be remedied in future legislation but meanwhile the relative advantages of incorporation have been substantially increased.

Financing the smaller company

Interest on money borrowed, whether by a company, an individual, or a partnership is, as one would expect, deductible in computing profits. Less obviously, interest on money borrowed by an individual to acquire an interest in a close company or a partnership is specifically eligible for relief (Schedule 1 Finance Act 1974 as amended). This suggests that someone starting a company, and who has personal taxable income (at least in that year) might be better advised to borrow as an individual and to put the money into the company.

There are three ways in which the tax system now facilitates the raising of finance for the smaller company. The most obvious, but not always the best, is the Business Expansion Scheme which was introduced in the Finance Act 1983 and superseded the largely unsatisfactory business start-up scheme. Under this, UK resident individuals can subscribe for up to £40 000 per annum in shares of a qualifying company. This investment can be claimed as a deduction against otherwise taxable income in the year of investment. This relief is not available to those connected with the company (directors, employees and their families or anyone entitled to more than 30 per cent of the ordinary share capital of the company). It is intended to encourage outside backing. It is also only available in respect of new money subscribed to the company and not to shares bought from third parties.

Needless to say, the detailed rules and safeguards are complex but this should not deter those seeking finance. The best type of business expansion finance is probably person-to-person, where a rising young business woman or man is backed financially (and also given friendly advice and support) by established members of the local business community, perhaps introduced by a banker or professional advisers. In practice, much of the Business Expansion Scheme money has been channelled through funds, some of which have been rather over-promoted without as yet much evidence that they have furthered the original objectives of the legislation. In addition, their methods of operation, often involving high management charges for the investor and options being taken in the qualifying company, have attracted criticism.

Relief under the Business Expansion Scheme is restricted to *qualifying individuals* and cannot apply to companies. The individual must subscribe for shares on his or her own behalf and must be both resident and ordinarily resident in the UK throughout the year of assessment in which shares are issued.

An individual is disqualified from obtaining relief if at any time during the relevant period the individual is connected with the company issuing the shares. (Generally, the 'relevant period' will be for the five years following the issue of the shares). An individual is 'connected with' a company if that individual or an associate is a director or employee of the company. An associate is defined to include a husband, wife, parent, or child but does not include a brother or sister. A director of a company may not be regarded as connected to that company if no payment is received as director during the period of five years commencing with the issue of shares. An individual is connected with a company if he or she directly or indirectly possesses more than 30 per cent of the issued ordinary share capital of the company or the voting power of the company. This is construed widely and covers options and other future rights.

The newcomer must *subscribe* for shares. Relief will not be available where shares are acquired by purchase from a former shareholder and the shares must be issued for the purpose of 'raising money for a qualifying trade which is being carried on by the company or which it intends to carry on'.

The shares must be '*eligible shares*' i.e., new ordinary shares which throughout the five-year period carry no preferential right to dividends or to assets on a winding up. Preference shares carrying the right to dividends at a fixed rate would not qualify.

A *qualifying company* must be incorporated in the UK and throughout the relevant period must be resident in the UK and not resident elsewhere. Throughout the relevant period the company must remain an unquoted company. This excludes companies with listings on the Stock Exchange or Unlisted Securities Market but does include companies traded on the over-the-counter market.

Throughout the relevant period (three years after the shares are issued or the trade commences for this purpose) a qualifying company must exist wholly, or substantially wholly, for the purpose of carrying on, wholly or mainly in the UK, one or more qualifying trades, or be a company whose business consists wholly of holding shares in or making loans to one or more qualifying subsidiaries, or a combination of the above.

The company must carry on a qualifying trade wholly or mainly in the UK. The trade must be conducted on a commercial basis and with a view to the realization of profit. There are a number of specifically excluded trades.

There is another approach to tax-efficient small business finance. Where an individual subscribes for shares in unquoted trading companies (and the detailed rules are met) any subsequent loss may be deducted from income in the year in which the loss was sustained (Section 37 Finance Act 1980). However, any gain is subject only to (indexed) Capital Gains Tax. There are fewer restrictions under this particular rule than under the BES and although it does not give immediate relief it could still have considerable appeal to the sophisticated investor willing to back risky new ventures.

Section 37 Finance Act 1980 provides that, 'where an individual who subscribes for shares in a qualifying trading company incurs an allowable loss (for Capital Gains Tax purposes) on the disposal of the shares in any year of assessment he may by notice in writing given within two years after that year make a claim for relief from Income Tax on an amount of his income equal to the amount of the loss.'

As with the BES the relief only applies to new subscribers in unquoted companies. The definition of 'qualifying trading company' rules out companies the purpose of which is simply to invest or trade in securities, but otherwise the restrictions are far less strict than those attached to the BES. There is also no limitation on the size of the investment.

24

Developments in Accounting Thought and Practice

Trevor Gambling

We conclude this book with a thought-provoking chapter by Professor Gambling. In it he examines certain fundamental ideas as to the nature of accountancy in an era of change – in society, in ways of doing business and in business organization. Attempts to capture the elusive concept of 'economic profit' are discussed in relation to the traditional valuation theory and the development of the 'events' approach to accounting. The financial statement, he points out, is concerned more with divisible profit than economic profit.

The quoted price of shares is influenced by the availability of information in corporate reports and by public relations exercises. What is needed is for the non-financial aspects of this information to be better organized, and for analyses to be presented of the events which affect efficiency in relation to the sector of the economy in which the business operates.

The successful business is one which concentrates on keeping markets, products and plant in a state of balance. The costs which matter are the loss of profit resulting from a sub-optimal plan; planning being now facilitated by fairly simple mathematical programming. The survival of a company depends on solvency, and this is a matter of fact rather than of valuation.

THE EFFECT OF CHANGE

We live in a society where just about everything can be expected to change. Any book which sets out to tell its readers how to do something, needs to say something about the changes which are taking place in its subject-area. Anything which goes on for more than a few months will almost certainly involve adaptation to change.

Financial planning and control are essential and ongoing parts of business management, so it would make sense to discuss the developments which are coming about in accounting *practice*, and to speculate about further developments as well. But why is it necessary to consider developments in accounting *thought*? Although it seems a down-to-earth affair, accounting is really just one way of thinking about a business. Financial planning and financial control are techniques for sorting out one's ideas about the business, and verifying them.

Obviously, there can be developments in techniques, without changes in whatever the techniques are working on. A new way of bottling milk need not imply any change in the sort of milk being bottled. Thus, it would be a good thing to say something about techniques of financial planning – mathematical programming, the use of matrix algebra in planning, electronic spread-sheets, and the psychological implications of different ways of planning and controlling the activities of people. None of these things is new, but it is a mark of the considerable advance in sophistication in business methods in this country, that it seems appropriate to acknowledge them in a book of this type.

However, this enhancement of sophistication in business as a whole has brought about a radical change in accounting thought. Since several of the techniques mentioned in the previous paragraph reflect this change, it is a good idea to start by describing these developments in thought. This change is a necessary consequence of the changing nature of the societies in which we live. Where there is a new sort of milk, if often does need a new bottle!

As well as new products and services, and new ways of providing them, we have new ways of doing business and new types of business organizations through which to handle them. Multinational corporations, conglomerates, consortia, institutional investors, capital leasing agreements, trading in futures and the like, mean that financial relationships are much more complex than they used to be. The need to capture the subtleties of these relationships is invalidating the principles upon which we base an assessment of the net income and capital states of all businesses. Thus, we see the accounting profession, all over the world, making heavy weather of defining Statements of Standard Accounting Practice for such things as inflation accounting, the treatment of expenditure on Research and Development, the valuation of inventories, and so on. Again, very practical questions as to whether conglomerates really grow, or whether redundant coalmines are really running at a loss, seem to elicit most uncertain answers at the present time.

THE CONCEPT OF ECONOMIC PROFIT

The conventional concern of accounting, and internal management information systems, has been economic profit, albeit hedged about by legal and social constraints. This has involved placing valuations on the undertaking at the beginning and end of a financial period. Once these two values have emerged, the figure of profit or loss is the difference between them, adjusted for investment and withdrawals of funds during the period. Details of what the enterprise actually did during the period are not directly relevant to economic profit. Such relevance as these details may have relates solely to any impact they are seen to have on valuation. For this reason, the traditional approaches to accounting are described as 'valuation theories of accounting'.

Until about forty years ago, published financial statements were very much of this type. They usually began with an undefined credit item called something like 'Surplus for the period, after provision for taxation and other adjustments'. The Companies Act 1948 changed this, and subsequent legislation, various accounting standards and the regulations of the Stock Exchange, have added more and more to the list of details to be disclosed in the published accounts of a company. A similar change has taken place in the USA, and in most other countries of the world. These additional disclosures do not often affect the valuations placed on the undertaking, so to that extent they do not affect its economic profit. This more recent development has been called the 'events approach to accounting theory'.

What are people doing with all this apparently surplus information? The older valuation theories all assumed that there was only one valuation which could be put upon a company's undertaking, and this would be a satisfactory basis for any economic decision by any reader of the accounts. One explanation of the events approach might be that this is not so, and the additional information enables people to make their own valuations to suit their own decision-rules.

443

That is to say, everyone could arrive at his or her own, private version of the firm's economic profit. On the other hand, if *this* were so, it is surprising that there should be any controversy about accounting theory *or* practice. Whatever valuation the company put upon its undertaking would be of little significance, so long as it provided enough information for account-users to make up their own minds about it.

THE EFFICIENT MARKET HYPOTHESIS

There are now grounds for supposing that the real answer to the question of how accounting information is used may be considerably more sophisticated than either the 'valuation' or the 'events' approach implies. About twenty-five years ago, an economist, I.M.D. Little, at Cambridge, England, formulated what has come to be known as 'the Efficient Market Hypothesis'. In its most usual form, this states that Stock Market prices of shares reflect all the publicly-available information about them. A great number of tests of this hypothesis have failed to disprove it, at least as regards generally-traded securities on the major markets of the world.

This means that investors can actually define the best possible portfolio of investments. This is one which minimizes its overall risk, by being spread across the whole spectrum of securities available. There are only two ways to out-perform this portfolio. The first is to select investments of more-than-average riskiness; if you are in luck, you will do better than the person who plays the safe game, but the downside is that you could be unlucky, and do worse. The other way is through 'insider trading'. If you can get hold of important information before it is publicly available, you may be able to do yourself a bit of good. It is also contrary to the regulations of the Stock Exchange, and a criminal offence.

A by-product of the massive research effort expended on the Efficient Market Hypothesis, has been a curious finding about the impact of accounting information on share prices. One would suppose that changes in the legislation, etc., affecting accounting disclosure, would be reflected by relative movements in share prices. Some companies have a more, or a less-than-average exposure to the effect of inflation, more-or-less-than-average investment in research and development, and so on. In fact, a considerable number of studies in the United Kingdom, and in the United States, have failed to find any significant effect from the promulgation (or the withdrawal!) of any accounting standard.

It is as if the stock market had already compounded the information into its prices, and these often bitterly-contested refinements in accounting practice are merely cosmetic embellishments of the corporate report. If this is the case, 'true economic profit' would seem to be an elusive beast, which can only exist in the interstices of a stock exchange's market-making activity. Moreover, if those market-makers are relying on information supplied by the companies themselves, it would be hard to see where the reporting of 'events' should end. Subject to the problems of an over-load of information, the more the market knew about the companies whose securities are listed on it, the more precisely could it distinguish their prices.

A general rule of science is that simple explanations are to be preferred to complex ones. There are two ways of analysing any activity, from the bottom-upwards, or the top-downwards. Human rationality, especially in the West, prefers the bottom-up approach. Everything is seen as being assembled from its basic components, like a Swiss watch. Using this approach to accounting and management, companies literally *make* profits – out of thin air! Everything they do must be contributing or detracting from this process.

The view from the top downwards is unfamiliar to business people and economists alike. Modern cosmology tells us (contrary to our own perceptions) that we live in a user-friendly Universe. It seems to be especially well-designed to support life, in a general way, on this Earth. The survival of individuals, and organizations too, depends upon their being sufficiently well-adapted to their environments to be able to secure what they need to sustain life and reproduce themselves.

A recent, ingenious proposal is that accounting has a dynamic dimension which could be reflected in the normal bookkeeping process. Income could be recorded as a flow, with a speed (or momentum), and a rate of acceleration (or force). Where do the flow and the initial force come from? It is probably equally untrue to claim that it arises from the efforts of the management and staff, as that it arises altogether externally in a benevolent economy-at-large. Rather it arises from the mutual activity of the Universe. Maybe what the Stock Market and others with passive, internal interests want to know about a company, is whether it is sufficiently well-organized to be able to seize its share of what is going. Those with more active, or external, interests will also be concerned with its efficiency as a contributor to the flow of income and (perhaps) more general welfare in its sector(s) of the community.

This suggests an admirably simple-minded explanation of market efficiency. Securities exist which are tapped into all available sectors of the economy, or flows of income. Also, a prerequisite of a quotation on a stock exchange is to be a fairly large company, with a long-ish history of well-organized activity. The information which is really needed relates to the state of the various sectors of the economy, and events within individual companies which are likely to affect their efficiency. It is unsurprising that the market seems to know the answers about any one company with such ease.

THE CORPORATE IMAGE

This, in turn, suggests a reasonable explanation for what we now see in published corporate reports, and a likely path of development for regulations on accounting and disclosure of information. The financial statements themselves are only one part of a modern corporate report. The remainder comprises a chairperson's statement about the condition, policies and expectations of the company, and what might be called a magazine section, covering markets, products, personnel, research and development and so on. At present, the various sections of the report seem disjointed, and the non-financial parts often lack discernible structure. As understanding of their true purpose grows, we may expect to see much better-integrated presentations in these documents.

All sections of the report probably have as their fundamental object the projection of the corporate image. There is nothing essentially meretricious about public relations, since the presentation of a false image is on all fours with the presentation of a false balance sheet. It can be done, but even if the deception remains undiscovered at the time, subsequent events tend to reveal whatever was being hidden, unless the bad news can be lost in a superabundance of good news!

Here is a new development, whose arrival seems largely unrecorded. Many firms are extending a formerly quite low-key commitment to PR to a more definite activity in what is called 'investor relations'. The remit of those concerned is with the market credibility of the corporation, in the broadest sense. The work involves all aspects of communication, in every medium, and is a largely independent specialism. Although the financial statements are reported by the finance staff, and the chairperson's statement by that officer, in consultation with the Board, the physical publication of the corporate report has much in common with the issue of a high-class glossy magazine.

Also, more and more companies arrange meetings with financial journalists, investment analysts, institutional investors and also individual investors, to present and explain their results. The physical presentation of these affairs, the handout material, scripts, visual aids and so on, are also part of the investor relations function. A very visible aspect of this activity is the current spate of mail-shots, videos, TV broadcast commercials and news conferences, which nowadays surround such events as takeover bids and major public issues of shares.

The information being put out in this way is essentially 'market sensitive'. It is evidence that the company is sufficiently well-organized to secure an appropriate share of some adequate income from the sectors in which it operates. Although very little of the material is scrutinized by the company's auditors, there is already a considerable apparatus to control the content of those communications which go directly to the public. All these transmissions are corporate (prestige) advertising, and are recognized as such. The Independent Broadcasting Authority and the Code of Advertising Practice Committee both have guidelines which make specific reference to financial advertising. While the bulk of such advertising deals with offers of unit trusts, if not second mortgages to hard-up householders, the requirements of the guidelines are drawn very broadly. In some respects, they are more stringent than those laid down by the Companies Acts themselves.

LIMITATIONS OF FINANCIAL STATEMENTS

This analysis suggests that the financial statements in themselves (essentially the profit and loss account and the balance sheet) may actually be telling us about a more limited aspect of the company's efficiency, or ability to survive. All businesses have to remain solvent, and solvency is a matter of fact, rather than of valuation. It is the question of whether the company can meet its debts as they fall due. The concern of the financial statement seems to be with divisible profit, as opposed to economic profit.

Divisible profit is calculated by the use of historical cost accounting. The chapter on inflation accounting has pointed out that historical cost accounting will overstate economic profit in times of rising price-levels. If the HCA profit is all paid out under those circumstances, it will erode the capital base of the company. However, this is not relevant to solvency; businesses will wind down quickly if the legally-divisible profits are paid out in a period of inflation, but they will not become insolvent. The legal requirement is to remain solvent, and not to maintain the capital of the company. Business people may choose to keep trading at the same level, to grow, or even to let the enterprise run down altogether.

As what might be called the extra-financial aspects of corporate reporting become more apparent and better-organized, one may expect a dying-away of the current attempts to capture economic profit for purposes of external reporting of corporate results. Instead, we might look forward to accounting standards and legislation more like those of continental Europe, which place emphasis on very conservative forms of historical cost accounting. The country's membership of the EEC has already begun this process. This is a tribute not so much to superior continental logic in financial matters as to the considerable and long-standing incidence of state-intervention in business affairs in those countries.

There, the concern is not so much for solvency as to ensure the formal, legally-defined 'enregistration' of items of income and expenditure. The highly-stylized financial data which results, is then presented in uniform final accounts, much as laid down in the Fourth Directive of the EEC, which has emerged in Schedule 1 of the Companies Act 1981. The purpose of uniform accounting was to facilitate the incorporation of the data into schemes for national and regional planning. It may be that this Act makes us pay the penalties of uniform accounting, without much opportunity to reap the benefits.

The demise of the current Anglo-American fixation with economic profit may be expected to have considerable effects on internal management accounting and financial control, as well as on external reporting. This would be especially the case if it were also to be recognized that the sources of income are outside the company, while costs emerge within it. As the earlier chapters of this book illustrate, present-day managerial accounting places a great deal of emphasis on a marginal approach to business opportunity. On the one hand, all production orders, etc., must cover their direct costs, and make a contribution towards overheads. On the other, it is not necessary that prices charged should provide a large enough margin to cover all the overheads, at least in the short run.

As a result, we are not supposed to deliver small orders to remote customers, until a good van-load is going their way. Nevertheless, when business is slack, it makes sense to accept lower prices for special contracts, so long as the contract makes some contribution to the fixed costs of the plant. This seems to be common sense, but the picture is at variance with what we learn about the policies of many especially-successful enterprises.

THE BALANCE OF MARKETS, PRODUCTS AND PLANT

In their book *In Search of Excellence*, Peters and Waterman (1982) observe that most highly-successful companies have a firm policy of going hell-for-leather after the best possible standards of service and reliability. At the same time, we learn that most Japanese firms live very dangerously, by Anglo-American standards. Their absence of buffer-stocks and paper-thin equity (and dividend-cover) means that things simply cannot go wrong – and everyone knows it. The lesson is quite simple to understand, if it is hard to put into practice. The firm's order book, production facilities and financial resources should be in perfect balance. Then everybody has only to do their very best, without thought of the financial consequences. A business that has to husband its resources, but still needs fat to survive, is probably making the wrong products, on the wrong machines, for the wrong people in the wrong place.

Several observers have noted a greater tendency to include financial data in management information systems in the United Kingdom and in the USA than is usual in Germany or Japan. Where the activity of the firm is planned, and the plans are expected to be fulfilled, the financial implications of the plan have been worked out in advance, as a budget. The management information needed to control the activity will be of a physical nature, rather than financial. Of course, some activities can only be planned within very short time-horizons; others can hardly be planned at all, and involve giving able and trustworthy people various resources, and telling them to do their best.

What is now developing is an approach to management which keeps markets, products, and plant in a reasonable state of balance.

The comparative ease or difficulty of forecasting a given activity is reflected in the elaboration of the plant, and the type of contracts for services and supplies which are placed. In short, we are turning Japanese. Britain and, to a lesser extent, America have been paying the price of being first in the field with large-scale commercial and industrial activity. When we started, the profits of the game handsomely covered the costs of inefficiency. 'Planning' was no more than the ample provision of resources, but now margins are much tighter and success depends absolutely on attention to detail and getting things *right*. A good deal of Anglo–American management *accounting* technique has the objective of controlling situations which somehow never do go quite according to plan.

This is a good point at which to return to those new developments in technique, referred to in the opening paragraphs of this chapter. They are not accounting techniques, as such, but they do deal in a more rigorous way with the costs of *not* getting things right! Since 'the right way' is presumably the most profitable way, any departure from the plan will be less profitable. In such circumstances, the 'costs' which matter are the loss of profit which results from following a sub-optimal plan.

The issue can be illustrated like this. It might seem that it would be useful to attach a money-cost to running every facility in the plant. One could say, 'Every minute that machine stands idle represents a dead loss of £127', and so make people aware of the relative priorities about the plant. However, the figure is misleading in that context. If there was nothing waiting for the machine to do, the real cost of leaving it idle is nil. On the other hand, if it is a bottleneck in production, the loss per minute is the loss of the profit from the additional production which could have occurred had an additional minute of capacity been available. Incidentally, the loss would be the same, whether the running-cost was £127 per minute, or £1.27 per minute.

MATHEMATICAL PROGRAMMING

This type of analysis comes from the technique of mathematical programming, but it is worth knowing that the technique is much more simple to use in practice than in theory! The reason is that a firm's capacity for production is usually fairly well balanced against what can be sold, so that bottlenecks are rarely so bad as to make it a good move to sacrifice output of more profitable products in favour of less profitable ones. It follows that a very good approximation of the optimal plan for the plant will always emerge immediately. There is never any need, in a real-life case, for the numerous 'iterations' and their accompanying calculation, which the text books set out.

Before giving an example of the simplified programming technique, which is really a method for solving simultaneous equations, it is useful to realize that just about every problem in planning anything is an exercise with simultaneous equations, anyway. Now problems with simultaneous equations are also problems in matrix algebra. Here again, the textbooks' complexities have little relevance to real industrial problems, because production tracks are almost never circular. The work rarely leaves a process, only to return later after further steps have been done. This means the matrices, or the simultaneous equations, are very easy to solve.

A small example will show just how easy all this is in practice. Please accept the writer's promise that a very large example is no more difficult to deal with! In fact, the arithmetic in the example is very easy and self-evident, but it will not be explained. This is because the many 'electronic spreadsheets' which are now available on any micro-computer, are really just devices for solving simultaneous equations through matrix algebra.

Here is a flow-chart for five interrelated processes of production. The figures on the arrows mean 'it requires 0.3 of a unit of A to make 1 unit of B', and so on:

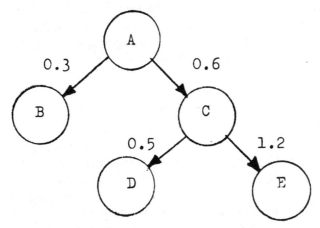

The information on this chart can be set up in spreadsheet format. If you like jargon, you could call it the 'next assembly matrix':

	Outputs				
	A	B	C	D	E
A	1.0	0.3	0.6	0	0
B	0	1.0	0	0	0
Inputs C	0	0	1.0	0.5	1.2
D	0	0	0	1.0	0
E	0	0	0	0	1.0

The '1.0's' along the diagonal just mean that 'it takes one shot of whatever outside inputs are needed to make a single unit of Product A, for example to be combined with the inputs from other processes, and make a finished product of product E'! The reason this is the 'next assembly matrix', is that while Products D and E are not direct users of Product A, they do include some A, through Product C. This can be shown in what could be called the 'total assembly matrix':

	Outputs				
	A	B	C	D	E
A	1.0	0.3	0.6	0.3	0.72
B	0	1.0	0	0	0
Inputs C	0	0	1.0	0.5	1.2
D	0	0	0	1.0	0
E	0	0	0	0	1.0

This matrix summarizes everything you need to know about how these products interrelate. Thus if we know the direct inputs of labour, material and overhead into each *process* it is easy to arrive at the full process-cost of each *product*. Given:

Process	A	B	C	D	E
Direct costs per unit	£4.00	5.00	2.00	3.00	6.00
Full cost of product	£4.00	6.20	4.40	6.70	11.28

Notice how this technique side-steps the formidable computations shown in most Anglo-American textbooks as necessary to work-out 'process costs'! Again, if we know the sales-price per unit of the products, we can arrive at the contribution to profit of each one. This example assumes that every product can either be sold externally, or in the cases of Product A and Product C, it can also be used internally to make other products:

Product	A	B	C	D	E
Full cost	£4.00	6.20	4.40	6.70	11.28
Sales-price	£5.00	8.00	6.40	8.00	13.00
Contribution	£1.00	1.80	2.00	1.30	1.72

If we also know the maximum sales which can reasonably be achieved at those prices, and the capacity of the plant to make each product, we have the largest quantities that can be made-and-sold in the period:

Product	A	B	C	D	E	
Market capacity	1200	600	500	700	400	units
Plant capacity	1000	400	1250	600	400	units
Make-&-sell	1000	400	500	600	400	units

Now you can load-up the plant with the make-and-sell quantities *in descending order of their contributions*, and this will give a very close approximation of the optimal production plan for the plant:

Process	A	B	C	D	E	
Plant capacity	1000	400	1250	600	400	units
Make-&-Sell 500 C's	300		500			
Unused capacity	700		750			
Make-&-Sell 400 B's	120	400				
Unused capacity	580	nil				
Make-&-Sell 400 E's	282		480		400	
Unused capacity	298		270		nil	
Make-&-Sell 540 D's[1]	162		270	540		
Unused capacity	136		nil	60		
Make-&-Sell 136 A's[1]	136					
	nil					

[1] Of course, you can't sell what you can't make. Process C is a bottleneck on the sales of Product D, while more profitable internal demands for Product A, restrict its sales below what could be sold at £5. The overcapacity in Process D represents a lack of balance in the plant. Further calculations using these matrices, etc., will product budgets and statements of profit, and more esoteric information about the real costs of bottlenecks, etc.

Finally, the academic literature on management accounting of the last twenty-five years or so has had a lot to say about 'behavioural aspects of budgeting'. If middle managers are being assessed by their performance against budgets, it is not likely that they will attempt to pad-out their budgets, underestimate possible production and so on. Anyone who has ever managed anything, even an academic department, might find the proposition credible. This 'game of budgeting' may be of less significance in the future. It is businesses where the relationships of market to products to plant are not well defined, which provide the nooks and crannies where 'organizational slack' of this sort can be deposited and retrieved, unseen.

REFERENCES AND FURTHER READING

Beaver, W.H., *Financial Reporting: An Accounting Revolution*, Prentice Hall, 1981.

Budd, J.F., Jr, *Corporate Video in Focus: A Management Guide to Private TV*, Prentice Hall, 1983.

Gambling, T., *Modern Accounting: Accounting as the Information System for Technological Change*, Macmillan, Reprinted 1979.

Ijiri, Y., 'A Framework for Triple-Entry Bookkeeping', *The Accounting Review*, **61**, pp. 745–759, 1986.

Kaplan, R.S., 'Measuring Manufacturing Performance: A New Challenge for Management Accounting Research', *The Accounting Review*, **58**, pp. 686–705, 1983.

Peters, T.J., and Waterman, R.H., *In Search of Excellence: Lessons from America's Best-Run Companies*, Harper and Row, 1982.

Sorter, G.H., 'An "Events" Approach to Basic Accounting Theory', *The Accounting Review*, **46**, pp. 12–19, 1969.

Index

security factor, 224
servicing factor, 225
see also Investment
Futures, commodity as a financial
  resource, 30, 163, 167

Gambling, Trevor, xiv, 441
Goch, Desmond, xiv, 93
Goodwill, 25
Groups:
  taxation planning for, 434
  see also Multinationals and Mergers
Growth factor in conditions of change,
  173

Hire purchase, 154
Hockey stick forecast, 46
Human resource accounting, 46, 385

Income, *see under* Budgeting
Industrial goods, forecasting demand
  for, 50
Inflation
  accounting for, 415
  current cost method, 424
  current purchasing power method,
    422
  distortions, effects of, 418
Information:
  for financial planning, 172, 317
Intangibles, resource factor of, 24
International companies, *see*
  Multinational; Taxation planning
Investments:
  overseas, 298
  ranking of (in budgeting), 119
  as a resource, 23

Jones, Philip, xiv, 365

Kennedy, R.Y., xiv, 18

Land, as a resource, 21
Leasing, 29, 154
Letter of credit, 293
Liquidity, resource factor in, 23
Lloyd, John, xv, 328
Loans, 27
Long-term cash flows, 27
Loss makers, 216

Machinery, *see* Plant
Magee, Prof. C.C., xx, 183
Management, facing up to changes by,
  see Change, planning in
  conditions of
Marginal costing, 11, 217
Market research for pricing, 77
Mepham, M.J., xv, 133
Mergers, 395
Metra potential method, 275
Milestone charts, 276
Miller, Elwood, xvi, 305
Modelling, financial, 133
Monte Carlo simulation, 141
Multinational companies, 305
  accounting problems, 307
    currency conversions, 314
    disclosures, segmented, 311
    standards of accounting, 311
    structural basis, 309
    taxation, 323
  managerial aspects, 316
    information, 317
    performance factor, 319
    transfer prices, 301, 318

Net present-value profile, 126
Network diagrams, 275
New products, *see* Product

Objectives, of business, 19, 50
Overheads, budgeting for, 101, 103, 205
Overseas development, 289
  credit insurance, 295
  European Investment Bank, 297
  financial controller, role of, 290
  foreign exchange, 291
  investment of capital, 298
    reporting element, 303
    taxation aspects, 301
    transfer of funds, 303
  letter of credit, 293
  payment procedure, 293
  statistical techniques, 295
  see also Multinational companies

Parkinson, Christine, xvi, 395
Pearson, Alan, xvi, 268
Performance, control of, 181
  assessment, 183
  capital employed, return on, 192